MICROSOFT

FrontPage 98

Introductory Concepts and Techniques

Gary B. Shelly
Thomas J. Cashman
Kurt A. Jordan

COURSE TECHNOLOGY
ONE MAIN STREET
CAMBRIDGE MA 02142

an International Thomson Publishing company 

CAMBRIDGE • ALBANY • BONN • CINCINNATI • LONDON • MADRID • MELBOURNE
MEXICO CITY • NEW YORK • PARIS • SAN FRANCISCO • TOKYO • TORONTO • WASHINGTON

© 1999 by Course Technology — I(T)P®

Printed in the United States of America

For more information, contact:

Course Technology
One Main Street
Cambridge, Massachusetts 02142, USA

ITP Europe
Berkshire House
168-173 High Holborn
London, WC1V 7AA, United Kingdom

ITP Australia
102 Dodds Street
South Melbourne
Victoria 3205 Australia

ITP Nelson Canada
1120 Birchmount Road
Scarborough, Ontario
Canada M1K 5G4

International Thomson Editores
Saneca, 53
Colonia Polanco
11560 Mexico D.F. Mexico

ITP GmbH
Konigswinterer Strasse 418
53227 Bonn, Germany

ITP Asia
60 Albert Street, #15-01
Albert Complex
Singapore 189969

ITP Japan
Hirakawa-cho Kyowa Building, 3F
2-2-1 Hirakawa-cho, Chiyoda-ku
Tokyo 102, Japan

All rights reserved. This publication is protected by federal copyright laws. No part of this publication may be reproduced, stored in a retrieval system, or transmitted in any form or by any means, electronic, mechanical, photocopying, recording, or otherwise, or be used to make a derivative work (such as translation or adaptation), without prior permission in writing from Course Technology.

TRADEMARKS
Course Technology and the Open Book logo are registered trademarks and CourseKits is a trademark of Course Technology.

I(T)P® The ITP logo is a registered trademark of International Thomson Publishing.

SHELLY CASHMAN SERIES® and **Custom Edition**® are trademarks of International Thomson Publishing. Some of the product names and company names used in this book have been used for identification purposes only and may be trademarks or registered trademarks of their respective manufacturers and sellers. International Thomson Publishing and Course Technology disclaim any affiliation, association, or connection with, or sponsorship or endorsement by, such owners.

DISCLAIMER
Course Technology reserves the right to revise this publication and make changes from time to time in its content without notice.

ISBN 0-7895-4624-8

PHOTO CREDITS: *Project 1, pages FP 1.4-5* Alex Haley, ©Christian Vioujard/The Gamma Liaison Network; Allen Ginsberg, UPI/Corbis-Bettman; Ernest Hemmingway, Archive Photos; woman at computer, woman's boots, Hemmingway's shoes, Ginsberg's shoes, oval atlas, Courtesy of Corel Professional Photos CD-ROM Image usage; Haley's shoes, Courtesy of Expert Software; *Project 2, pages FP 2.2-3* Hands on keyboard, hands on piano, MRI, Courtesy of PhotoDisc, Inc.; *Project 3, pages FP 3.2-3* Camel, satellite, Courtesy of Corel Professional Photos CD-ROM Image usage.

1 2 3 4 5 6 7 8 9 10 BC 03 02 01 00 99

MICROSOFT

FrontPage 98

Introductory Concepts and Techniques

CONTENTS

PROJECT THREE

USING GRAPHICS AND IMAGES IN WEB PAGE DESIGN

Preface

The Shelly Cashman Series® Internet books reinforce the fact that you made the right choice when you use a Shelly Cashman Series book. Earlier Shelly Cashman Series Internet books were used by more schools and more students than any other series in textbook publishing. Yet the Shelly Cashman Series team wanted to produce an even better book for Microsoft FrontPage, so the step-by-step pedagogy was refined to include larger screens (800 x 600) to present material in an even easier to understand format. Features such as OtherWays and More Abouts enhance the book to give students an in-depth knowledge of Microsoft FrontPage. Each project opens with a fascinating perspective of the subject covered in the project. Completely redesigned student assignments include the unique Cases and Places. This book provides the finest educational experience for students learning about how to create Web pages.

The World Wide Web

In the ten years since its birth, the World Wide Web, or Web for short, has grown beyond all expectations. During this short period of time, the Web has increased from a limited number of networked computers to more than twenty million computers offering millions of Web pages on any topic you can imagine. Schools, businesses, and the computing industry all are taking advantage of this new way of delivering information.

Web pages do not just happen. Someone must create and manage them. You have the option of creating a Web page by coding directly in HTML (hypertext markup language) or by using a higher-level tool, such as Microsoft FrontPage.

Objectives of This Textbook

Microsoft FrontPage 98: Introductory Concepts and Techniques is intended for use in combination with other books in an introductory course on creating Web pages. This book also is suitable for use in a one-credit hour course or a continuing education course. Specific objectives of this book are as follows:

- To expose students to creating Web pages
- To teach students how to use Microsoft FrontPage 98
- To provide an introduction to managing collections of related Web pages
- To expose students to common Web page formats and functions
- To encourage curiosity and independent exploration of World Wide Web resources
- To develop an exercise-oriented approach that allows students to learn by example
- To encourage independent study and help those who are learning about the Internet on their own in a distance education environment

Other Ways

1. On Edit menu click FrontPage Component Properties
2. Right-click to select, press ALT+ENTER
3. Right-click to select, press ALT+E, I

More About

URLs

The first part of a URL indicates the protocol, or method of communication to be used. Some other protocols are ftp://, telnet://, and gopher://.

Organization of This Textbook

Microsoft FrontPage 98: Introductory Concepts and Techniques is comprised of three projects that introduce students to creating and publishing Web pages. Neither World Wide Web nor Internet experience is necessary. Each project begins with a statement of Objectives. The topics in the project are presented in a step-by-step, screen-by-screen manner.

Each project ends with a Project Summary and a section titled What You Should Know. Questions and exercises are presented at the end of each project. Exercises include Test Your Knowledge, Use Help, Apply Your Knowledge, In the Lab, and Cases and Places. The projects are organized as follows:

Project 1 – Creating a FrontPage Web Using a Template In Project 1, students are introduced to HTML and how to use FrontPage templates. After learning the basics of HTML, students create a simple three-page web consisting of a Home page, an Interests page, and a Favorites page. Topics include basic Web page editing and customization techniques; changing the templates using FrontPage commands and features; and saving, printing, and publishing the three pages to an available Web server. Students then can use a browser to view their own personal Web pages.

Project 2 – Creating a New FrontPage Web In Project 2, students learn how to create a new FrontPage web. Topics include basic Web page design criteria; setting up the page background; inserting tables and images; adding, replacing, and applying special formatting features to text; and adding linked targets to the page. After creating the Web page, students save it and publish it to a Web server and then test it.

Project 3 – Using Graphics and Images in Web Page Design In Project 3, students are introduced to the various techniques for using graphics and images in Web pages. Topics include adding a new page to the FrontPage web; setting up a tiled background image; copying and pasting objects from another Web page; applying special formatting techniques to images, such as washout and resizing; creating an image map and assigning URLs to the image map hotspots; inserting a photographic image; and using the picture to create a thumbnail image. Finally, students save, publish, and test their Web pages.

End-of-Project Student Activities

A notable strength of the Shelly Cashman Series Internet books is the extensive student activities at the end of each project. Well-structured student activities can make the difference between students merely participating in a class and students retaining the information they learn. These activities include all of the following sections.

- **What You Should Know** A listing of the tasks completed within a project together with the pages where the step-by-step, screen-by-screen explanations appear. This section provides a perfect study review for students.
- **Test Your Knowledge** Four or five pencil-and-paper activities designed to determine students' understanding of the material in the project. Included are true/false questions, multiple-choice questions, and two short-answer exercises.
- **Use Help** Any user of FrontPage must know how to use Help. Therefore, this book contains two Help exercises per project. These exercises alone distinguish the Shelly Cashman Series from any other set of instructional materials.

- **Apply Your Knowledge** A substantive exercise intended to be completed in a few minutes that provides practice with project skills.
- **In the Lab** Several assignments per project that require students to apply the knowledge gained in the project to solve problems.
- **Cases and Places** Seven unique case studies allow students to apply their knowledge to real-world situations.

Instructor's Resource Kit

A comprehensive Instructor's Resource Kit (IRK) accompanies this textbook in the form of a CD-ROM. The CD-ROM includes an electronic Instructor's Manual and teaching and testing aids. The CD-ROM (ISBN 0-7895-4637-X) is available through your Course Technology representative or by calling one of the following telephone numbers: Colleges and Universities, 1-800-648-7450; High Schools, 1-800-824-5179; and Career Colleges, 1-800-477-3692. The contents of the CD-ROM are listed below.

- **Instructor's Manual** The Instructor's Manual is made up of Microsoft Word files. The files include lecture notes, solutions to laboratory assignments, and a large test bank. The files allow you to modify the lecture notes or generate quizzes and exams from the test bank using you own word processor. The Instructor's Manual includes the following for each project: project objectives; project overview; detailed lesson plans with page number references; teacher notes and activities; answers to the end-of-project exercises; test bank of 110 questions (50 true/false, 25 multiple-choice, and 35 fill-in-the blanks); transparency references; and selected transparencies. The transparencies are available on the Figures in the Book described below. The test bank questions are numbered the same as in Course Test Manager. Thus, you can print a copy of the project and use the printed test bank to select your questions in Course Test Manager.
- **Figures in the Book** Illustrations for every figure in the textbook are available. Use this ancillary to create a slide show from the illustrations for lecture or to print transparencies for use in lecture with an overhead projector.
- **Course Test Manager** Course Test Manager is a powerful testing and assessment package that enables instructors to create and print tests from the large test bank. Instructors with access to a networked computer lab (LAN) can administer, grade, and track tests online. Students also can take online practice tests, which generate customized study guides that indicate where in the textbook students can find more information for each question.
- **Lecture Success System** The Lecture Success System is a set of files that allows you to explain and illustrate the step-by-step, screen-by-screen development of a project in the textbook. The Lecture Success System requires that you have a copy of Microsoft FrontPage, a personal computer, and a projection device.
- **Instructor's Lab Solutions** Solutions and required files for all the In the Lab assignments at the end of each project are available.
- **Student Files** All the files that are required by students to complete the Apply Your Knowledge exercises are included.
- **Interactive Labs** Eighteen hands-on interactive labs that take students from ten to fifteen minutes to step through help solidify and reinforce computer concepts. Student assessment requires students to answer questions about the contents of the interactive labs.

Shelly Cashman Online

Shelly Cashman Online is a World Wide Web service available to instructors and students of computer education. Visit Shelly Cashman Online at www.scseries.com. Shelly Cashman Online is divided into four areas:

- **Series Information** Information on the Shelly Cashman Series products.
- **Teaching Resources** Designed for instructors teaching from and using Shelly Cashman Series textbooks and software. This area includes password-protected instructor materials that can be downloaded, course outlines, teaching and tips, and much more.
- **Student Center** Dedicated to students learning about computers with Shelly Cashman Series textbooks and software. This area includes cool links, data that can be downloaded, and much more.
- **Community** Opportunities to discuss your course and your ideas with instructors in your field and with the Shelly Cashman Series team.

Acknowledgments

The Shelly Cashman Series would not be the leading computer education series without the contributions of outstanding publishing professionals. First, and foremost, among them is Becky Herrington, director of production and designer. She is the heart and soul of the Shelly Cashman Series, and it is only through her leadership, dedication, and tireless efforts that superior products are made possible.

Under Becky's direction, the following individuals made significant contributions to these books: Doug Cowley, production manager; Ginny Harvey, series specialist and developmental editor; Ken Russo, graphic designer and Web developer; Mike Bodnar, Stephanie Nance, Dave Bonnewitz, and Mark Norton, graphic artists; Jeanne Black, Quark expert; Nancy Lamm, proofreader; Marlo Mitchem, production/administrative assistant; Cristina Haley, indexer; Sarah Evertson of Image Quest, photo researcher; and Susan Sebok contributing writer.

Special thanks go to Jim Quasney, our dedicated series editor; Lisa Strite, senior editor; Lora Wade, associate product manager; Tonia Grafakos and Meagan Walsh, editorial assistants; and Kathryn Coyne, product marketing manager. Special mention must go to Becky Herrington for the outstanding book design; Mike Bodnar for the logo designs, and Ken Russo for the cover design and illustrations.

Gary B. Shelly
Thomas J. Cashman
Kurt A. Jordan

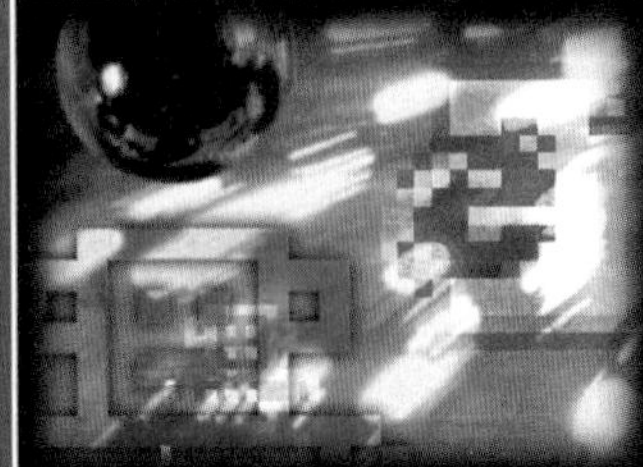

Microsoft FrontPage 98

Creating a FrontPage Web Using a Template

OBJECTIVES

You will have mastered the material in this project when you can:

- Describe HTML
- Explain the use of HTML tags
- Identify common Web page elements
- Describe FrontPage webs
- Create a FrontPage web using a template
- Assign a theme to a FrontPage web
- Alter text in a Web page using the FrontPage Editor
- Print a Web page
- Add items to a bulleted list
- Change WebBot component properties
- Delete a Web page from a FrontPage web
- Add hyperlinks to a Web page
- Publish a FrontPage web
- Use FrontPage Help

Web Authors
and the
Complete Web Site Creation Tool

At first glance, the best-selling authors Allen Ginsberg, Ernest Hemingway, and Alex Haley appear to have little in common. Each wrote unique works for distinct audiences, at certain historical moments. Yet despite the apparent differences, these authors have at least one common trait: editors had the final say in the design of their books.

Would-be authors of World Wide Web pages have the best of both worlds: they are writers and editors of their own work.

In traditional publishing, an author writes a manuscript and an editor marks up the pages with instructions for layout. The designer, in conjunction with the markups, lays out the pages accordingly. Adjustments are made by the editor and author, and the designer revises the layout until it is complete.

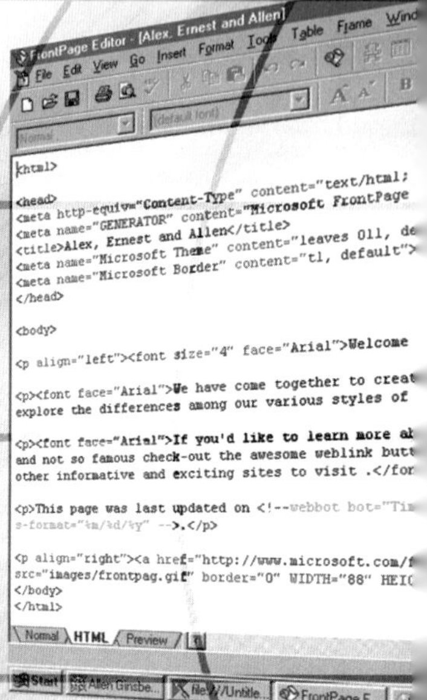

In traditional Web page publishing, the author writes a text file and marks up the words with special HTML (hypertext markup language) character

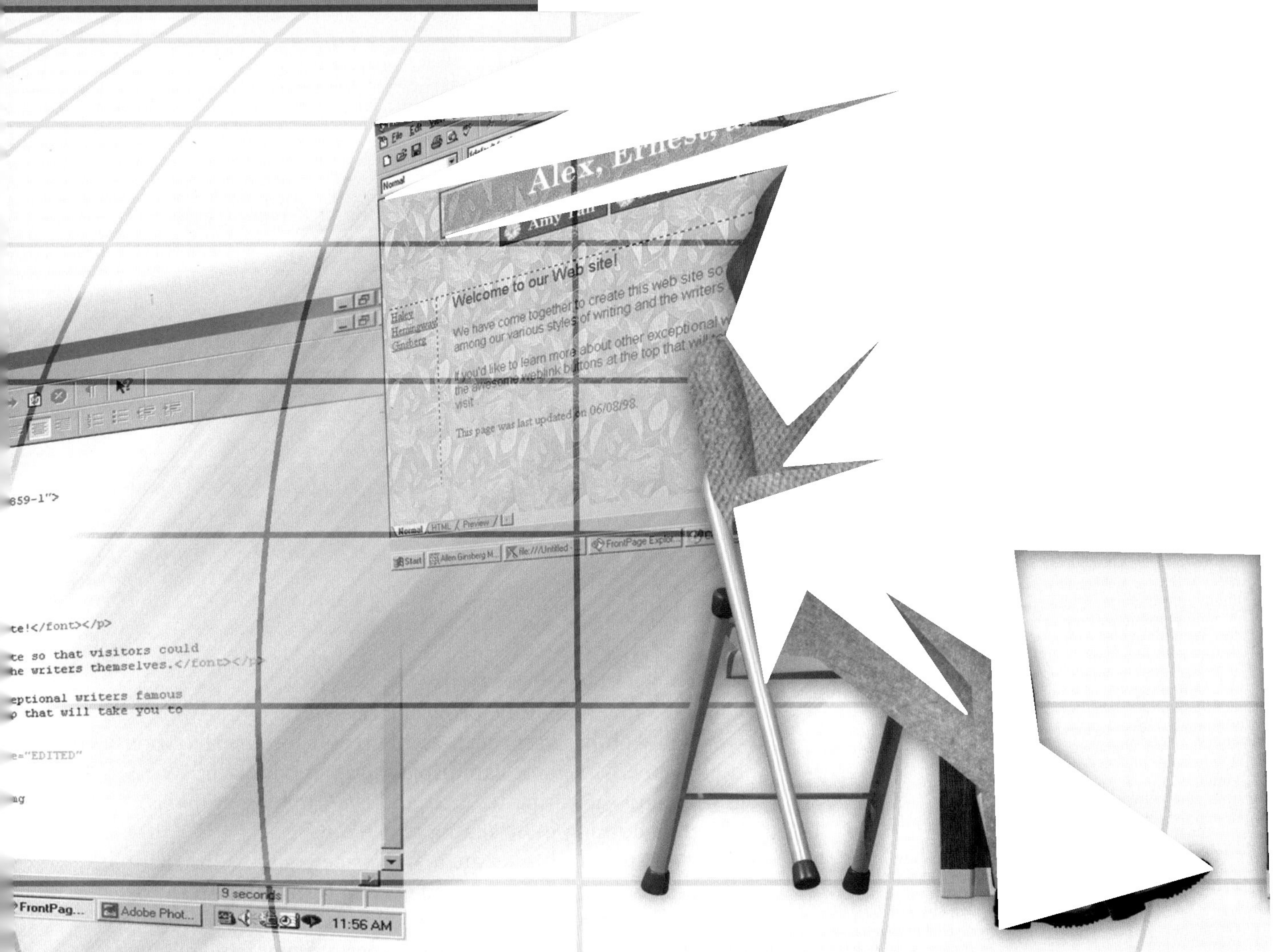

sequences, called tags, to indicate the various formatting features. HTML tags begin and end with brackets (< and >) and usually come in pairs to indicate the beginning and ending of a formatting feature such as headings, bulleted lists, placement of inline images, hyperlinks to other pages, and more. HTML is a coding scheme that can be interpreted by a Web browser, such as Internet Explorer. Creating Web pages by writing HTML can be tedious and confusing, but a basic understanding of the process is valuable.

As an HTML document stored on an Internet server, a Web page can be retrieved and displayed on a computer with a Web browser. The HTML tags specify how the Web page displays and indicates links to other documents. These links to other documents are called hyperlinks. Hyperlinks can be text, graphics, sound, or other media. Text links are known as hypertext.

The Web page creation capabilities of Microsoft FrontPage are designed for both experienced and beginning Web site developers with a simple yet powerful tool for designing and building great-looking, easy-to-navigate World Wide Web sites.

With FrontPage, Web pages are constructed in an environment similar to word processing that requires no programming knowledge. For example, formatting attributes such as fonts, borders, and bulleted lists look very close to the way they appear in your browser, and many features and options are available using familiar elements such as toolbars, dialog boxes, and templates.

This project illustrates using the two components of FrontPage: the FrontPage Explorer and the FrontPage Editor. The FrontPage Explorer is a tool for organizing, creating, and publishing your FrontPage webs. The FrontPage Editor is a Web page editor that allows you to create and edit individual Web pages without needing to know HTML. You will learn the ease of Web page creation using FrontPage templates modeled after popular World Wide Web site styles. Then, you customize your page by adding, deleting, and editing as needed.

As an aspiring Web site developer, you have everything you need to design, create, and manage a Web site. Plus, you are the author, editor, designer, and publisher.

Microsoft FrontPage 98

Creating a FrontPage Web Using a Template

CASE PERSPECTIVE

In the early days of the World Wide Web, most Web pages were designed for use in education and research. Although some visually stunning Web pages did exist, most were simple, using text and basic graphics to convey content. Today, the Web has extended its reach to entertainment, business, and marketing. Organizations without Web sites are considered behind the times. This change has created opportunities for professional Web developers, who design, develop, and manage complex Web sites.

Initially, Web page development was difficult because of the elaborate method used to create them. Today, software programs called Web page editors greatly simplify the process. More powerful Web page editors, such as Microsoft FrontPage 98, hide the complexity of the instructions used to create the page and allow a developer to focus on design and style. Web page editors can be purchased from dealers or manufacturers or can be downloaded free on the Internet.

As an entry-level Web page developer recently hired by a busy advertising firm, your job is to learn Microsoft FrontPage 98 so you can design and develop Web pages for the firm's clients.

Introduction

If you have spent any time browsing the World Wide Web, you know that Web browsers such as Microsoft Internet Explorer and Netscape Navigator can display dramatic-looking Web pages. Behind the formatted text and eye-catching graphics, however, is nothing more than a text file.

The **text file** used to create a Web page contains instructions that describe the page layout and special formatting to the browser. The **language**, or code, used to write these instructions for displaying Web pages is called hypertext markup language, or HTML.

In this project, you will learn about basic Web page elements and the HTML used to create them. You also will learn how to use one of Microsoft FrontPage's pre-formatted sets of Web pages called a **template**. You will create and modify a simple collection of related Web pages and make them available for viewing on the World Wide Web.

The three Web pages you will create in this project are: a **Home Page** that introduces you to other Web users (Figure 1-1a); an **Interests page** that lists some of your hobbies and interests (Figure 1-1b); and a **Favorites page** that contains links to some of your favorite Web sites (Figure 1-1c). Before you begin creating these Web pages, you should familiarize yourself with some important concepts and definitions.

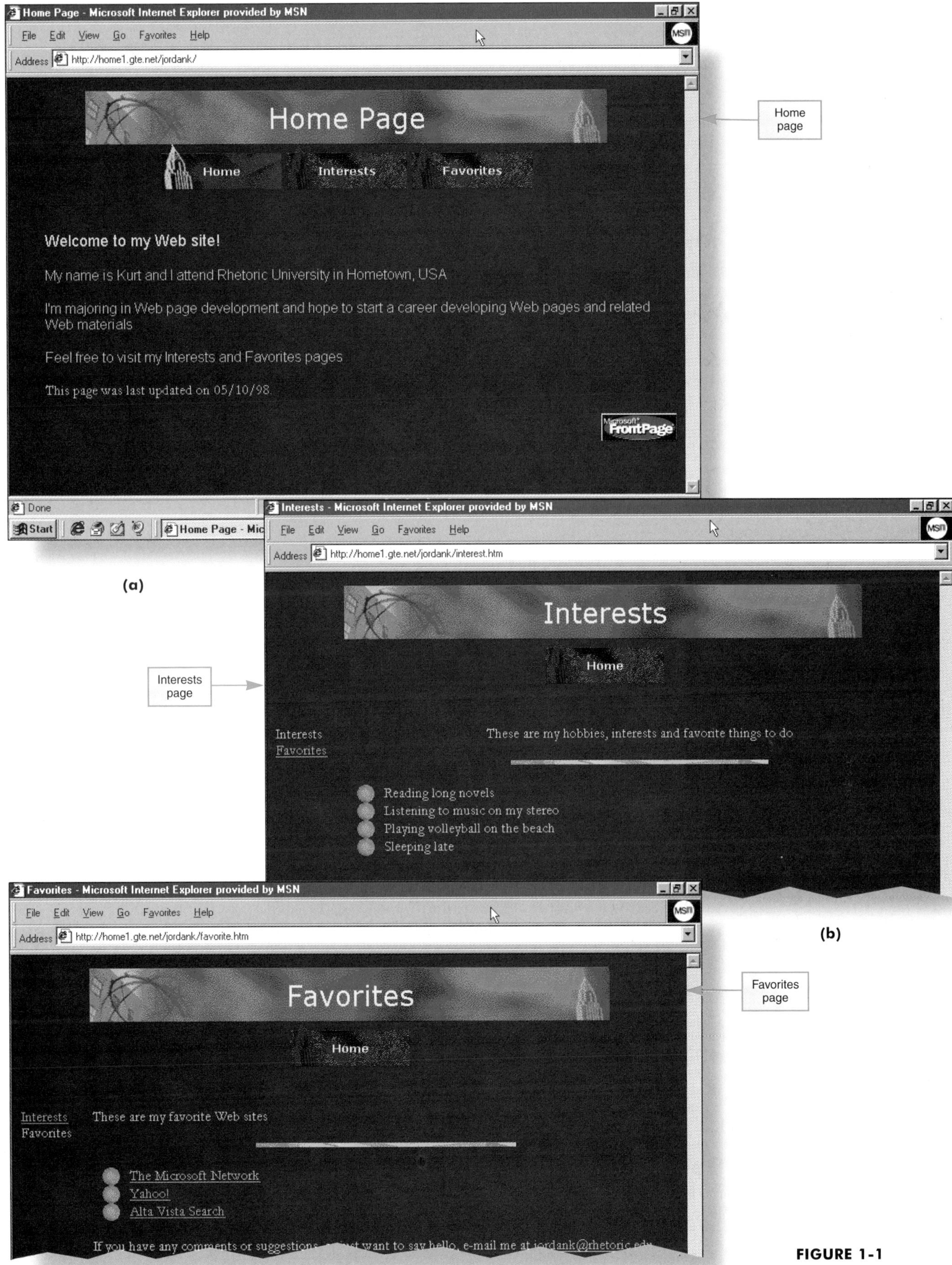

Home Page - Microsoft Internet Explorer provided by MSN
File Edit View Go Favorites Help
Address http://home1.gte.net/jordank/
Home Page
Home
Interests
Favorites
Welcome to my Web site!
My name is Kurt and I attend Rhetoric University in Hometown, USA
I'm majoring in Web page development and hope to start a career developing Web pages and related Web materials
Feel free to visit my Interests and Favorites pages
This page was last updated on 05/10/98.
Microsoft FrontPage
Done
Start
Home Page - Mic
Home page
(a)
Interests - Microsoft Internet Explorer provided by MSN
File Edit View Go Favorites Help
Address http://home1.gte.net/jordank/interest.htm
Interests
Home
Interests
Favorites
These are my hobbies, interests and favorite things to do
Reading long novels
Listening to music on my stereo
Playing volleyball on the beach
Sleeping late
Interests page
(b)
Favorites - Microsoft Internet Explorer provided by MSN
File Edit View Go Favorites Help
Address http://home1.gte.net/jordank/favorite.htm
Favorites
Home
Interests
Favorites
These are my favorite Web sites
The Microsoft Network
Yahoo!
Alta Vista Search
Favorites page
(c)

FIGURE 1-1

Web Servers

Many organizations such as large corporations or big universities have several Web servers. This provides better response times and divides control of those servers among several individuals or groups.

Accessing a Web Page on the World Wide Web

Two programs are needed to access a Web page on the World Wide Web. The first is called a Web browser. A **Web browser**, or **browser**, is a software program that requests a Web page, interprets the codes used to create the page, and then displays the Web page on your computer screen. **Microsoft Internet Explorer** and **Netscape Navigator** are just two of the many Web browsers available.

The second program needed to access a Web page is called Web server software. **Web server software** allows a computer to receive the requests for Web pages and sends the pages over the Internet where they are displayed by the Web browser. The computer that runs the Web server software and responds to Web page requests is called a **Web server**, or **host**. Every Web site is stored on and run from one or more Web servers; a Web server can have thousands of Web pages available for viewing. Each Web page is comprised of one of more files that are stored on the hard disk of the Web server or other computer.

To access a Web page, you use a special address called a **Uniform Resource Locator**, or **URL**. A URL has two parts: a domain name, and a path and file name. The **domain name** identifies the computer on the Internet where the Web document is located. The path and file name indicate where the Web document is stored on that computer. For example, in the URL shown in Figure 1-2, the domain name is www.nationalgeographic.com, the path to the file is /ngs/maps/, and the file name is cartographic.html.

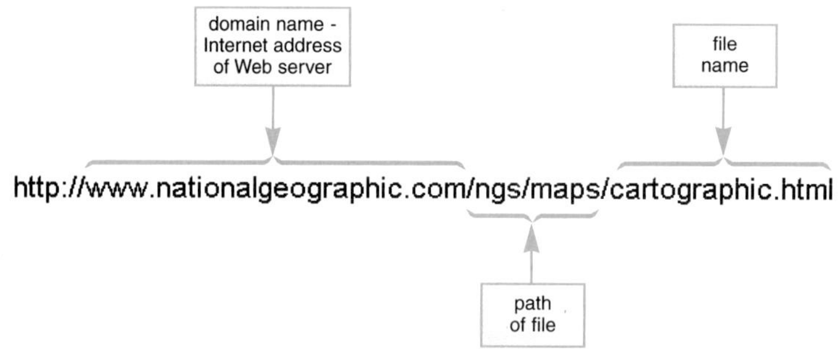

FIGURE 1-2

When you enter a URL in a Web browser, it sends a request for a Web page to the Web server located at the domain name in the URL. The Web server looks at the path and file name in the URL, locates the file, and sends it to your browser. Your browser then displays the Web page on your computer screen. The process repeats when you enter another URL.

Web pages are created using special codes that instruct the browser how to display the Web page. These codes are called hypertext markup language (HTML).

More About

URLs

The first part of a URL indicates the protocol, or method of communication to be used. Some other protocols are ftp://, telnet://, and gopher://.

Hypertext Markup Language (HTML)

Hypertext markup language, or **HTML**, is a special formatting language used to create Web pages. HTML tells the browser how to display text and images; how to set up list and text boxes, option buttons, and hyperlinks; and how to include sound, video, and other multimedia you would expect to find on a Web page.

HTML uses specific codes called **tags** that contain information about items such as formatted text, images, hyperlinks, lists, and forms. These tags are used throughout a Web document to indicate how certain items should display and function on the Web. HTML thus is considered a markup language, because the document is *marked up* with the HTML tags.

To ensure that Web page developers use the same HTML tags in the same manner, an official standard for HTML language exists. The most current specification — called **HTML 4.0** — describes the tags and how to use them. You can view the HTML 4.0 specification by connecting to http://www.w3.org/TR/REC-html40-971218/. Although many HTML tags are available, most Web developers use just a small subset when building Web pages. Table 1-1 shows some of the more commonly used HTML tags and a brief explanation of their functions. Every Web page element is created using one or more HTML tags.

HTML Specifications

The World Wide Web Consortium is an international industry consortium founded in 1994 to develop common protocols for the evolution of the World Wide Web. For more information, visit their Web site at www.w3.org.

Table 1-1

HTML TAG	FUNCTION
<HTML> </HTML>	Indicates the start and end of a Web document
<HEAD> </HEAD>	Indicates the start and end of the header section of the Web document (used for the title and other document header information)
<TITLE> </TITLE>	Indicates the start and end of the Web page title; the title displays in the title bar of the browser, not on the Web page itself
<BODY> </BODY>	Indicates the start and end of the main section of the Web page (as opposed to the header)
<H1> </H1>	Indicates the start and end of a section of text called a heading, which uses a larger font size than normal text; a heading's font size is defined by the integer used in the tag (H1 is largest, H6 is smallest)
<HR>	Inserts a horizontal rule
<P>	Indicates the start of a new paragraph; inserts a blank line above the new paragraph
<B> </B>	Indicates the start and end of a section of bold text
<I> </I>	Indicates the start and end of a section of italic text
<BLINK> </BLINK>	Indicates the start and end of a section of blinking text
<UL> </UL>	Indicates the start and end of an unordered (bulleted) list of items
<LI>	Indicates that the text after the tag is an item within a list
<A> </A>	Indicates the start and end of a hyperlink
HREF="URL"	Indicates a hyperlink to a file in the location specified by the URL in quotation marks
<IMG>	Inserts an inline image into the page
<CENTER> </CENTER> or ALIGN=CENTER	Causes the text or graphic specified between these tags to be centered on the Web page

Web Page Elements

Although Web pages can be as distinctive and different as the individuals who create them, a relatively small set of basic features, or **elements**, are common to most. As you begin to look at Web pages through the eyes of a Web page developer, you will notice that most pages are variations on the use of the elements identified in Figures 1-3a and 1-3b on the next page.

Markup Language

HTML was derived from Standard Generalized Markup Language (SGML). SGML focuses on the elements of the document, freeing the viewer from any hardware- or software-specific choices made by the originator of the document.

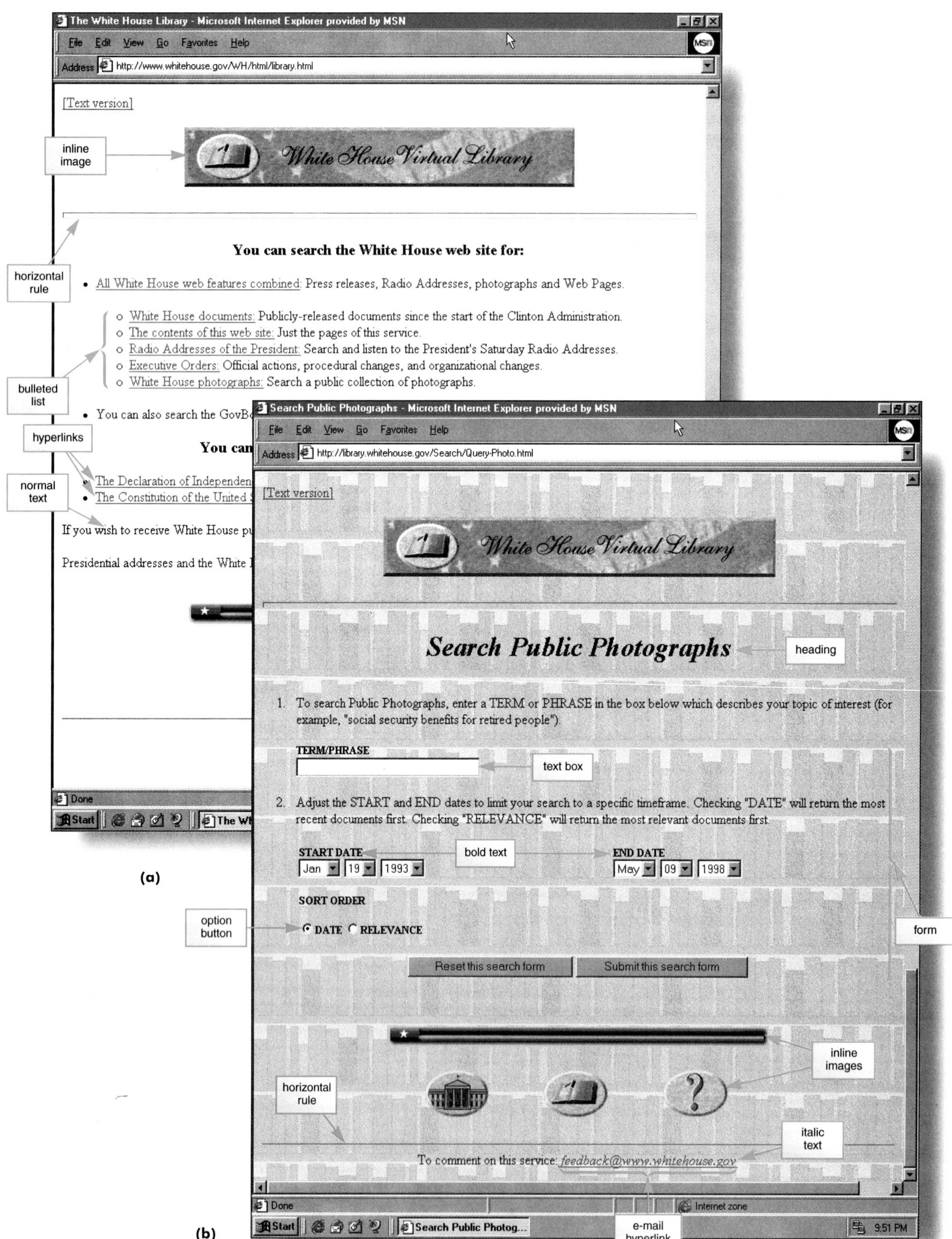
The White House Library - Microsoft Internet Explorer provided by MSN
http://www.whitehouse.gov/WH/html/library.html
[Text version]
inline image
White House Virtual Library
horizontal rule
You can search the White House web site for:
All White House web features combined: Press releases, Radio Addresses, photographs and Web Pages.
White House documents: Publicly-released documents since the start of the Clinton Administration.
The contents of this web site: Just the pages of this service.
Radio Addresses of the President: Search and listen to the President's Saturday Radio Addresses.
Executive Orders: Official actions, procedural changes, and organizational changes.
White House photographs: Search a public collection of photographs.
bulleted list
hyperlinks
normal text
(a)
Search Public Photographs - Microsoft Internet Explorer provided by MSN
http://library.whitehouse.gov/Search/Query-Photo.html
[Text version]
White House Virtual Library
Search Public Photographs
heading
1. To search Public Photographs, enter a TERM or PHRASE in the box below which describes your topic of interest (for example, "social security benefits for retired people").
TERM/PHRASE
text box
2. Adjust the START and END dates to limit your search to a specific timeframe. Checking "DATE" will return the most recent documents first. Checking "RELEVANCE" will return the most relevant documents first.
START DATE
bold text
END DATE
Jan 19 1993
May 09 1998
SORT ORDER
option button
DATE RELEVANCE
form
Reset this search form
Submit this search form
inline images
horizontal rule
italic text
To comment on this service: feedback@www.whitehouse.gov
e-mail hyperlink
(b)

FIGURE 1-3

The **title** of a Web page is the text that displays on the title bar of the browser window when the Web page displays. The **background** of a Web page is either a solid color or a small graphic image that provides a backdrop against which the other elements are shown. Like the wallpaper in Windows, a background color or graphic can be tiled, or repeated, across the entire page. **Normal text** is the text that makes up the main content of a Web page. Normal text also can be formatted to display as bold, italic, or underlined or in different colors. **Headings** are used to separate different paragraphs of text or different sections of a page. Headings are a larger font size than normal text and usually are bold or italic.

The TITLE Tag

The TITLE tag is used extensively by Web search engines. Search engines use the text inside a TITLE tag as part of the search criteria to determine a successful match.

A **hyperlink**, or **link**, is an area of the page that you click to instruct the browser to go to a location in a file or to request a file from a server. On the World Wide Web, hyperlinks are the primary way to navigate between pages. Links not only point to Web pages, but also to graphics, sound, multimedia, e-mail addresses, and program files. The most commonly used hyperlinks are text links. When text is used to identify a hyperlink, it usually is given a color different from the normal text.

An **inline image** is a graphic or picture file that is not part of the page's HTML file itself. Rather, these separate graphic and picture files are merged into the Web page as it is displayed. The HTML file contains <IMG> tags that tell the browser which graphic file to request from the server, where to locate it on the page, and how to display it. Some inline images are animated, meaning they include motion and can change in appearance. Inline images also can be used as hyperlinks on a Web page.

An **image map** is a special type of inline image. The image is divided into sections, with a URL assigned to each section. Clicking one of the sections of the image instructs the browser to display a different area of the current page or a different page altogether.

Horizontal rules are lines that display across the page to separate different sections of the page. Although the appearance of horizontal rules varies, often on a Web page, a horizontal rule actually is an inline image.

Many Web pages present a series of text items as a **list**. Typically, lists are numbered or bulleted. A **numbered list** presents an ordered list of items, such as the steps in this project. Numbers precede the items in a numbered list. A **bulleted list** presents an unordered list of items and often uses small images called **bullets** preceding each item. Different shapes of bullets are available and, as with horizontal rules, many Web pages actually use inline images as bullets. Bulleted lists also are called **unordered lists.**

Forms are areas of a Web page that allow a person displaying a Web page to enter information to be sent back to the Web server. The information is supplied using input elements within the form such as option buttons or text boxes. **Tables** are used to present text and graphics in rows and columns. The intersection of a row and column is called a **cell**. The text or graphic in a cell often is used as a hyperlink. The **border width** of a table determines the width of the grid lines surrounding the cells. When the border width is set to zero, grid lines do not display.

Frames allow you to divide the display area of the browser into sections. A different Web page can be displayed in each frame. Web pages with frames have many possible applications. For example, you can keep a table of contents for your Web site always visible in one frame while displaying different pages in another. Users can click different hyperlinks in the table of contents frame and display the corresponding Web page in one of the other frames. All of these Web page elements are defined using HTML.

Web Page Design

The purpose of the Web page will determine which HTML items are included. Do not clutter the page with unnecessary objects just to show off. See Project 2 for Web page design criteria and guidelines.

HTML Tags

HTML tags are not case-sensitive. For example, the body element tag can be typed as <BODY>, <body>, or even <BoDy>.

HTML Basics

Defining the type and layout of an element on a Web page requires one or more HTML tags. As shown in Table 1-1 on page FP 1.7, HTML tags begin with the less than sign (<) and end with the greater than sign (>). Tags often are used in pairs to indicate the start and end of an element or format. The end tag contains a forward slash (/). For example, <H1> indicates the start of a size 1 (largest) heading, and </H1> indicates the end of a size 1 (largest) heading. These tags would be used to display the text, My Favorite Web Sites, as a size 1 heading as follows:

<H1>My Favorite Web Sites</H1>

Tags can be used in combination to apply multiple formatting features at the same time. For example,

<CENTER><H1>My Favorite Web Sites</H1></CENTER>

would center the size 1 heading on the page. If tags are used in combination, as in the example above, then the closing tags are in the opposite order as the beginning tags.

HTML tags can contain keywords that further define the appearance of the element created by the tag. Keywords take the form

keyword=value

For example, an alternative to the previous example is to use the keyword ALIGN. ALIGN=CENTER tells the browser to center text on the page, and it can be used within the <H1> tag as follows:

<H1 ALIGN=CENTER>My Favorite Web Sites</H1>

Two of the more frequently used tags are those for creating a hyperlink and inserting an inline image. Hyperlinks are added using the <A> </A> tag and the HREF tag. The HREF tag takes the form:

HREF="URL"

where the keyword HREF defines this as a hypertext reference and the URL in quotation marks indicates the location of the linked file. The HREF tag is included within the beginning hyperlink tag <A>. You then can insert text or the URL of an image between the beginning and ending hyperlink tags. The person viewing the Web page will see the text or image and can click it to initiate the link. When text is used in a hyperlink, called **hypertext**, it often displays as underlined text. For example, to create a hypertext link to NASA's Jupiter page, you would type

```
<A HREF="pds.jpl.nasa.gov/planets/welcome/jupiter.htm">Jupiter</A>
```

To insert an inline image in a Web page, you would use the <IMG> tag. The <IMG> tag takes the form:

<IMG SRC="URL">

where the <IMG> tag indicates this element as an inline image and the SRC keyword and the URL in quotation marks indicates the source or location of the desired graphic file. For example, <IMG SRC="mypicture.gif"> inserts a graphic with the file name mypicture.gif into the Web page at the location where the <IMG> tag is located.

Multiple HTML Attribute Tags

The order of placement for attributes, such as centering or italics, is not important. As long as all of the attributes are contained within the HTML tag brackets, they can appear in any order.

With both the HREF and SRC keywords, the way the URL is specified defines where the browser looks for the specified file. If only a file name is supplied after the HREF or SRC keywords, as in the preceding example, the browser will look for that file in the directory on the Web server where the current Web page is located. If both a path and file name are specified (for example, <IMG SRC="/images/mypicture.gif">), then the browser will look in the specified path on the Web server where the current page is located. If you use a complete URL, such as <IMG SRC="http://www.myschool.edu/images/mypicture.gif">, then the browser looks for the file on a different Web server.

The HTML used to create a Web page often is called the **HTML source**, or **source code**. Figure 1-4 shows the HTML source for the page in Figure 1-3b on page FP 1.8. Most Web browsers allow you to view the HTML source for the currently displayed Web page. If you are using Internet Explorer, you click the Source command on the View menu to view the HTML.

```
Query-Photo - Notepad
File  Edit  Search  Help
      <H1>
        <I>Search Public Photographs</I>
        <H2></H2>
      </H1>
    </CENTER>

    <BR clear=all>

    <OL>
      <li>To search Public Photographs, enter a TERM or
      PHRASE in the box below which describes your topic of interest (for
      example, "social security benefits for retired people").<BR><BR>

      <FONT SIZE=2><B>TERM/PHRASE</B></FONT><BR>
      <INPUT TYPE=HIDDEN NAME="fields" VALUE="TITLE">
      <INPUT NAME="query_TITLE" SIZE=30><BR>
      <BR>
      <li>Adjust the START and END dates to limit your search to a specific
      timeframe. Checking "DATE"
      will return the most recent documents first.  Checking "RELEVANCE" will return
      the most relevant documents first.<BR><BR>

      <TABLE WIDTH=100%><TR VALIGN=TOP><TD>
```

HTML tags

FIGURE 1-4

Many other HTML tags exist to help you design a Web page exactly as you want. It is not necessary for you to understand every HTML tag; with FrontPage, you simply determine how best to convey the information and then make those changes on the Web page using FrontPage commands. FrontPage inserts the appropriate HTML tags for you.

FrontPage Webs

A typical Web server stores anywhere from one to several thousand Web pages. Some of the pages will have hyperlinks to a group of other pages on the Web server. In FrontPage, a group of related Web pages is called a **FrontPage web**. A FrontPage web consists of the Web pages, images, documents, multimedia, and other files, folders, and programs that make up related content at a Web site. The Web pages in a FrontPage web usually are related by topic or purpose, and most webs use a series of hyperlinks to connect the related pages to each other.

A FrontPage web also can be composed of groups of other smaller FrontPage webs. For example, a school's Admissions office develops certain Web pages and the Financial Aid office develops other Web pages. The Admissions Web pages could be considered one FrontPage web; all of the Financial Aid Web pages could be considered another Web.

Groups of Web pages within the Financial Aid web also could be organized into webs. For example, one web might include a group of Web pages that contain descriptions of different financial aid packages; another web might include a group of Web pages used for online applications for financial aid. The person designing the Web pages decides which ones belong to a particular FrontPage web.

HTML Editors

Even if FrontPage does not support the latest HTML tags and features, you always can add them later using any text editor. Because HTML files are plain text, you can adjust your documents using your favorite word processor.

Web Authoring Tools

More than seventy different HTML editors are available for the Windows operating system alone. Several Internet newsgroups are devoted just to HTML editors.

Once created, a FrontPage web can be stored on the computer on which FrontPage is installed or on a Web server anywhere on the World Wide Web. Using FrontPage, you can upload and download a complete web to and from your computer to a Web server. **Publishing** involves sending copies of Web pages, image files, multimedia files, and any folders to a server where they then become available to the World Wide Web. To publish a FrontPage web, you would need proper security clearance to store files on the Web server on which you publish your FrontPage web. FrontPage thus not only helps you create Web pages, but also helps you manage an entire Web site on the World Wide Web.

Starting FrontPage

FrontPage 98 consists of two components, the Microsoft FrontPage Explorer and the FrontPage Editor. The **FrontPage Explorer** is a tool for organizing, creating, administering, and publishing FrontPage webs. Using the FrontPage Explorer, you can create new webs, administer existing webs, and publish the completed webs on a Web server.

The **FrontPage Editor** is a Web page editor that allows you to create and edit individual Web pages without needing to know hypertext markup language (HTML). The FrontPage Editor will be explained in more detail later in the project. When developing a Web site, you first use the FrontPage Explorer to lay out the relationship between the Web pages within a web. You then use the FrontPage Editor to add, delete, or edit each individual Web page — adding images, text, hyperlinks, and other elements to convey the desired information.

To learn how to use Microsoft FrontPage 98 to create a Web site, you will create a Personal Pages web, which is a set of Web pages (Figure 1-1 on page FP 1.5) that describes you, your interests, and some of your favorite Web sites. The following steps show how to start Microsoft FrontPage 98 and then begin developing your Personal Pages web.

Steps To Start FrontPage

1 Click the Start button on the taskbar. Point to Programs. Point to Microsoft FrontPage.

The Start menu and Programs submenu display (Figure 1-5).

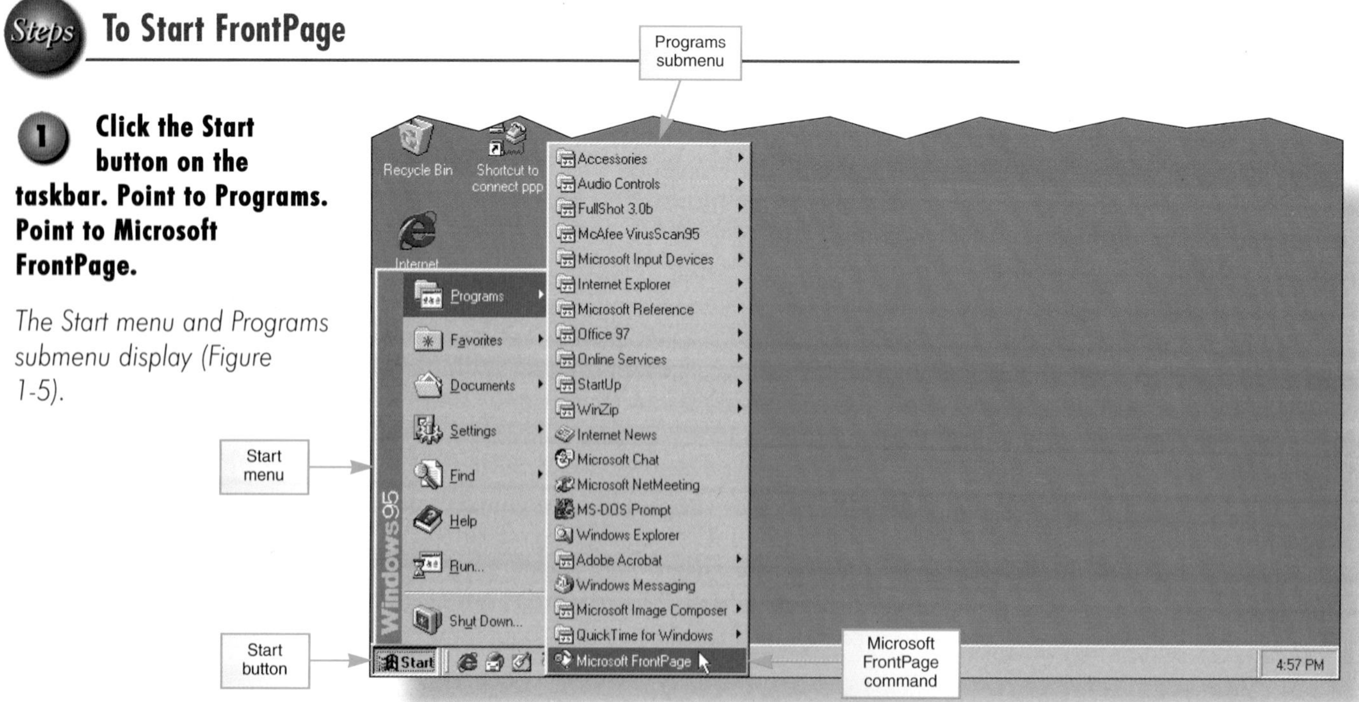

FIGURE 1-5

2 Click Microsoft FrontPage on the Programs submenu.

The FrontPage Explorer window opens and the Getting Started dialog box displays (Figure 1-6). This dialog box contains options to open an existing FrontPage web or create a new FrontPage web.

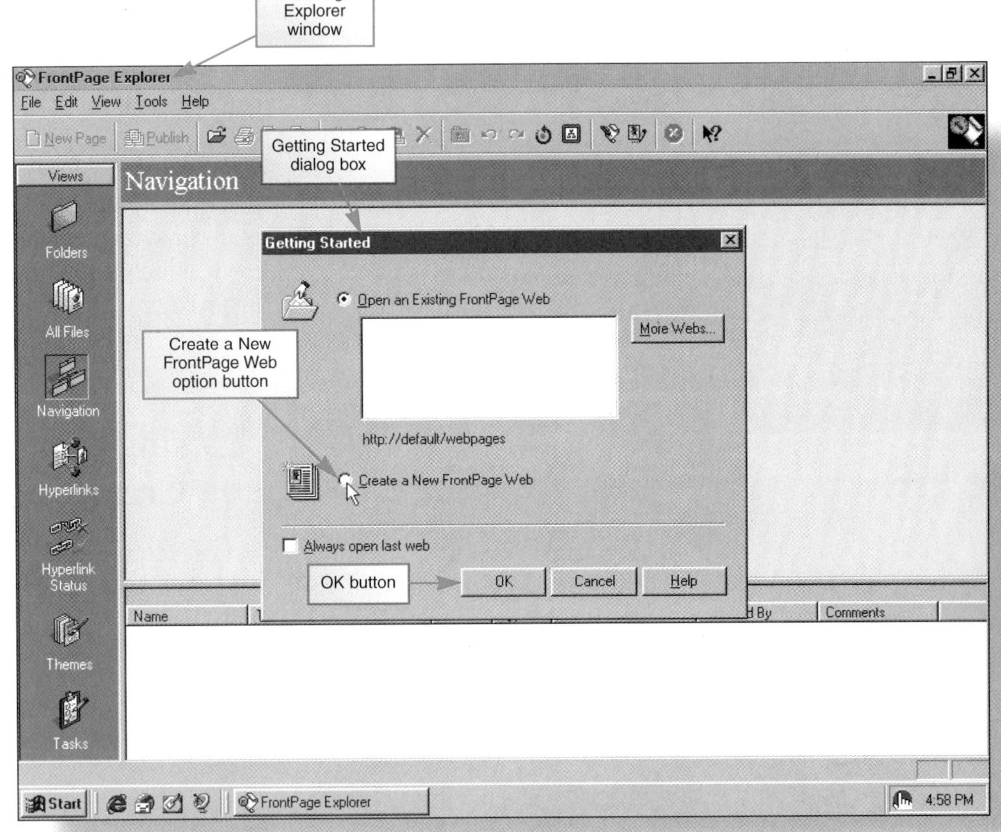

FIGURE 1-6

3 Click Create a New FrontPage Web and then click the OK button.

The New FrontPage Web dialog box *displays, prompting you for information needed to create a new FrontPage web (Figure 1-7).*

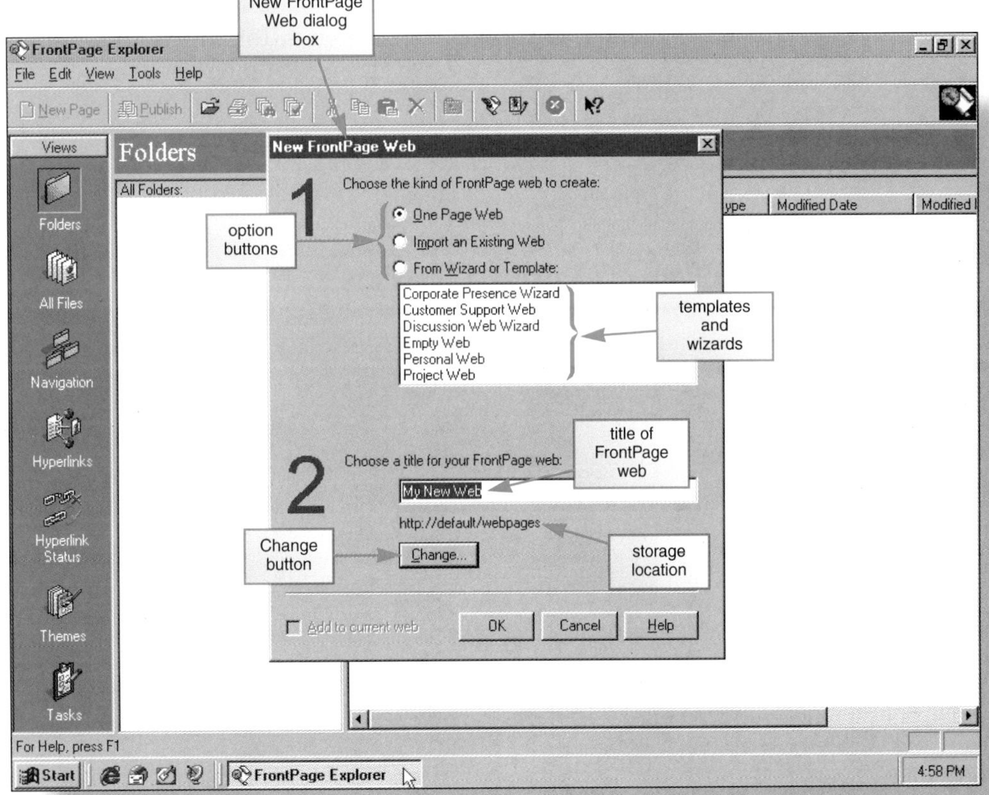

FIGURE 1-7

Table 1-2

TYPE	DESCRIPTION
One Page Web	Creates a FrontPage web with a single page (a home page). Used to create a FrontPage web from scratch with no suggested content.
Import an Existing Web	Imports an existing web into a new FrontPage web. Starts the Import Web Wizard, which guides you through the process of importing an existing Web site.
From Wizard or Template	Creates a new FrontPage web with suggested content using wizards and templates.

In the New FrontPage Web dialog box, you can select the type of FrontPage web you want to create. FrontPage allows you to create a one-page Web, import a Web from a Web server or your personal computer, or create a Web using a template or wizard. Table 1-2 describes the options from which you can choose when creating a new FrontPage web.

Using a Template to Create a FrontPage Web

Designing a Web site is a complex process that requires you to make decisions concerning the appearance and content of each Web page. For example, when developing a web composed of several Web pages, you should use a consistent design and layout on each. This means the pages should be similar in their use of features such as background color, margins, buttons, and headings. To support this objective, FrontPage 98 provides several preformatted webs as a start for your web. These preformatted Web pages are called templates.

FrontPage Templates

A FrontPage **template** is a series of Web pages that have been organized and formatted with a basic framework of content on which new pages and new FrontPage webs can be based. Each template consists of linked Web pages that already include basic elements such as headings, formatted text, graphics, and hyperlinks. After a page or web is created using a template, you can customize the page or web. The closer the template is to your desired design, the less editing work you have to do to complete your Web site. The following steps show how to create a FrontPage web using a template.

To Create a FrontPage Web Using a Template

1 With the New FrontPage Web dialog box displaying, click From Wizard or Template. Click Personal Web in the From Wizard or Template list box.

The From Wizard or Template option button is selected. Personal Web is highlighted in the From Wizard or Template list box (Figure 1-8).

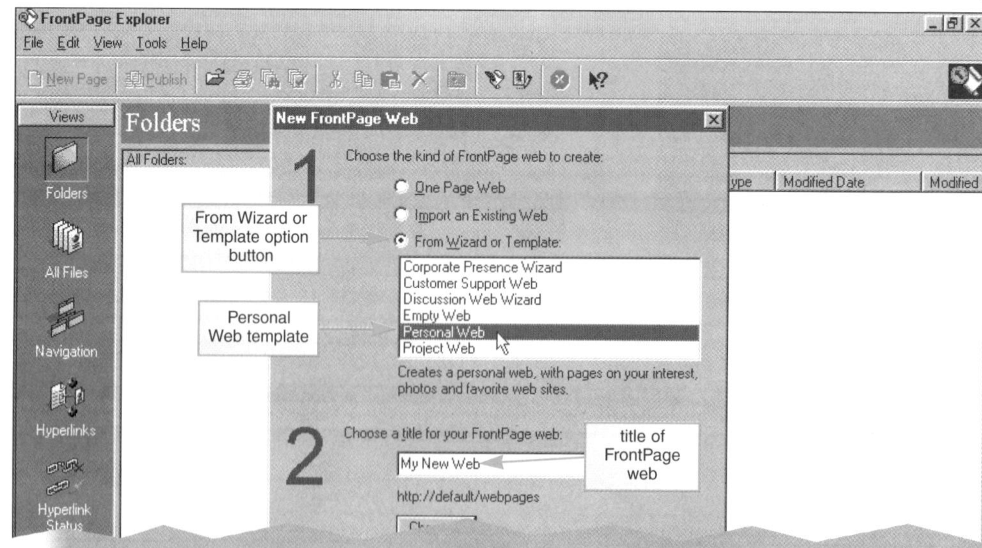

FIGURE 1-8

2 Click the Choose a Title for your FrontPage web text box to highlight the title, My New Web. Type `Personal Pages` **as the title for your new FrontPage web.**

The title, Personal Pages, displays in the text box (Figure 1-9). The title is used to identify the web within the FrontPage Explorer. Next, you have to specify the location where this Web will be stored.

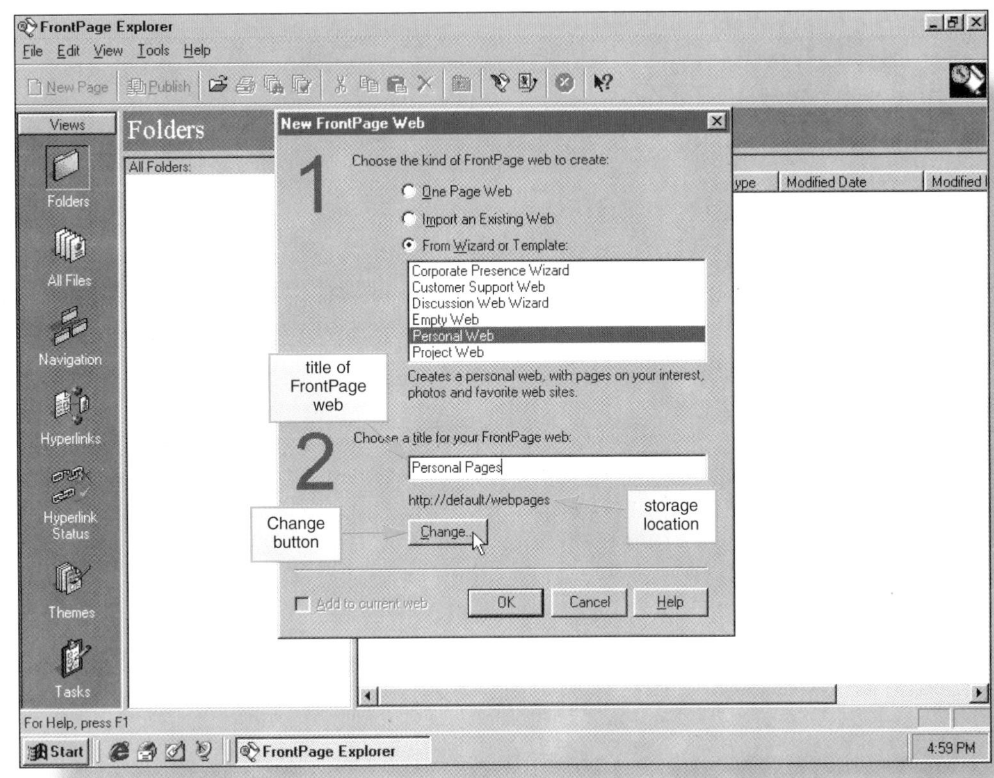

FIGURE 1-9

Click the Change button.

The Change Location dialog box displays (Figure 1-10). The text box contains the location where this web will be stored.

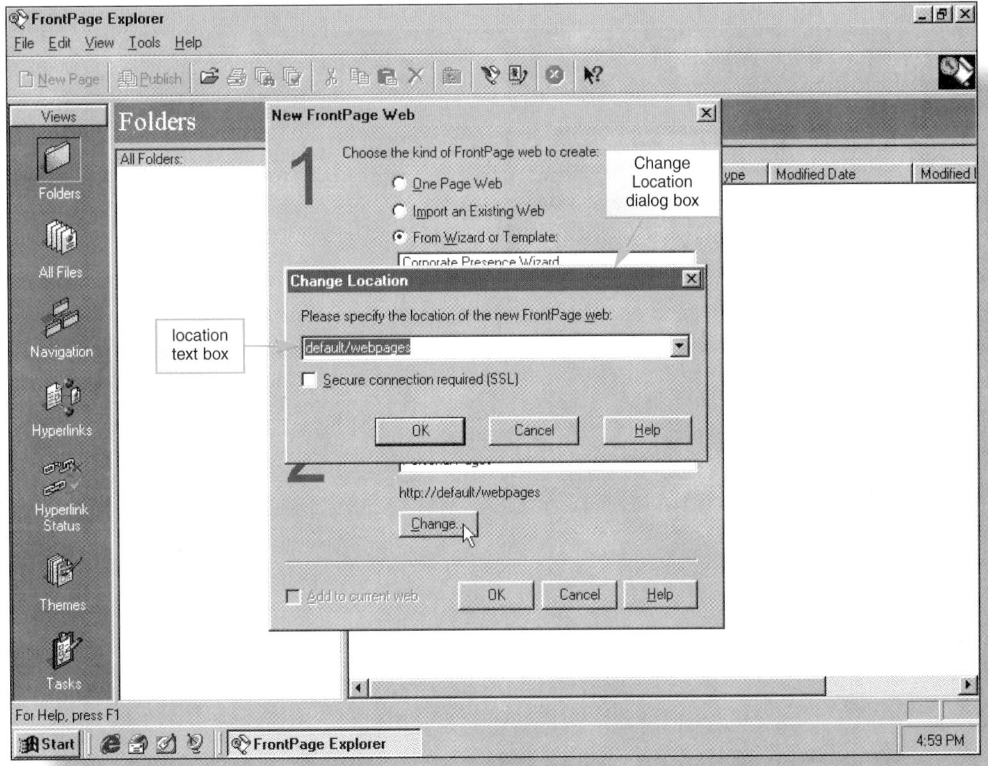

FIGURE 1-10

4 **Insert a floppy disk in drive A. Type** a:\webpages **in the text box.**

The new location displays in the text box (Figure 1-11).

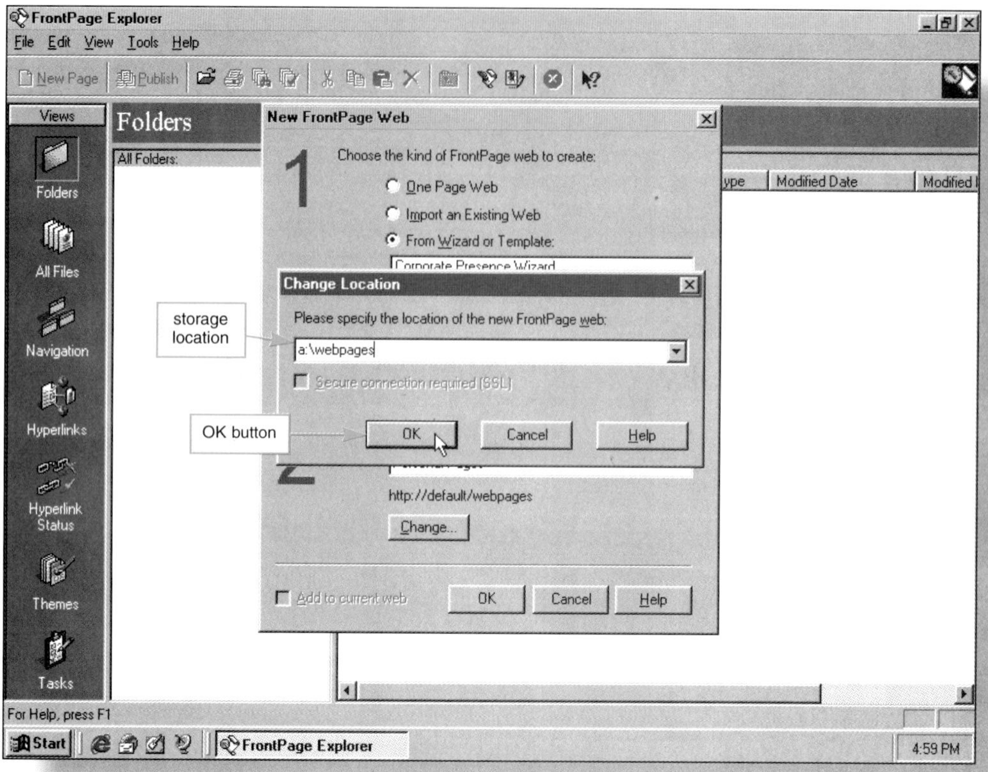

FIGURE 1-11

5 **Click the OK button in the Change Location dialog box.**

The New FrontPage Web dialog box displays with a:\webpages as the location where this web will be stored (Figure 1-12).

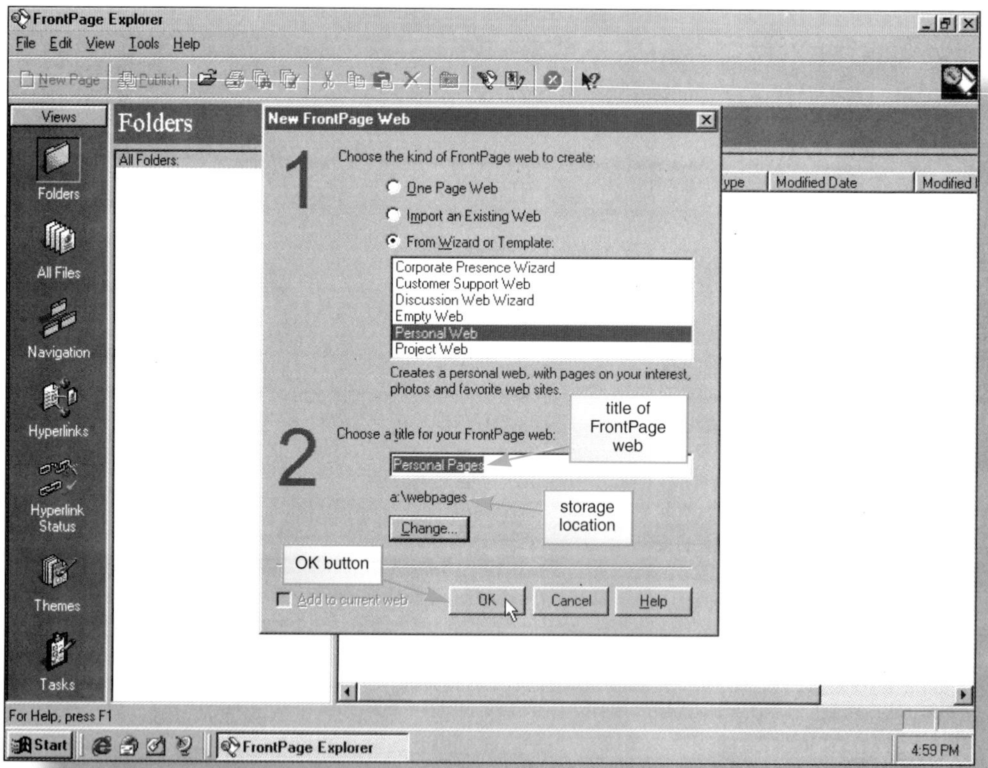

FIGURE 1-12

6 Click the OK button in the New FrontPage Web dialog box.

The FrontPage Explorer dialog box *displays, asking if you want to create the a:\webpages folder on drive A (Figure 1-13).*

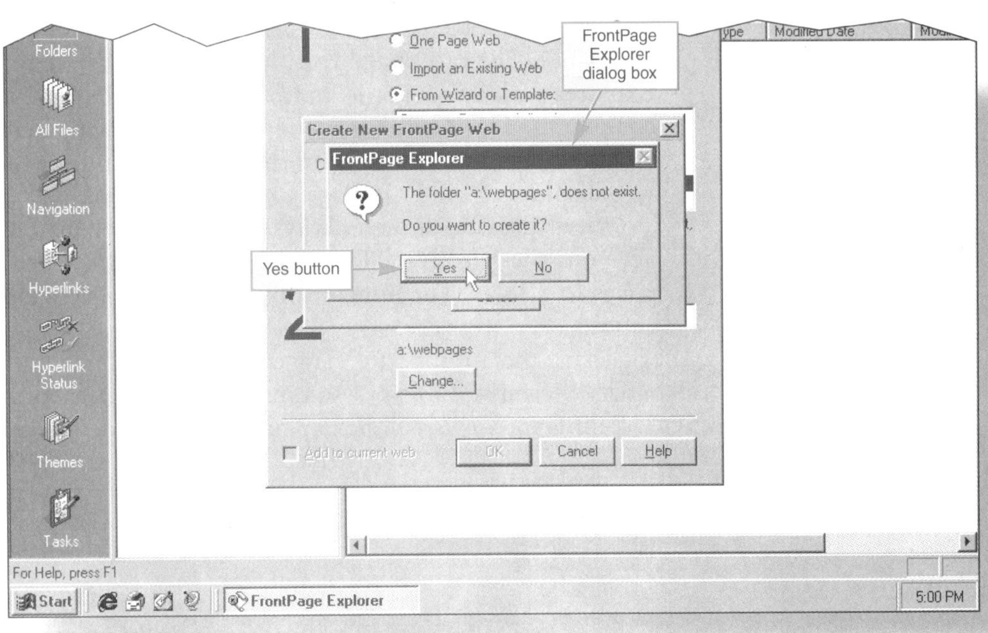

FIGURE 1-13

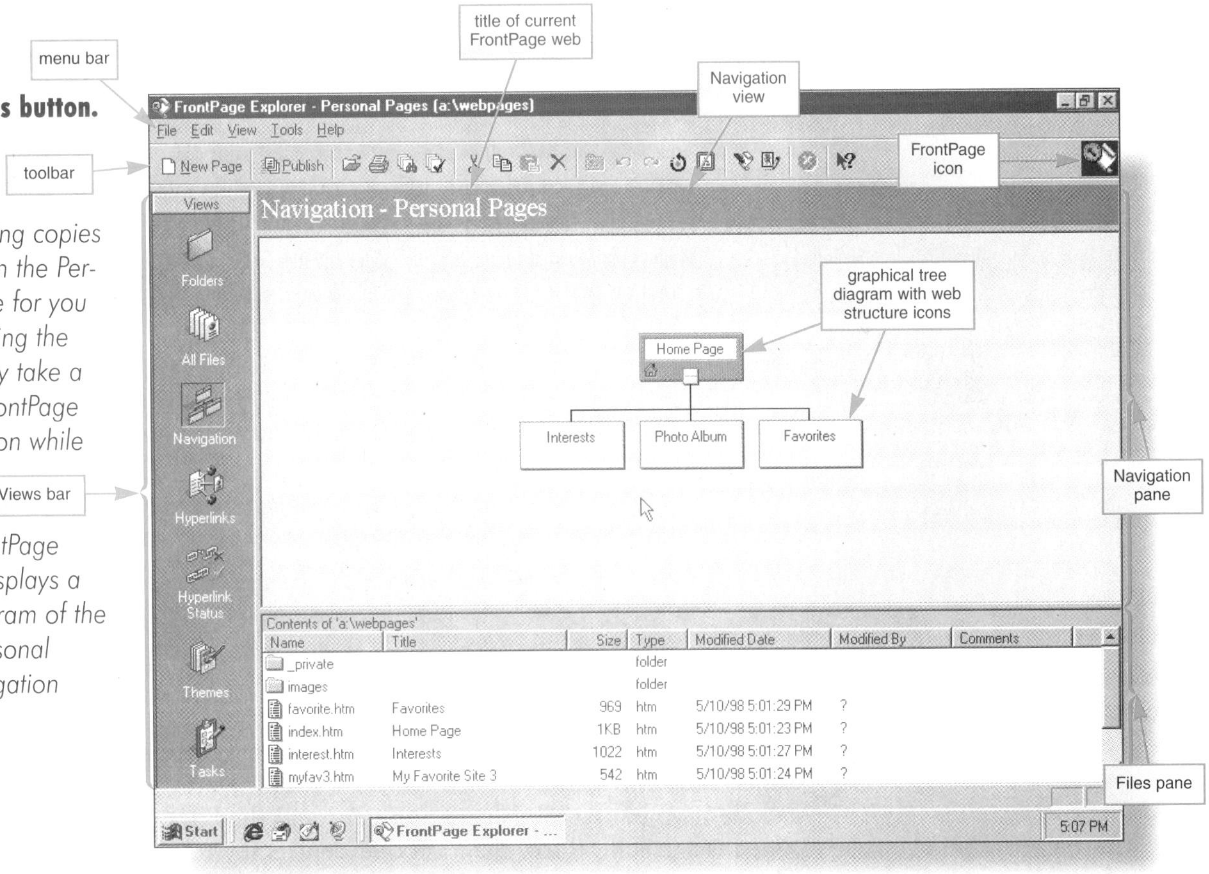

menu bar

title of current FrontPage web

Navigation view

7 Click the Yes button.

toolbar

FrontPage icon

FrontPage begins creating the set of folders and making copies of the Web pages in the Personal Web template for you to customize. Copying the template pages may take a few minutes; the FrontPage icon will be in motion while this takes place. When FrontPage is finished, the FrontPage Explorer window displays a graphical tree diagram of the structure of the Personal Pages web in Navigation view (Figure 1-14).

graphical tree diagram with web structure icons

Views bar

Navigation pane

Files pane

FIGURE 1-14

1. On File menu click New, click FrontPage Web
2. Press ALT+F, N, W

The FrontPage Explorer window has a menu bar, a toolbar, a Views bar, and several panes. The FrontPage Explorer **toolbar**, located at the top of the FrontPage Explorer window, contains buttons that execute the most commonly used menu commands. The **Views bar** is the vertical bar at the left of the FrontPage Explorer window. The seven buttons on the Views bar allow you to control how the current web displays in the FrontPage Explorer window.

Views provide different ways of looking at your FrontPage web so you can manage your site effectively. Clicking a button on the Views bar will cause different panes to display. The number of panes and their content depend on the view you choose.

Using the appropriate view can save you time and help you manage your webs more efficiently. Table 1-3 summarizes the buttons and their corresponding views. The different views will be explained in more detail as they are used.

Table 1-3

BUTTON	VIEW	DESCRIPTION
	Folders	Displays the files and folder structure of the current web. This view allows you to manage the files and folders with an interface similar to Windows Explorer. You can drag and drop files between folders, and right-click any file to display a shortcut menu from which you can copy, rename, open, or delete the selected file.
	All Files	Displays all the files that make up the current web, including information about each individual file. The folders are not displayed. All of the files in folders and subfolders in the current web are displayed. This view is useful because it displays the complete path to files in the current web. You can verify the path to a particular file with just one click of the All Files button.
	Navigation	Displays a graphical tree diagram of the relationship among pages in the current web. The Navigation view has two panes, with the structure of the current web in the upper pane, the Navigation pane, and a Windows Explorer-like file and folder list in the bottom pane, the Files pane. The structure of the web is organized similarly to an organizational chart, with the Home Page at the top and linked pages on the lower levels.
	Hyperlinks	Displays the hyperlinks connecting the pages and files in the current web, starting with the Home Page. You can select any page in the current web and all the pages and files that are the targets of hyperlinks in the page are displayed. The hyperlinks are drawn as arrows to the pages or files.
	Hyperlink Status	Verifies and reports on the status of any hyperlinks in the current web. This view simplifies the management of complex sites by automatically verifying any hyperlinks in the current web. An option is available to verify any hyperlinks that point to files or pages outside the current web or on a remote Web server.
	Themes	Previews and applies a preformatted design to the current web. A theme can consist of background images, bullets, inline images, navigation bars, and other items that are applied to each of the pages in the current web. Applying a theme gives your pages a consistent, attractive appearance.
	Tasks	Displays a list of activities that have yet to be completed for the current web. Acting as a project manager to some extent, the Tasks view can be used to help manage your web by flagging important reminders and prerequisites.

After making a copy of the Personal Web template pages, the FrontPage Explorer displays the Navigation view (Figure 1-14 on the previous page). Navigation view includes two panes: the Navigation pane and the Files pane. The **Navigation pane** contains a graphical tree diagram that depicts the relationships among the various Web pages in the current FrontPage web. The title of the web, Personal Pages, displays at the top of the pane.

The **Files pane** shows the files and folders that make up the Personal Pages web. You can sort the files and folders by clicking the column heading buttons in the pane, just as you would in Windows Explorer. Two folders currently display in the Files pane. FrontPage automatically creates these folders when you create a new FrontPage web. The **images folder** holds any graphic files used in the current web.

The **_private folder** holds files you can use on the Web pages in the current web, but do not want people who are browsing your web to access individually. For example, you can place image files that are used as inline images in the _private folder. You can use these on the Web pages, but others cannot access the graphic files individually.

Applying a Theme to a FrontPage Web

When creating a web that consists of many Web pages, it is important to maintain a consistent, professional appearance throughout all the pages. FrontPage includes more than 50 built-in collections of design elements — bullets, background patterns, fonts and graphics — called **themes**, that you can apply to an entire web or to a single page. The themes vary in style, color, and fonts. You also can create your own themes and store them for use when developing other webs.

Once you apply a theme to a web, every page in the web will have a uniform appearance. Everything on a Web page, from its bullets to its background patterns, matches all the other pages in the web. When you insert new elements in a page that uses a theme, FrontPage automatically formats those elements to match the theme. FrontPage also automatically applies the theme to any new pages you create in the web.

Each FrontPage template uses a default theme. Thus, when you selected the Personal Web template in the previous set of steps, FrontPage automatically applied a theme to the Personal Pages web. The following steps show how to display the Themes view, preview the theme used in the current web, and then apply a different theme to your Personal Pages web.

Steps To Apply a Theme to a FrontPage Web

1 Click the Themes button.

The Personal Pages web displays in Themes view (Figure 1-15). Using this view, you can control how themes are used in the current web. The Use Selected Themes list box contains all of the themes provided with FrontPage. The Theme Preview area displays a sample page using the currently selected theme. The preview shows how the color scheme, background image, and headings will display on each Web page. The current theme for the Personal Pages web template is Global Marketing.

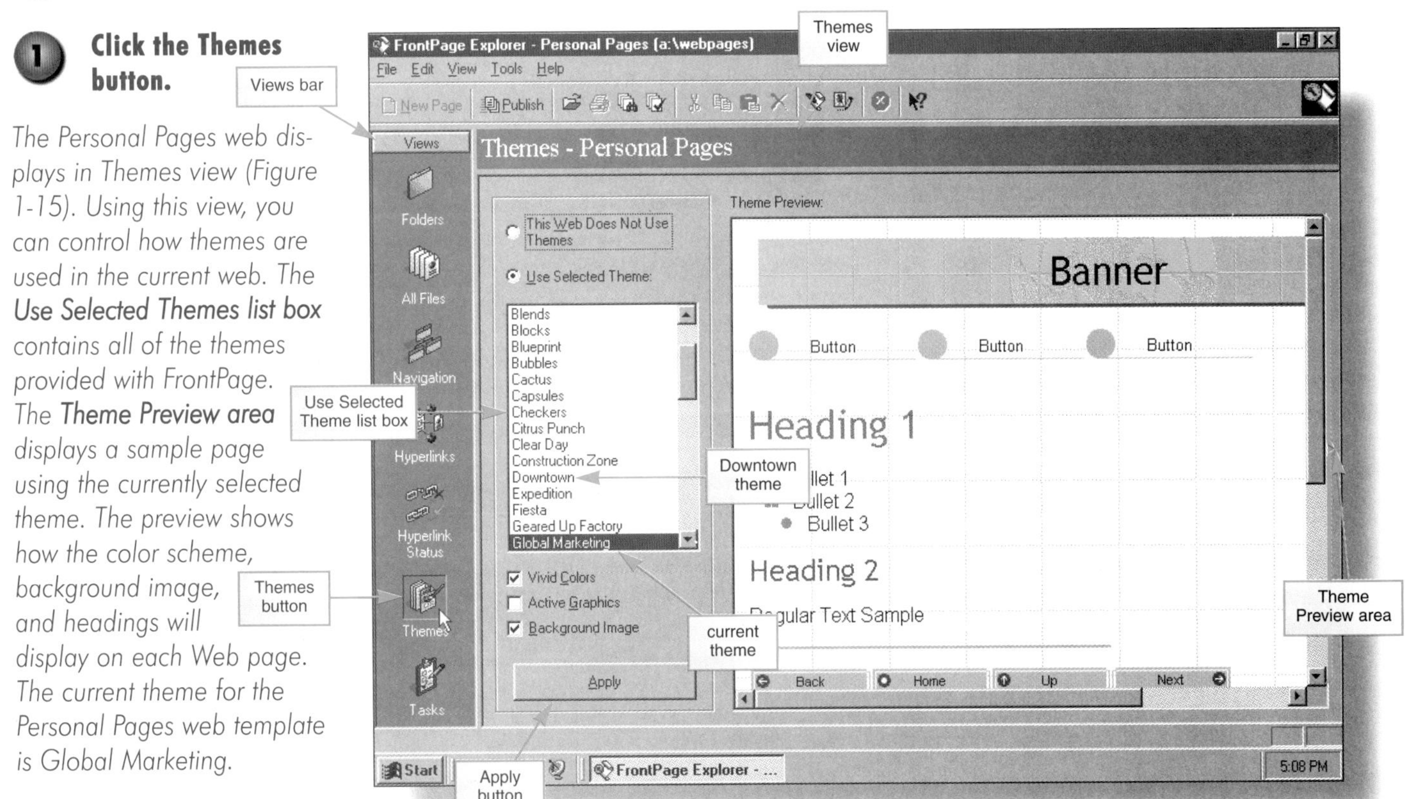

FIGURE 1-15

2 **Click Downtown in the Use Selected Theme list box.**

A sample of the Downtown theme displays in the Theme Preview area (Figure 1-16).

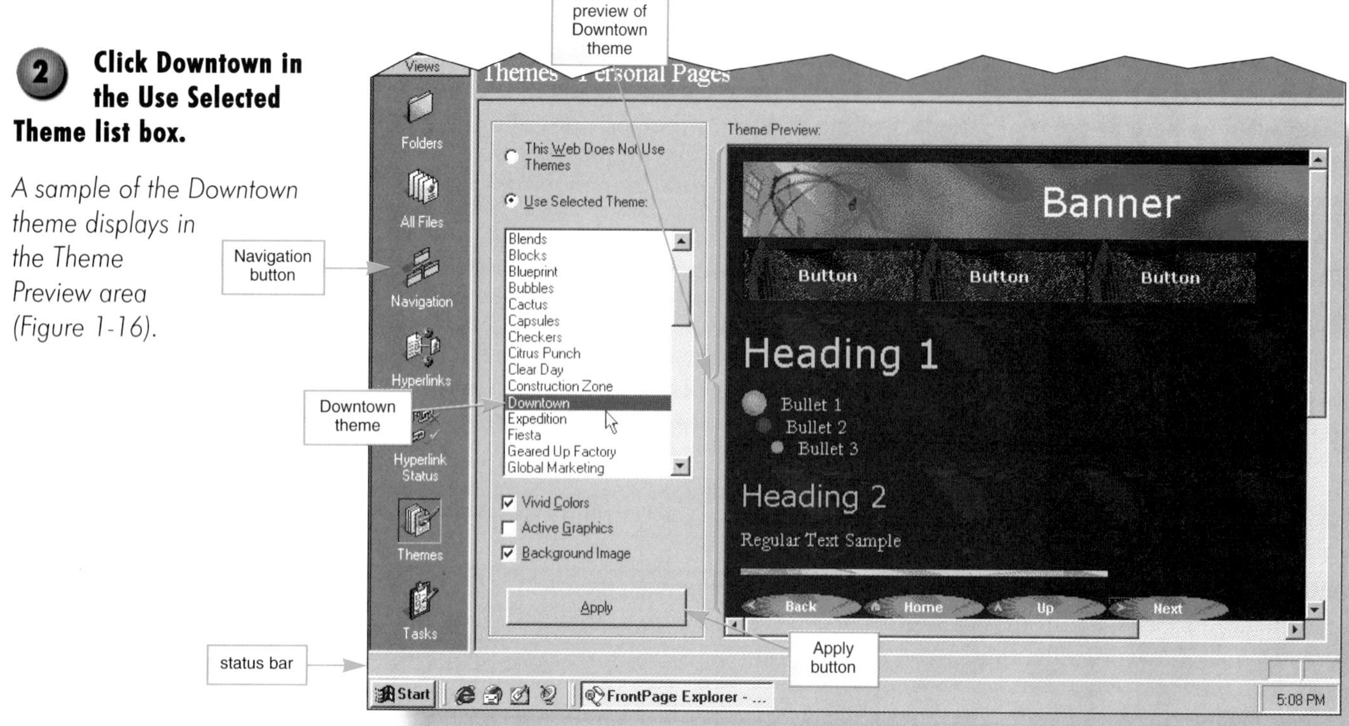

FIGURE 1-16

3 **Click the Apply button to apply the Downtown theme to the entire current web.**

FrontPage displays a message on the status bar in the lower-left corner of the FrontPage Explorer window indicating FrontPage is applying the new theme to all the Web pages in the current web. This can take anywhere from a few seconds to a few minutes, depending on the number of pages in the current web.

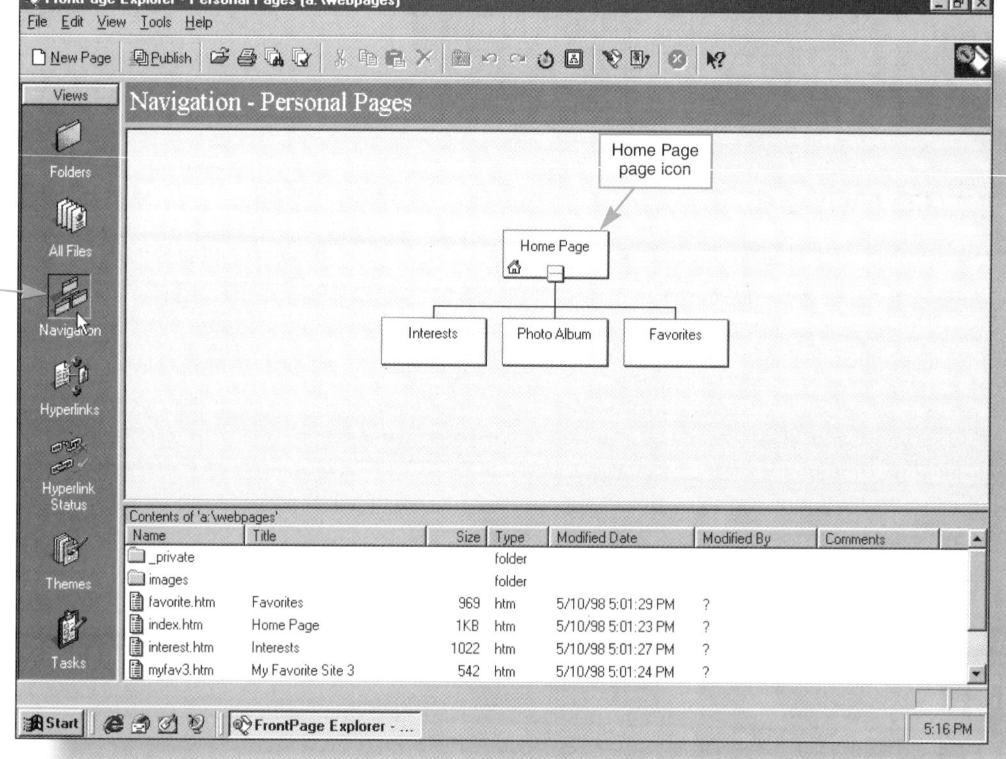

FIGURE 1-17

4 **When FrontPage is finished applying the Downtown theme, click the Navigation button on the Views bar to return to Navigation view.**

The Personal Pages web displays in Navigation view (Figure 1-17).

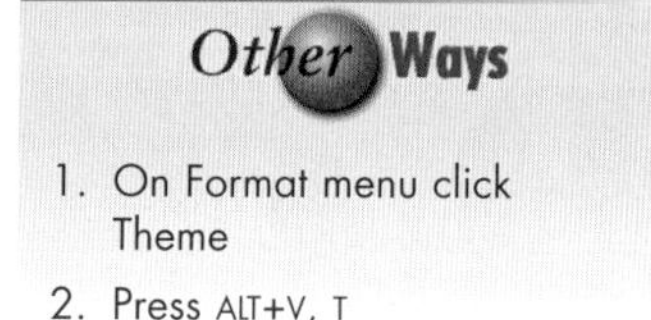

Other Ways

1. On Format menu click Theme
2. Press ALT+V, T

You successfully have previewed and applied a theme to a FrontPage web using Themes view. While applying a new theme, FrontPage displays information about the operation in progress on the **status bar**, which is an area at the bottom of the window. Once the theme is applied, the background, fonts, and graphics used on the pages in the web are changed. For example, applying the Downtown theme to the web changes the background from white to blue (Figure 1-16). Clicking **Vivid Colors** in the Themes view applies brighter colors to text and graphics. Selecting **Active Graphics** animates certain elements on the pages. Selecting **Background Image** applies a textured background image to the pages in the current web.

Although the templates provided with Microsoft FrontPage are useful for quickly setting up a FrontPage web, you will want to customize them further to convey your message. To modify a Web page, you use the Microsoft FrontPage Editor. The next section describes how to modify a Web page using the FrontPage Editor.

More About

Templates

If you are going to create several similar Web pages, it will help first to create a simple Web page containing common elements found on all pages and then save it. By opening this file instead of starting from scratch, you will save some time.

Modifying a Web Page Using the FrontPage Editor

The **FrontPage Editor** is a tool for creating, designing, and editing the individual pages in a web. The FrontPage Editor allows you to add and modify text, images, tables, form fields, and other elements on each individual Web page. You do not need to know or learn HTML to modify Web pages using the FrontPage Editor. For example, if you insert a graphic on a page, the FrontPage Editor will insert the proper HTML code for you (in this case, the <IMG> tag).

If you want to edit the HTML code directly, you can use the FrontPage Editor's **HTML view**. In this view, you can enter text and HTML tags just as you would with a word processor. HTML views will be discussed later in the project.

Starting the FrontPage Editor

To start the FrontPage Editor, you simply double-click a page icon in the graphical tree diagram in Navigation view. The FrontPage Editor window will display with that page in the FrontPage Editor window. The steps on the next page show how to start the FrontPage Editor and customize the Web pages in your Personal Pages web.

More About

The FrontPage Editor

You do not have to open a FrontPage web to use the FrontPage Editor. Click the Cancel button when prompted to open a FrontPage web and then click Show FrontPage Editor on the Tools menu.

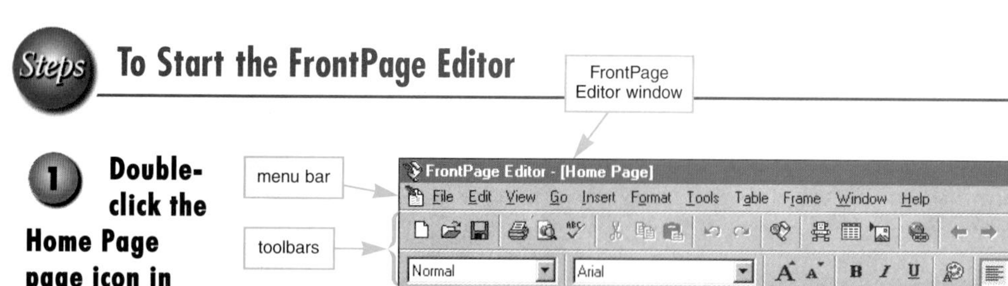

To Start the FrontPage Editor

1 Double-click the Home Page page icon in the Navigation pane.

The FrontPage Editor window opens with the Home Page in the display area (Figure 1-18). The tab at the bottom of the page indicates that the page displays in Normal view.

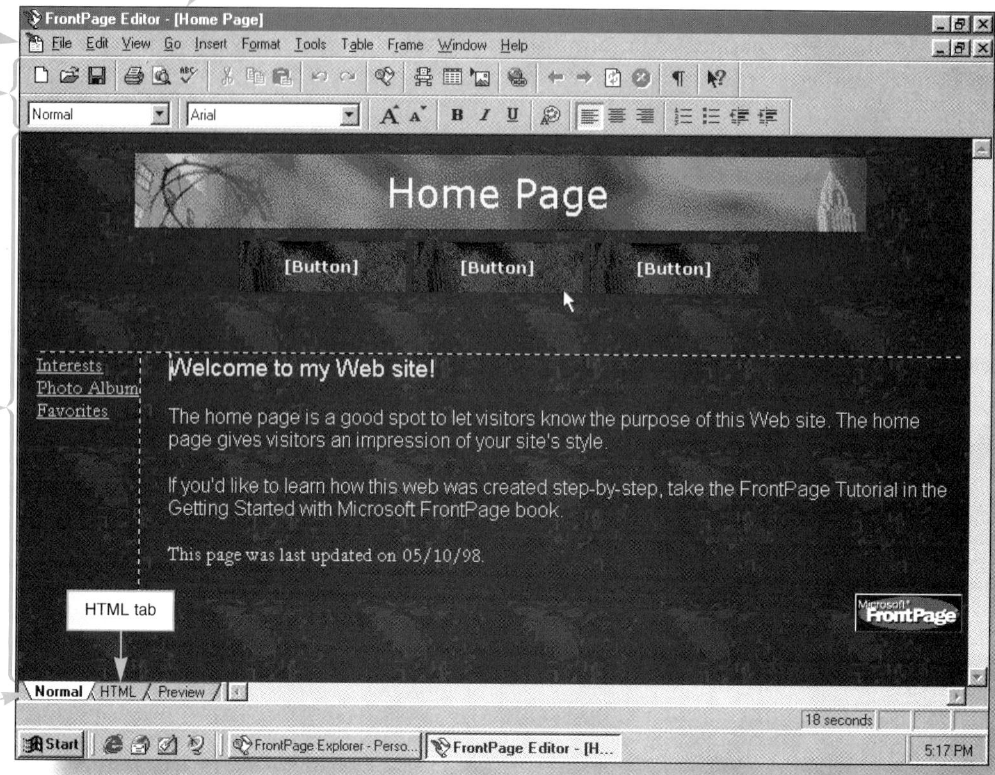

FIGURE 1-18

Other Ways

1. Right-click page icon, click Open
2. Press CTRL+O
3. Press ALT+E, O

You also can start the FrontPage Editor by clicking the Show FrontPage Editor button on the Standard toolbar. The FrontPage Editor window will open, with a new page in the display area.

The FrontPage Editor Window

The **FrontPage Editor window** has a menu bar, toolbars, a display area showing the current Web page you are editing, and three tabs that provide different views of the Web page. Like the FrontPage Explorer toolbar, the **Standard toolbar** at the top of the FrontPage Editor window contains the most commonly used menu commands. The FrontPage Editor also has a **Format toolbar** that contains buttons that format selected paragraphs or text. You can display or remove additional toolbars using commands on the View menu. Figure 1-19 summarizes the various toolbars available in the FrontPage Editor.

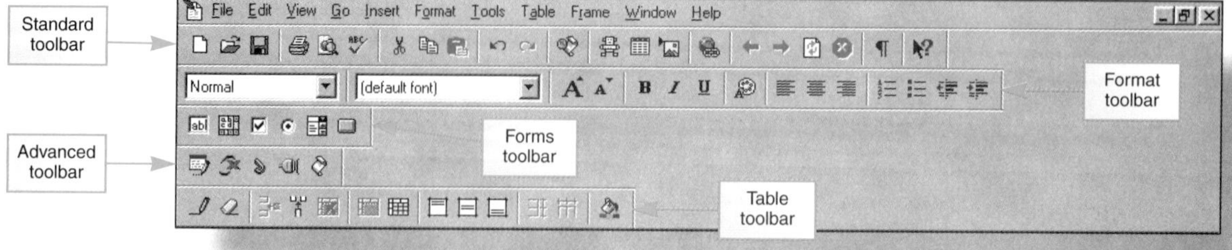

FIGURE 1-19

The FrontPage Editor is a **WYSIWYG** (what you see is what you get) editor, meaning that, as a Web page or file is created, it displays the HTML document as it will appear on the Web. Using a WYSIWYG editor such as the FrontPage Editor eliminates the need to continuously save a partially completed Web page, load it in your Web browser to test it, switch to the editor to make additions and changes, and so on.

Viewing the HTML Source for a Web Page

The tabs at the bottom left of the display area provide different views of the Web page in the FrontPage Editor. Clicking the **Normal tab** allows you to work with the Web page in a WYSIWYG environment, or Normal view. Clicking the **Preview tab** displays the Web page as anyone browsing the Web would see it. Clicking the **HTML tab** displays the HTML source for the Web page. Using this view, you can edit the HTML. Perform the following steps to view the HTML source for the Home Page Web page.

To View the HTML Source for a Web Page

1 Click the HTML tab at the bottom of the FrontPage Editor window.

The Web page displays in HTML view (Figure 1-20). This view shows the HTML tags used to describe how the Home Page displays when viewed with a Web browser. This view also allows you to make changes directly to the HTML source.

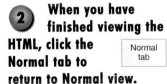

2 When you have finished viewing the HTML, click the Normal tab to return to Normal view.

The Web page displays in Normal view. With FrontPage, most Web page development and modification takes place in Normal view.

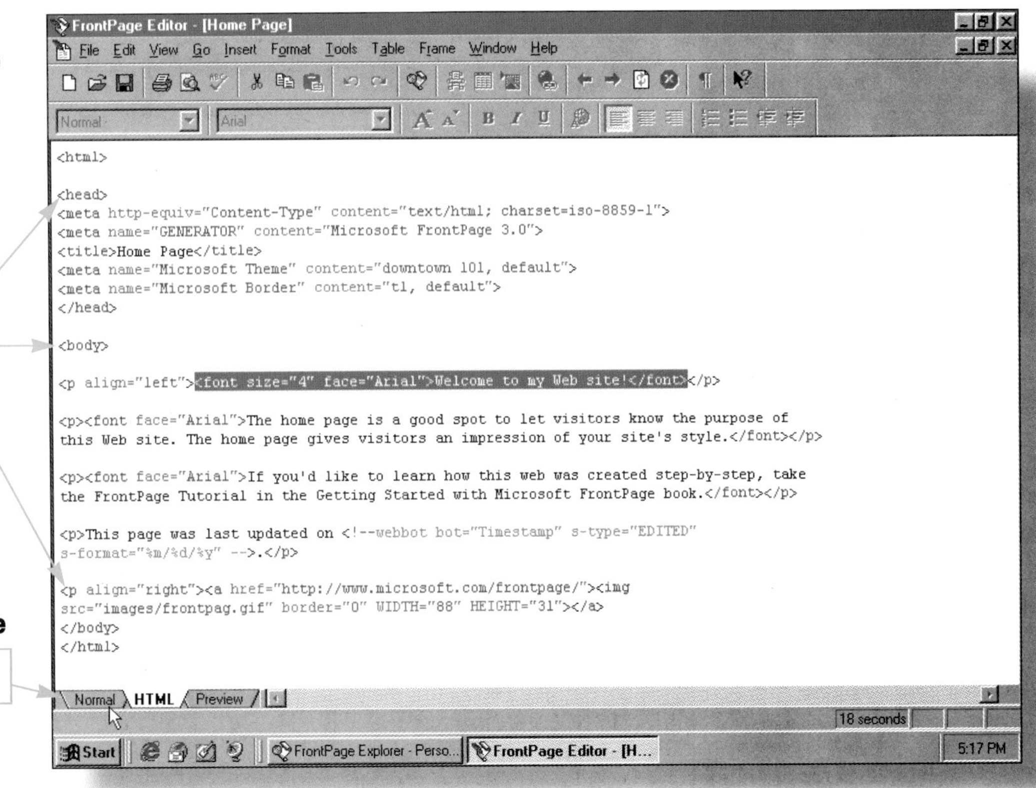

FIGURE 1-20

Microsoft FrontPage 98

Recall that you can edit a page's HTML source using the FrontPage Editor's HTML view. As you type changes, the FrontPage Editor color-codes the HTML. If you choose to edit the HTML, you must enter carefully the HTML tags along with any keywords, text, and file names. Using Normal view is easier, because FrontPage inserts the HTML codes for you.

Editing Text on a Web Page

Even though the template contains pleasant-looking Web pages, the pages are not yet ready for publication on the Web. The templates still include *placeholders* for certain elements on the page. You can change these placeholders to convey the desired information or you can delete them altogether. For instance, you probably will want to change the text that instructs the viewer to go through the FrontPage tutorial.

Before you publish the pages on the Web, you should review all of the pages in the web and edit or delete template items so they reflect the desired information. The following steps demonstrate how to edit the text on a Web page.

To Edit Text on a Web Page

1 Point to the beginning of the first paragraph that begins with the text, The home page is a good spot (Figure 1-21).

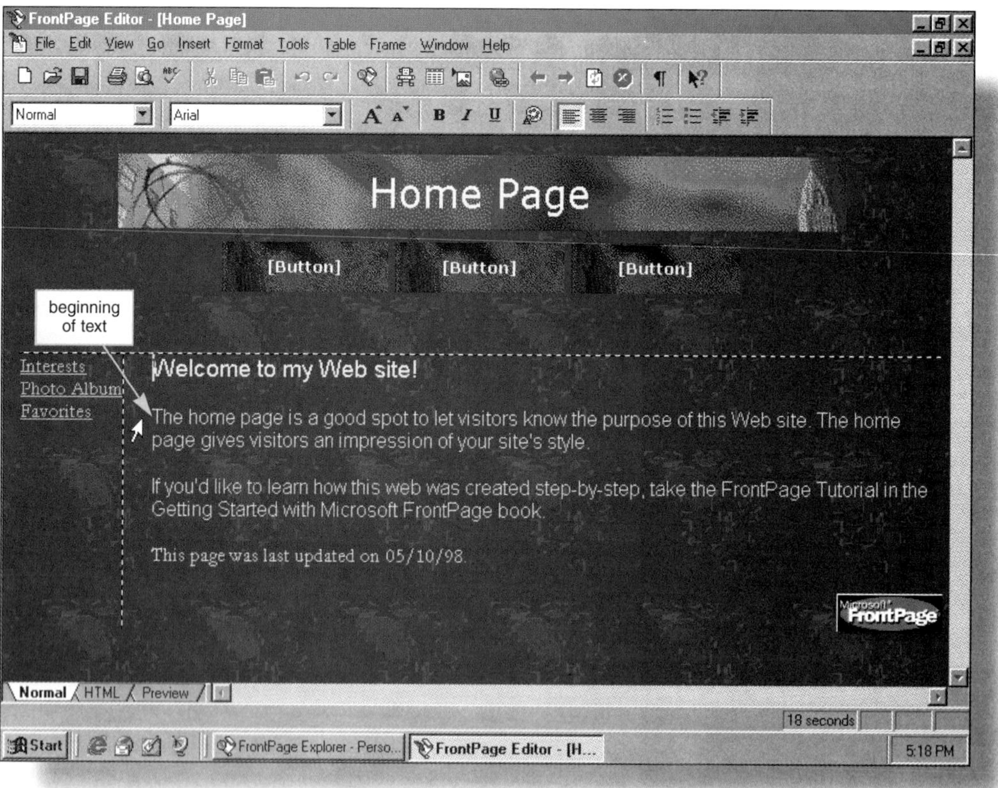

FIGURE 1-21

2 Drag through the first paragraph of text to select it.

The selected text is highlighted (Figure 1-22).

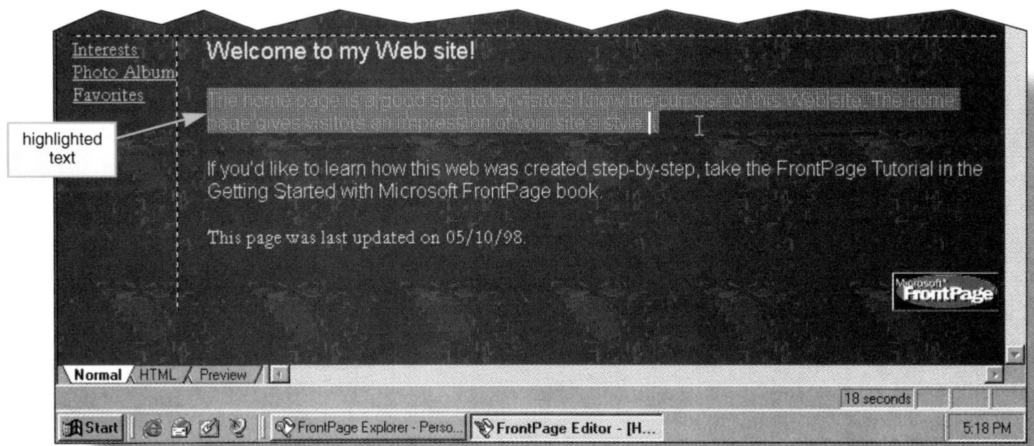

FIGURE 1-22

3 Type `My name is Kurt and I attend Rhetoric University in Hometown, USA` **as the first paragraph. (If you wish, substitute your own personal information here).**

The new text replaces the selected text (Figure 1-23).

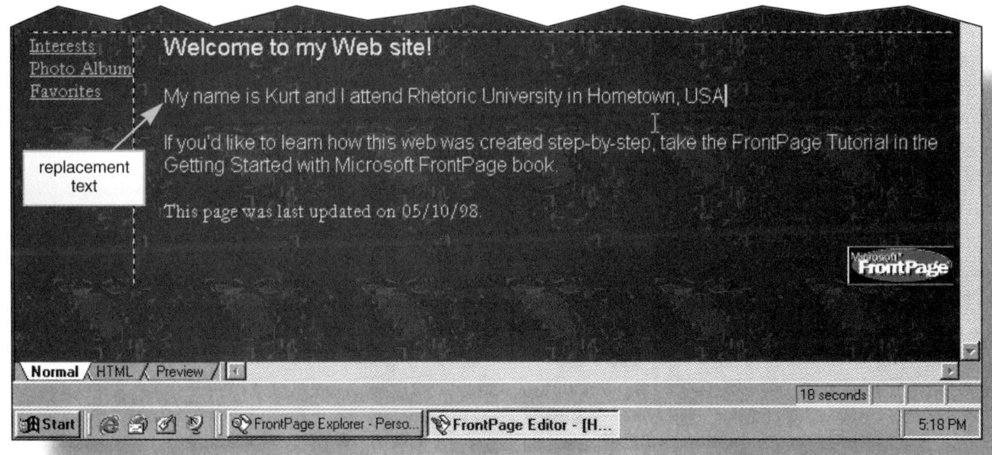

FIGURE 1-23

4 Drag through the second paragraph that begins with the text, If you'd like to learn. With the paragraph selected, type `I'm majoring in Web page development and hope to start a career developing Web pages and related Web materials` **as the new text.**

The new text replaces the selected text (Figure 1-24). The text automatically wraps to the next line as you type.

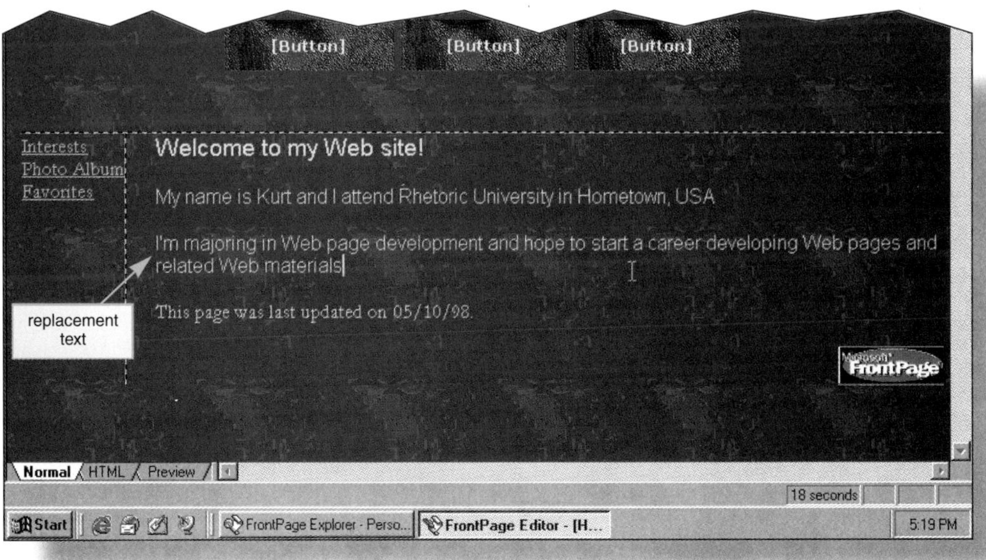

FIGURE 1-24

You can move around the text on the Web page using the ARROW keys. If you make a mistake typing, you can use the BACKSPACE key and back up to correct the mistake and then continue typing.

Adding New Text to a Web Page

Adding new text to a Web page is simply a matter of positioning the insertion point where you want the new text to appear, and then typing the new text. The following steps show how to add new text to a Web page.

To Add New Text to a Web Page

1. **Press the ENTER key to start a new paragraph below the paragraph you just changed.**

The insertion point is positioned at the beginning of a new paragraph (Figure 1-25).

FIGURE 1-25

2. **Type** `Feel free to visit my Interests and Favorites pages` **as the new paragraph.**

The new paragraph displays on the Web page (Figure 1-26).

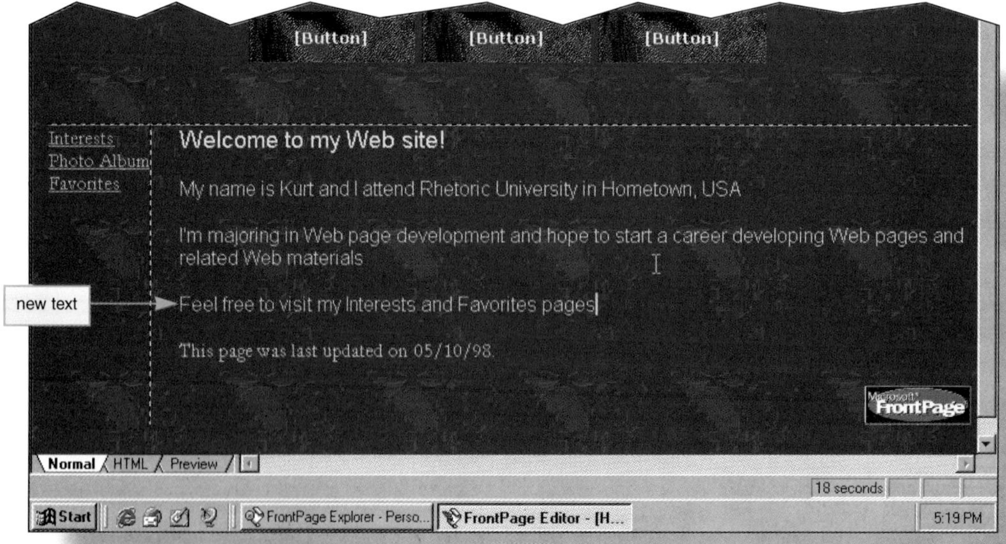

FIGURE 1-26

Editing and adding text on a Web page using the FrontPage Editor is similar to editing a word processing document. In the Normal view of the FrontPage Editor, you can insert, delete, cut, copy, and paste text, just as you would with a word processor. To begin editing, you position the insertion point where you want to make a change and then perform the desired action.

Saving a Web Page

Now that you have edited the Web page using the FrontPage Editor, you should save it on a disk to preserve the changes.

To Save a Web Page

1 Point to the Save button on the Standard toolbar (Figure 1-27).

2 Click the Save button.

The current page is saved in the webpages folder on the floppy disk in drive A.

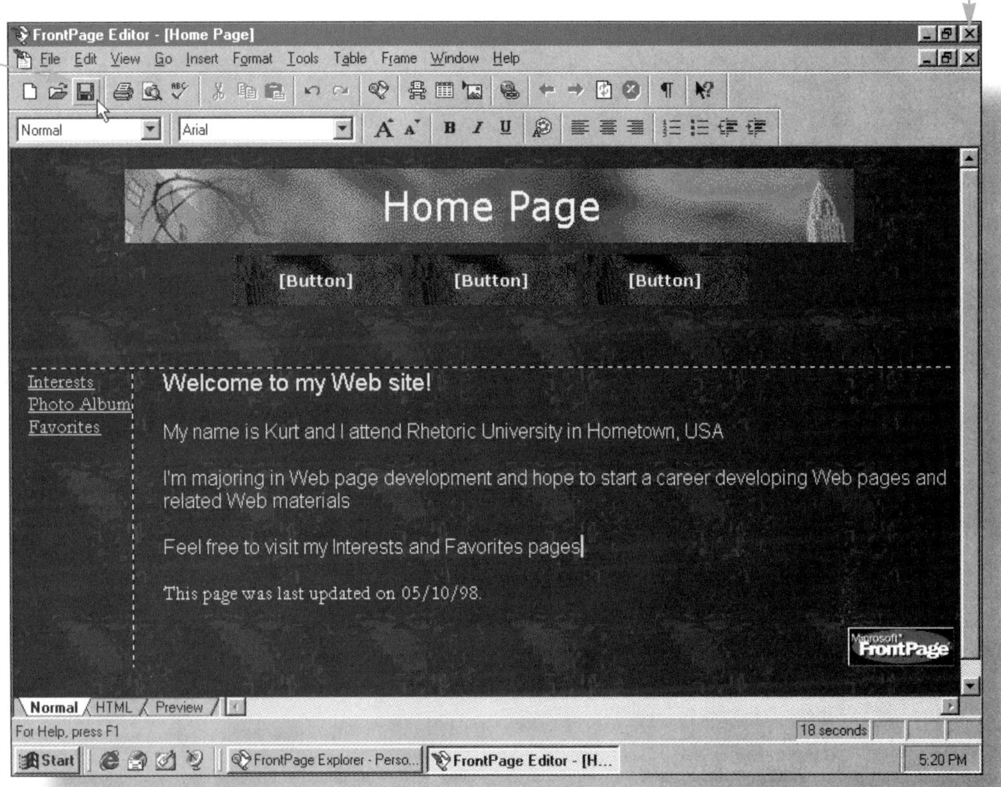

FIGURE 1-27

Other Ways

1. On File menu click Save
2. Press CTRL+S
3. Press ALT+F, S

Clicking the Save button saves the active page in HTML format. Recall that a Web page is simply a file that contains HTML source (see Figure 1-20 on page FP 1.23). HTML files have an .htm file extension by default. When you saved the Web page in the previous steps, FrontPage saved the page as an HTML file using the file name index.htm.

Because the page was opened from the current web, the Save command saves the page without prompting you. If the page has never been saved, the Save command displays the Save As dialog box and prompts you to enter a file name.

Quitting the FrontPage Editor

Once the page has been saved, you can quit the FrontPage Editor, return to the FrontPage Explorer, and select another page for editing. The following steps demonstrate how to quit the FrontPage Editor.

Other Ways

1. On File menu click Exit
2. Press ALT+F, X

TO QUIT THE FRONTPAGE EDITOR

Click the Close button on the title bar of the FrontPage Editor window.

The FrontPage Editor window closes and the FrontPage Explorer window displays, as shown in Figure 1-17 on page FP 1.20.

In the previous steps, you edited the Home Page, which is represented by the page icon at the top of the graphical tree diagram. The other pages in the current web also need to be edited. The template for the Interests page, for example, includes a bulleted list of interests for you to customize.

Editing a Bulleted List

Recall that a bulleted list is an unordered list of items, usually indicated by a bullet image. Using the FrontPage Editor, you can change, add, and remove entries from the bulleted list on the Interests page to include your interests. For example, if the current list does not include enough items to list all of your interests, you can add other items to the list. Follow these steps to edit items and add a new item to a bulleted list.

Steps To Edit a Bulleted List

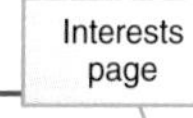

1 Double-click the Interests page icon in the Navigation pane.

The FrontPage Editor window opens and the Interests Web page displays in Normal view (Figure 1-28). The template page for the Interests page includes a bulleted list of items. A bullet image precedes each item in the list.

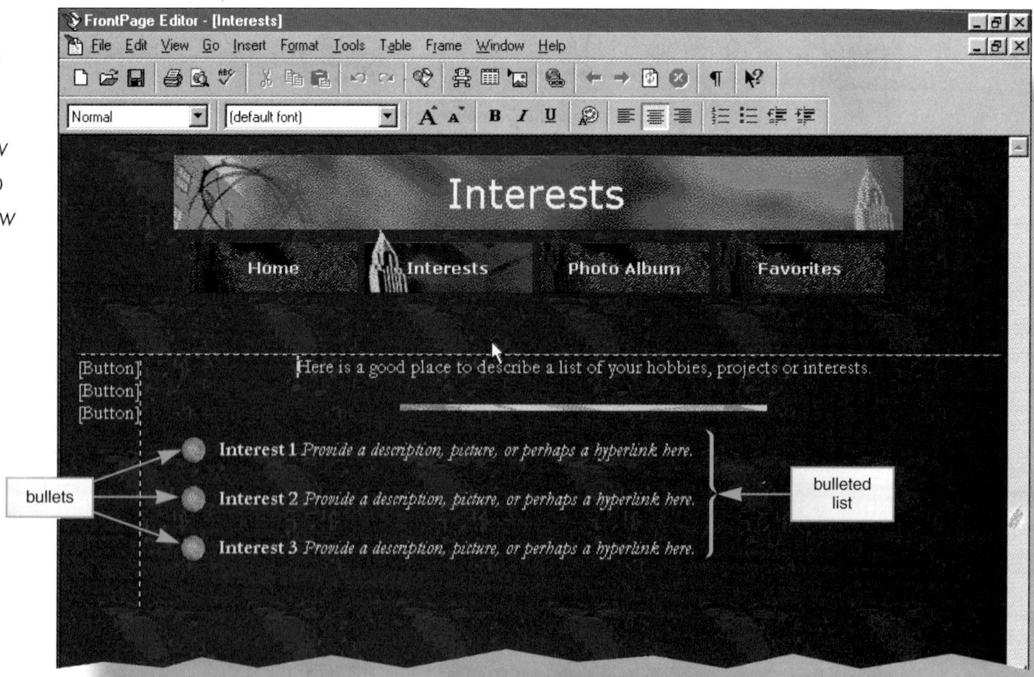

FIGURE 1-28

2 **Drag through the first line of text to select it. Type** These are my hobbies, interests and favorite things to do **as the new text.**

The new text replaces the selected text (Figure 1-29).

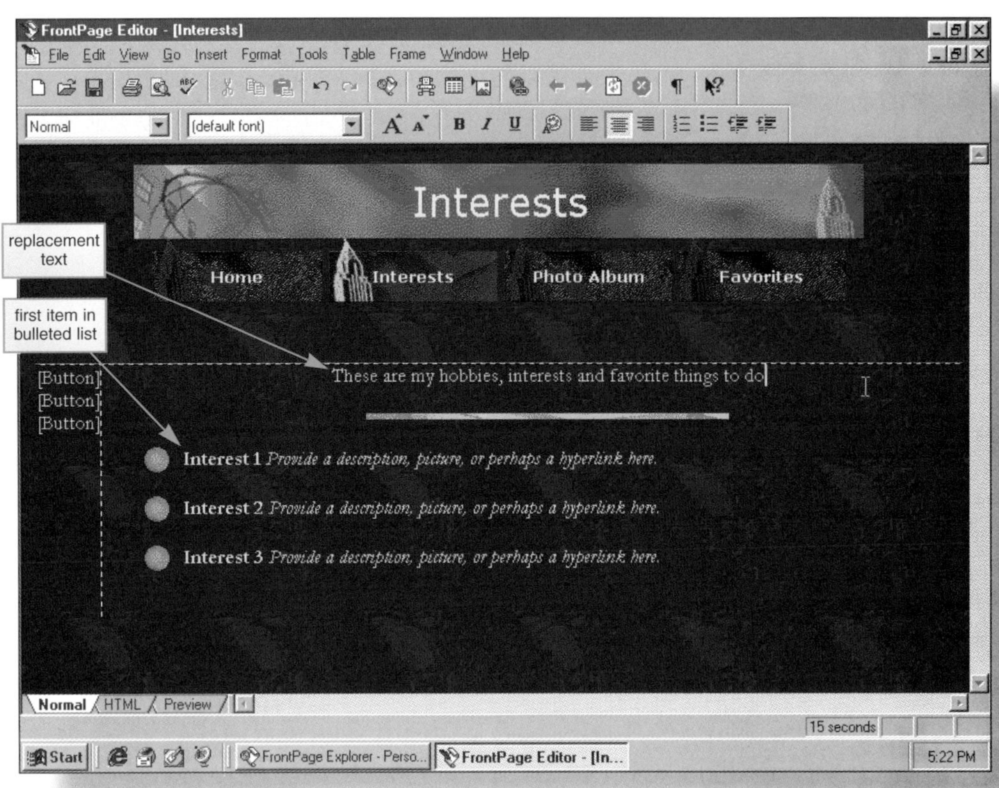

FIGURE 1-29

3 **Drag through the first line of text in the bulleted list and then type** Reading long novels **as the first item. Drag through the second line of text in the list and then type** Listening to music on my stereo **as the second item. Drag through the third line of text in the list and then type** Playing volleyball on the beach **as the third item.**

The new text replaces the placeholder text in the bulleted list (Figure 1-30).

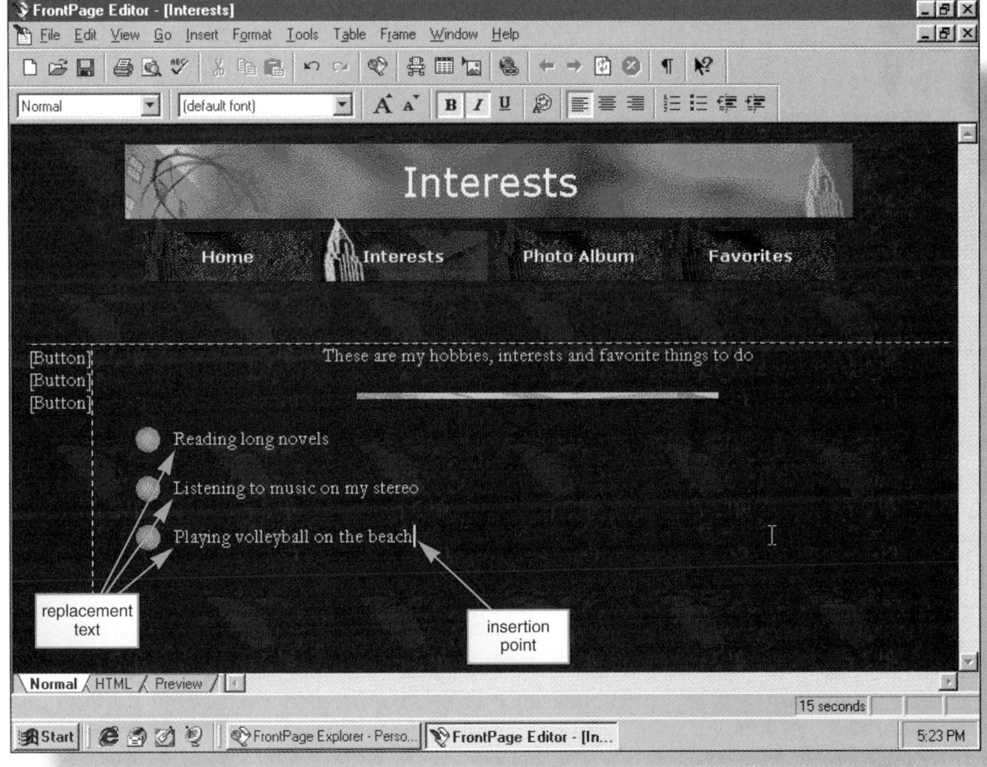

FIGURE 1-30

4 **If necessary, click the end of the text of the last item on the bulleted list to position the insertion point. Press the ENTER key.**

A new bullet displays under the last item in the list (Figure 1-31).

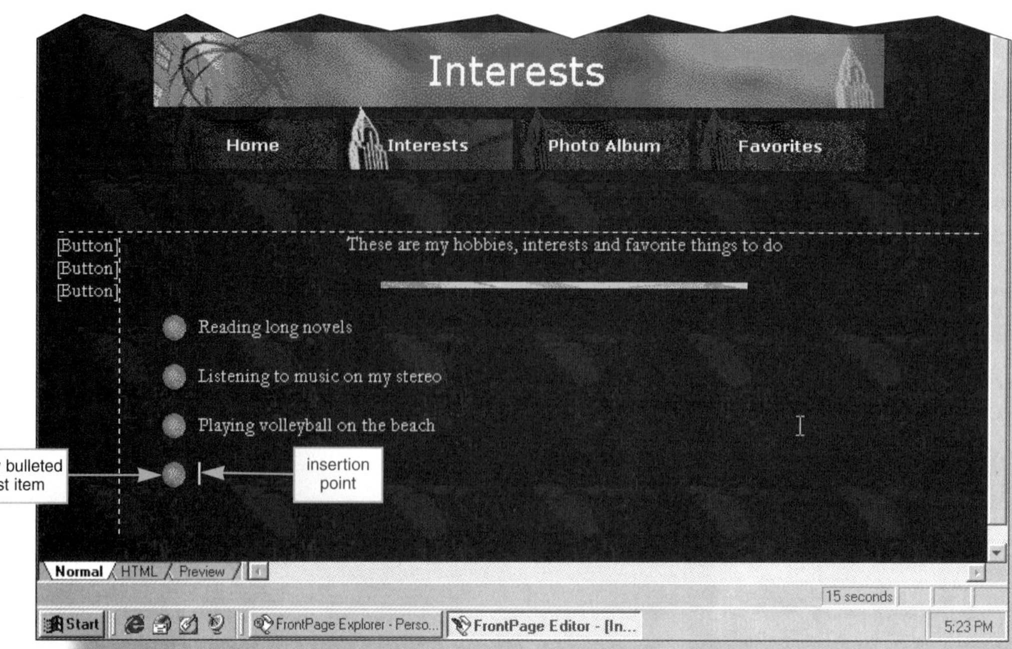

FIGURE 1-31

5 **Type** `Sleeping late` **as the fourth item in the list.**

The text displays next to the new bullet (Figure 1-32).

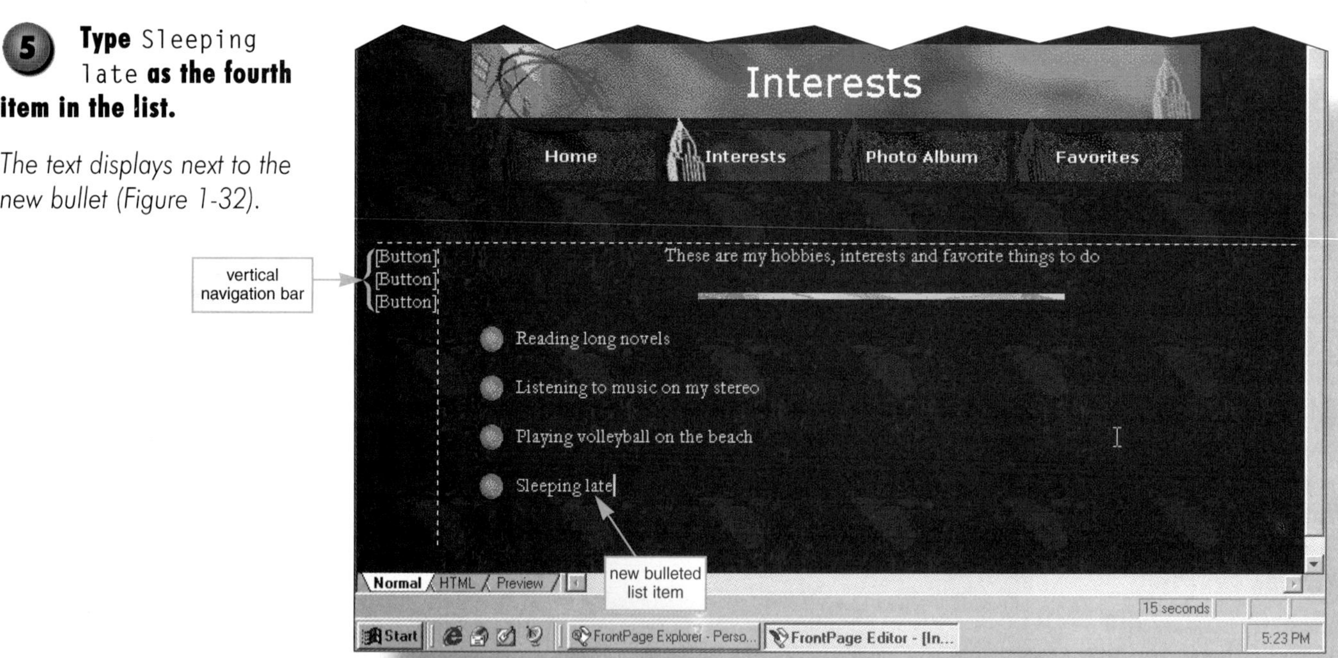

FIGURE 1-32

You successfully have edited the items in a bulleted list — and even added an item. Before you publish your pages on the Web, you will want to add other elements to the page, such as the current date or a set of hyperlinks to the other pages in the web. All of these elements are considered active elements, or WebBot components.

Modifying WebBot Components

Active elements, also called **WebBot components**, are dynamic objects on a page that are evaluated and executed when the page is saved or, in some cases, when the page is displayed with a Web browser. Most WebBot components generate HTML automatically using the text, image files, and other items you supply. For example, with a **banner ad** WebBot component, a series of designated images is shown for a specified amount of time, before the banner ad transitions to the next image. You can identify a WebBot component by clicking it: when a WebBot component is clicked, the mouse pointer changes to a special, robot-shaped **WebBot component cursor**.

A commonly used WebBot component is a navigation bar. A **navigation bar** provides hyperlinks to related Web pages in the FrontPage web. The Downtown theme you selected in previous steps includes two navigation bars. The top navigation bar can be used for **parent-child navigation**, which allows you to move between the Home Page (the parent) and the Interests or Favorites pages (the children). The left-hand navigation bar can be used for **same-level navigation**, which allows you to move back and forth between the Interests and Favorites pages. Perform the following steps to modify the navigation bars.

WebBot Components

Many built-in FrontPage components, such as search forms, banner ads, and save results form handlers, are implemented as WebBot components. You can add your own WebBot components to the FrontPage Editor.

To Modify a Navigation Bar WebBot Component

1 Click the vertical navigation bar to select it.

FrontPage highlights the WebBot component (Figure 1-33). The mouse pointer changes to the WebBot component cursor. This indicates the selected item is a WebBot component.

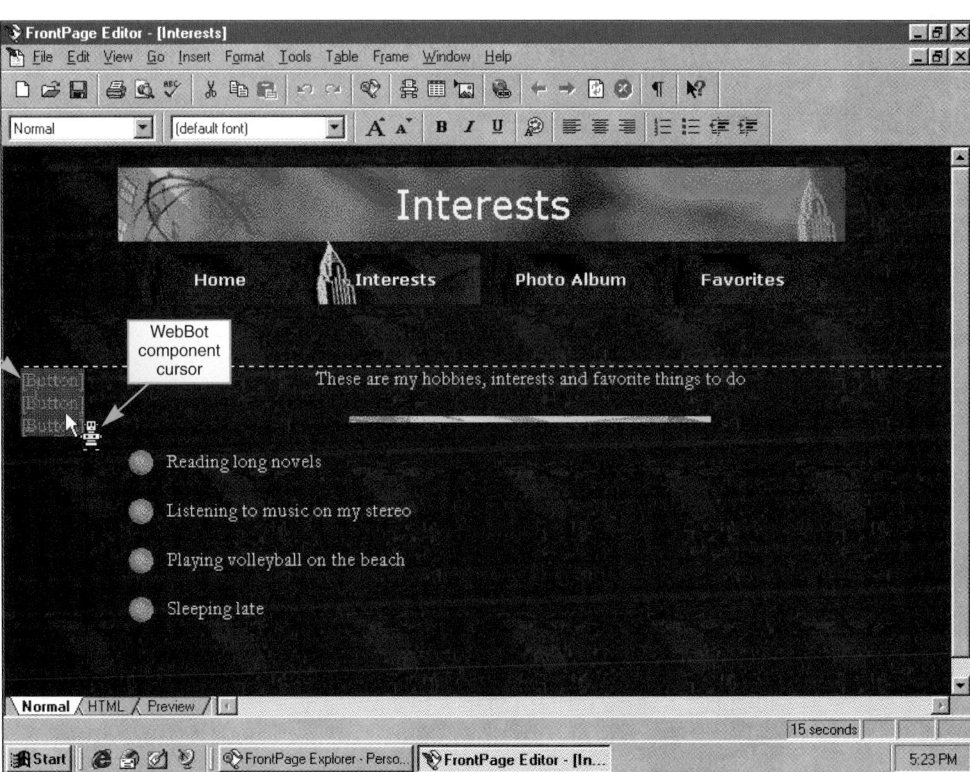

FIGURE 1-33

2 **Double-click the navigation bar WebBot component.**

The Navigation Bar Properties dialog box displays (Figure 1-34). It contains options that control how the navigation bar is organized and its appearance. In the Personal Pages web, this navigation bar will link the Interests page to the Favorites and Photo Album pages, all of which are at the same hierarchical level. The Same level option button thus is the correct choice.

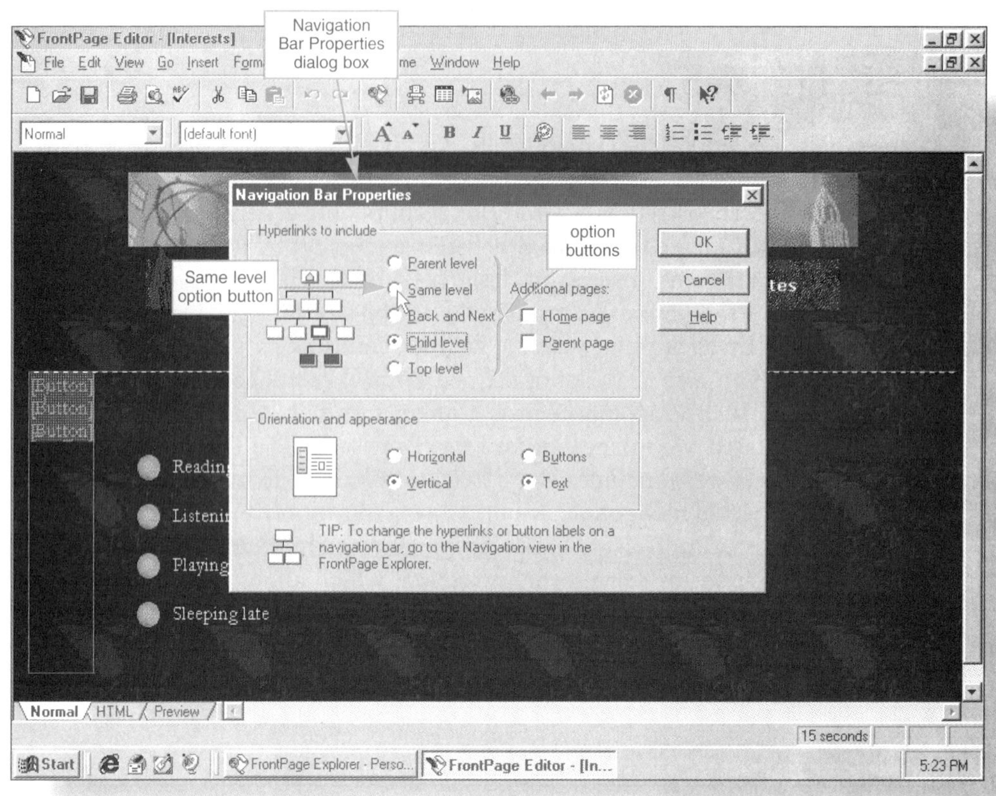

FIGURE 1-34

3 **Click Same level.**

The Same level option button is selected (Figure 1-35). The graphic changes to indicate how the pages will be linked.

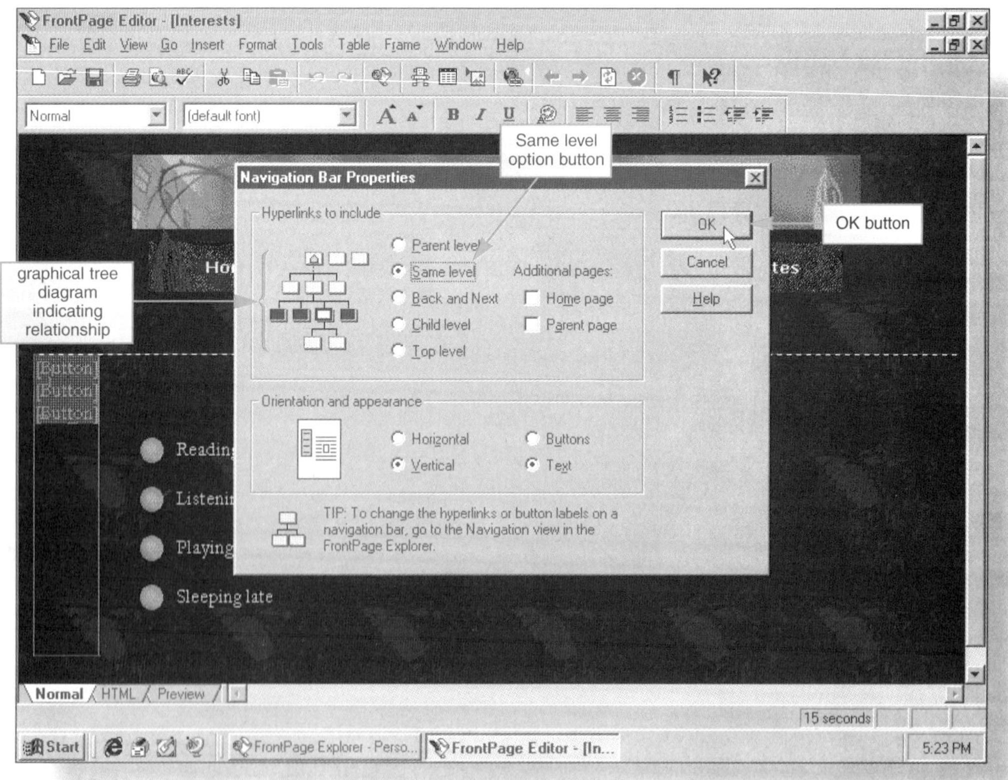

FIGURE 1-35

4 **Click the OK button.**

The FrontPage Editor window re-displays (Figure 1-36). The button labels on the navigation bar now indicate the title of the Web page that will display when that button is clicked. FrontPage automatically changes the navigation bar buttons on all of the other pages in the current web.

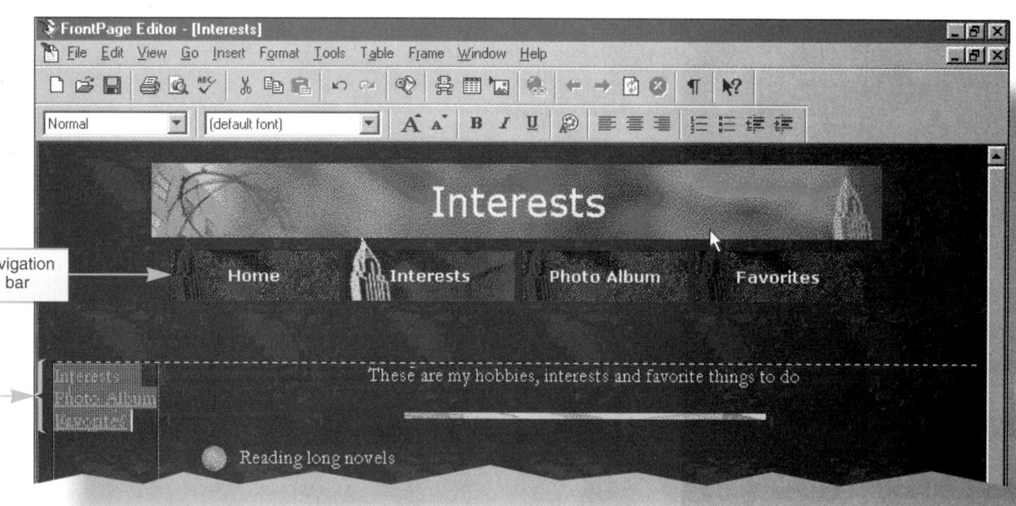

FIGURE 1-36

5 **Click the navigation bar at the top of the page to select it.**

FrontPage highlights the navigation bar WebBot component (Figure 1-37).

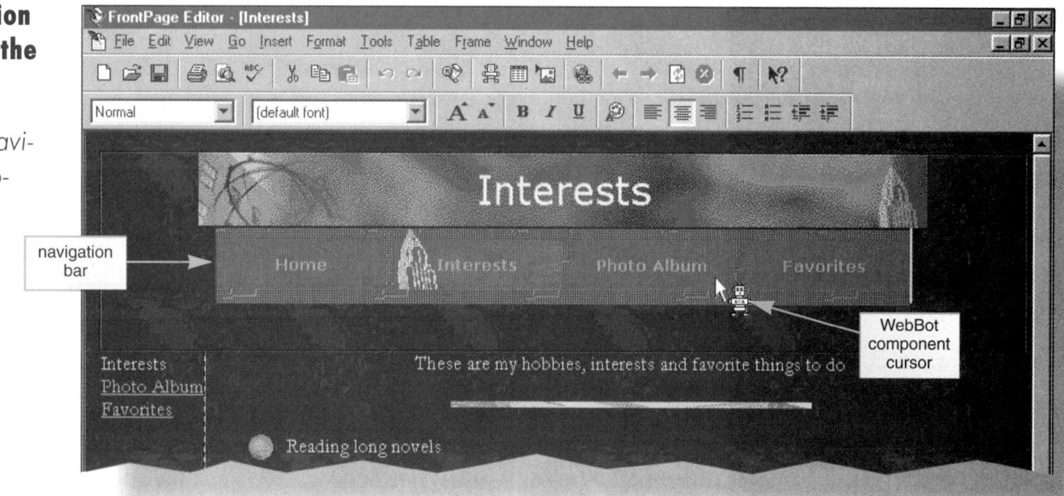

FIGURE 1-37

6 **Double-click the navigation bar WebBot component to display the Navigation Bar Properties dialog box. Click Child level.**

The Navigation Bar Properties dialog box displays and the Child level option button is selected (Figure 1-38). Choosing this option causes the navigation bar on the Interests page to point back to the Home page. The graphic changes to indicate how the pages will be linked.

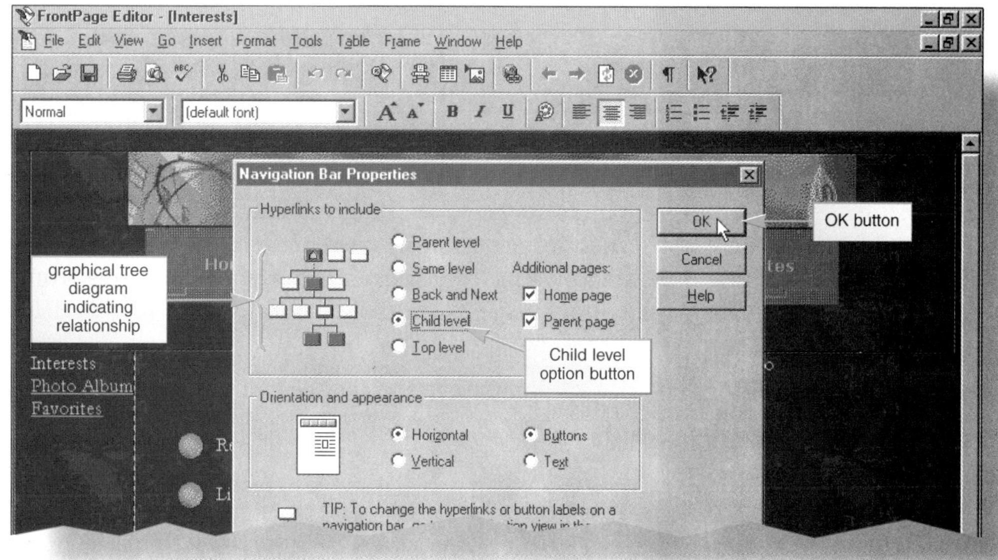

FIGURE 1-38

7 Click the OK button.

The FrontPage Editor window displays (Figure 1-39). The button label on the top navigation bar now points to the Home Page. FrontPage automatically makes the changes to the navigation bars on all pages in the current web.

8 Click the Save button on the Standard toolbar to save the active page. Click the Close button on the title bar of the FrontPage Editor window.

The changes you made to the page are saved. The FrontPage Editor window closes and the FrontPage Explorer window displays.

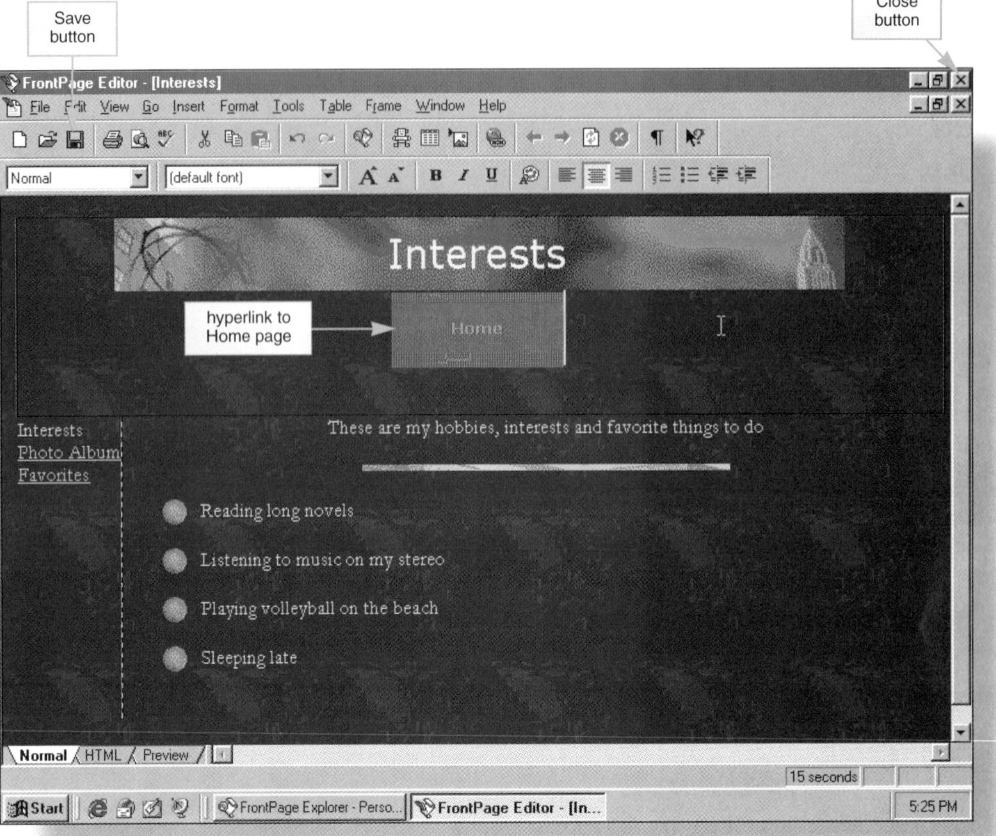

FIGURE 1-39

Other Ways

1. On Edit menu click FrontPage Component Properties
2. Right-click to select, press ALT+ENTER
3. Right-click to select, press ALT+E, I

You successfully have changed the properties of a WebBot component — in this case, a navigation bar. Be aware that different WebBot components have different properties. The options that display in the component Properties dialog box will be different, depending on what type of WebBot component you selected.

In the process of creating and editing the pages in your web, you may decide to delete a page from the web. You can do this in the Navigation view of the FrontPage Explorer.

Deleting a Page from a FrontPage Web

The navigation bar you just changed now links three same-level pages in the web — the Interests page, the Photo Album page, and the Favorites page. If you delete one of these pages from the current web, the navigation bar WebBot component automatically removes hyperlinks to the deleted page from the navigation bars in all remaining pages. Complete the following steps to delete a Web page from the current web.

To Delete a Page from the FrontPage Web

1 If necessary, click the Navigation button on the Views bar to display the Personal Pages web in Navigation view. Right-click the Photo Album page icon in the Navigation pane.

A shortcut menu displays (Figure 1-40). It contains commands to manage individual Web pages within a FrontPage web.

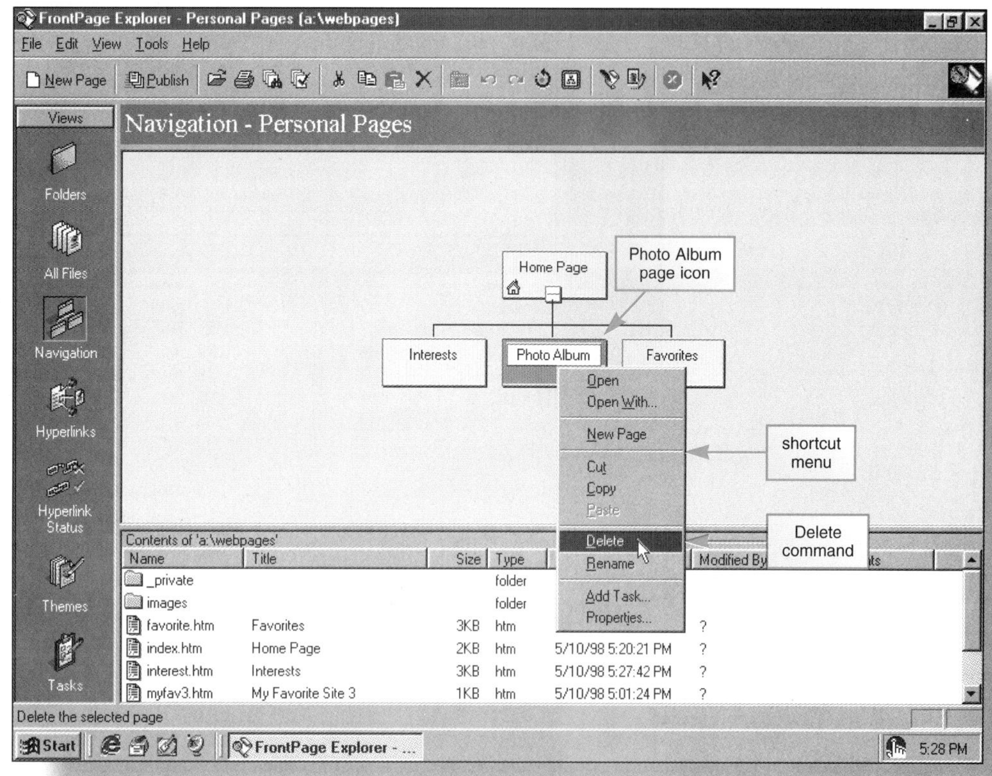

FIGURE 1-40

2 Click Delete on the shortcut menu.

The Delete Page dialog box displays, asking you what you want to do (Figure 1-41). The dialog box provides two options: you can remove this Web page from all navigation bars or delete the Web page from the current FrontPage web.

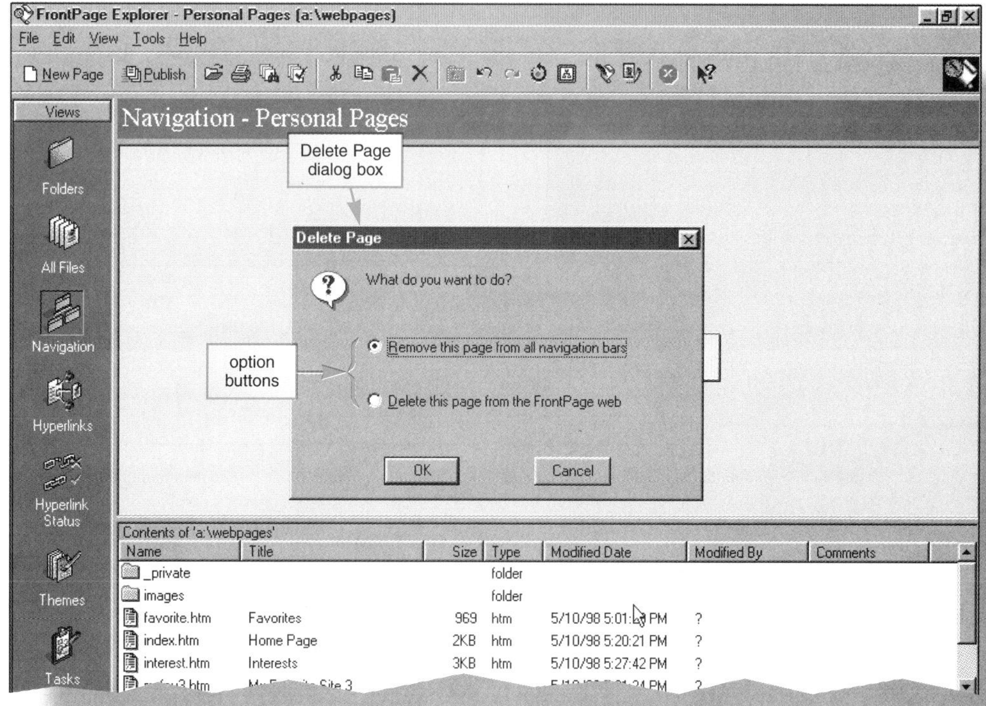

FIGURE 1-41

3 Click Delete this page from the FrontPage web.

The Delete this page from the FrontPage web option button is selected (Figure 1-42).

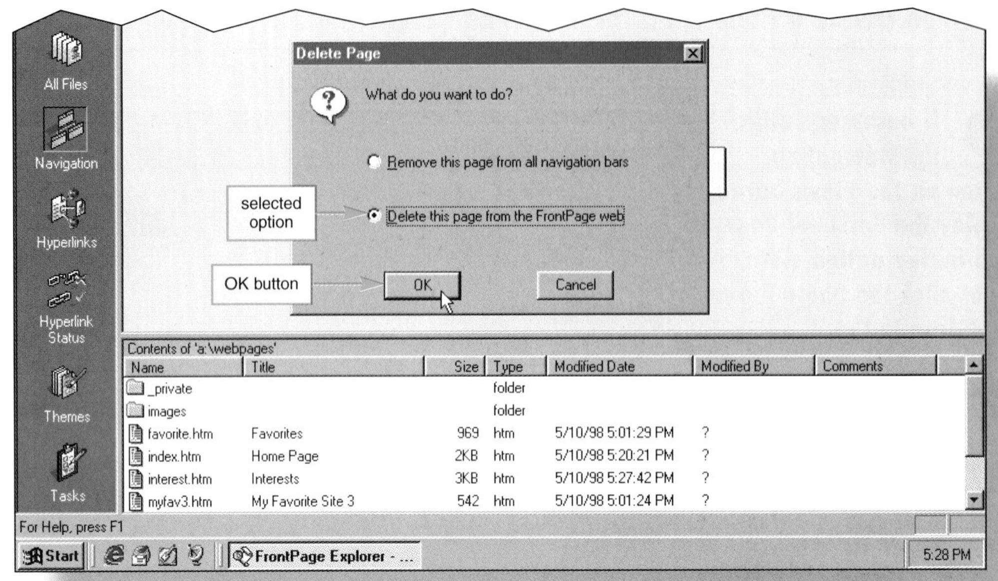

FIGURE 1-42

4 Click the OK button.

After a few moments, the Personal Pages web redisplays in Navigation view. The Photo Album page icon no longer is part of the web structure (Figure 1-43).

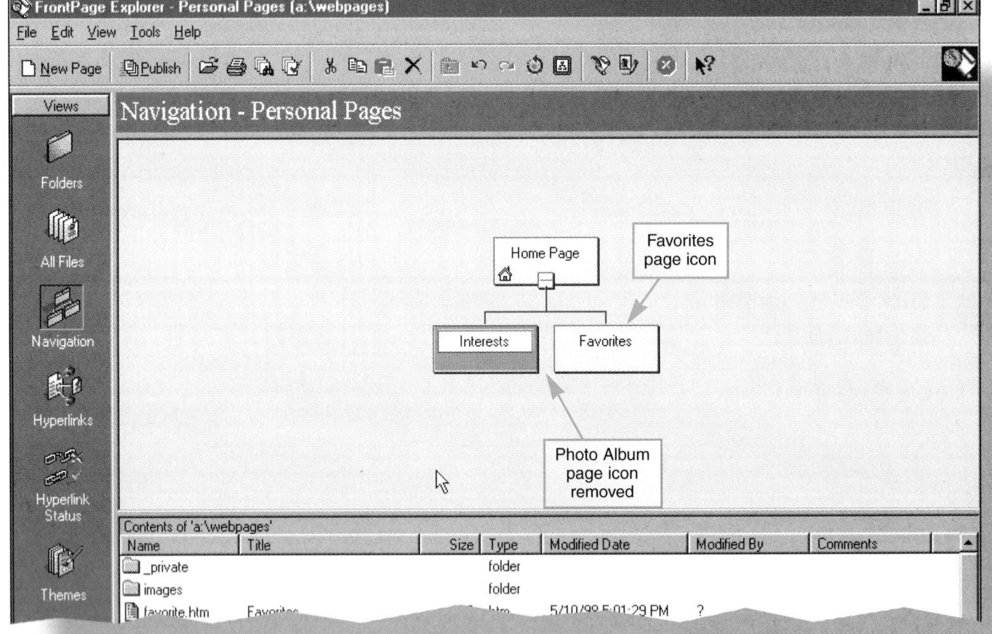

FIGURE 1-43

Other Ways

1. Click page icon to select page, press DELETE
2. Click page icon to select page, press ALT+E, D
3. Click file name in Files pane, press DELETE

If you choose to remove the Web page from all navigation bars, the Web page is still saved on the disk and can be linked to other pages. If you choose to delete a Web page from the FrontPage web, as you did in the previous steps, the Web page file is deleted from the disk and removed from all the navigation bars.

The final page to edit in your Personal Pages web is the Favorites page, which contains a list of hyperlinks to some of your favorite Web sites. Because you are using a template, the page already includes placeholder hyperlinks. You can edit the hyperlinks using FrontPage Editor just as you did with the bulleted list in the Interests Web page.

Managing Hyperlinks on a Web Page

Recall that a *hyperlink* is an area of the page that you click to instruct the browser to go to a location in a file or to request a file from a server. Often, a hyperlink consists of text or a picture that is associated with a URL that points to a page on the World Wide Web. Using the FrontPage Editor, you can create text or graphic hyperlinks in your Web page. You insert the text or the picture on the Web page and then associate the text or picture with a URL.

FrontPage provides several ways to associate the URL with the text or picture on a Web page. You can type the URL or select a file within the current Web. You also can browse the Web using Internet Explorer and display the page to which you want to link; FrontPage automatically displays the URL in the appropriate text box.

To learn how to manage the hyperlinks on a Web page, you will alter the existing hyperlinks on the Favorites Web page and add a new hyperlink. The following steps show you how to change existing hyperlinks on a Web page.

More About

Hyperlinks

If you create a hyperlink to a Web page that is not your own, be sure to check periodically to make sure the link is still active. It is important for you to maintain your hyperlinks, as the World Wide Web is a constantly changing environment.

Steps To Change a Hyperlink on a Web Page

1 Double-click the Favorites page icon in the Navigation pane.

The FrontPage Editor window opens and the Favorites page displays (Figure 1-44). The vertical navigation bar shows only two buttons, because you deleted the Photo Album page.

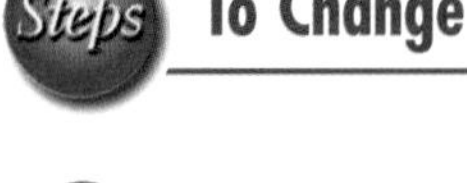

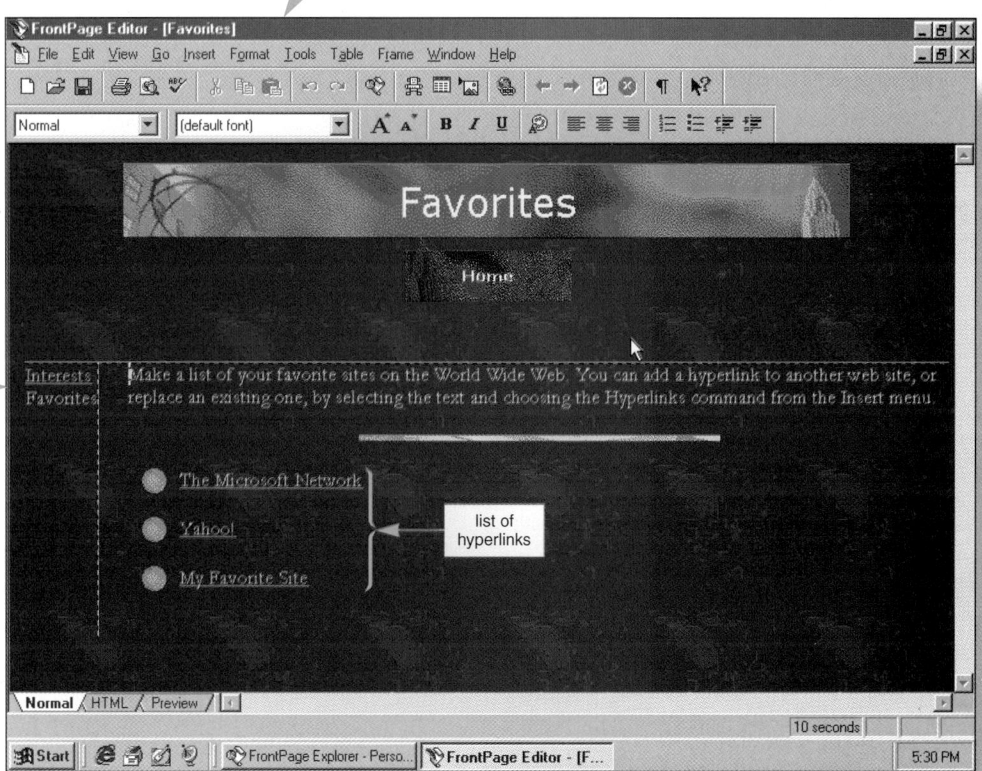

FIGURE 1-44

2 Drag through the first paragraph of text that begins with, Make a list of your favorite sites, to highlight the text and then type `These are my favorite Web sites` **as the new text.**

The new text replaces the highlighted text (Figure 1-45). The list entries are underlined, which identifies them as hyperlinks.

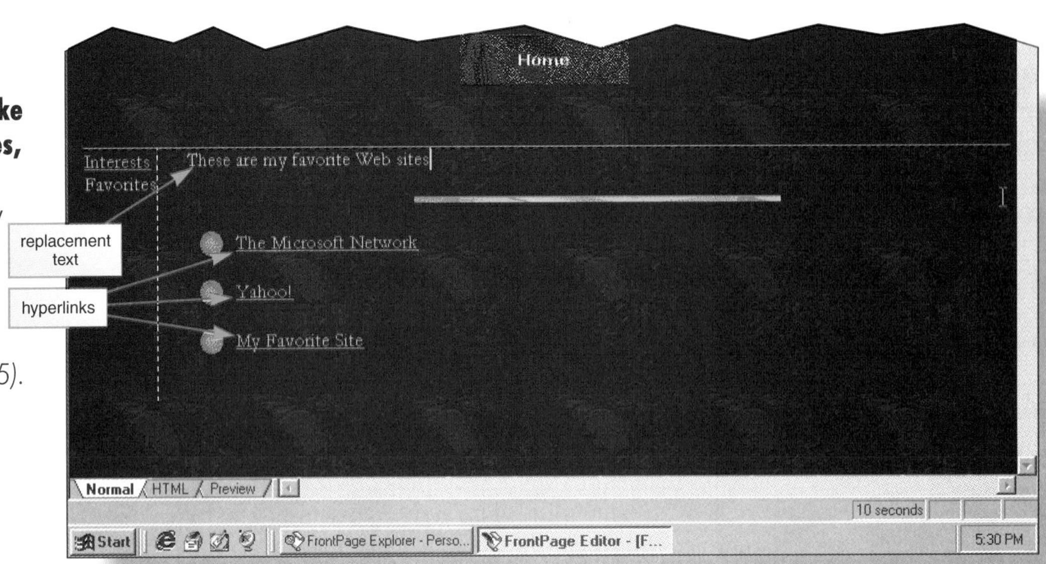

FIGURE 1-45

3 Drag through the hyperlink text, My Favorite Site, to select it and then type `Alta Vista Search` **as the new hyperlink text.**

The new hyperlink text replaces the old hyperlink text (Figure 1-46). Remember that you have changed only the text that identifies the hyperlink. The URL behind the hyperlink still must be changed.

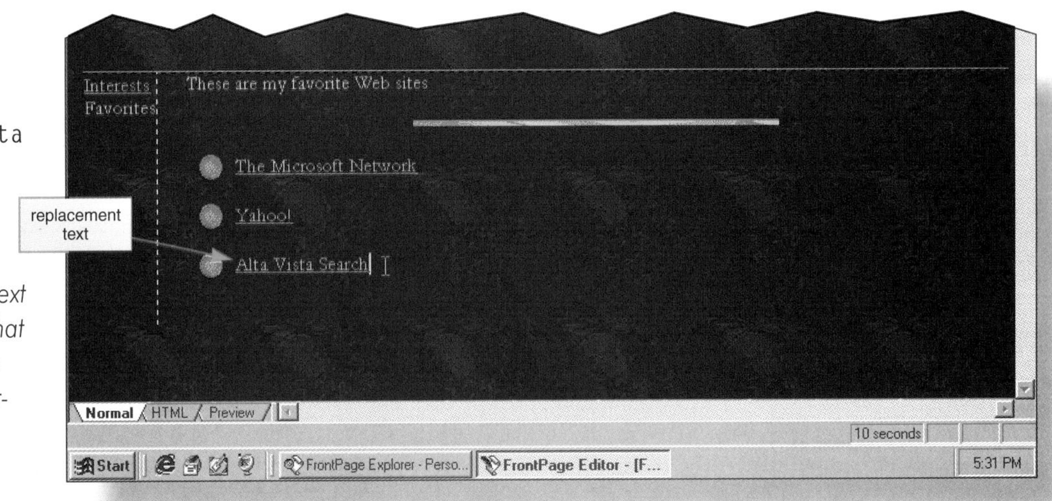

FIGURE 1-46

4 Right-click the Alta Vista Search hyperlink.

A shortcut menu displays (Figure 1-47). The shortcut menu contains commands to manage items on the current Web page. The **Hyperlink Properties command** *allows you to manage a hyperlink.*

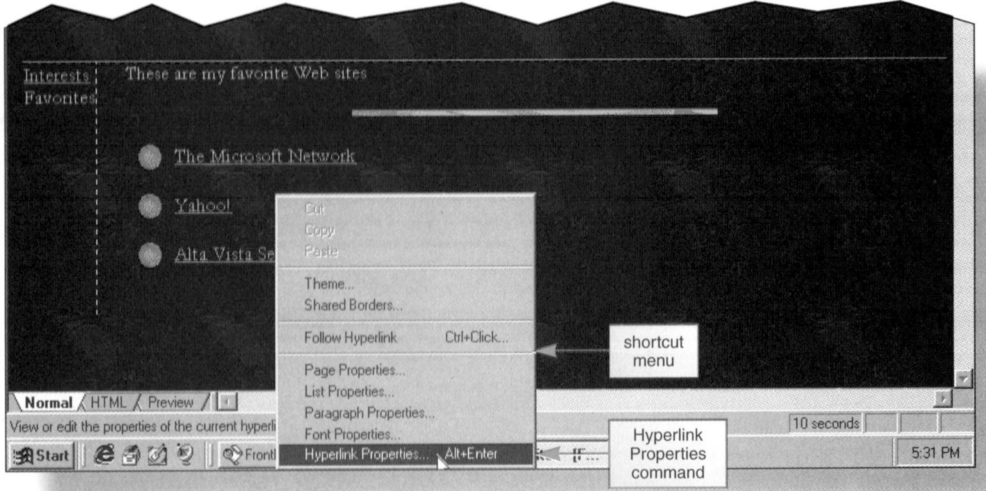

FIGURE 1-47

5 Click Hyperlink Properties on the shortcut menu.

The Edit Hyperlink dialog box displays (Figure 1-48). It contains buttons and list boxes that allow you to specify the URL of the Web resource to which you want to link. The current URL is myfav3.htm, which is another page that comes with the Personal Web template. You can specify another page within the current FrontPage web, another Web page on the local Web server, or any Web page on the World Wide Web.

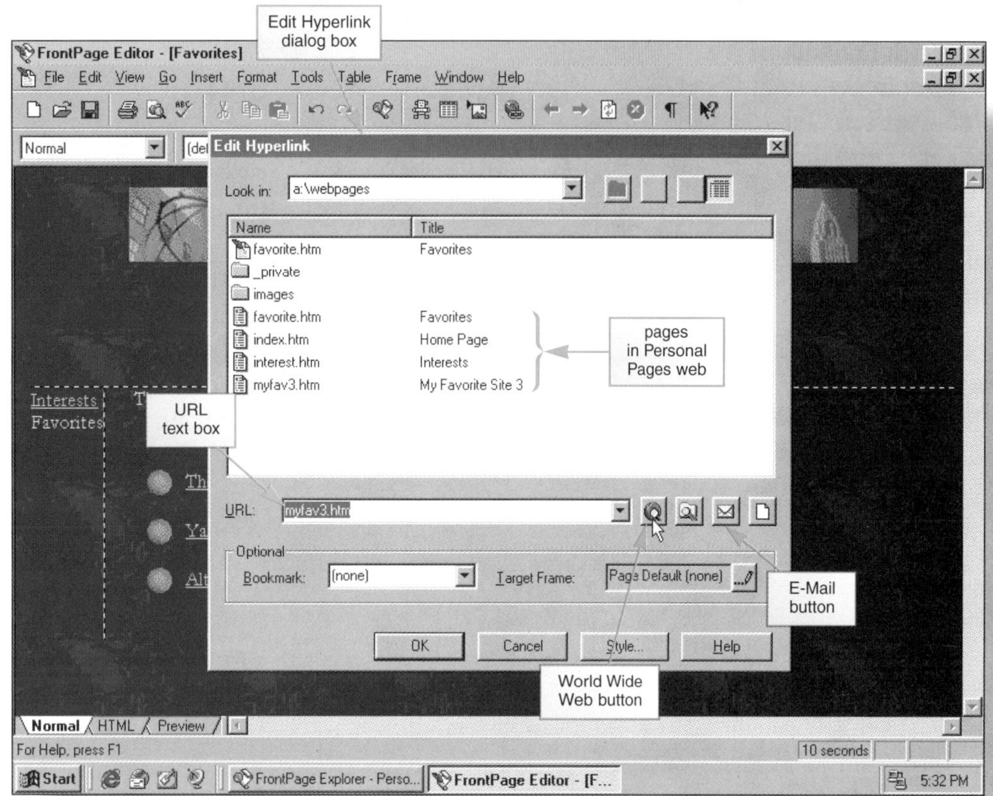

FIGURE 1-48

6 Click the World Wide Web button to the right of the URL text box.

The Internet Explorer window opens with a message indicating how to proceed (Figure 1-49). You should browse to the page to which you want to link and then return to the FrontPage Editor using the FrontPage Editor button on the taskbar.

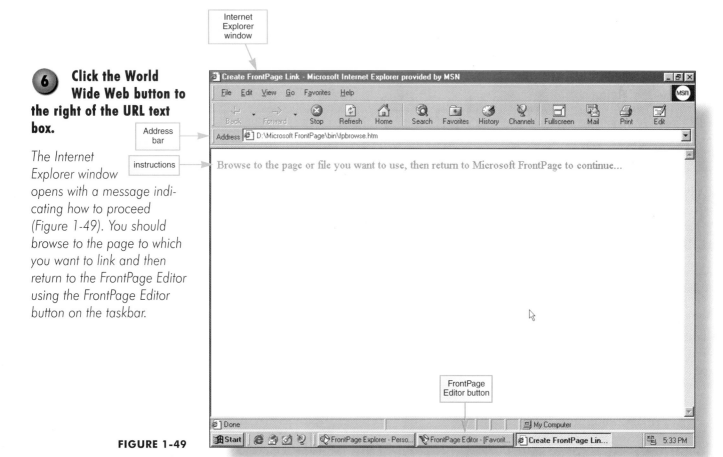

FIGURE 1-49

Microsoft FrontPage 98

7 Click the Address bar in the Internet Explorer window. Type `go altavista` **and then press the ENTER key. Scroll down to display the search results.**

The search results display, with several matches containing the word, altavista (Figure 1-50).

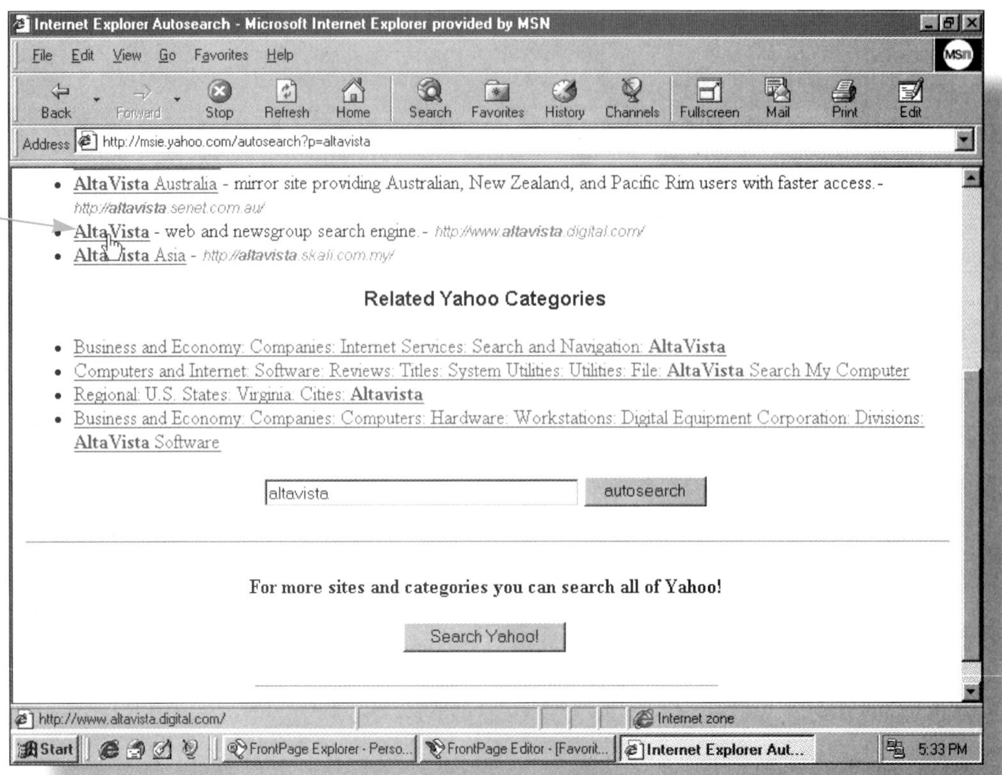

FIGURE 1-50

8 Click the AltaVista hyperlink for www.altavista.digital.com.

The AltaVista Main Page displays in the Explorer content area (Figure 1-51). With the target page in Internet Explorer, you can return to the FrontPage Editor and Internet Explorer will return the URL automatically.

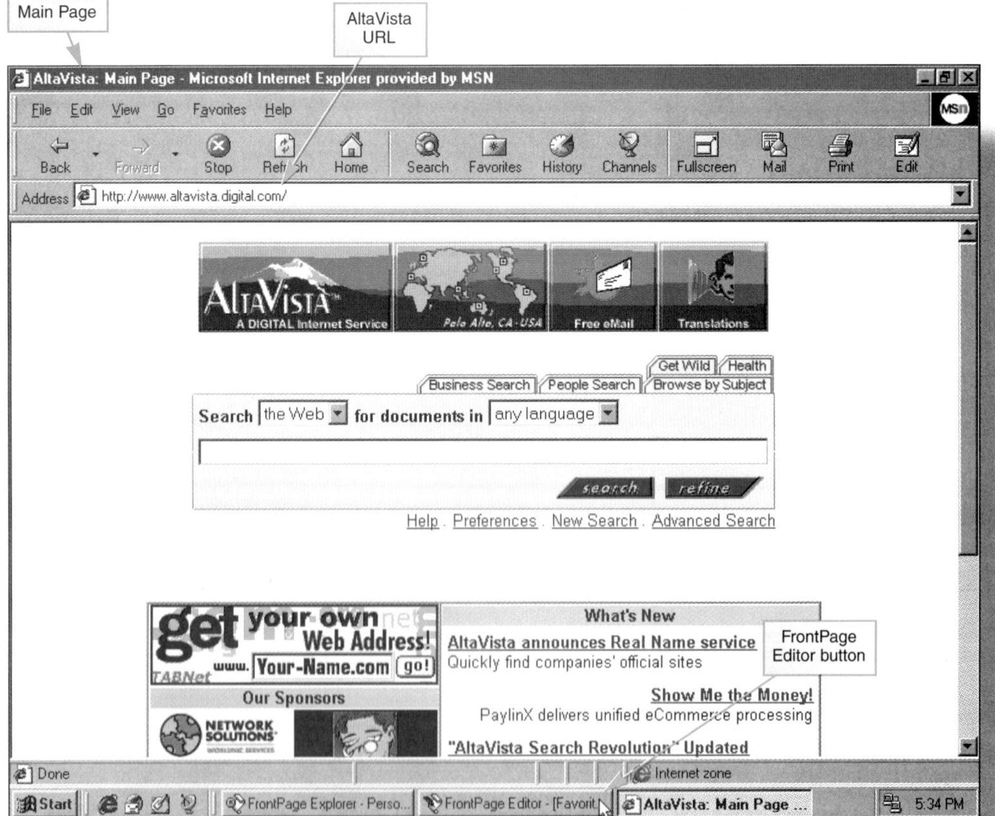

FIGURE 1-51

9 Click the FrontPage Editor button on the taskbar.

The FrontPage Editor window with the Edit Hyperlink dialog box displays (Figure 1-52). The AltaVista URL displays in the URL list box.

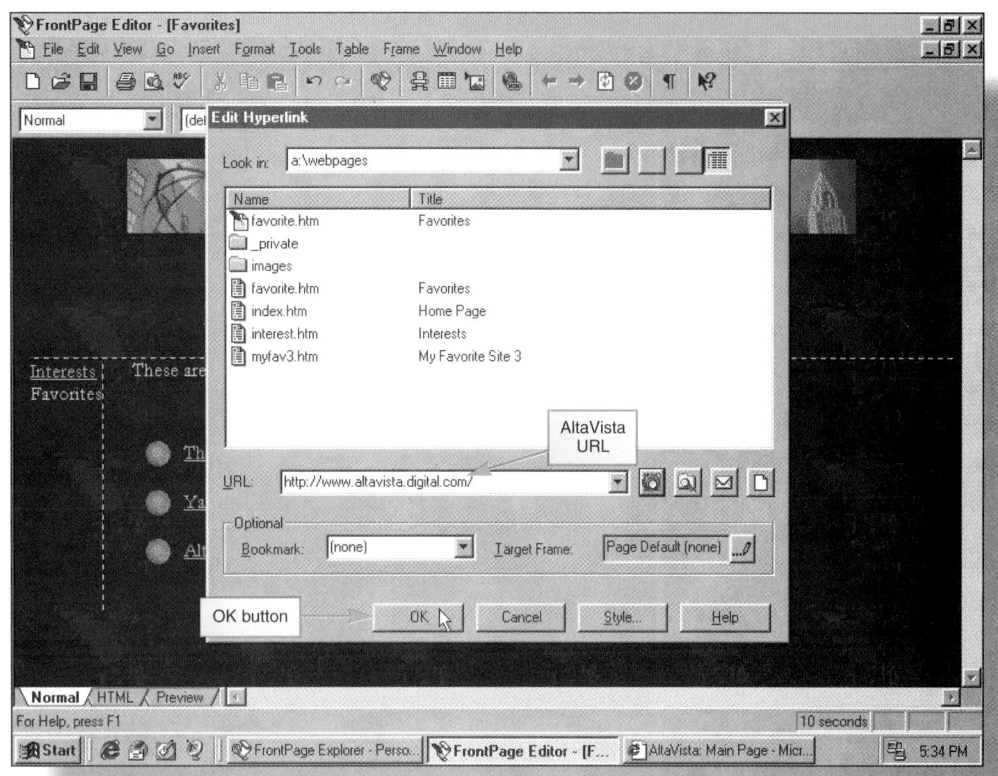

FIGURE 1-52

10 Click the OK button. Position the mouse pointer on the Alta Vista Search hyperlink in the Favorites page.

The AltaVista Main Page URL displays in the status bar (Figure 1-53).

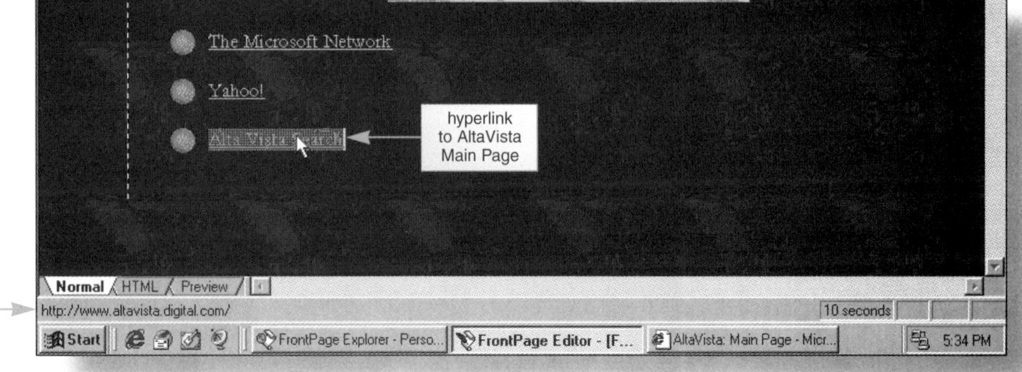

FIGURE 1-53

Other Ways

1. Click hyperlink text, click Create or Edit Hyperlink button on Standard toolbar
2. Click hyperlink text, press ALT+ENTER
3. Click hyperlink text, press ALT+E, I

You successfully have changed the hyperlinks on a Web page by browsing the Web using Internet Explorer. Adding a new hyperlink consists of entering new text on the Web page, and then associating a URL with the text.

Adding a Hyperlink to a Web Page

You also can create mailto hyperlinks by clicking the E-mail button in the Create Hyperlink dialog box and typing an e-mail address. When a user clicks a **mailto hyperlink** in your Web page, the Web browser will start a designated mail program, such as Microsoft Outlook Express, and prompt the user for a message. The message automatically is addressed to the e-mail address specified in the hyperlink. Not all Web browsers support mailto hyperlinks, so be sure to specify the e-mail address somewhere on the Web page. Perform the following steps to add a mailto hyperlink to the Favorites Web page.

Steps To Add a Mailto Hyperlink to a Web Page

1 Position the mouse pointer approximately one inch below the text, Alta Vista Search, and then click.

An insertion point displays (Figure 1-54). If the insertion point displays at the end of the AltaVista Search text, you did not point far enough below the text before you clicked, in which case you must position the mouse pointer a little lower and try again.

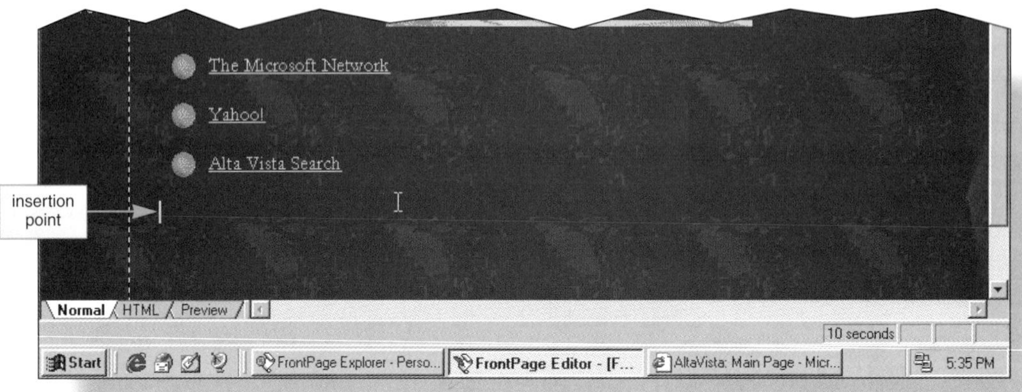

FIGURE 1-54

2 Type `If you have any comments or suggestions, or just want to say hello, e-mail me at jordank@rhetoric.edu` **as the mailto hyperlink.**

The text displays on the Web page (Figure 1-55). To finish creating the mailto hyperlink, you must select the text you want to represent the hyperlink and then supply the URL.

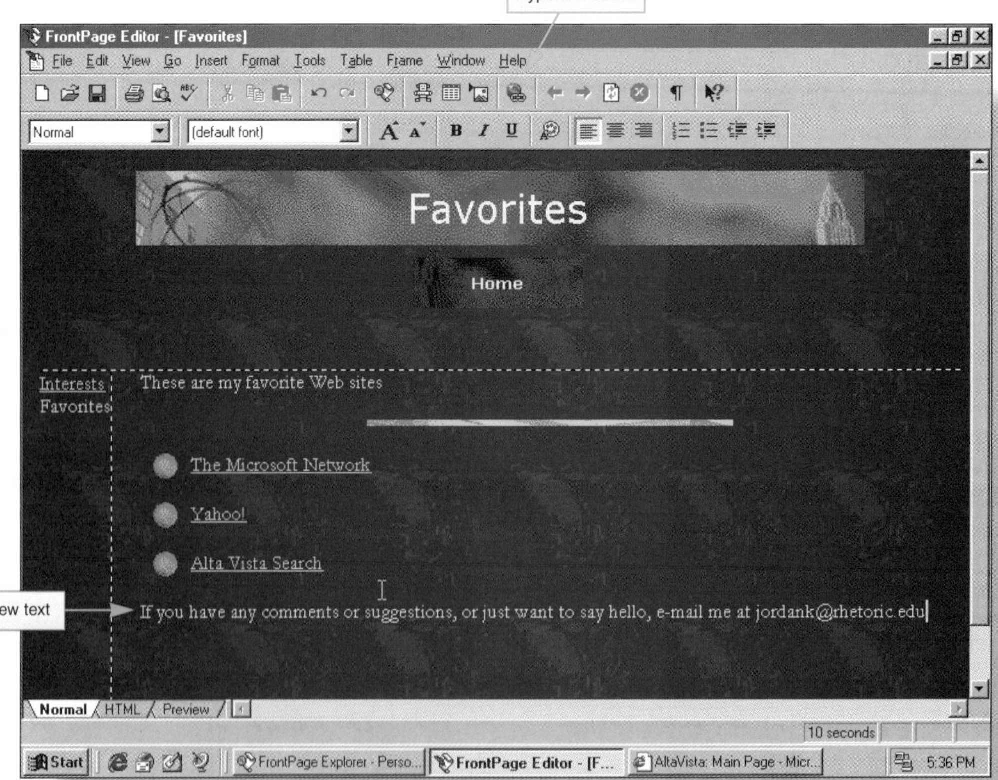

FIGURE 1-55

3 Drag through the text, jordank@rhetoric.edu, to select it and then click the Create or Edit Hyperlink button on the Standard toolbar.

The Create Hyperlink dialog box displays (Figure 1-56).

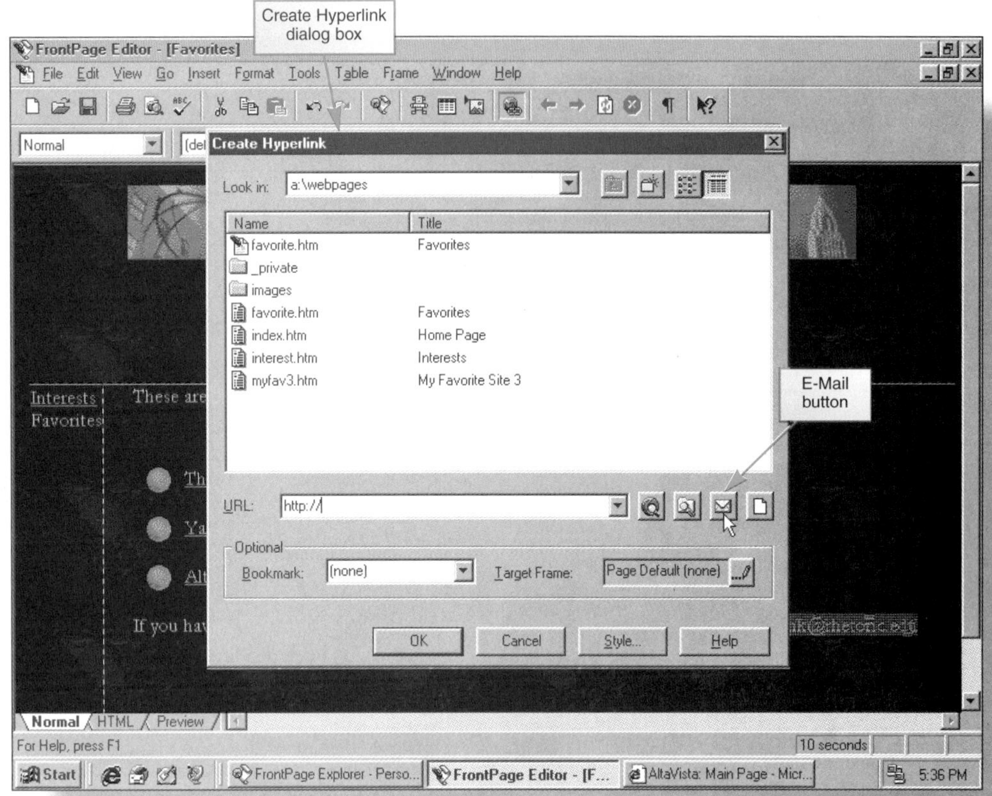

FIGURE 1-56

4 Click the E-Mail button to the right of the URL box.

The Create E-mail Hyperlink dialog box displays (Figure 1-57).

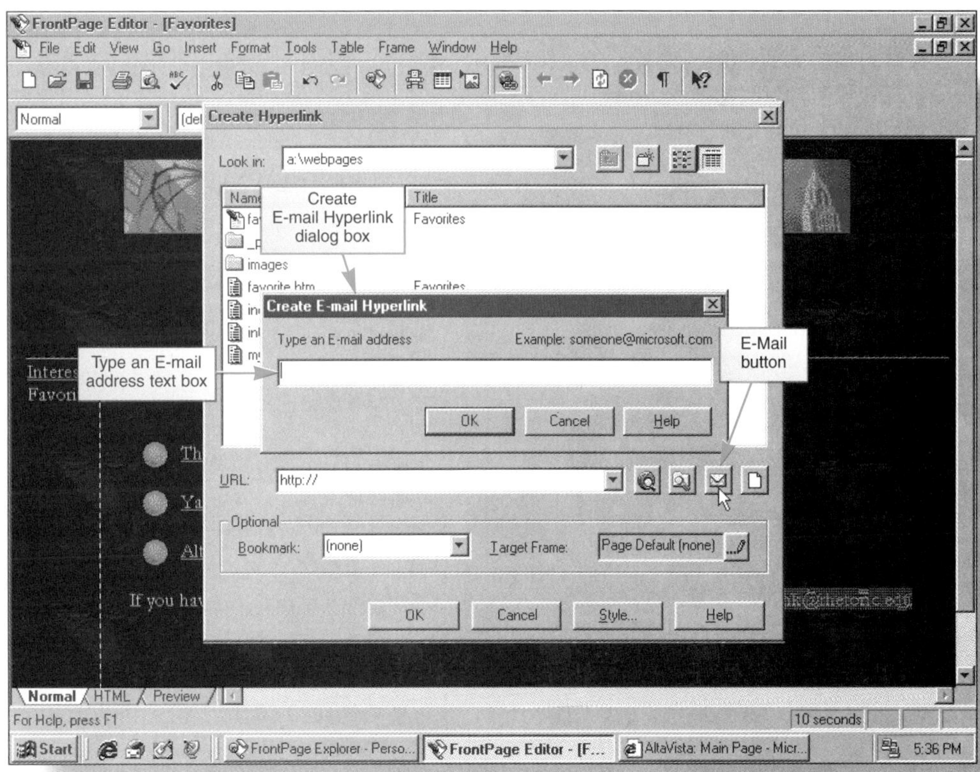

FIGURE 1-57

5 **Type** `jordank@rhetoric.edu` **in the Type an E-mail address text box.**

The e-mail address displays in the text box (Figure 1-58).

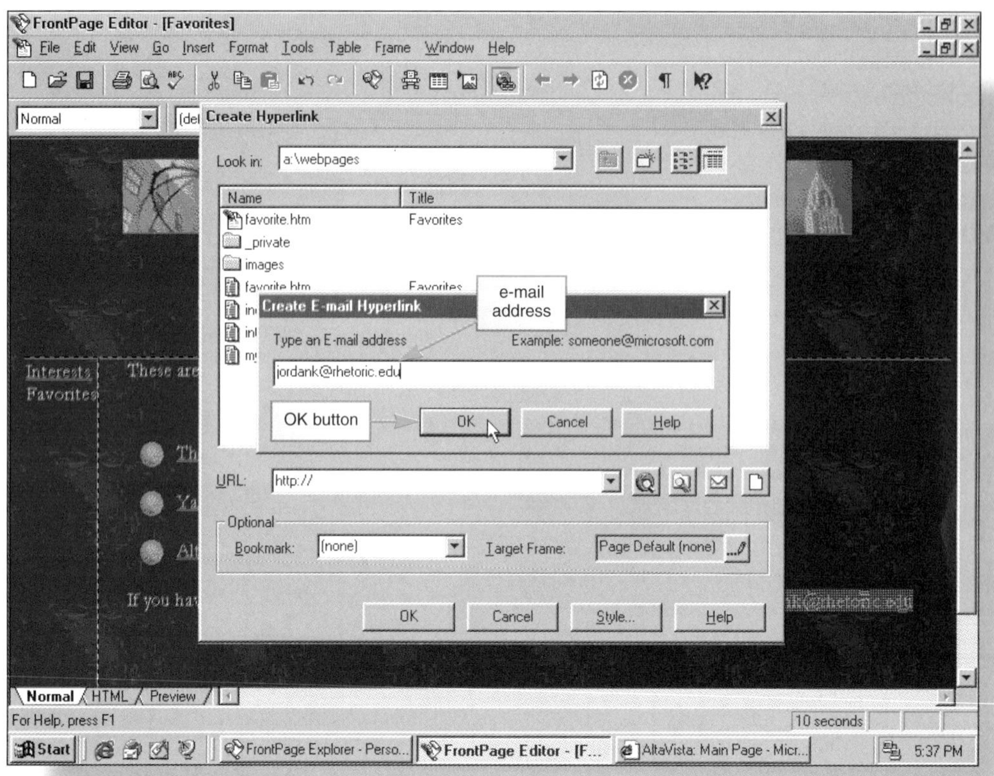

FIGURE 1-58

6 **Click the OK button in the Create E-mail Hyperlink dialog box.**

The completed mailto URL displays in the URL text box (Figure 1-59).

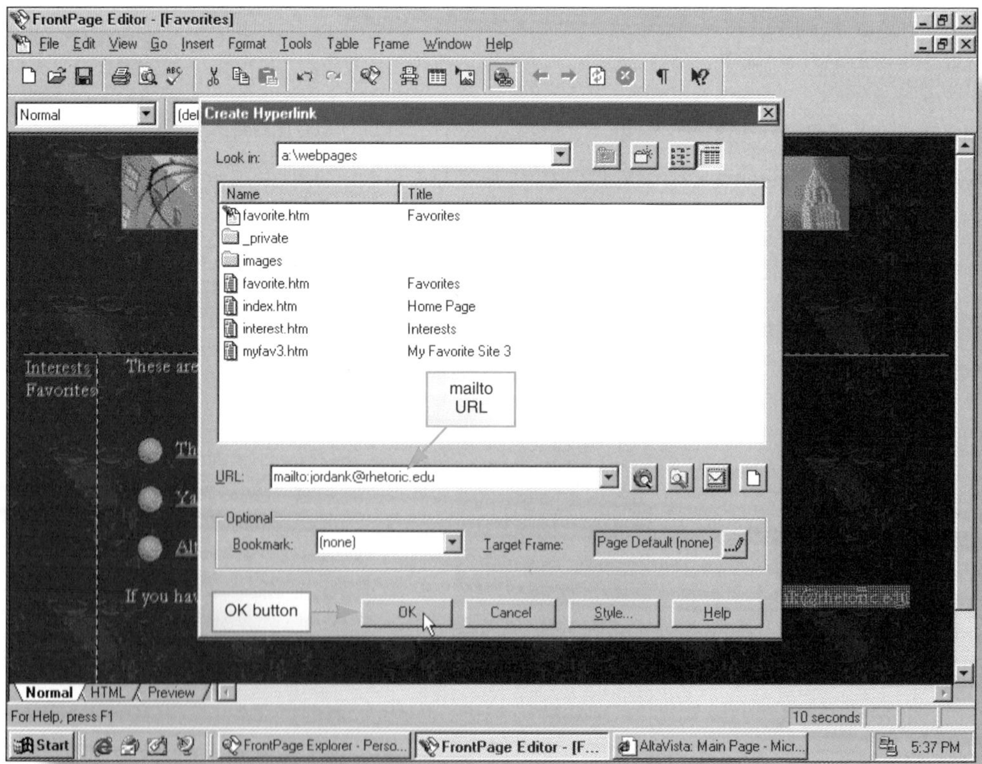

FIGURE 1-59

7 **Click OK in the Create Hyperlink dialog box. Position the mouse pointer over the jordank@rhetoric.edu hyperlink on the Favorites page.**

The mailto hyperlink you provided in the Create Hyperlink dialog box displays on the status bar (Figure 1-60).

8 **Click the Save button on the Standard toolbar to save the Web page.**

The Favorites Web page is saved on a disk file.

9 **Click the Close button to close the FrontPage Editor. If necessary, click the Close button on the Internet Explorer window to close Internet Explorer.**

The FrontPage Editor window closes and the FrontPage Explorer window displays (Figure 1-17 on page FP 1.20).

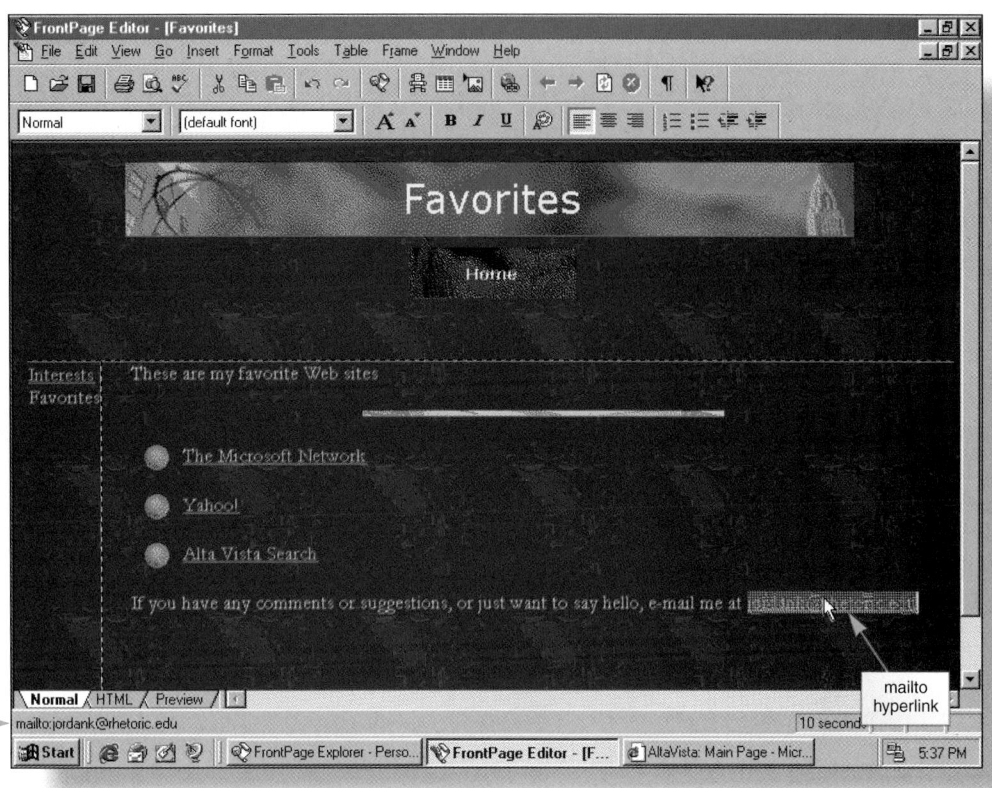

FIGURE 1-60

1. Type hyperlink text, on Insert menu click Hyperlink
2. Type hyperlink text, click Create or Edit Hyperlink button on Standard toolbar
3. Type hyperlink text, press ALT+ENTER
4. Type hyperlink text, press ALT+E, I

You successfully have added and altered text hyperlinks in a Web page. As noted, you also can use an image as a hyperlink. Using an image as a hyperlink will be explained in a later project.

Printing a Web Page from the FrontPage Editor

Once you have created a Web page and saved it on disk, you might want to print it. A printed version of the Web page is called a **hard copy** or **printout**.

To print a Web page, you must open the Web page in the FrontPage Editor. Recall that you selected a Web page to open in the FrontPage Editor by clicking the corresponding page icon in the Navigation pane of the FrontPage Explorer. After you print the first page, you then can open the additional Web pages to print while in the FrontPage Editor using the Open button on the Standard toolbar. To print the three Web pages in the Personal Pages web, you will open each page in the FrontPage Editor and then print each page.

With the Web page opened in the FrontPage editor, you can print the active page. The easiest way to print is to use the Print button on the Standard toolbar. The following section demonstrates how to print the three Web pages in your Personal Pages web.

To Print a Web Page from the FrontPage Editor

1 Ready the printer. Double-click the Home Page page icon in the Navigation pane to open the Home Page in the FrontPage Editor. Click the Print button on the Standard toolbar.

The Print dialog box displays (Figure 1-61). The All option button is selected in the Print range area indicating the entire document will print, regardless of its length.

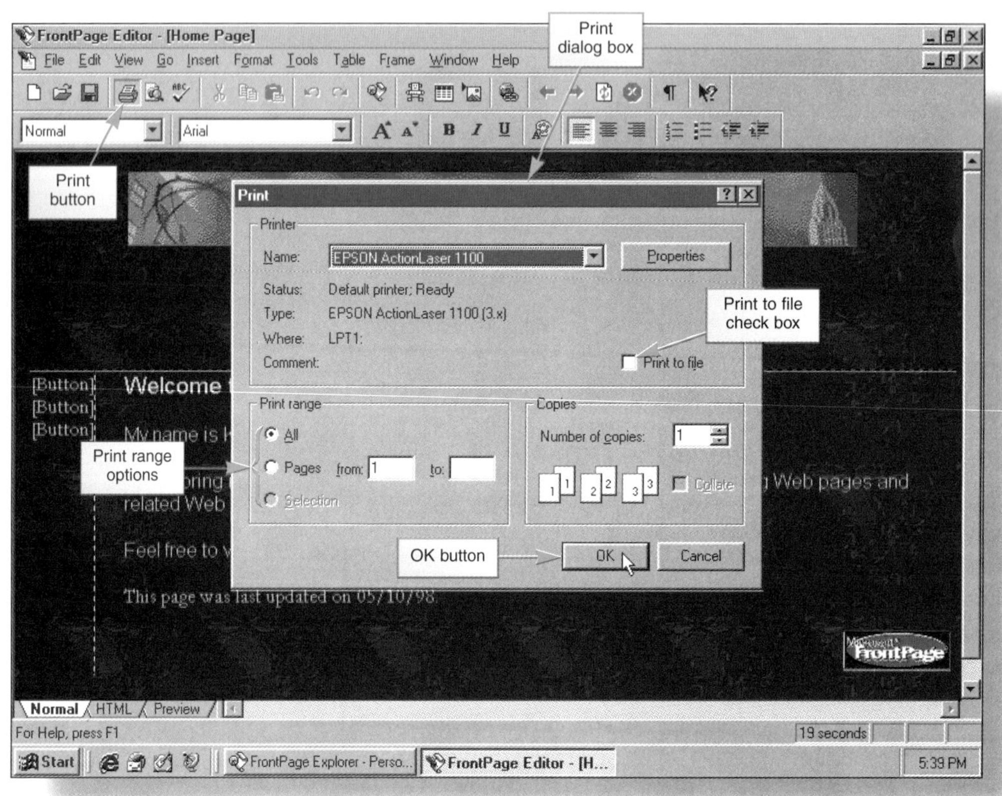

FIGURE 1-61

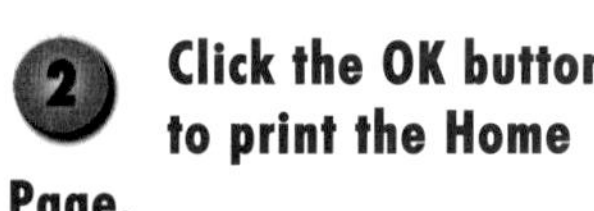

2 Click the OK button to print the Home Page.

The Home Page prints (see Figure 1-68a on page FP 1.49). The next two pages in your Personal Pages web will be opened using the Open button on the Standard toolbar and then printed.

3 Click the Open button on the Standard toolbar.

The Open dialog box displays showing the files and folders that comprise the Personal Pages web (Figure 1-62). Notice the file names ending with .htm. The file name of the Favorites page is favorite.htm.

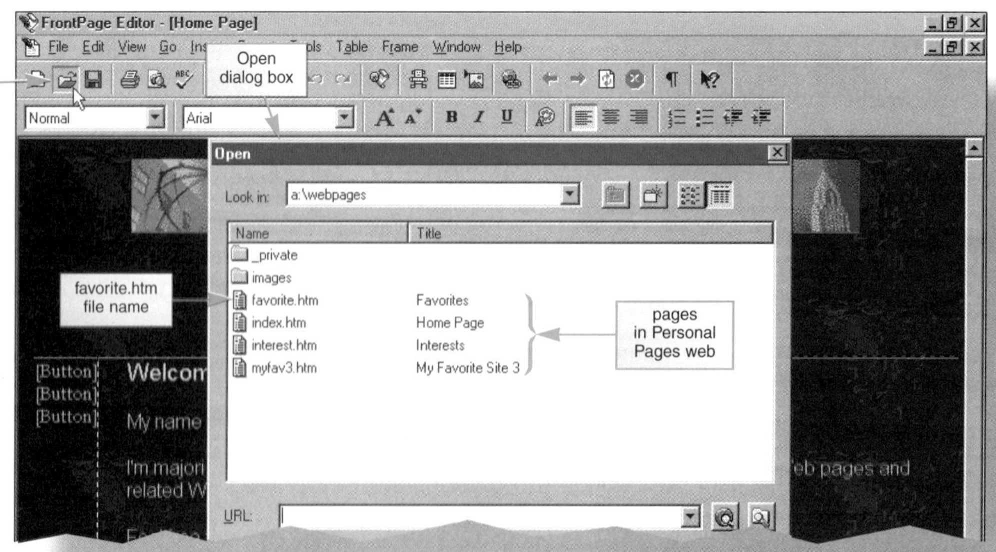

FIGURE 1-62

4 Click the file name, favorite.htm, to select it and then point to the OK button.

The file name, favorite.htm, is highlighted (Figure 1-63).

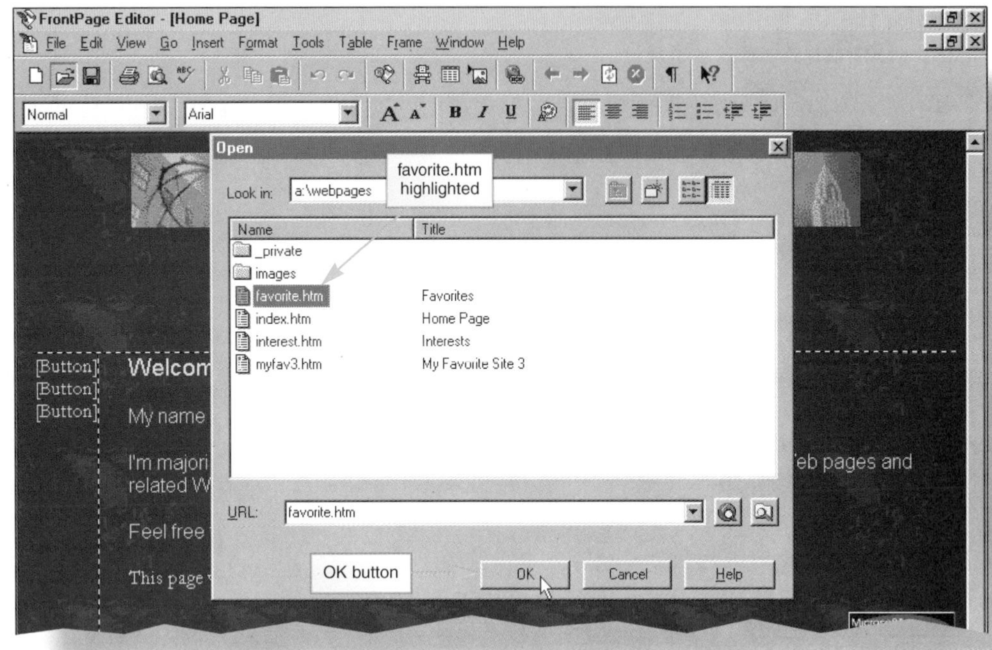

FIGURE 1-63

5 Click the OK button.

The Favorites page displays in the FrontPage Editor window (Figure 1-64).

Favorites page

FIGURE 1-64

6 Click the Print button on the Standard toolbar.

The Print dialog box displays (Figure 1-65).

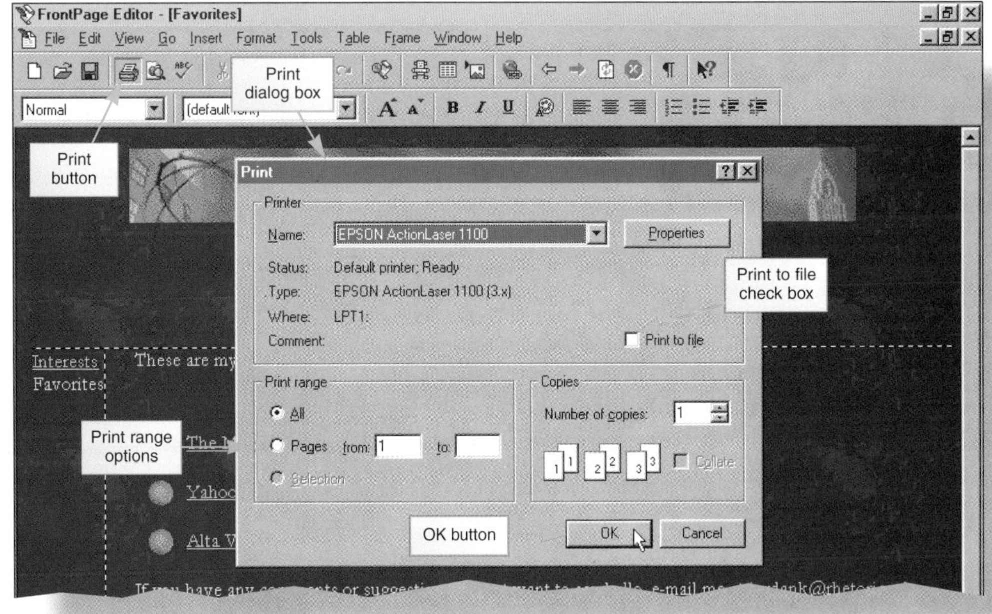

FIGURE 1-65

7 **Click the OK button to print the Web page.**

The Favorites page prints (see Figure 1-68b). The Interests page, with the file name interest.htm, will be printed next.

8 **Click the Open button on the Standard toolbar. Click the file name, interest.htm, to select it and then point to the OK button.**

The Open dialog box displays (Figure 1-66). The file name, interest.htm, is highlighted.

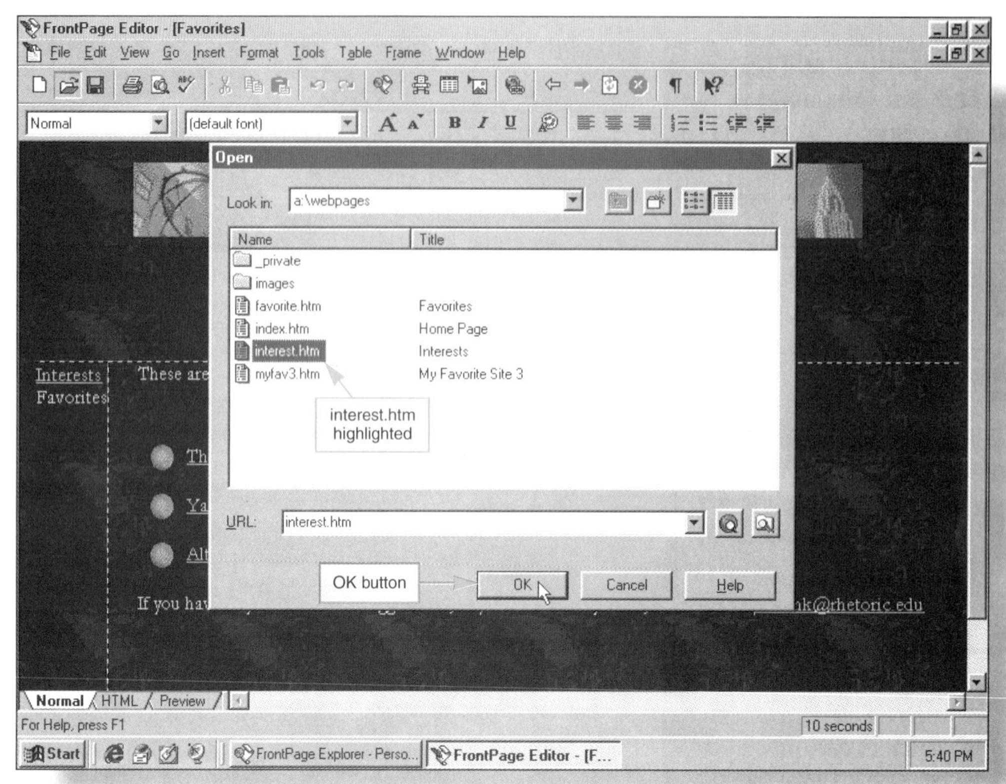

FIGURE 1-66

9 **Click the OK button.**

The Interests page displays in the FrontPage Editor window (Figure 1-67).

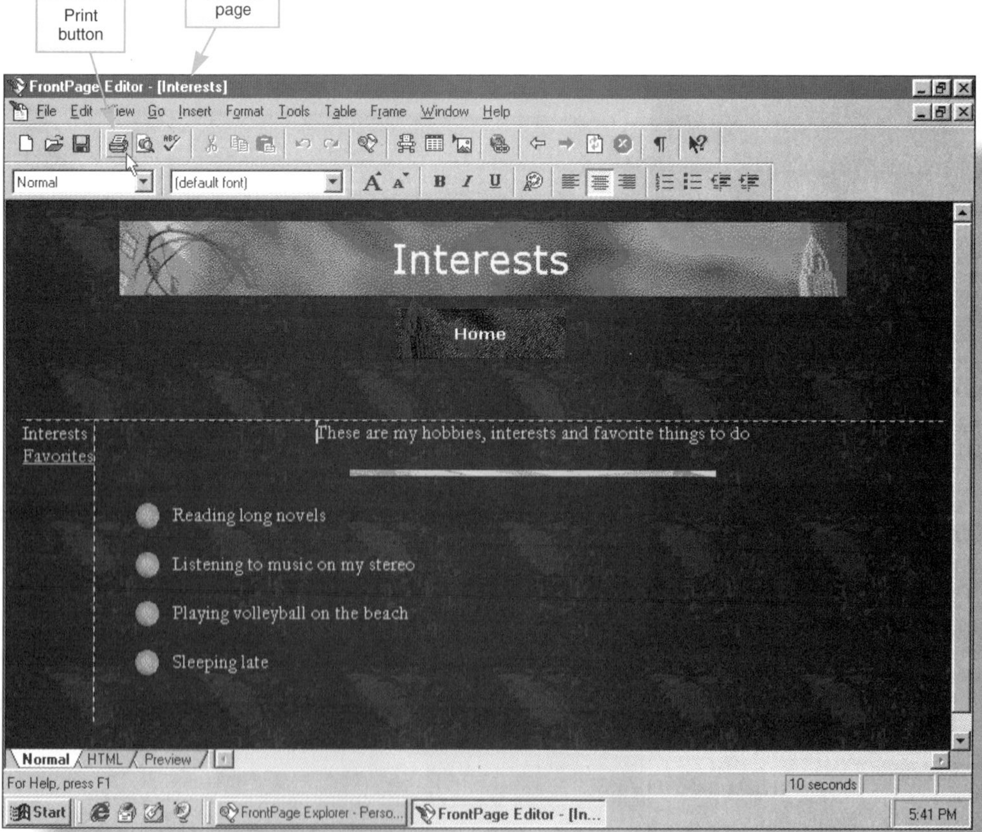

FIGURE 1-67

10 **Click the Print button on the Standard toolbar. Click the OK button in the Print dialog box.**

The Interests page prints (Figure 1-68c). The three Web pages print with all the changes you have made to the Personal Pages web. Hyperlinks and images are printed as they look in the FrontPage Editor's Normal view.

11 **Click the Close button on the FrontPage Editor title bar to close the FrontPage Editor.**

The FrontPage Editor window closes, and the FrontPage Explorer window displays.

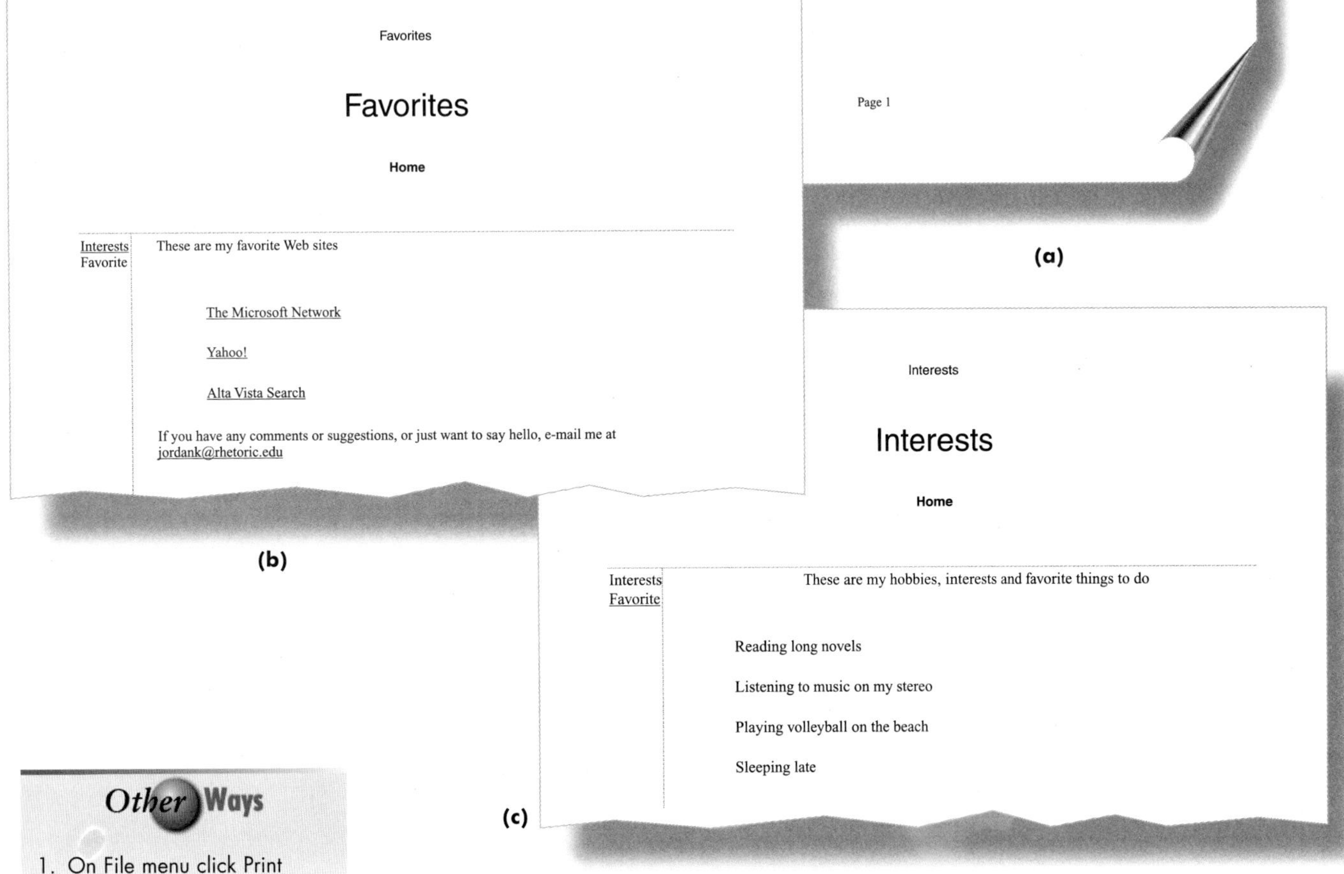

Home Page

Home Page

Home Interests Favorites

[Button
[Button
[Button

Welcome to my Web Site!

My name is Kurt and I attend Rhetoric University in Hometown, USA

I'm majoring in Web page development and hope to start a career developing Web pages and related Web materials

Feel free to visit my Interests and Favorites pages

This page was last updated on 05/10/98

Page 1

(a)

Favorites

Favorites

Home

Interests
Favorite

These are my favorite Web sites

The Microsoft Network

Yahoo!

Alta Vista Search

If you have any comments or suggestions, or just want to say hello, e-mail me at jordank@rhetoric.edu

(b)

Interests

Interests

Home

Interests
Favorite

These are my hobbies, interests and favorite things to do

Reading long novels

Listening to music on my stereo

Playing volleyball on the beach

Sleeping late

(c)

FIGURE 1-68

Other Ways

1. On File menu click Print
2. Press CTRL+P
3. Press ALT+P, P

To print a Web page, the FrontPage Editor must be in Normal view, as indicated by the tab at the bottom of the window. Printing while the FrontPage Editor is in HTML view prints the HTML source. Viewing the page in Preview view disables printing.

Notice the printing options in the **Print dialog box** in Figure 1-61 on page FP 1.46. In the Print range area, the **All option** allows you to print the entire document. The **Pages option** lets you print selected pages of a multiple-page document. Using the **Number of copies box** specifies how many copies you want to print. Clicking the **Print to file check box**, you can choose to print the selected page on to a disk.

Publishing

A FrontPage web can be published on your Windows 95 or Windows 98 PC, on a local intranet, or on the World Wide Web. You need access via an Internet service provider (ISP) to publish on the World Wide Web.

Publishing a FrontPage Web

If you have access to a Web server, FrontPage provides an easy way to publish your Web pages on the Internet. As noted, *publishing* a Web page is the process of sending copies of Web pages, image files, multimedia files, and any folders to a Web server where they then become available to the World Wide Web. With FrontPage, you can publish your Web by clicking a single button.

Many schools provide some facilities for their students to publish a small amount of Web materials. For a modest fee, Internet service providers, or ISPs, will provide space for you to publish personal Web materials. Contact your instructor, or your ISP to see if these facilities are available and how you can access them.

FrontPage 98 comes packaged with a program that will turn your Windows system into a Web server. The program, called **Personal Web Server**, can be installed when you install FrontPage 98. You then can publish your custom Web pages on your Windows system using the Personal Web Server.

Because your Web currently is on drive A, you will have to use an Internet service program called a **File Transfer Program**, or **FTP**, to copy the files in your FrontPage web to the Web server. FTP is a method of transferring files over the Internet.

The following steps demonstrate how to publish your FrontPage Web on a Web server. These steps will work only if you have write access to an account on the Web server computer. Be sure to substitute your own URL where you see home1.gte.net/jordank, or your FrontPage web will not be published successfully. If you do not know what URL to use, ask your instructor.

To Publish the FrontPage Web

1 Point to the Publish button on the FrontPage Explorer toolbar (Figure 1-69).

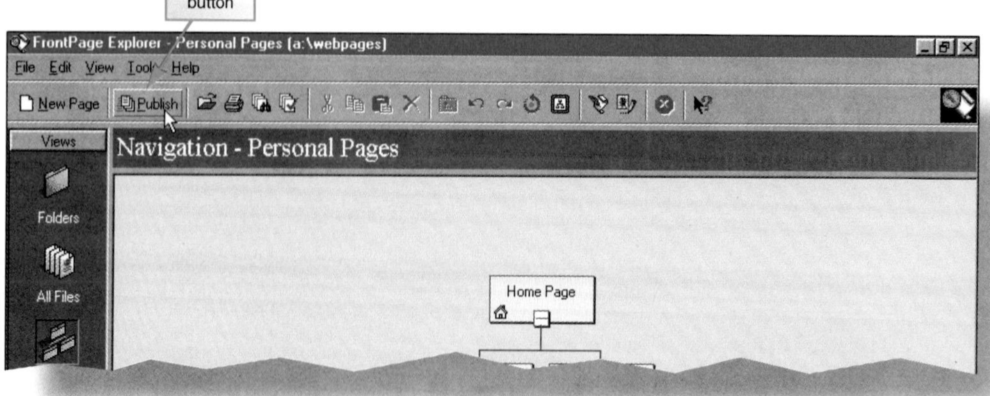

FIGURE 1-69

2 Click the Publish button. If necessary, click the Cancel button in the Microsoft Web Publishing Wizard dialog box, and click Cancel in the Publish dialog box.

The Publish FrontPage Web dialog box displays (Figure 1-70). The location text box displays the URL of the location where the current web will be published. This URL is the location of the Home Page; the other files in the Web will be located below this URL.

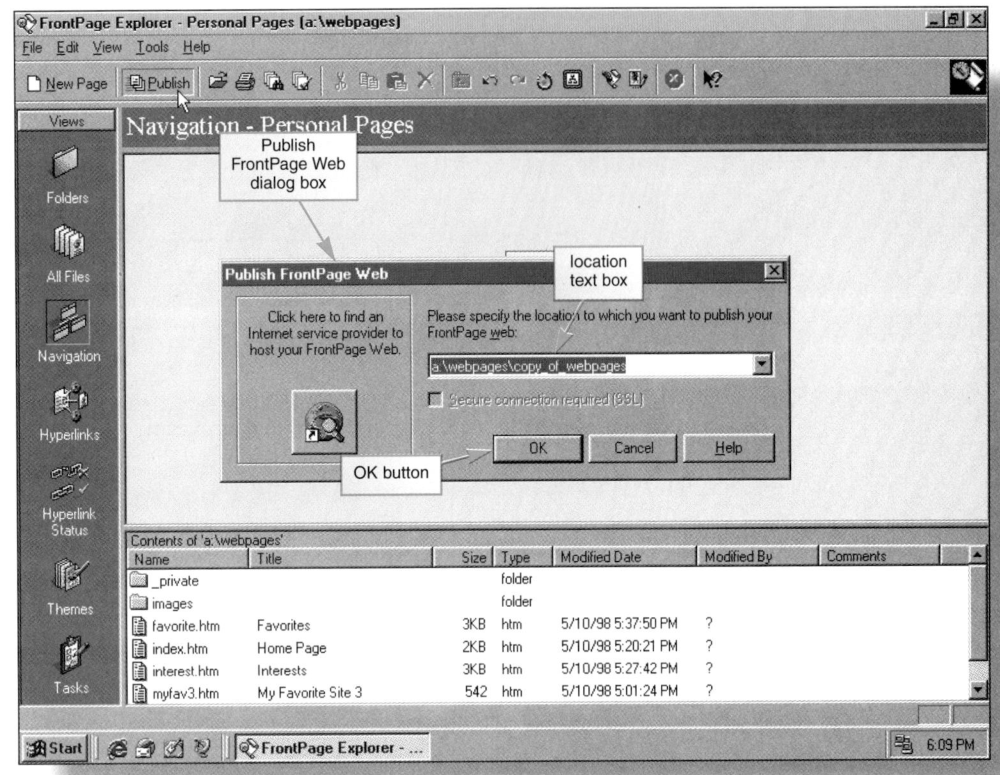

FIGURE 1-70

3 Type `http://home1.gte.net/jordank` **in the text box. Be sure to substitute your own URL where you see http://home1.gte.net/jordank.**

The destination URL displays in the location text box (Figure 1-71).

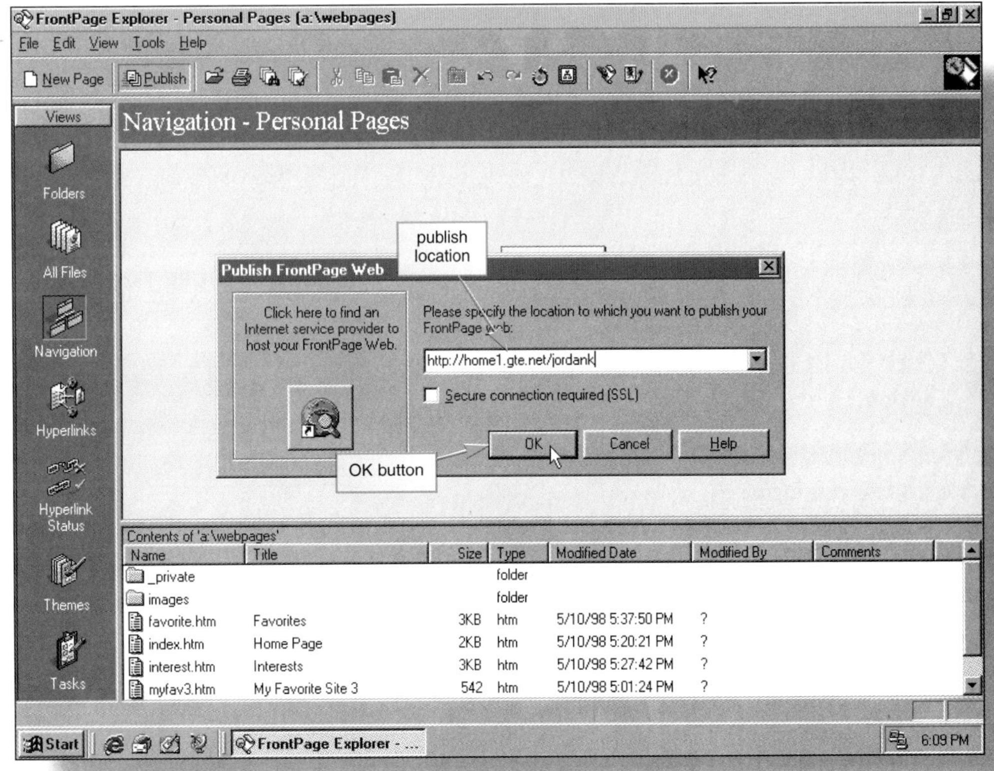

FIGURE 1-71

4 Click the OK button.

The Microsoft Web Publishing Wizard dialog box displays (Figure 1-72). The wizard will prompt you for all the necessary information needed to transfer the entire FrontPage Web to the Web server computer.

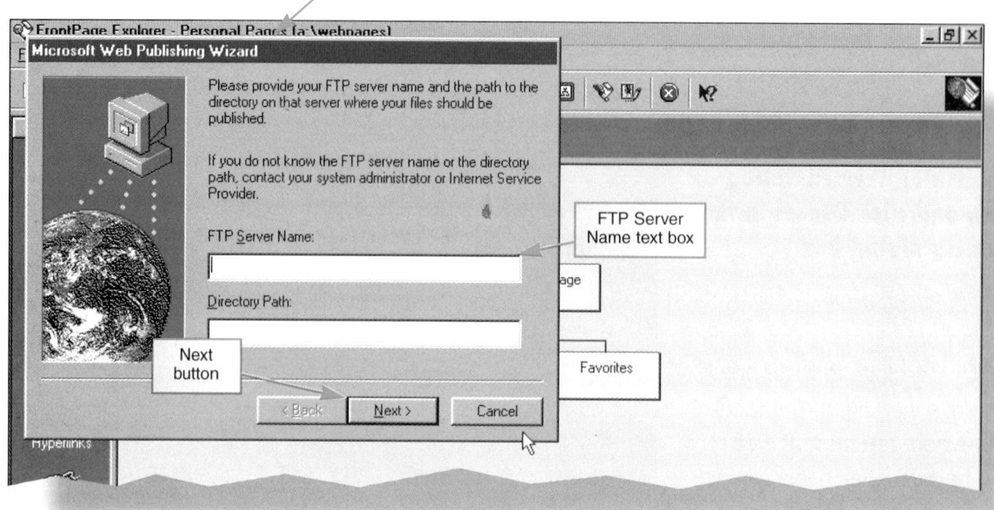

FIGURE 1-72

5 Type `ftphome1.gte.net` **in the FTP Server Name text box. If you do not know what FTP server name to use, ask your instructor.**

The server name displays in the text box (Figure 1-73). You did not have to supply a directory path because you specified the path in the destination URL in earlier steps.

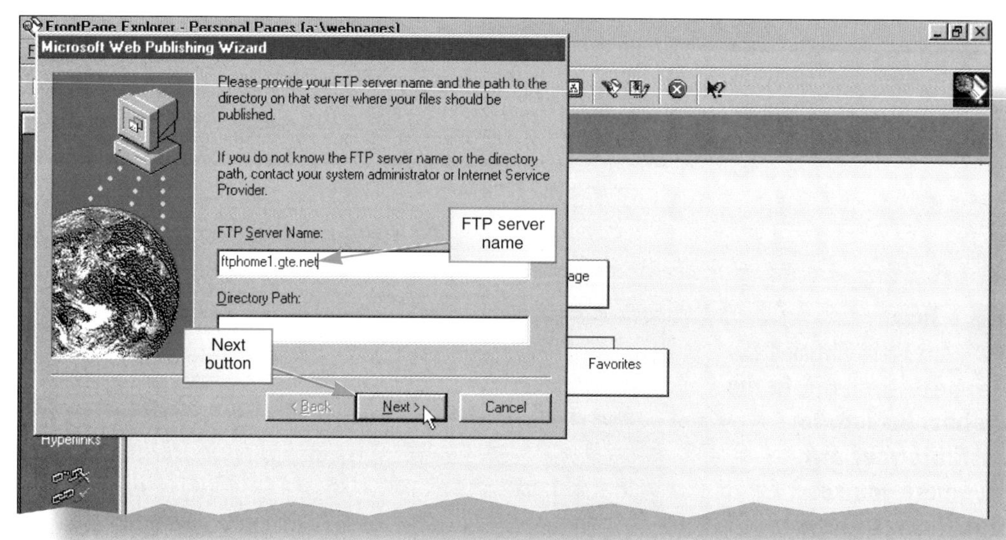

FIGURE 1-73

6 Click the Next button.

The User Name and Password text boxes display (Figure 1-74). Before you can place files in the FTP server, you must identify yourself.

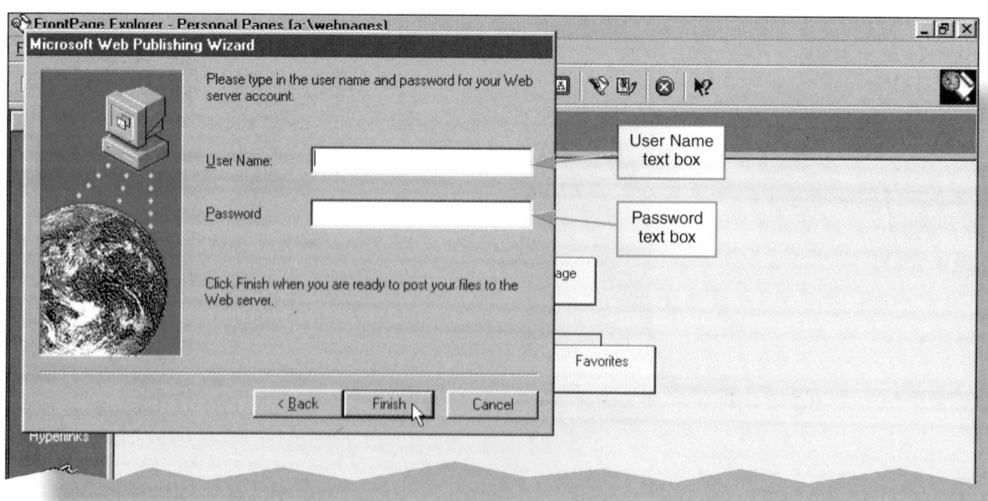

FIGURE 1-74

7 Type `jordank` **in the User Name text box. Type the password in the Password text box. If you do not know what user name and password to use, ask your instructor.**

The user name and password display in the text boxes (Figure 1-75). The password displays as asterisks (*).

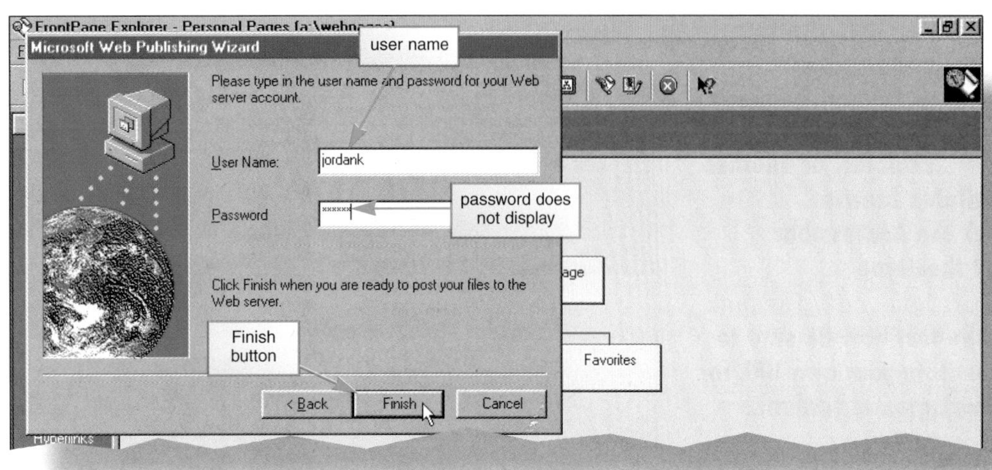

FIGURE 1-75

Click the Finish button.

A Transferring Files dialog box displays indicating the progress of the transfer (Figure 1-76). Seventy-two files are to be transferred. Most of these files contain components of the Downtown theme you selected for use with the FrontPage web. The transfer may take a few moments. When the FrontPage Explorer has completed the publication of the Web, a message displays on the status bar.

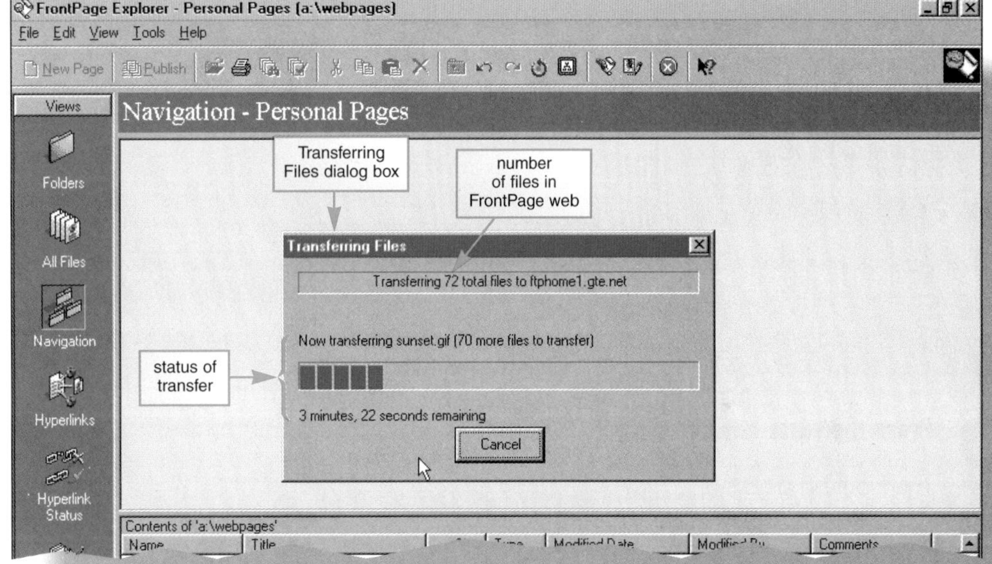

FIGURE 1-76

Other Ways

1. On File menu, click Publish FrontPage Web
2. Press CTRL+B
3. Press ALT+F, B

FrontPage remembers the location where the current web was published, so the next time you click the Publish button on the toolbar, FrontPage will prompt for only your FTP user name and password. FrontPage will publish the current web in the same location as the last time the web was published. That is the reason you might have to cancel the two dialog boxes before you can enter the URL you will use to publish your own Web pages.

Testing the FrontPage Web You Created

Now that the web has been published, it is available to anyone on the World Wide Web. You should take time to test the newly published web to make sure the pages look as you expected and that hyperlinks work. The steps on the next page test the Personal Pages web.

To Test the FrontPage Web

1 **Start Internet Explorer, or another available browser. Click the Address bar and then type** `home1.gte.net/jordank` **in the text box. Be sure to substitute your own URL for home1.gte.net/jordank.**

The new URL displays in the Address bar (Figure 1-77). You did not have to supply a path or file name on the URL because the Web server will display a default Web page, called index.htm, and this is the name that FrontPage used to store your Home Page.

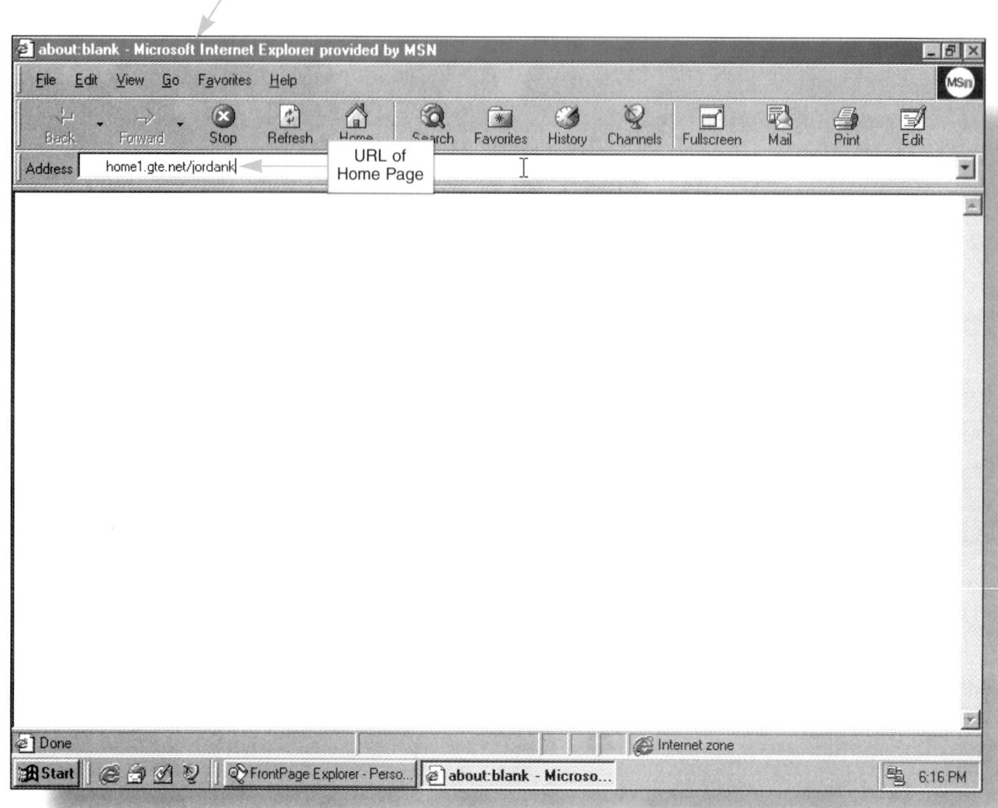

FIGURE 1-77

2 **Press the ENTER key.**

The Home Page displays in the browser display area (Figure 1-78). Notice the buttons that were on the vertical navigation bar while in the FrontPage Editor (see Figure 1-61 on page FP 1.46) do not display. This is because you changed that navigation bar to do same level navigation and there are no other pages at the same level as the Home Page.

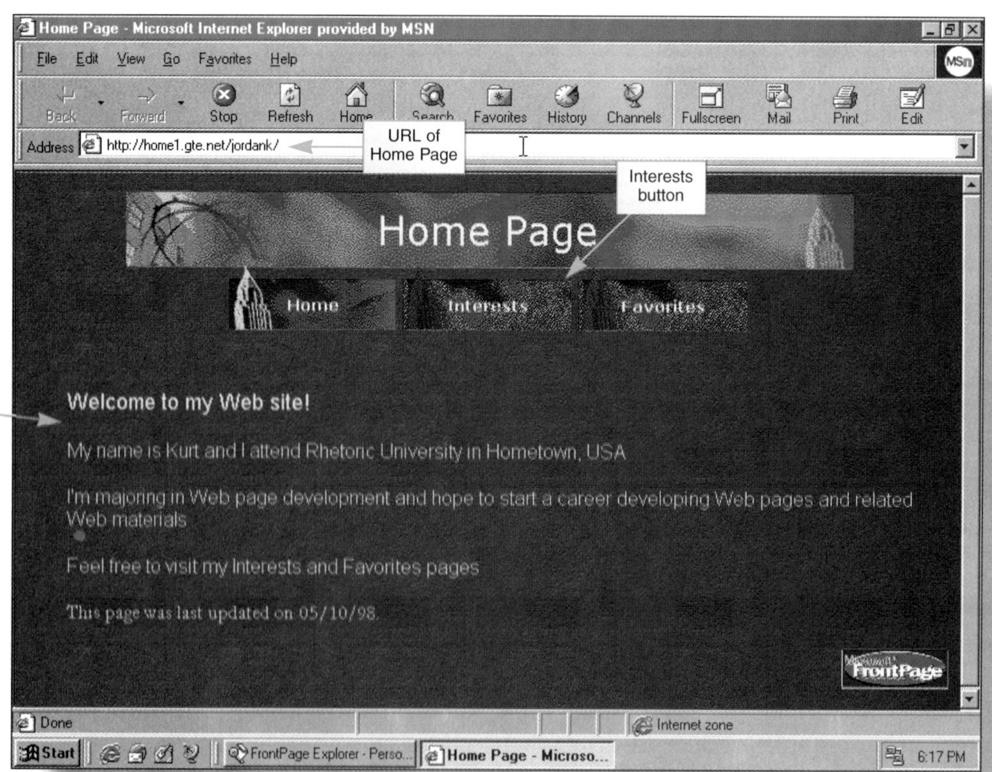

FIGURE 1-78

3 Click the Interests button on the navigation bar.

The Interests page displays (Figure1-79). Notice the changes you made to the Web page in the FrontPage Editor.

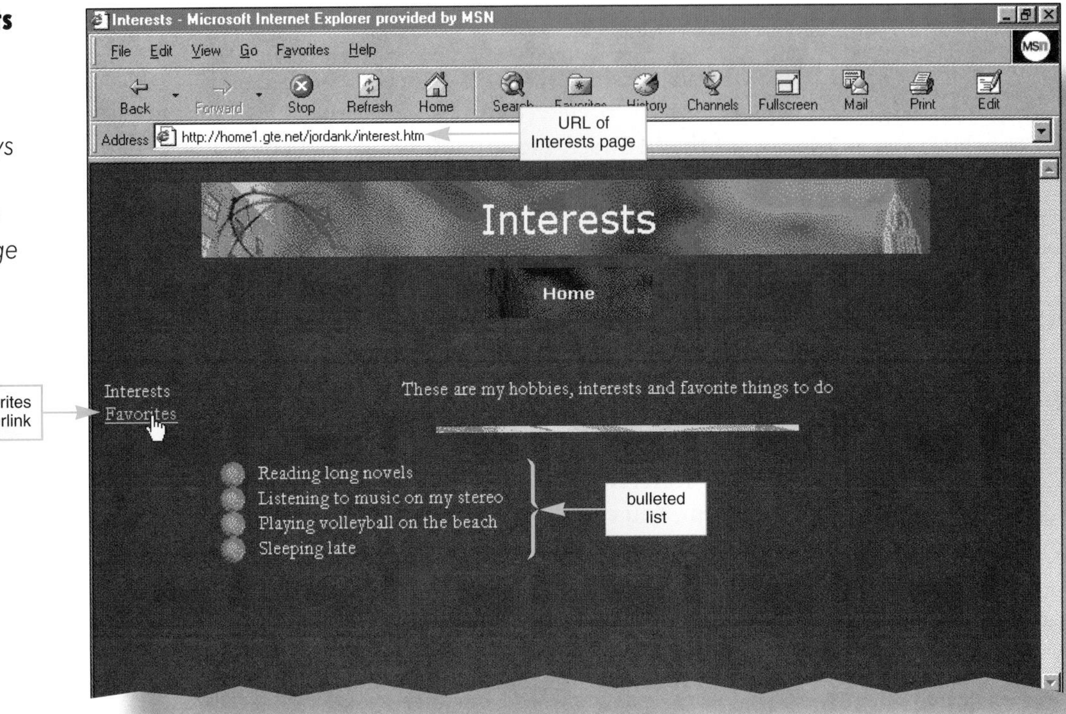

FIGURE 1-79

4 Click the Favorites hyperlink on the vertical navigation bar.

The Favorites page displays (Figure 1-80). You can continue to test the hyperlinks and check the correctness and visual aspects of the Personal Pages web pages.

5 After viewing the Web pages for correctness and ensuring all the hyperlinks function properly, click the Close button on the Internet Explorer title bar to close the browser.

The Internet Explorer window closes and the FrontPage Explorer window displays.

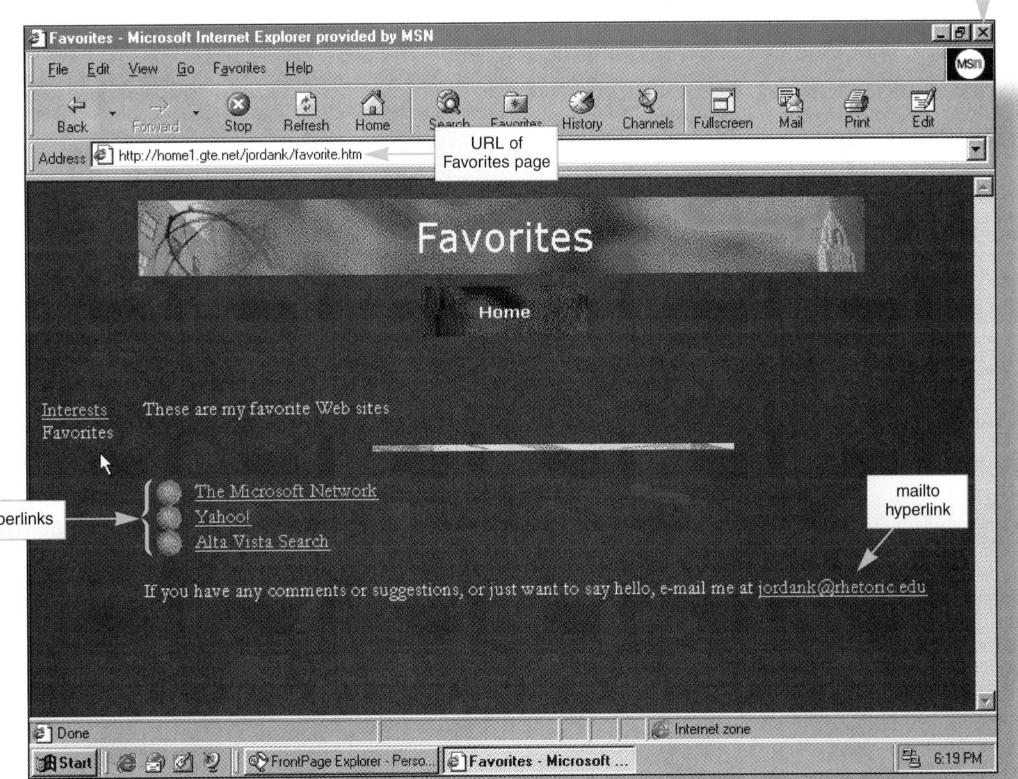

FIGURE 1-80

The Contents Sheet

Use the Contents sheet in the same manner you would use a table of contents at the front of a textbook – simply browse through topics and subtopics to find the desired information.

You successfully have published and tested a series of related Web pages on the World Wide Web. You could have used any browser to display your Web pages. Testing your Web pages is important because some Web pages will look slightly different when viewed in different browsers. This is because of the different capabilities of the browser, the capabilities of the computer system running the browser program, and the browser preferences set by the user.

FrontPage Help

FrontPage is a program with many features, procedures, and options. Although you will master some of these features and procedures, it is not necessary for you to remember everything about each one of them.

Reference materials and other forms of assistance are available using **FrontPage Help**. You can display these materials and print or copy them to other Windows applications. Table 1-4 summarizes the four categories of online help available to you.

Table 1-4

TYPE	DESCRIPTION	ACTIVATE BY CLICKING
Contents sheet	Groups Help topics by general categories. Use when you know only the general category of the topic in question.	Click Microsoft FrontPage Help on the Help menu and then click the Contents tab.
Index sheet	Similar to an index in a book. Use when you know exactly what you want.	Click Microsoft FrontPage Help on the Help menu and then click the Index tab.
Find sheet	Searches the index for all phrases that include the search term.	Click Microsoft FrontPage Help on the Help menu and then click the Find tab.
Question mark button	Identifies unfamiliar elements in a dialog box.	In a dialog box, click the question mark button and then click an element in the dialog box.
Help button	Identifies unfamiliar elements on the screen.	In the FrontPage Explorer, click the Help button on the toolbar. In the FrontPage Editor, click the Help button on the Standard toolbar. Then, click an element on the screen.

When you click Microsoft FrontPage Help on the Help menu, the **Help Topics: Microsoft FrontPage Help dialog box** displays. It contains three sheets that access Help in different ways. The **Contents sheet** organizes topics in general categories, such as Using FrontPage and What's New. A book icon identifies general categories. A question mark icon identifies specific information on a topic.

The Index Sheet

If you have used a book's index to look up terms, then you will feel comfortable with the Index sheet. It works in much the same way, except that you type the term on which you want information, rather than paging through the index to find it.

The **Index sheet** displays an extensive index to FrontPage Help topics. Like the index in the back of a book, the Index sheet helps when you know the first few letters of the term or the exact term you want to find.

The **Find sheet** allows you to type a keyword to find information on specific topics. It will return a list of all topics pertaining to the word or phrase you type in the text box. From that point, you can select words to narrow your search further.

When displaying information about a topic, a **Help toolbar** displays containing buttons for frequently used actions such as navigation and printing. For example, you can print a Help topic using the **Print button** on the Help toolbar.

You also can select sections of a Help topic and then drag the selected text into another Windows application. You can return to the Help Topics: Microsoft FrontPage Help dialog box to search for more information by clicking the **Help Topics button** on the Help toolbar.

When you are working in the FrontPage Explorer or the FrontPage Editor, you have access to Help to identify unfamiliar elements on the screen by clicking the **Help button** on the toolbar.

Quitting FrontPage

Once you have finished the activities in the project, you can quit FrontPage. The following steps demonstrate how to quit FrontPage.

TO QUIT FRONTPAGE

Click the Close button on the FrontPage Explorer title bar.

If necessary, click the Close button on the Internet Explorer title bar to quit Internet Explorer.

The Windows desktop displays.

Other Ways

1. On File menu click Exit
2. Press ALT+F, X
3. Press ALT+F4

Project Summary

Having completed Project 1, you now are ready to assist in developing Web pages for your advertising firm. In this project, you learned how hypertext markup language, or HTML, is used to create Web pages. You also learned how to create a FrontPage web using a template. You learned how to apply a theme to a FrontPage web. The FrontPage Editor was used to change and add text. You also learned how to modify a bulleted list, add hyperlinks to a Web page, change the properties for a WebBot component, and publish a FrontPage Web on the World Wide Web. Finally, you learned how to use FrontPage Help.

What You Should Know

Having completed this project, you now should be able to perform the following tasks.

- Add a Mailto Hyperlink to a Web Page *(FP 1.42)*
- Add New Text to a Web Page *(FP 1.26)*
- Apply a Theme to a FrontPage Web *(FP 1.19)*
- Change a Hyperlink on a Web Page *(FP 1.37)*
- Create a FrontPage Web Using a Template *(FP 1.14)*
- Delete a Page from the FrontPage Web *(FP 1.35)*
- Edit a Bulleted List *(FP 1.28)*
- Edit Text on a Web Page *(FP 1.24)*
- Modify a Navigation Bar WebBot Component *(FP 1.31)*
- Print a Web Page from the FrontPage Editor *(FP 1.46)*
- Publish the FrontPage Web *(FP 1.50)*
- Quit FrontPage *(FP 1.57)*
- Quit the FrontPage Editor *(FP 1.28)*
- Save a Web Page *(FP 1.27)*
- Start the FrontPage Editor *(FP 1.22)*
- Start FrontPage *(FP 1.12)*
- Test the FrontPage Web *(FP 1.54)*
- View the HTML Source for a Web Page *(FP 1.23)*

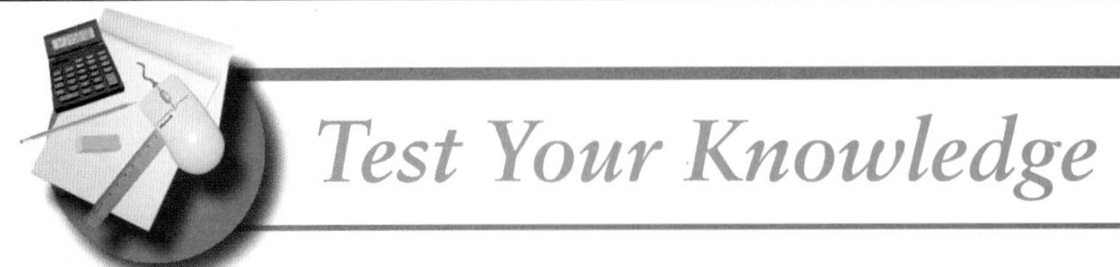

Test Your Knowledge

1 True/False

Instructions: Circle T if the statement is true or F if the statement is false.

T F 1. The Web page text file contains instructions that describe elements such as page layout and special formatting.

T F 2. A Web server is a special program that requests and interprets the HTML in Web pages.

T F 3. A URL consists of the Internet address of the computer where the Web page is located and the path to the file containing the Web page.

T F 4. HTML is similar to a computer programming language.

T F 5. HTML uses special character sequences, called markups to indicate the various formatting features on a Web page.

T F 6. In FrontPage, a group of related Web pages is called a FrontPage web.

T F 7. FrontPage themes allow you to look at your FrontPage web from several perspectives.

T F 8. Themes are built-in collections of design elements that you can apply to an entire FrontPage web.

T F 9. The FrontPage Editor creates and formats Web pages using HTML in a what you see is what you get, or WYSIWYG, style.

T F 10. Bulleted lists, image maps, and forms are examples of WebBot components.

2 Multiple Choice

Instructions: Circle the correct response.

1. A ___________ is a special program that requests and interprets the HTML in Web pages.
   a. Web server
   b. Web browser
   c. theme
   d. FrontPage web
2. A ___________ consists of the Internet address of the computer where a Web page is located and the path to the file containing the Web page.
   a. theme
   b. Web server
   c. URL
   d. WebBot component
3. Web pages are created using a special formatting language called ___________.
   a. hypertext markup language, or HTML
   b. Java
   c. themes
   d. secure socket layer, or SSL
4. An inline image is inserted in a Web page with the ___________ tag.
   a. <H1>
   b. <HREF>
   c. <SRC>
   d. <IMG>
5. In FrontPage, a group of related Web pages is called a FrontPage ___________.
   a. web
   b. frame
   c. view
   d. site
6. A Web ___________ is a series of files that has been organized and formatted with a basic framework of content.
   a. site
   b. template
   c. view
   d. frame

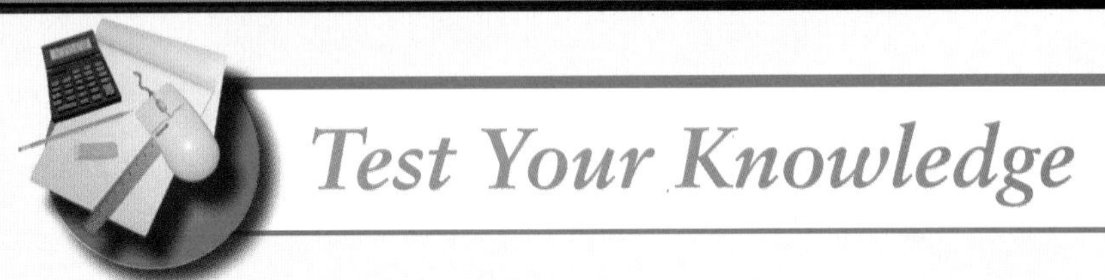

7. FrontPage is packaged with more than 50 built-in collections of design elements called ___________.
   a. views
   b. clipart
   c. templates
   d. themes
8. Dynamic objects on a Web page that are evaluated or executed when the page is saved or displayed with a browser are called active components, or ___________.
   a. WebBot components
   b. browser components
   c. HotBot components
   d. intranet components
9. You can determine if an object on a Web page is an active component because the ___________ is added to the mouse pointer when pointing to the object.
   a. browser icon
   b. HotBot cursor
   c. insertion point
   d. WebBot component cursor
10. ___________ a Web page is the process of sending copies of the Web page and corresponding image and other multimedia files to a Web server where they become available to the World Wide Web.
    a. Saving
    b. Publishing
    c. Serving
    d. Installing

3 Understanding HTML

Instructions: Perform the following tasks with a computer.

1. Start Internet Explorer or another browser. Display the Home Page Web page you created in this project.
2. Click the Interests hyperlink to display the Interests page.
3. Click Source on the View menu to display the HTML for the Interests page (Figure 1-81).
4. Click File on the Notepad menu bar and then click Print to print the HTML. Close Notepad.
5. Click the Favorites hyperlink to display the Favorites page. Print the HTML.
6. Compare the HTML used in the two documents. List the tags that are common to both documents and the tags in one but not the other.
7. Determine the functions of the tags that are not in both documents.
8. Write your lists, your answers, and your name on the printouts and hand them in to your instructor.

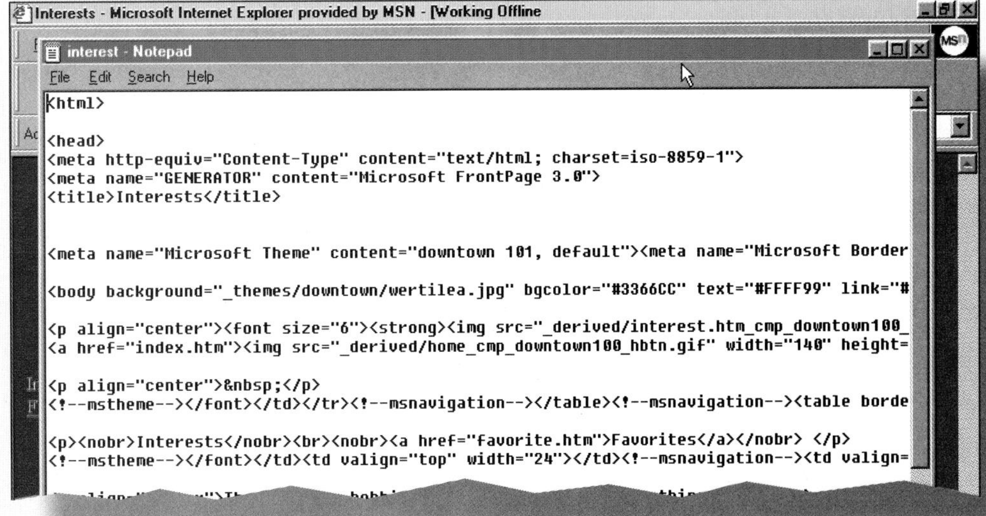

FIGURE 1-81

Test Your Knowledge

4 Understanding the FrontPage Explorer Views

Instructions: The FrontPage Explorer views allow you to manage a FrontPage web. In Figure 1-82, arrows point to the views available on the Views bar. In the spaces provided, briefly explain the purpose of each view.

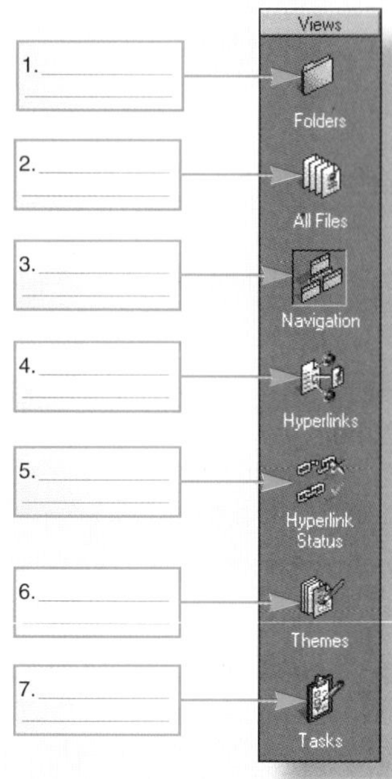

FIGURE 1-82

Use Help

1 Setting Margins

Instructions: The FrontPage Editor allows you to edit a Web page in a manner similar to a word processor, such as setting margins on the page. Using FrontPage Help (Figure 1-83), find and display information for setting the margins on a Web page. Write the steps along with your name and hand them in to your instructor.

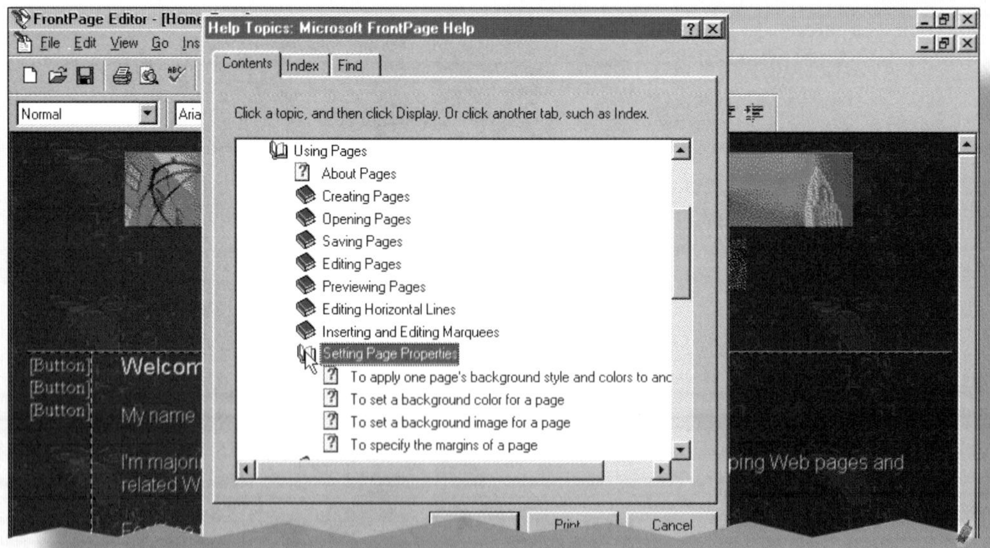

FIGURE 1-83

2 Deleting a FrontPage Web

Instructions: Using FrontPage Help, find and display information for deleting a FrontPage web. Write the steps to delete a FrontPage web along with your name and hand them in to your instructor.

1 Creating a Web Page Using a Template

Instructions: Start FrontPage 98. Perform the following steps with a computer.

1. In the Getting Started dialog box, click Create a New FrontPage Web and then click the OK button.
2. Insert a formatted disk in drive A. In the New FrontPage Web dialog box, click From Wizard or Template, click Corporate Presence Wizard, and click the Change button. In the Change Location dialog box, type `a:\ayk1` and then click the OK button. The Corporate Presence Wizard window opens.
3. Click the Next button. Be sure that only the What's New check box is selected. Click the Finish button.
4. Click the Themes button on the Views bar and then apply a theme of your choice to the Web.
5. Click the Navigation button on the Views bar. Edit the Home Page (double-click the page icon).
6. Click the first paragraph to select it, and then type `Welcome to Ruler-Rite Ruler Company, makers of rulers, pointers, and other fine educational products` as the new text.
7. Select the second paragraph. Type `To make the best wood products while being a friend to the environment` as the new text.
8. Select the third paragraph. Press the DELETE key to delete the text from the page (Figure 1-84).
9. Print the Web page, save the page, and then close the FrontPage Editor.
10. Edit the News page by double-clicking the News page icon.
11. Select the navigation bar below the News banner and then edit the properties to include hyperlinks at the child level. Make sure the Home Page check box is selected.
12. Select the vertical navigation bar and then edit the properties to include hyperlinks at the same level.
13. Select the second paragraph. Type `Watch for the announcement of our new year 2000 model ruler. Slim, sleek and precise, it's a must for the new school year` as the new text.
14. Print and save the Web page, and then close the FrontPage Editor. Hand in the printouts to your instructor.

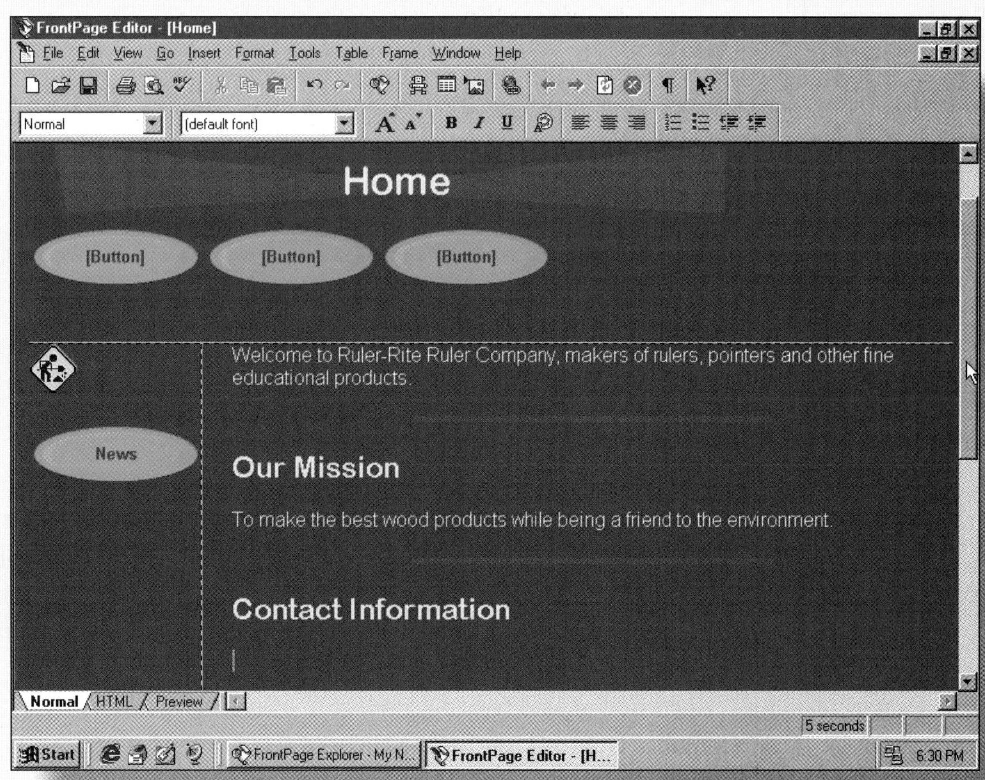

FIGURE 1-84

1 Customizing the Navigation Bar

Instructions: You can change the hyperlinks in the navigation bar so they provide access to Web pages in the current web in several different ways. Perform the following steps to change the navigation bar hyperlinks.

1. Start Microsoft FrontPage and create a new Personal Pages web.
2. Double-click the Home Page page icon in the Navigation pane to start the FrontPage Editor.
3. Click the WebBot component in the navigation bar at the top of the page to select it (Figure 1-85).
4. Double-click the WebBot component. In the Navigation Bar Properties dialog box, change the Hyperlinks to include option to Same level. Click the OK button.
5. What happened to the buttons in the navigation bar?
6. Print the Home Page.
7. Double-click the WebBot component. In the Navigation Bar Properties dialog box, change the Hyperlinks to include option to Back and Next. Click the OK button. How has the navigation bar changed?
8. Print the page, write your name and the answers to the questions on the printouts and hand them in to your instructor.

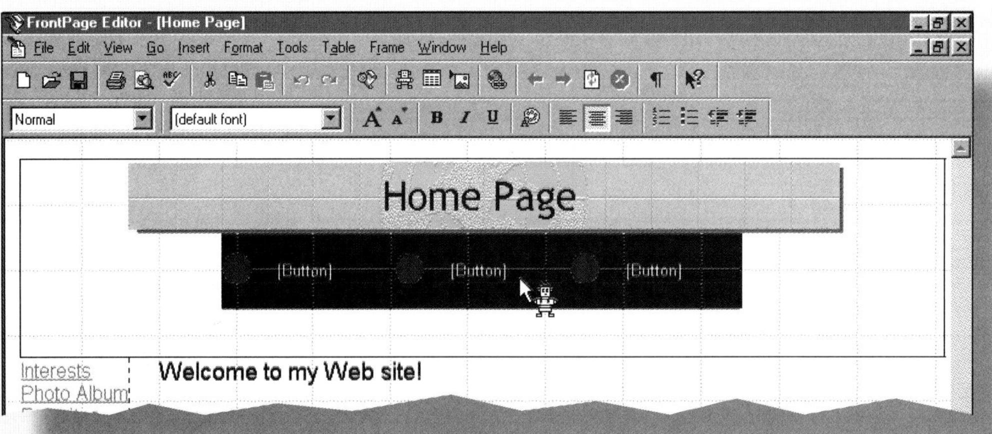

FIGURE 1-85

2 Add a Hyperlink to a Web Page

Instructions: Perform the following steps with a computer.

1. Start the FrontPage Explorer and create a new Personal Pages web.
2. Double-click the Home Page page icon in the Navigation pane to open that page in the FrontPage Editor.
3. Drag through the first paragraph of text and then type `Hello, my name is Kurt and I attend Rhetoric University`. You can substitute your name where you see Kurt and the name of your school where you see Rhetoric University.
4. Drag through the Rhetoric University text to select it (Figure 1-86).
5. Click the Create or Edit Hyperlink button on the toolbar to display the Edit Hyperlink dialog box.
6. Click the World Wide Web button to launch Internet Explorer.

7. Display your school's or another home page.
8. Click the FrontPage Editor button on the taskbar to return to the FrontPage Editor.
9. Click the OK button in the Edit Hyperlink dialog box to accept the URL in the URL text box.
10. Click the HTML tab to display the HTML source for the Home Page. Print the HTML source.
11. Write your name on the page and hand it in to your instructor.

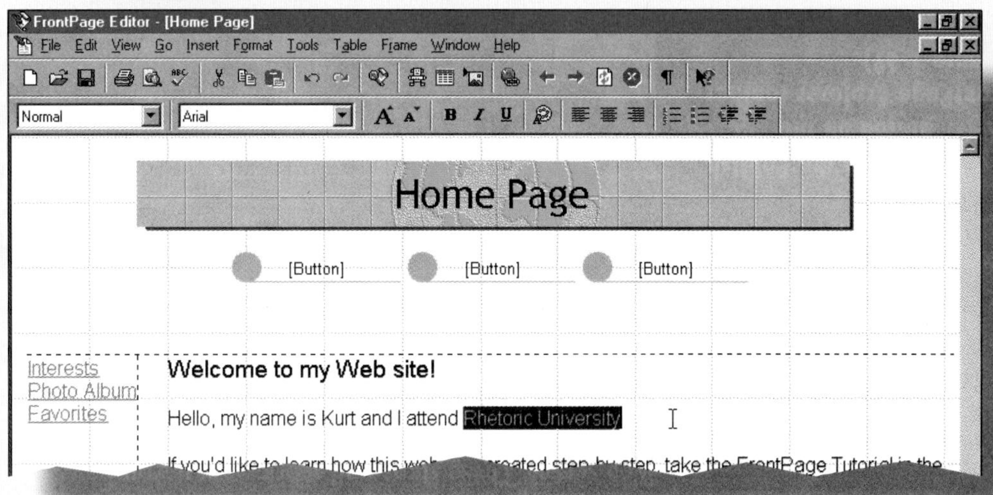

FIGURE 1-86

3 Change the Theme Used with a FrontPage Web

Instructions: Perform the following steps with a computer.

1. Start the FrontPage Explorer and create a new Personal Pages web. If necessary, click the Home Page page icon to select it.
2. Scroll down the Views bar and then click the Themes button to display the Themes view (Figure 1-87).
3. Apply the theme to the Personal Pages web and then click the OK button.
4. Double-click the Home Page page icon to start the FrontPage Editor.
5. Print the Home Page with the new theme, write your name on it, and hand it in to your instructor.

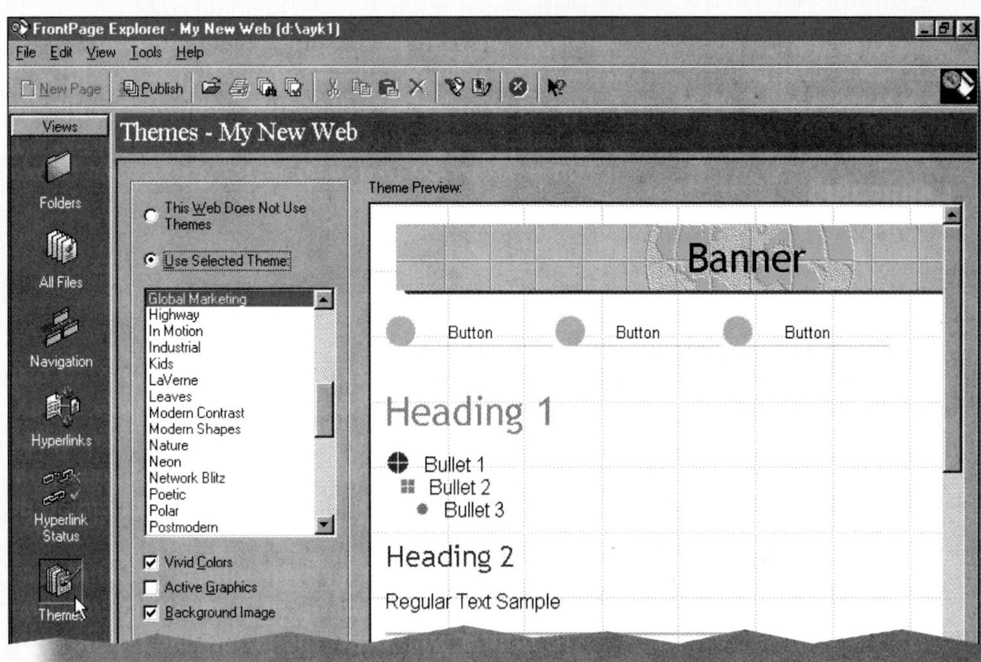

FIGURE 1-87

Cases and Places

The difficulty of these case studies varies:
◗ are the least difficult; ◗◗ are more difficult; and ◗◗◗ are the most difficult.

1 ◗ Your instructor wants his course syllabus available on the Web. Use FrontPage and the One Page Web template to create a text-only course home page that includes information from the syllabus.

2 ◗ The HTML in Web pages can be edited using any word processor, such as WordPad. Using an available Web browser, save any prominent Web page to a file on a floppy disk. Edit the Web page using WordPad and insert some HTML code for your name and the name of your school. Use appropriate HTML code to cause your name and the name of your school to display properly in a browser.

3 ◗ Many software products such as Microsoft Word and Microsoft FrontPage are packaged with a library of images, graphics, pictures, and other clip art. Libraries of clip art also are available for download on the Web. Using the Web search engine of your choice, search for five sites that offer clip art for use in Web pages. Print a few of the images from each site.

4 ◗◗ Themes and templates allow you to create artistic, consistent Web pages. Find out how to create your own themes and templates. Using a Web search engine of your choice, see if any sites exist that contain themes and templates you can use. Write a report detailing your findings.

5 ◗◗ The hypertext markup language (HTML) contains many more tags than those presented in this project. It is evolving continuously and additional tags are being added to each new version. Find some sources of information about HTML on the Web. What are some of the new features of the current version of HTML? Learn about some new tags that are being considered for the next version of HTML.

6 ◗◗◗ Many Internet Service Providers (ISPs) provide a small amount of space for individuals to publish their own Web pages. Contact several local ISPs and find out which ones provide space for customer's Web pages. Record how large the space is, how much it costs, and any other restrictions, such as a limit on the amount of data uploaded or downloaded per month. Write a report detailing your findings.

7 ◗◗◗ Many schools allow students to publish Web pages using the school's Web facilities. At some schools, this has raised questions about censorship and free speech. Find out if your school has an official policy or set of rules for publishing Web pages. Contact several other schools to see if they have a Web page publishing policy. Write a report comparing the different Web page publishing policies.

Microsoft FrontPage 98

Creating a New FrontPage Web

OBJECTIVES

You will have mastered the material in this project when you can:

- List Web page design criteria
- Create a new one-page web
- Change the title of a Web page
- Set the Web page background
- Insert a table in a Web page
- Undo and redo actions in the FrontPage Editor
- Insert an image in a Web page
- Copy and paste items on a Web page
- Align items on a Web page
- Change table border properties
- Add a heading to a Web page
- Add horizontal rules
- Add normal text
- Create hyperlinks
- Preview a Web page

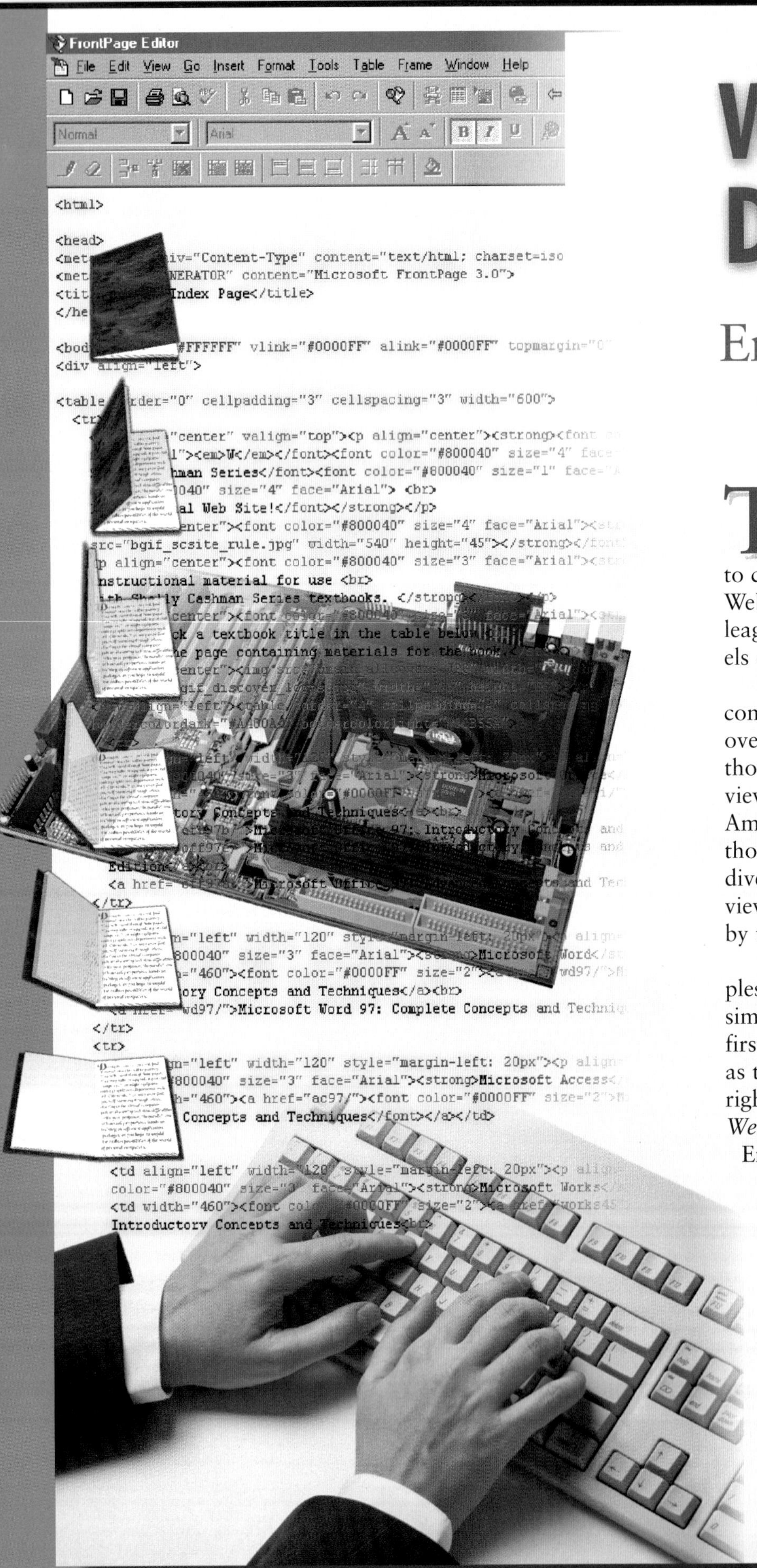

Web Page Designers

Eminent Among Composers

The objective of an accomplished Web page designer is to create high-quality, noteworthy Web pages that are admired by colleagues, win awards, and are models of exceptional style.

This appreciation does not come from verbose, complex, overanimated designs, but from thoughtful planning, sensitivity to viewers, and focus on detail. Among the skills required are a thorough understanding of the diverse community of potential viewers and the goal to be achieved by the Web page.

Literature abounds with examples of authors who pursue very similar objectives as they prepare a first draft and continue to rewrite as they struggle to get the words right. In his book, *On Writing Well*, respected Yale University English professor William Zinsser states, "Writing improves in direct ratio to the things we can keep out of it that shouldn't be there."

In the world of musical arrangements, celebrated composers exhibit the struggles they experience as they toil to score their greatest pieces in scrupulous detail and thought.

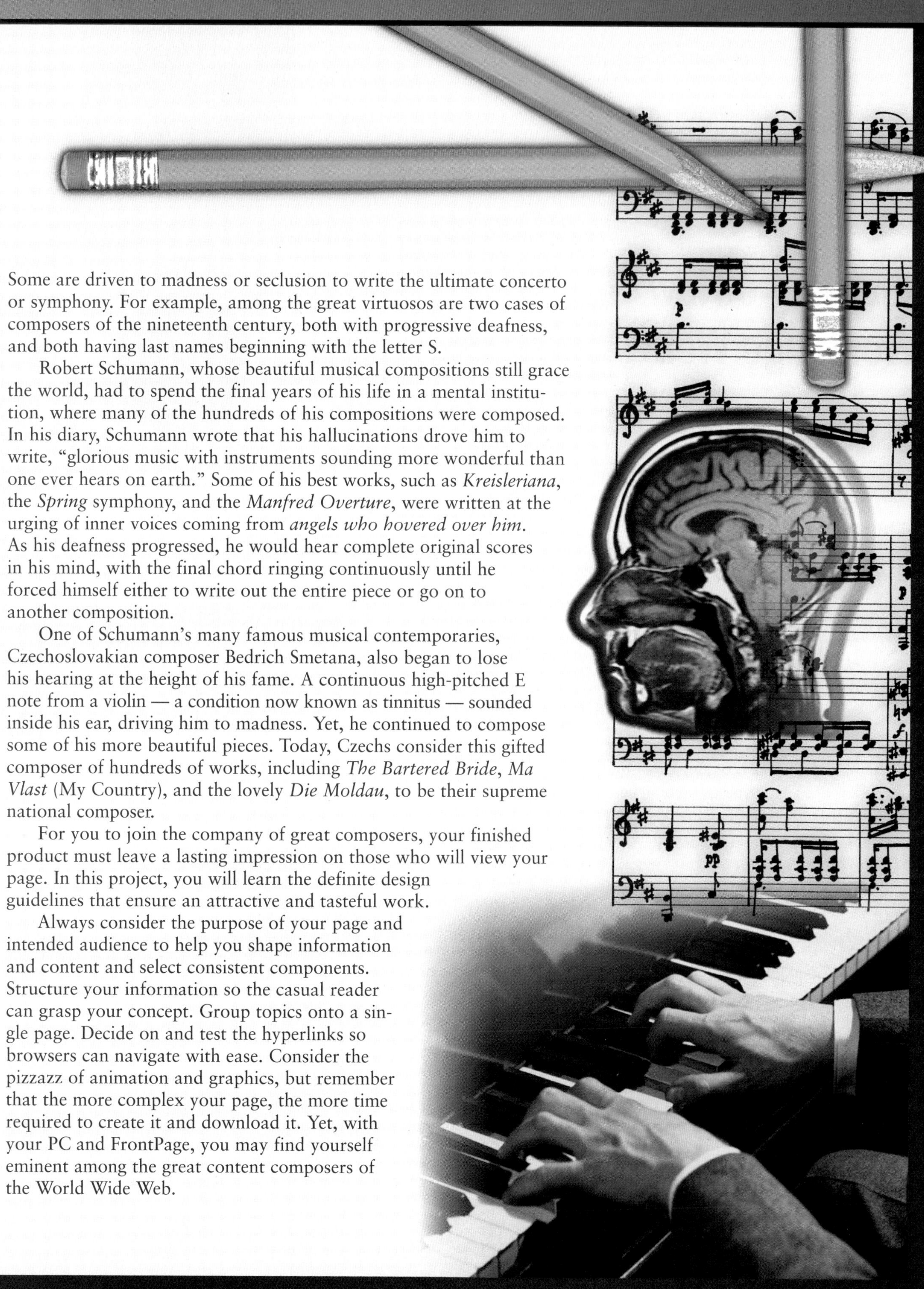

Some are driven to madness or seclusion to write the ultimate concerto or symphony. For example, among the great virtuosos are two cases of composers of the nineteenth century, both with progressive deafness, and both having last names beginning with the letter S.

Robert Schumann, whose beautiful musical compositions still grace the world, had to spend the final years of his life in a mental institution, where many of the hundreds of his compositions were composed. In his diary, Schumann wrote that his hallucinations drove him to write, "glorious music with instruments sounding more wonderful than one ever hears on earth." Some of his best works, such as *Kreisleriana*, the *Spring* symphony, and the *Manfred Overture*, were written at the urging of inner voices coming from *angels who hovered over him.* As his deafness progressed, he would hear complete original scores in his mind, with the final chord ringing continuously until he forced himself either to write out the entire piece or go on to another composition.

One of Schumann's many famous musical contemporaries, Czechoslovakian composer Bedrich Smetana, also began to lose his hearing at the height of his fame. A continuous high-pitched E note from a violin — a condition now known as tinnitus — sounded inside his ear, driving him to madness. Yet, he continued to compose some of his more beautiful pieces. Today, Czechs consider this gifted composer of hundreds of works, including *The Bartered Bride*, *Ma Vlast* (My Country), and the lovely *Die Moldau*, to be their supreme national composer.

For you to join the company of great composers, your finished product must leave a lasting impression on those who will view your page. In this project, you will learn the definite design guidelines that ensure an attractive and tasteful work.

Always consider the purpose of your page and intended audience to help you shape information and content and select consistent components. Structure your information so the casual reader can grasp your concept. Group topics onto a single page. Decide on and test the hyperlinks so browsers can navigate with ease. Consider the pizzazz of animation and graphics, but remember that the more complex your page, the more time required to create it and download it. Yet, with your PC and FrontPage, you may find yourself eminent among the great content composers of the World Wide Web.

Microsoft FrontPage 98

Creating a New FrontPage Web

CASE PERSPECTIVE

Early Web pages consisted of simple text documents that were developed by computer programmers or university researchers. Today's Web pages can be complex, highly animated objects. Web page developers now are individuals being recruited from the ranks of computer interface designers, graphic designers, and artists. People with little computer or design training, however, are creating outstanding Web sites.

The law firm of Morgan, Turner and Lock has hired you as a part-time assistant. Because of your Internet experience, you have been asked to develop a Web site for the firm. The site is to consist of several pages that introduce the firm and its people, describe the services available, and provide a means of obtaining some preliminary information from potential clients. Your current task is to design and develop a Home page for Morgan, Turner and Lock.

Introduction

Every Web page designer wants to build a high-quality, eye-popping Web page that is admired by colleagues, wins awards, and frequently is imitated. This appreciation does not come from long-winded, complicated, over-animated designs, but from thoughtful planning, sensitivity to viewers, and careful attention to detail. You must have a thorough understanding of the diverse community of potential viewers, and the goal to be accomplished by the Web page.

Web page development consists of two phases: design and implementation. **Design** consists of understanding the audience, determining the purpose of the Web page, and then selecting and organizing the individual elements that, together, will achieve that purpose. **Implementation** consists of writing the HTML statements and organizing files and folders to give life to the design. Sometimes the design and implementation tasks are separated, with a design group rendering the designs and another group responsible for the implementation.

Designing a Web page is an *iterative* process. You would perform some analysis concerning the requirements of the Web page, and then call upon your creativity to arrive at a design that satisfies those requirements, is functional, and attractive.

Once a page is designed, it is a simple matter to create it using an HTML editor, such as Microsoft FrontPage. The Microsoft FrontPage Editor has many rich features that will assist you in implementing Web page designs, from the simple to the complex. In this project, you will learn some of the criteria used to arrive at well-designed Web pages, and then implement the design for the Morgan, Turner and Lock Home page, shown in Figure 2-1.

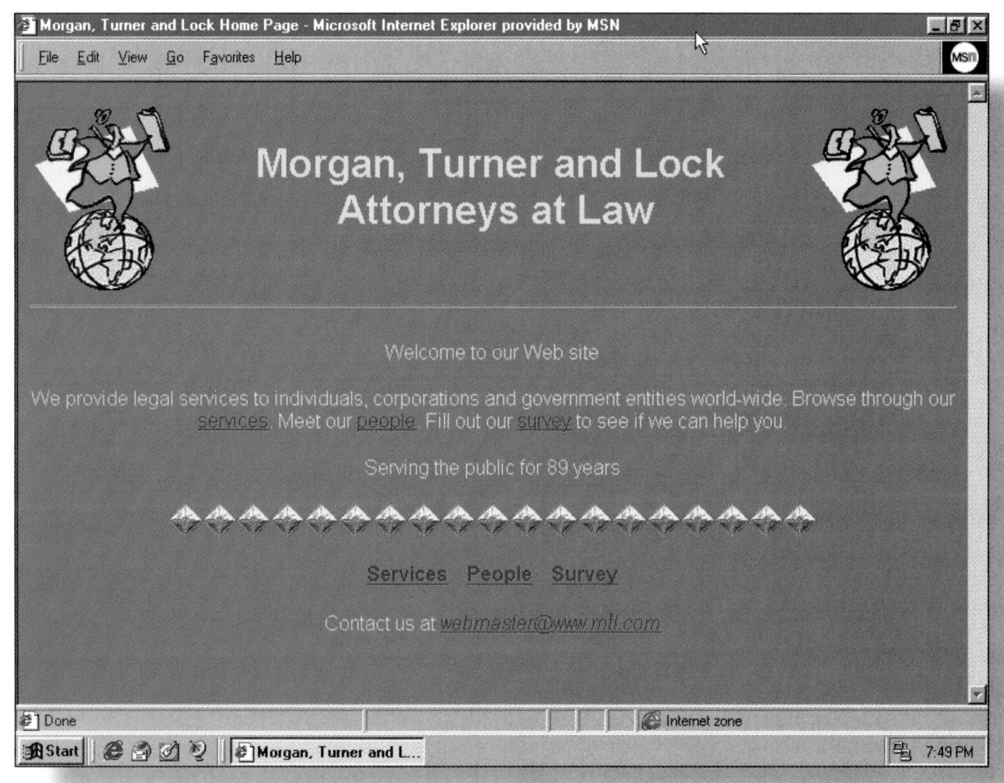

FIGURE 2-1

Web Page Design Criteria

If you ask several experienced Web page designers what the criteria are for a good Web page design, you will get as many different answers. Each designer will emphasize different elements that he or she thinks are important. A basic set of common criteria exists, however, on which all developers can agree.

When a Web page is well designed, the mechanics of the page almost disappear, enabling the users to concentrate on their research, exploration, or pleasure. Table 2-1 on the next page lists several important criteria with their associated guidelines for designing and developing Web pages. The list is by no means exhaustive.

Well-Designed Web Pages

Discover tricks and techniques to designing Web pages by perusing the numerous formal and informal *Best of the Web* sites. These sites contain links to outstanding Web pages. Use a Web search engine to find *Best of the Web* sites.

Table 2-1

CRITERIA	• GUIDELINES
Authentication	• Announce who is responsible for the existence of the Web page. • Name the sponsoring organization and author of the Web page. • Use clear, concise titles that identify or announce the purpose of the page. • List appropriate dates, such as the date written or the date the page was last changed. • List the sources for information or other data used on the Web page.
Aesthetics	• Ensure the Web page looks good and is easy to navigate. • Provide functionality and clear organization. • Select good metaphors to represent your concepts and ideas. • Use complementary color schemes. • Eliminate the use of too many animated graphics on a single page. • Avoid long paragraphs of plain text.
Performance	• Keep the pages relatively short. Long pages take time to display. • Web page design should be a compromise between many graphics vs. speed of display. • Use the 10 second response rule when possible: A user will wonder if something is wrong after waiting about 10 seconds without a response.
Consistency	• Use the same colors, locations, and navigation techniques for all related pages. • Maintain a uniform look and feel for all related pages. • Utilize themes and templates to ensure consistency.
Validity	• As with any paper, story, or other literary piece, proofread the text for accuracy. • Verify all the hyperlinks to ensure they are valid. • Check the image, sound, or movie files used in the Web pages. • View the Web page using different browsers. Not every neat HTML trick or every file format is supported in all browsers.
Images	• Use alternate text in your Web page to provide support for text-only browsers. • Note the size of a large image next to a hyperlink so viewers can decide whether or not to download it. • Use thumbnail images to provide a preview of larger images. • Use universally recognized images for items such as Forward and Back buttons. Remember that you have a global audience.
Hyperlinks	• Ensure that each Web page stands on its own; users can come in from anywhere. • Provide hyperlinks to resources mentioned in the page. • Use clear navigation hyperlinks such as Next, Back, and Home. • At a minimum, always have a hyperlink to the site's Home page. • Limit the number of hyperlinks. • Avoid click here hyperlinks.
External Files	• Note the type of file, such as avi for compressed video files, or jpg for image files. • Include a notation of the size of the file next to the hyperlink.

Web Page Design

For a fee, most Internet service providers will provide Web page design and development services. You can find computer artists who create custom logos, diagrams, and images in electronic format suitable for publishing on the Web.

Each individual Web page should have one purpose or present one concept. Avoid splitting one concept into two parts simply to reduce the size of a page. Likewise, refrain from combining two unrelated ideas just to make a Web page larger.

To help you learn new tips and techniques, examine a number of well-designed pages. View the HTML source to see how other developers created the effects that interest you.

Many HTML style guides are accessible on the Web. Style guides can contain rules, guidelines, tips, and templates that assist you in creating Web pages. Use any Web search engine and search for the keywords, html style guide. Your school or local library also may have an HTML style guide available.

Web Page Components

A typical Web page is composed of three common sections: a header, the body, and the footer (Figure 2-2). The **header** can contain text or images that identify the sponsoring site, the author, or the purpose of the page. Many business Web sites will place an advertisement in the header area, because this is the first part of the Web page that shows in the browser's display area. The header also can contain hyperlinks to related pages at the Web site. The header is an important part of the Web page. Viewers evaluate your site from their first impression of the header information. An appealing header will peak their interest, so they will want to see what else is on the page.

The **body** of the Web page contains information and other materials that initially bring visitors to the Web page. The information will be conveyed with combinations of text, images, animation, and hyperlinks.

The **footer** of the Web page provides contact information and navigation controls. You would expect to find the name and perhaps the e-mail address of the author of the Web page or other official contact person responsible for the Web site. Hyperlinks to other resources at the Web site, such as the Home page or help information also will be included in this section.

It is useful, when designing a Web page, to divide the page into these three logical sections to ease the design process. You can focus your attention on completing one of the three sections, test it, and then move on to the next one.

FIGURE 2-2

Designing the Web Page

Ideally, you would create several Web page design alternatives and then discuss with other designers the merits and shortcomings of each. The leading contenders are then refined, until a final design is agreed upon. In practice, usually you will work alone and thus be responsible for these tasks yourself.

Several techniques including brainstorming and word association are available for use during the creative process. As with any artistic endeavor, form follows function. If something appears on the Web page, then it serves some purpose. If something serves no purpose, then it should not be on the Web page.

After receiving input from the Morgan, Turner and Lock representative, you design a Home page. In a second session with the Morgan, Turner and Lock representative the design shown in Figure 2-3 is approved. Notice the page is divided easily into the header, body, and footer sections.

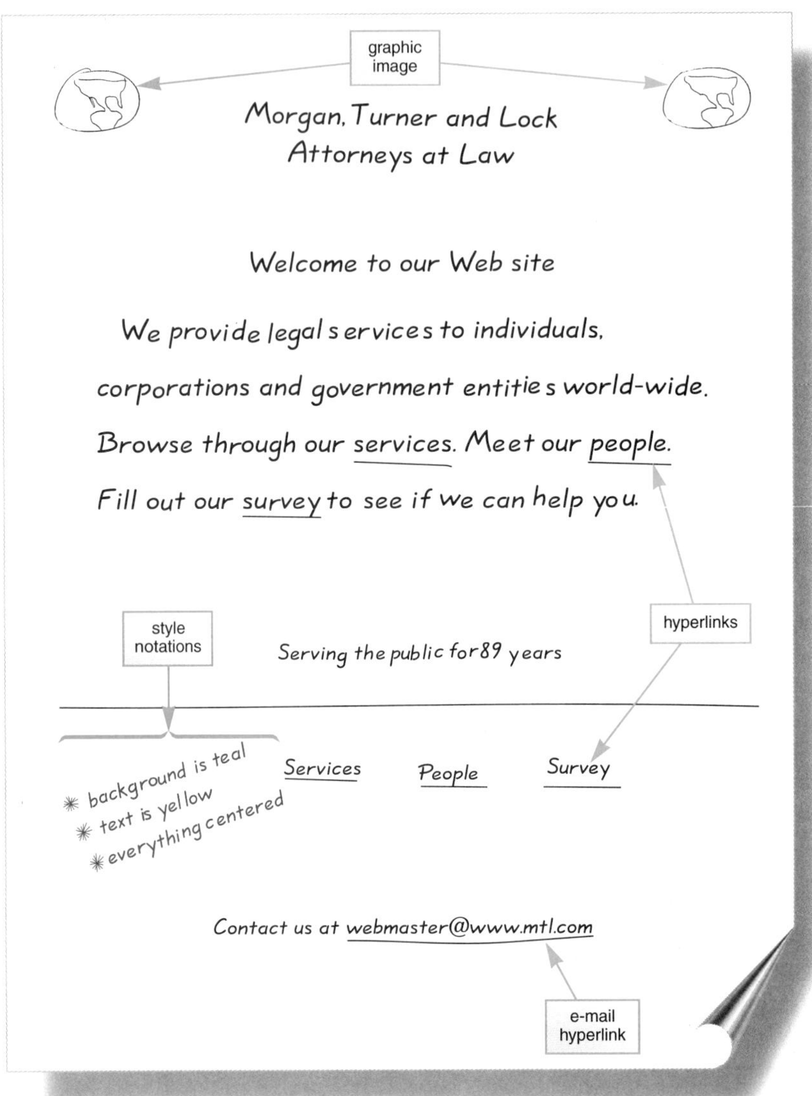

FIGURE 2-3

Web Page Design Guidelines

Numerous books and Internet resources on Web design have been published. You will find a large selection of Web authoring books at the library or local bookstores. Online style guidelines also are available on the World Wide Web.

The header contains two images and a heading that identifies the company. The body of the page contains descriptive information and hyperlinks to other Web pages in the Morgan, Turner and Lock web. The footer contains navigation hyperlinks and contact information in the form of an e-mail hyperlink.

Notice the **notations** on the design document indicating special formatting requirements such as color, text size, and alignment. With the design of the page completed, you can now implement the design using Microsoft FrontPage 98.

Starting Microsoft FrontPage and Creating a New FrontPage Web

Web Page Themes

Try to use an appropriate metaphor or theme in your Web pages. For example, if the topic of the Web page is needlepoint, you might use some sort of needlepoint pattern as the background, and use crossed needles as the bullets in unordered lists.

Recall from Project 1 that several ways exist to create a new FrontPage web. You can import an existing Web from a Web server. You can use a template or wizard. Finally, you can create a simple, one-page web. But before using any of these options, you must start Microsoft FrontPage. The following steps summarize how to start Microsoft FrontPage.

TO START FRONTPAGE 98

1. Click the Start button on the taskbar. Point to Programs on the Start menu.
2. Click Microsoft FrontPage on the Programs submenu.

The FrontPage window opens and the Getting Started dialog box displays.

Creating a One-page Web

Templates and wizards, such as the one used in Project 1, are wonderful work-saving devices. Sometimes, however, the requirements necessitate the design of Web pages that do not fall neatly into any of the available template or wizard categories. In this case, you can create a one-page Web and add new pages as necessary. Adding pages to an existing FrontPage web will be discussed in Project 3. The following steps demonstrate how to create a new FrontPage web consisting of a single page.

Steps To Create a New One-page Web

1 Insert a formatted disk in drive A.

2 With the Getting Started dialog box displayed on the screen, click Create a New FrontPage Web (Figure 2-4).

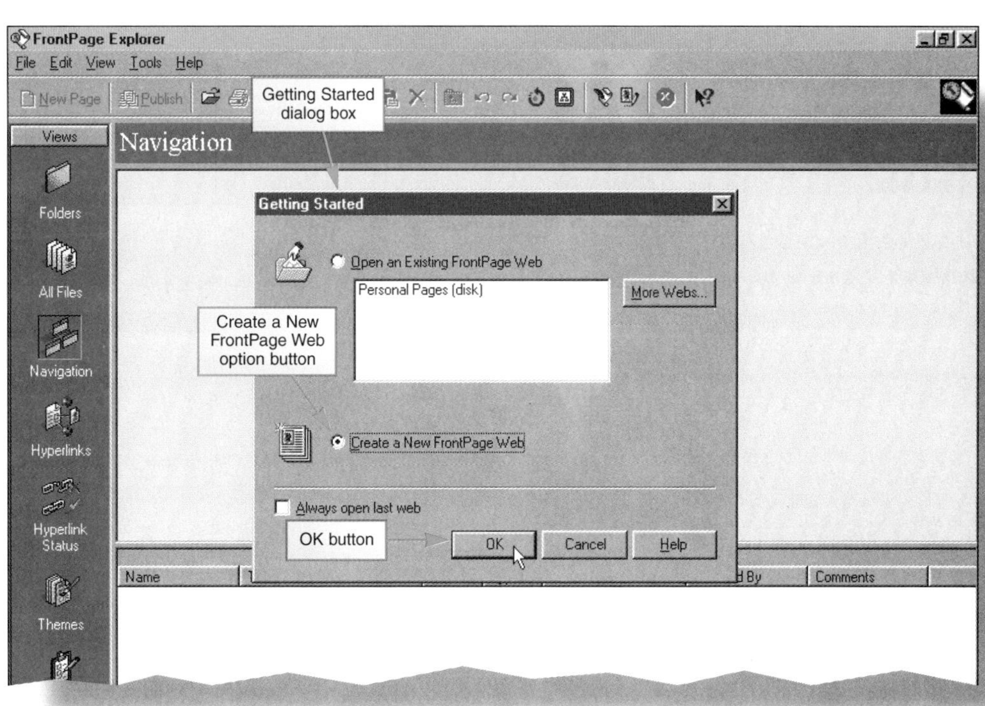

FIGURE 2-4

3 **Click the OK button.**

The New FrontPage Web dialog box displays (Figure 2-5). The Morgan, Turner and Lock Home page is a one-page Web.

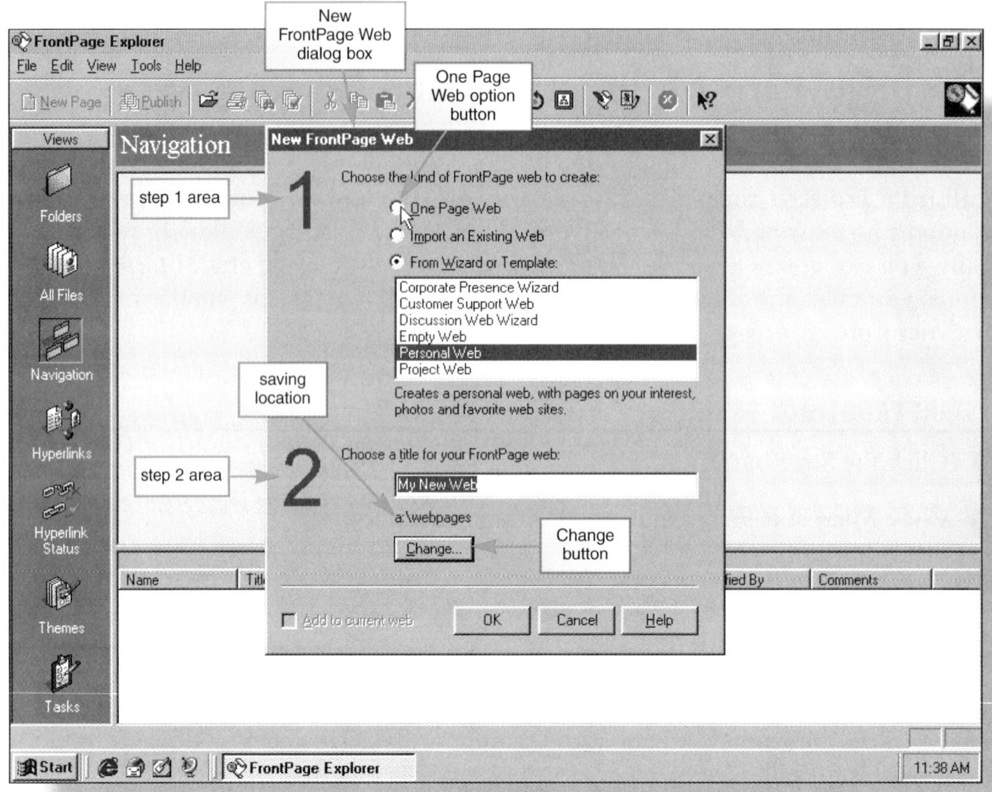

FIGURE 2-5

4 **Click One Page Web in the step 1 area and then click the Change button in the step 2 area.**

5 **When the Change Location dialog box displays, type** `a:\legal` **in the text box.**

The new location displays in the text box (Figure 2-6).

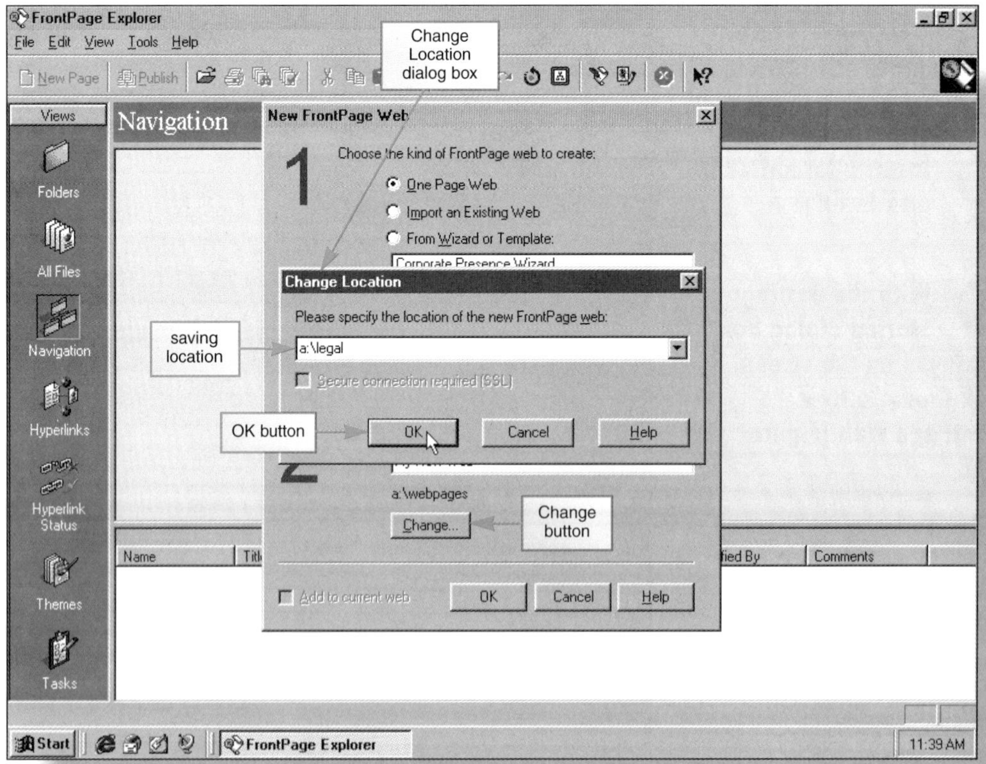

FIGURE 2-6

6 Click the OK button in the Change Location dialog box.

The New FrontPage Web dialog box indicates that a One Page Web will be created in a folder named legal on drive A (Figure 2-7).

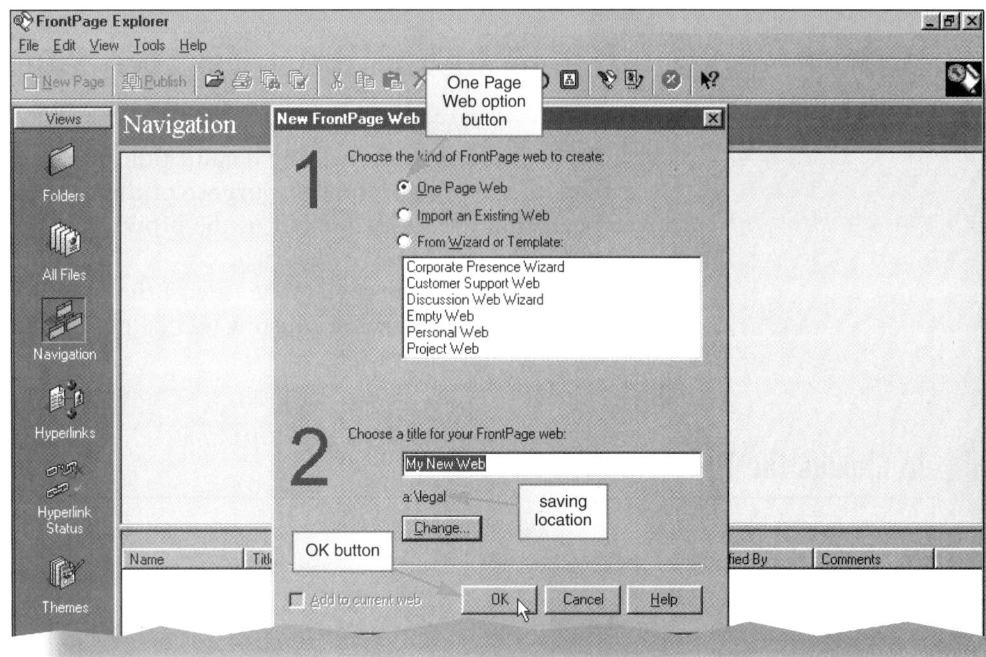

FIGURE 2-7

7 Click the OK button. When the FrontPage Explorer box displays, click the Yes button.

FrontPage creates the folder on the floppy disk in drive A and then copies several files. When the creation process is complete, the FrontPage Explorer window displays in Navigation view (Figure 2-8).

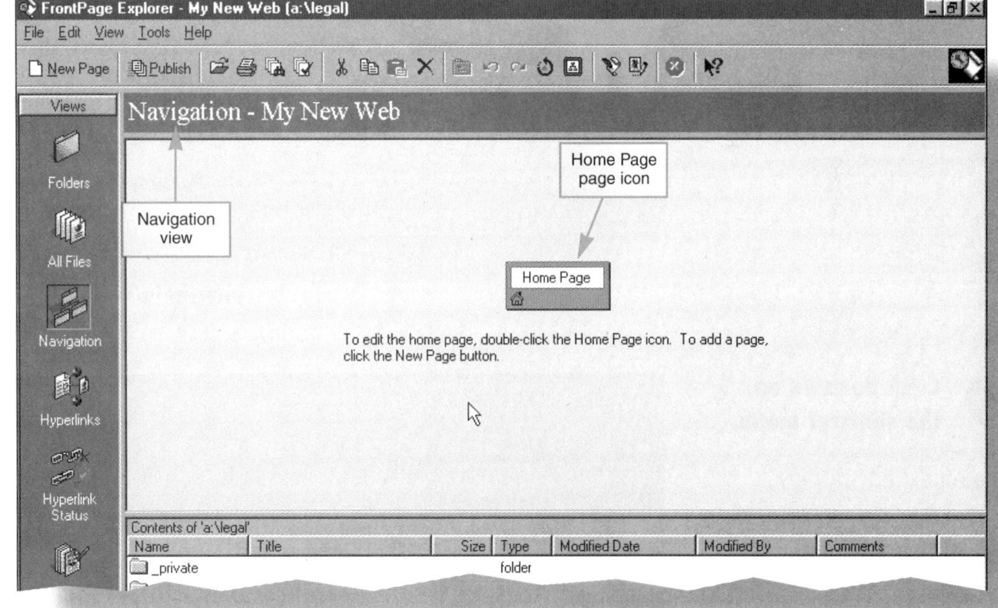

FIGURE 2-8

In Project 1, you learned that FrontPage creates several folders and files that together compose a FrontPage web. Once FrontPage has created the files and folders, you can begin to customize the Web page.

Changing the Title of a Web Page

The title of the Web page appears in the page icon in the Navigation pane of the FrontPage Explorer window. The default title is Home Page. Titles should reflect the name of the organization or purpose of the Web page. Recall that the title of a Web page appears in the title bar of the browser displaying the page and in any bookmarks or favorites for that page.

The following steps change the title of the Morgan, Turner and Lock Home page to the name of the organization so it will be placed in the title bar of browsers and in favorite or bookmark lists.

Steps To Change the Title of a Web Page

Right-click the Home Page page icon in the Navigation pane of the FrontPage Explorer.

A shortcut menu displays (Figure 2-9). The **Rename command** *will change the title of the Web page.*

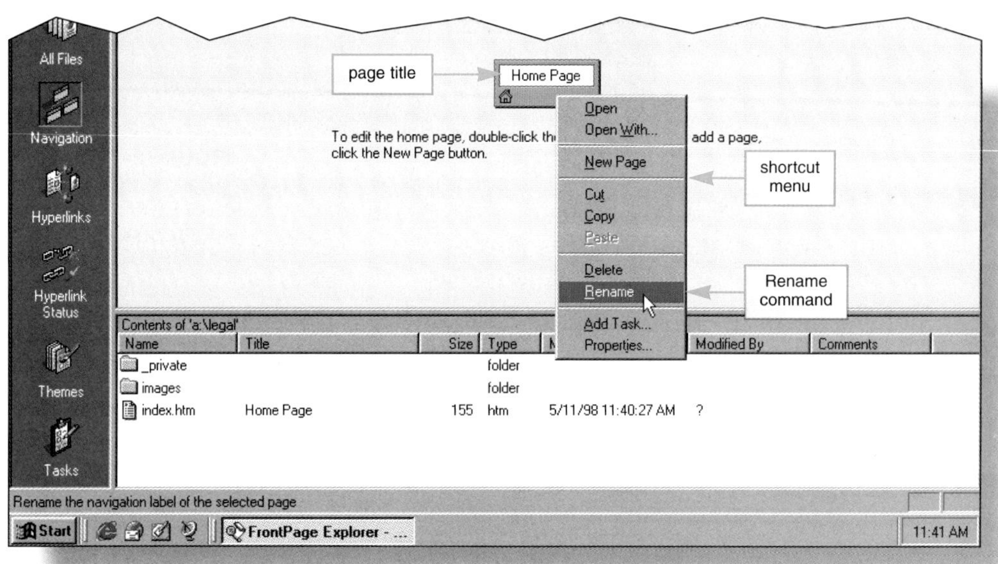

FIGURE 2-9

Click Rename on the shortcut menu.

An edit text box displays around the default title and the title is highlighted (Figure 2-10).

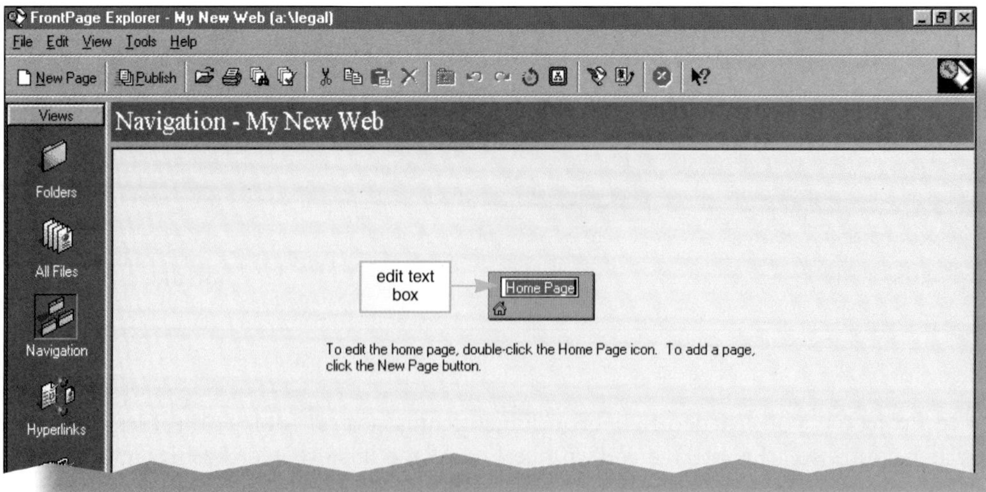

FIGURE 2-10

3 **Type** `Morgan, Turner and Lock Home Page` **in the edit text box.**

The new text replaces the old text (Figure 2-11).

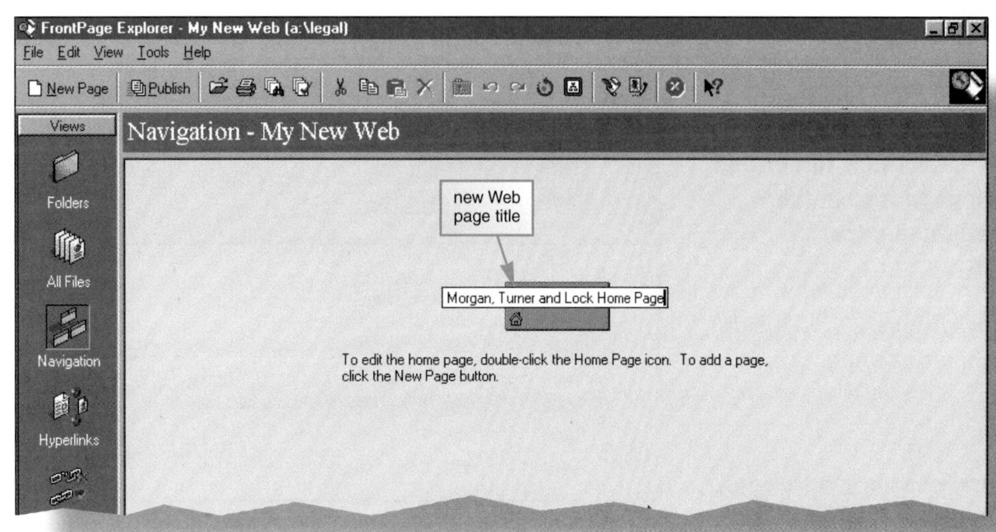

FIGURE 2-11

4 **Press the ENTER key to save the new title.**

The edit text box closes, and the new title displays in the page icon (Figure 2-12). The new title does not display in its entirety because it is longer than the room available in the page icon. The entire title exists, however.

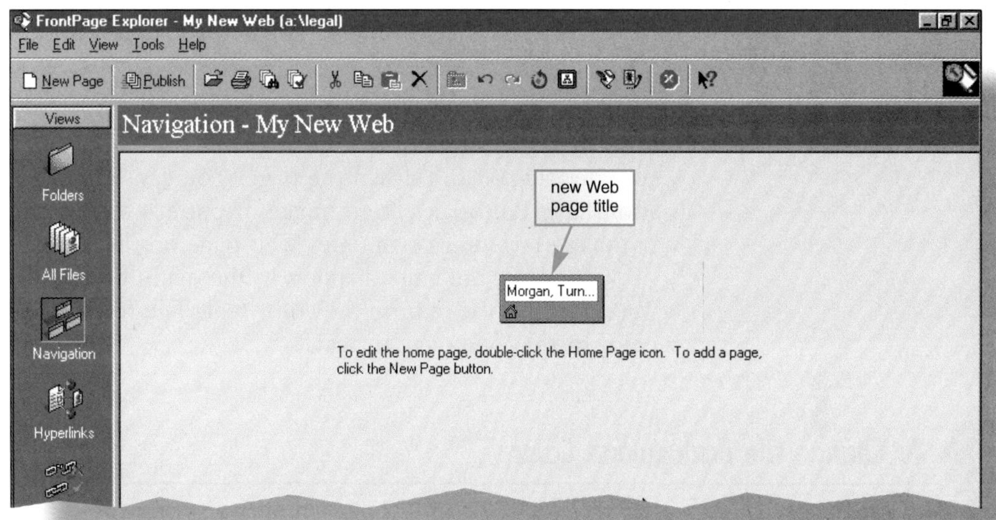

FIGURE 2-12

Other Ways

1. On Edit menu click Properties, click General tab
2. Press ALT+E, I, click General tab
3. Press ALT+ENTER, click General tab

You can change the titles of other new or existing Web pages using the same techniques. Although the FrontPage Explorer will allow you to enter very long titles, browser title bars display approximately 80 to 90 characters, so keep this limitation in mind when entering the title. Once you have changed the title, you can start the FrontPage Editor and begin to edit the Web page.

Editing the Web Page

Activities required to create the Morgan, Turner and Lock Web page consist of selecting the page background, inserting headings, images, and text, establishing hyperlinks, and then testing the page. Perform the steps on the next page to start the FrontPage Editor and then open the Morgan, Turner and Lock Home page.

To Edit the Web Page

1 Double-click the Morgan, Turner and Lock page icon in the Navigation pane.

The FrontPage Editor window opens (Figure 2-13). The display area is empty.

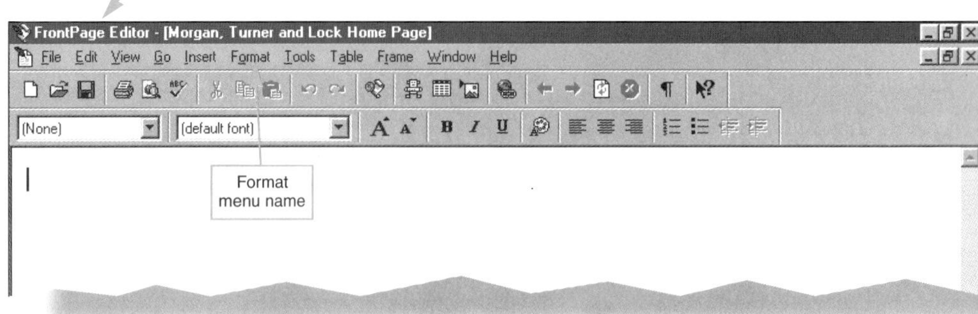

FIGURE 2-13

Other Ways

1. On Edit menu click Open
2. Press ALT+E, O
3. Press CTRL+O

With the page open in the FrontPage Editor, you can start customizing the Web page to implement the design shown in Figure 2-3 on page FP 2.8. The first step is to change the background color.

Changing the Background Color of a Web Page

The **background** of a Web page can be a solid color, an image, or a pattern that is repeated across and down the page. You can select a color from within the FrontPage Editor, select an image or pattern stored on your local computer, or copy an image or pattern from any Web page on the World Wide Web.

Currently, the page displays in the default background color white. Morgan, Turner and Lock require the color teal. The following steps change the background color of the Web page to teal.

To Change the Background Color

1 Click Format on the menu bar and then point to Background.

The Format menu displays (Figure 2-14). The Format menu contains commands to manage Web page formatting items such as themes, style sheets, and backgrounds.

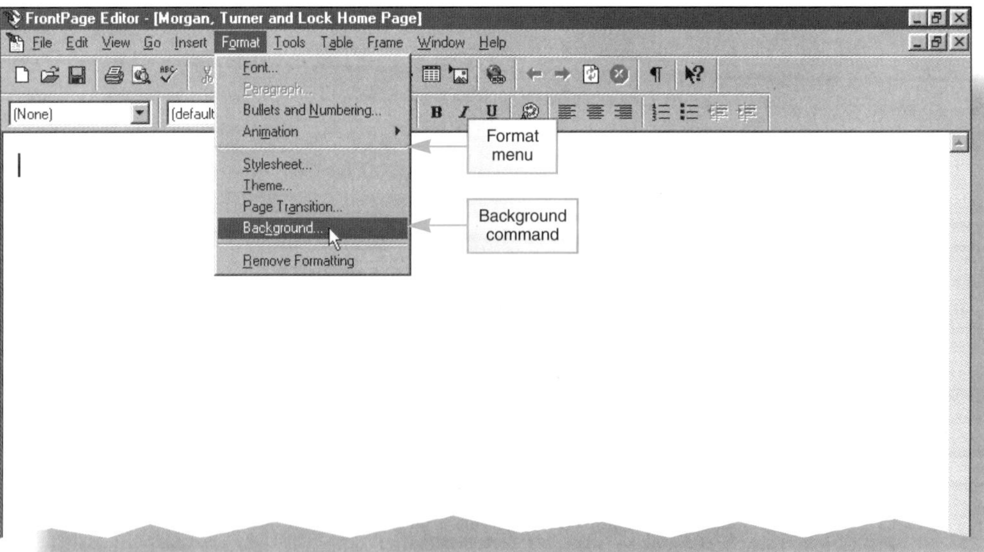

FIGURE 2-14

2 Click Background. If necessary, click the Background tab.

*The Page Properties dialog box displays with the Background sheet on top (Figure 2-15). The **Background sheet** contains settings to control the background image or color.*

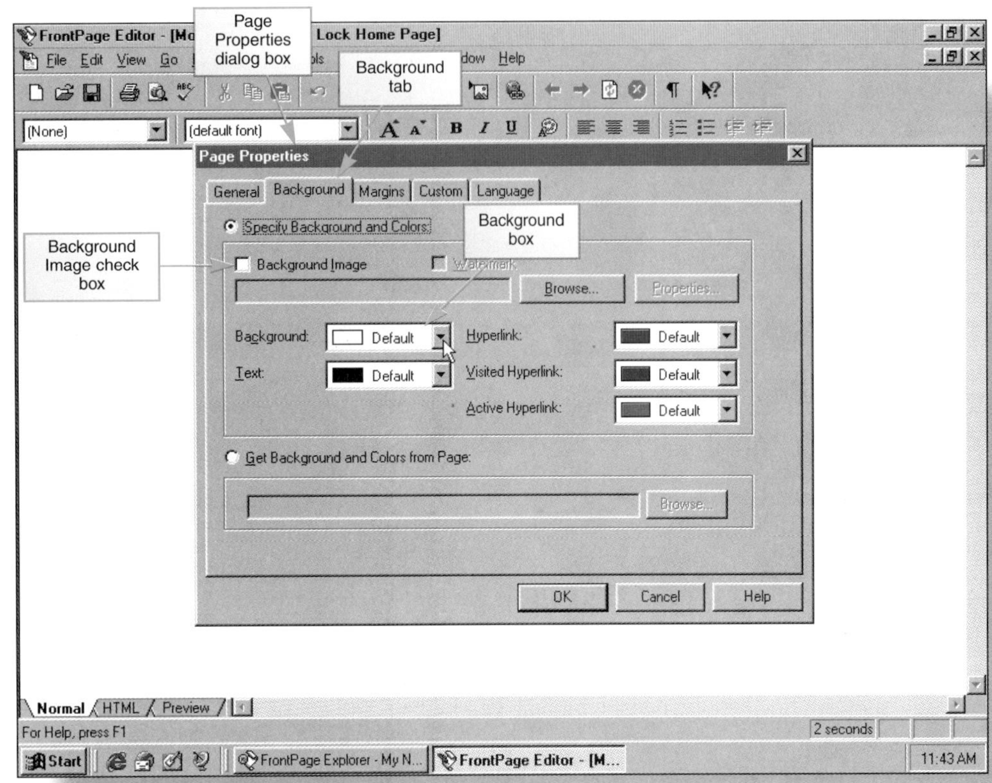

FIGURE 2-15

3 Click the Background box arrow. Point to the color Teal.

The list of available background colors displays and the color Teal is highlighted (Figure 2-16).

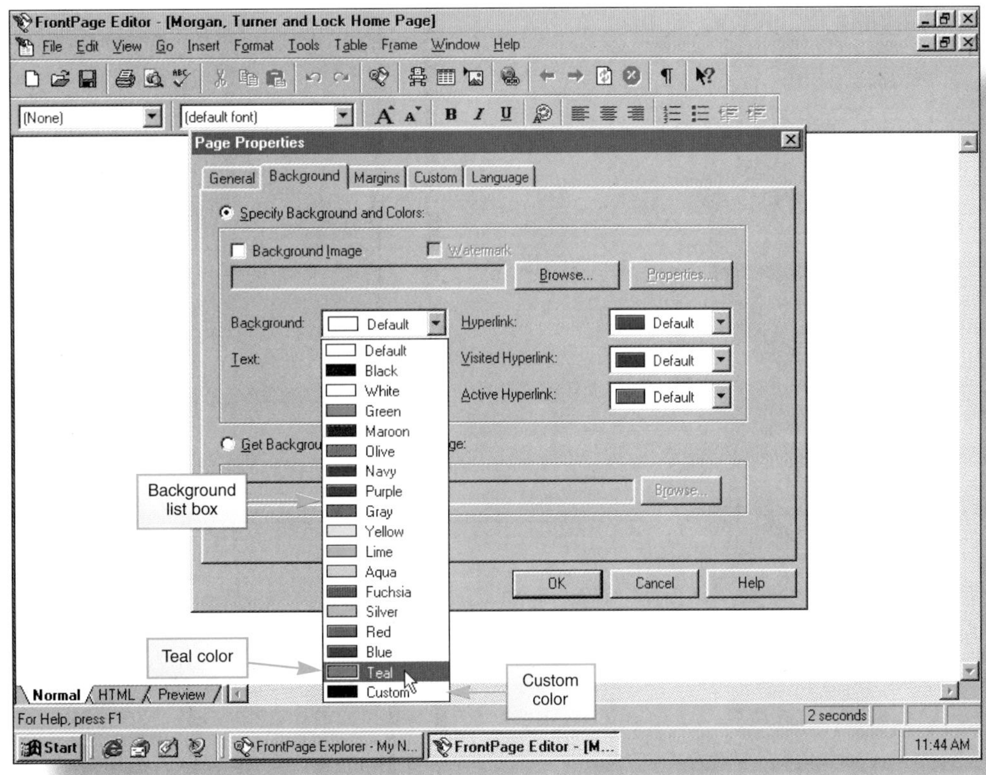

FIGURE 2-16

Click the color Teal.

Teal is selected as the background color in the Background box (Figure 2-17).

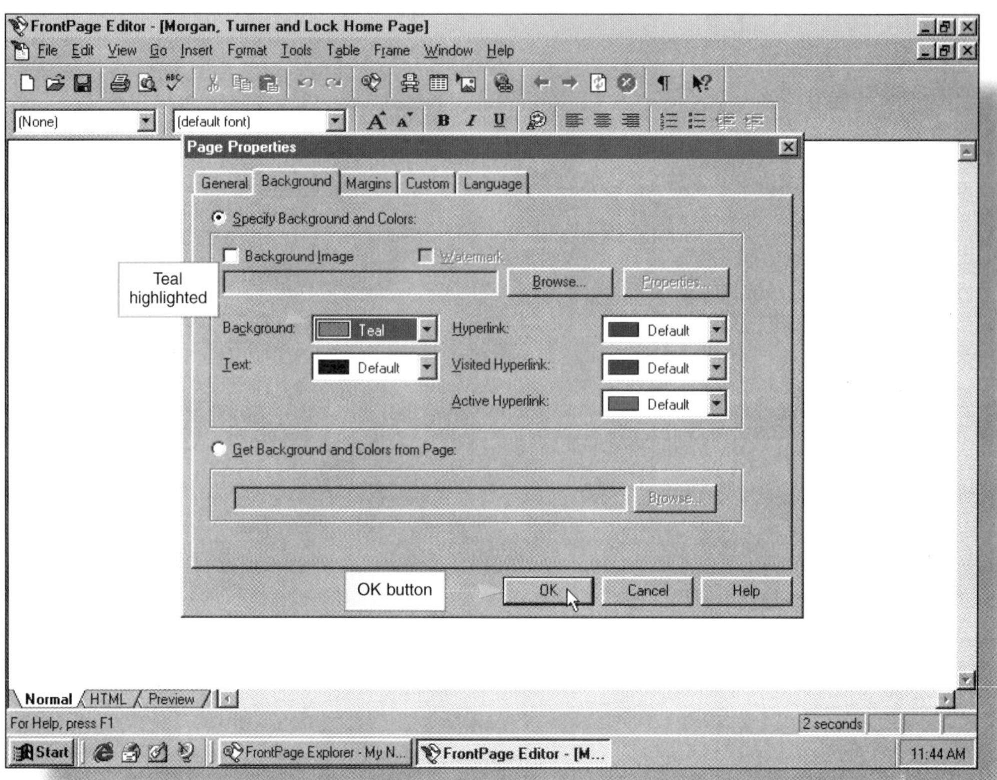

FIGURE 2-17

Click the OK button.

The FrontPage Editor window displays with the Teal background color (Figure 2-18).

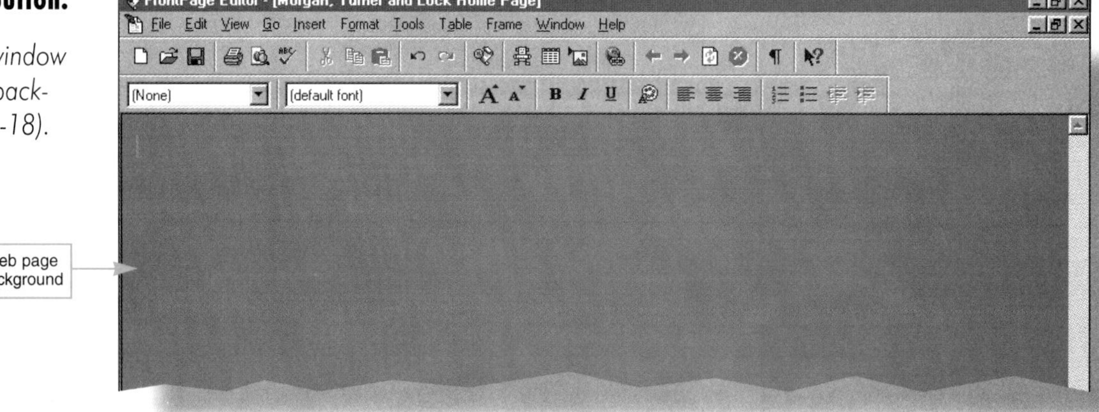

FIGURE 2-18

Other Ways

1. Right-click Web page, click Page Properties on shortcut menu, click Background tab
2. Press ALT+O, K

When you click the Background box arrow, the list of available colors displays and allows you to select the color of your choice. If you happen to prefer another color, simply click the Background box arrow and select the desired color.

Selecting the **Custom color** displays a Color dialog box (Figure 2-19) in which you can mix your own color, save it as a custom color, and then use it as the background color.

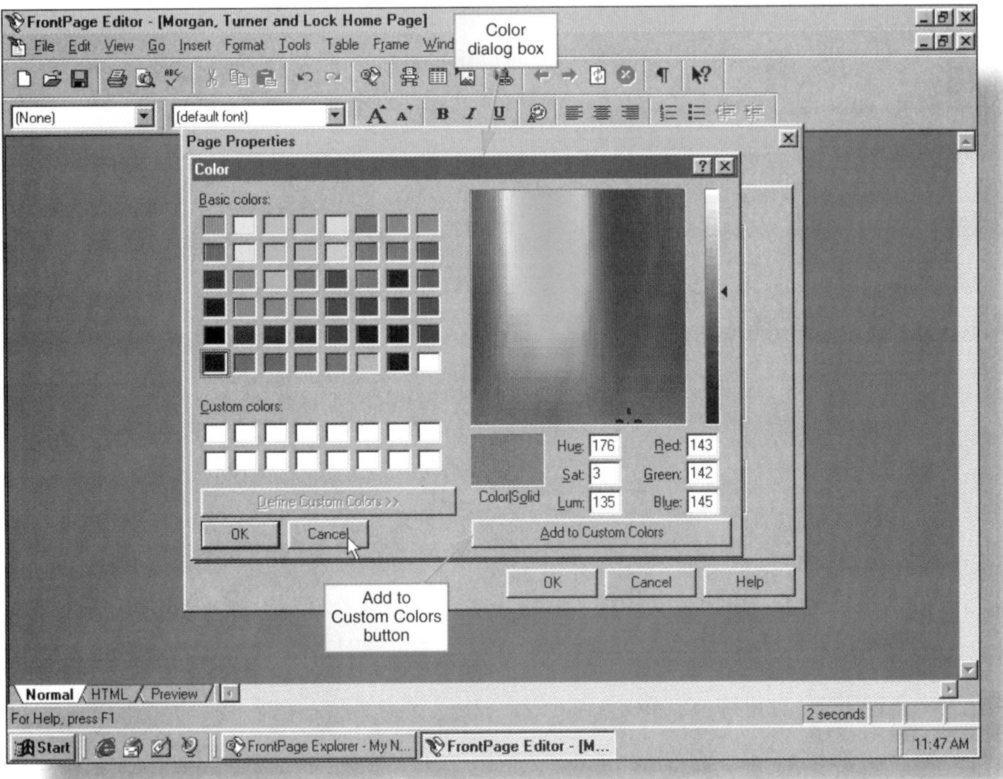

FIGURE 2-19

Using Tables on a Web Page

Tables are used frequently in applications to present information in a clear, concise format. Disciplines such as mathematics, engineering, and chemistry all take advantage of tables. A computer spreadsheet is laid out in the form of a table with rows and columns. Many different applications exist for which tables are an ideal solution.

As noted earlier, an HTML table consists of one or more rows containing one or more columns. The intersection of a row and column is called a **cell**. Any Web page component, such as text or an image, can be placed in a cell.

Normally, you would use tables on a Web page to display any type of information that looks best in rows and columns, such as a list of products and their corresponding prices. In Web pages, tables also can be used to accomplish special design effects.

You can create a table and insert your entire Web page in the cells. Using tables, you can define headings, sidebars, and captions and use other creative design techniques.

In the Morgan, Turner and Lock Web page, you will use a table with one row and three columns to control the horizontal spacing between the two outside images and the company name in the header at the top of the page (Figure 2-1 on page FP 2.5). The steps on the next page demonstrate how to insert a table in a Web page.

More About

Web Page Background Colors

Microsoft FrontPage uses the hue, saturation and luminosity method to specify colors. Hue represents a gradation of color, such as red or blue. Saturation is the amount of color in a hue. Luminosity is the brightness of a hue.

More About

Tables

A table can have a different background color or image than the rest of the Web page. The Table Properties dialog box contains options that allow you to select a different background color or image file.

To Insert a Table in a Web Page

1 Click the Insert Table button on the Standard toolbar.

The Insert Table box displays (Figure 2-20). You can indicate how many rows and columns the table will have by dragging through the cell matrix.

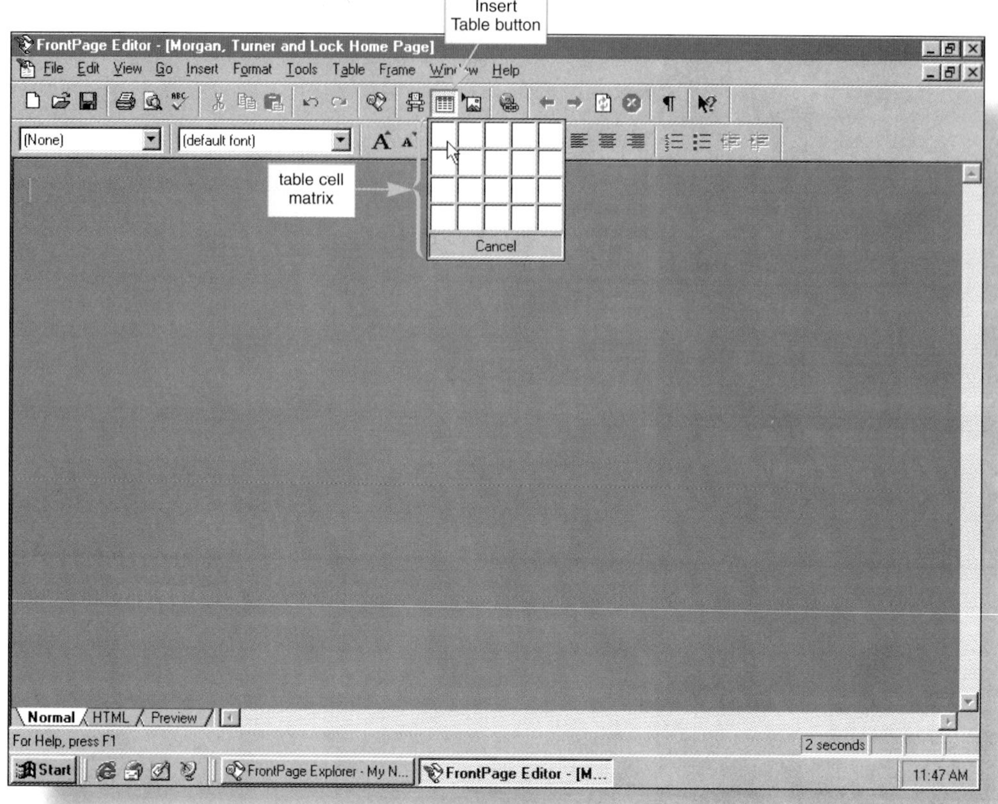

FIGURE 2-20

2 Drag through the top three squares in the cell matrix.

The three squares become highlighted (Figure 2-21). This indicates you want a one-row table with three columns, for a total of three cells.

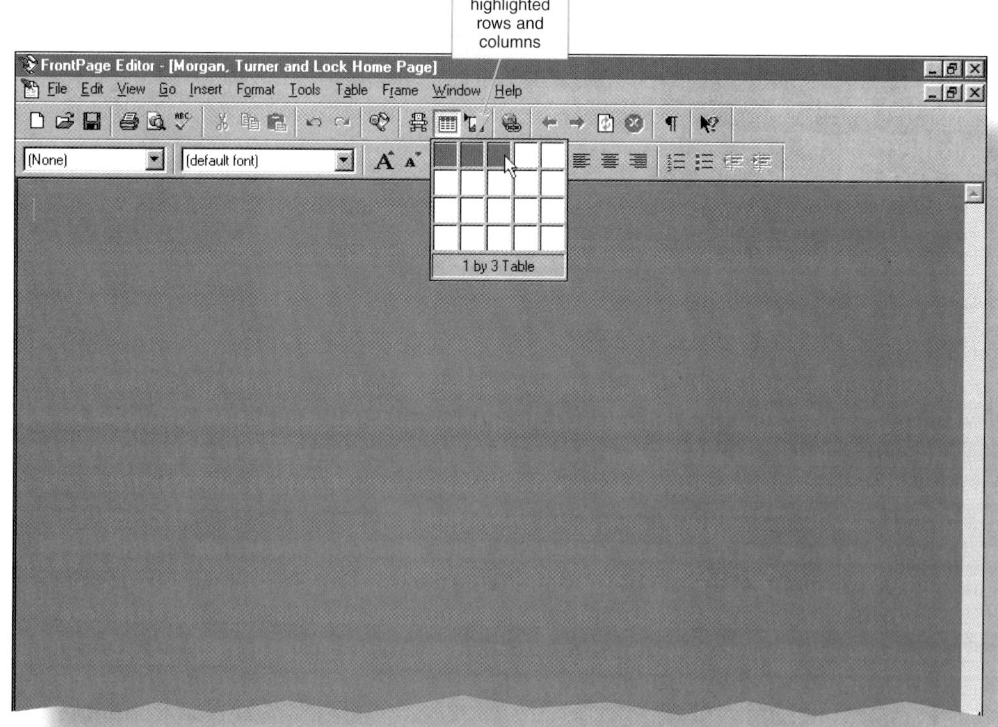

FIGURE 2-21

3 Release the mouse button.

A table displays in the Web page with one row and three columns (Figure 2-22). The table extends across the width of the Web page. Each cell is the same size.

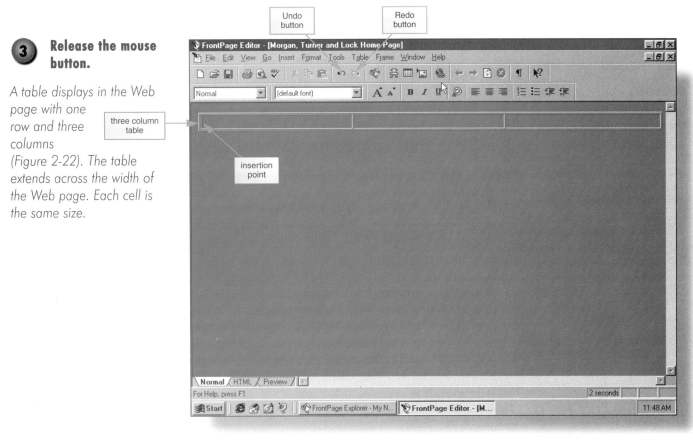

FIGURE 2-22

1. On Table menu click Insert Table
2. Press ALT+A, I

The Insert Table box opens with only four rows and five columns. You can add more rows or columns simply by continuing to drag through the cell matrix. The FrontPage Editor will add more rows and columns automatically.

Extra rows can be added to the bottom of the table on the Web page by positioning the insertion point in the last column of the last row and then pressing the TAB key. Likewise, you can insert rows anywhere in the table by positioning the insertion point on the row above the desired new row and then clicking Insert Rows or Columns on the Table menu. Extra columns can be inserted in a similar fashion.

Tables and HTML

Tables were not included in the original HTML specifications. Tables became available, but not officially supported, in HTML 2. Now, the HTML 3 specification allows for advanced formatting and customization of HTML tables.

Undoing the Last Action

Although you will take great care when creating your Web pages, you may make possible mistakes or you might want to make an immediate change. FrontPage provides facilities to help you undo errors with the **Undo button** on the Standard toolbar or the **Undo command** on the Edit menu. Thus, if you make a change or a mistake, undo it using either the Undo button or the Undo command. FrontPage will reverse your action up to thirty consecutive actions.

Also available for quick reversal of errors and changes are the **Redo button** on the Standard toolbar and the **Redo command** on the Edit menu (see Figure 2-22). Redo reverses the effect of the last Undo command. If you decide the undo is incorrect, you can click the Redo button or Redo command to restore the last change you made. Redo is available up to thirty consecutive actions.

Images

Do not overload your Web page with images and graphics. Too many graphics on a Web page can overwhelm the viewer, and will slow down the time it takes to display your Web page.

As you work with FrontPage, you will find that using the Undo and Redo buttons facilitate the creative process. You can add and rearrange items to see if they work, knowing you can return to a previous starting point with little effort.

Inserting an Image in a Web Page

Regardless of how impressive your written message, people always will respond to images. The viewer's eye is drawn naturally to a picture before reading any text. The choice and quality of images you use largely will determine whether someone will take the time to read your Web page or pass it by.

Much of the Web's success is due to its capability of presenting graphics. Because of the impact of images on the Web, it is important to master the graphic options necessary to include pictures on your Web pages.

Along with the company heading, the Morgan, Turner and Lock Home page has two images in the header. The table you inserted in earlier steps will be used to control the amount of horizontal spacing between the images and the company name. The image on the left will be left-aligned in the left cell of the table. The image on the right will be right-aligned in the right cell of the table. The company name, which will be inserted later in the project, will be centered in the middle cell.

More About

Obtaining Images

You can browse the Web and select an image to insert in your Web page. Be sure you have permission to use the image before placing it in your Web page. Some images on the Web are copyrighted.

The goal of the images at the top of the page is to reflect the concept that the Morgan, Turner and Lock law firm handles cases all around the world. Therefore, a graphic with a globe or world map is appropriate. Refer to Table 2-1 on page FP 2.6 for criteria on the appropriate use of metaphors in your Web designs.

FrontPage includes a library of ready-to-use images, called **clip art** and a selection of photographs you can insert into your Web pages. You will be selecting an image from the clip art gallery to use as the image on the Morgan, Turner and Lock Web page.

To insert an image, you first position the insertion point at the desired location, and then select the image. Perform the following steps to insert an image in the Web page.

Steps To Insert a Clip Art Image in a Web Page

1 If necessary, click in the leftmost cell of the table to position the insertion point and then click the Insert Image button on the Standard toolbar.

The Image dialog box displays (Figure 2-23). You can select an image file or clip art file from your local computer, or select an image from any Web page on the World Wide Web.

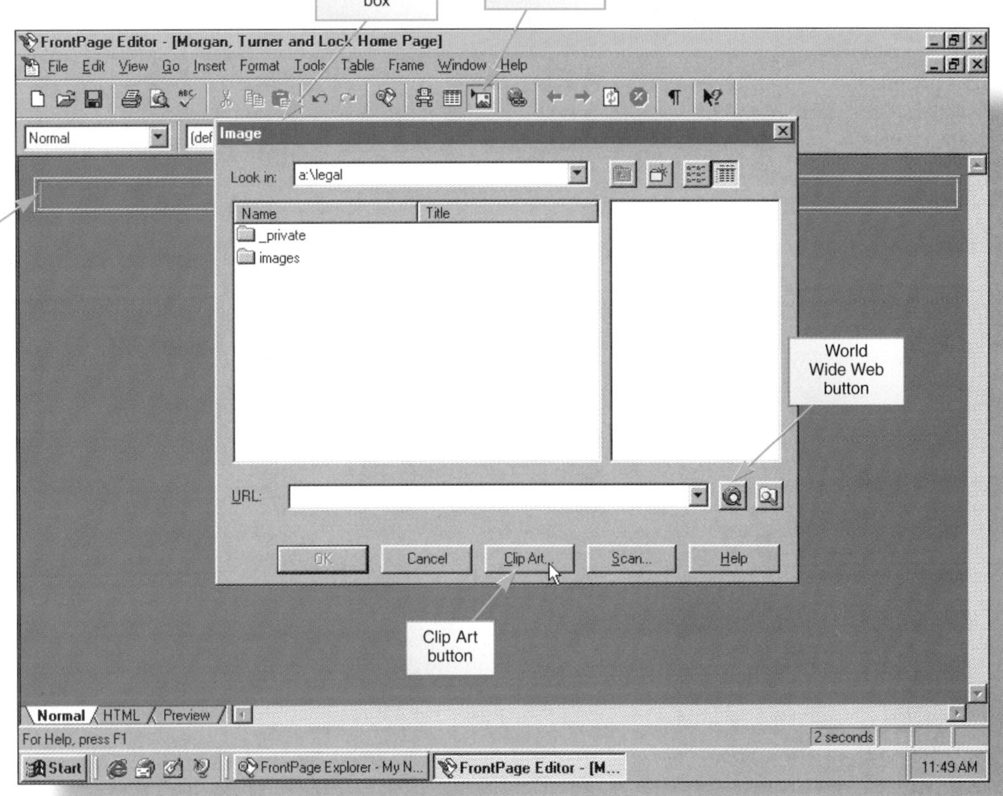

FIGURE 2-23

2 Click the Clip Art button. When the Microsoft Clip Gallery 3.0 dialog box displays, click the Clip Art tab.

The Microsoft Clip Gallery 3.0 dialog box displays (Figure 2-24). It contains two sheets, one containing clip art images and the other containing photographs that have been transferred into a computer-readable format using a scanner. The Clip Art sheet contains a list of clip art categories in the categories list box, and small samples of the images in the preview list box.

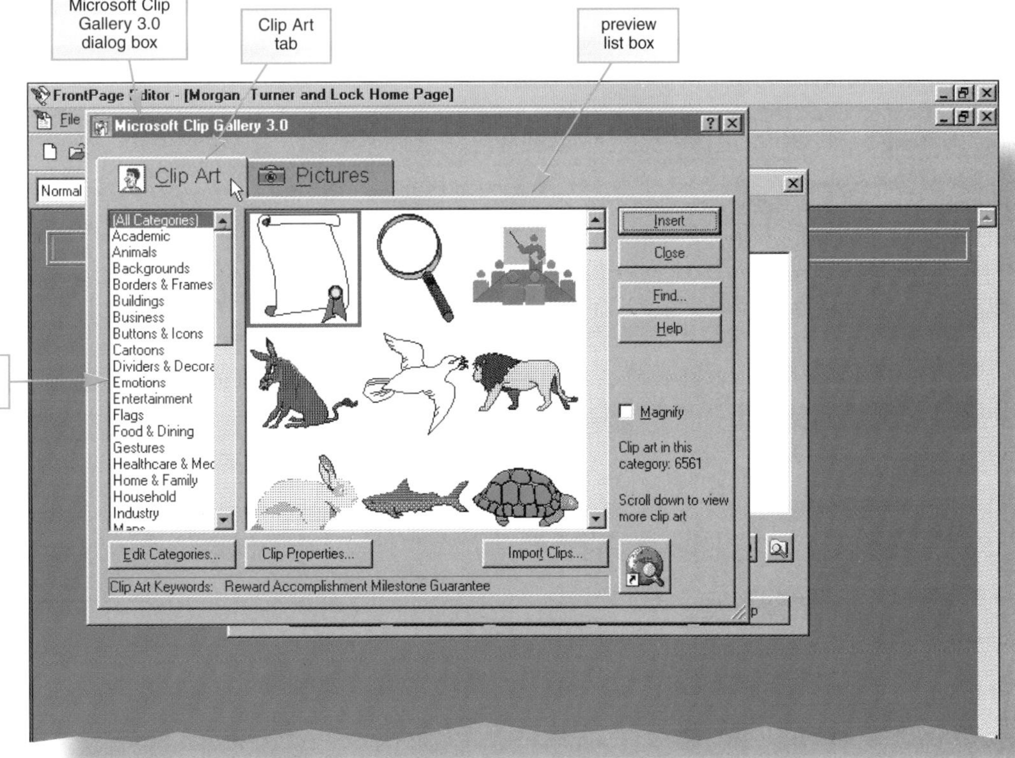

FIGURE 2-24

3 **Scroll down the categories list box until the Maps category displays. Click the Maps category.**

Clip art images of maps display (Figure 2-25).

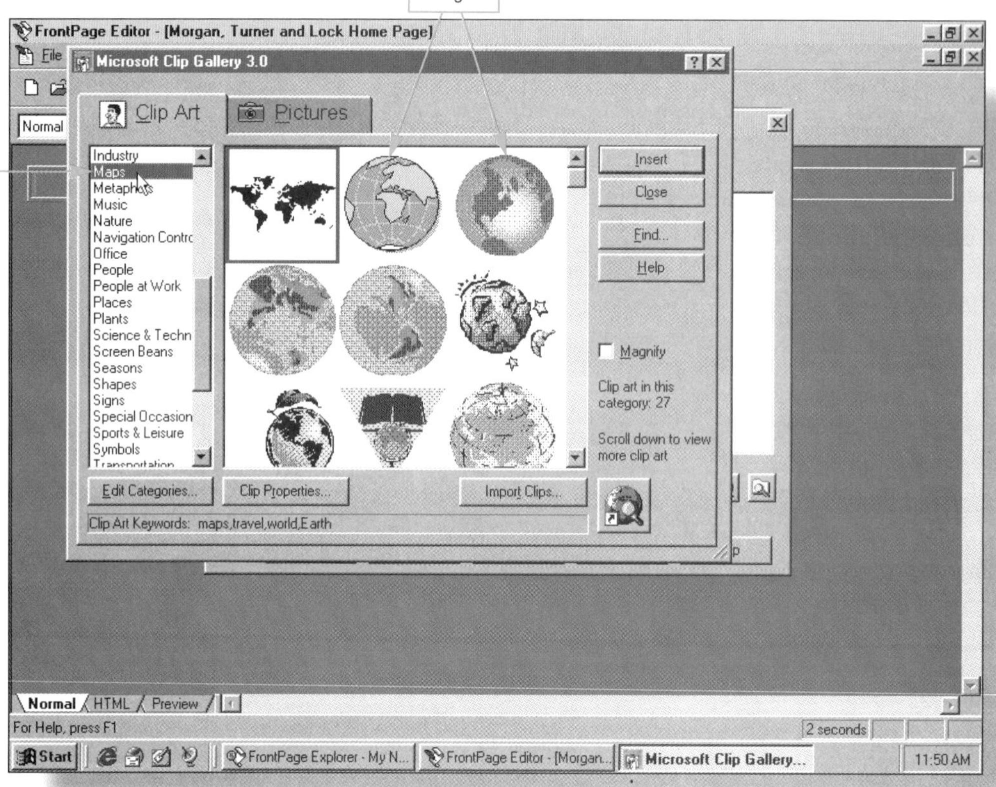

FIGURE 2-25

4 **Scroll down the preview list box until the image of a man standing on a globe displays, or another image of your choice. Click the image to select it.**

The clip art image of a man standing on a globe displays (Figure 2-26). A selected image contains a blue border, as the image does in Figure 2-26.

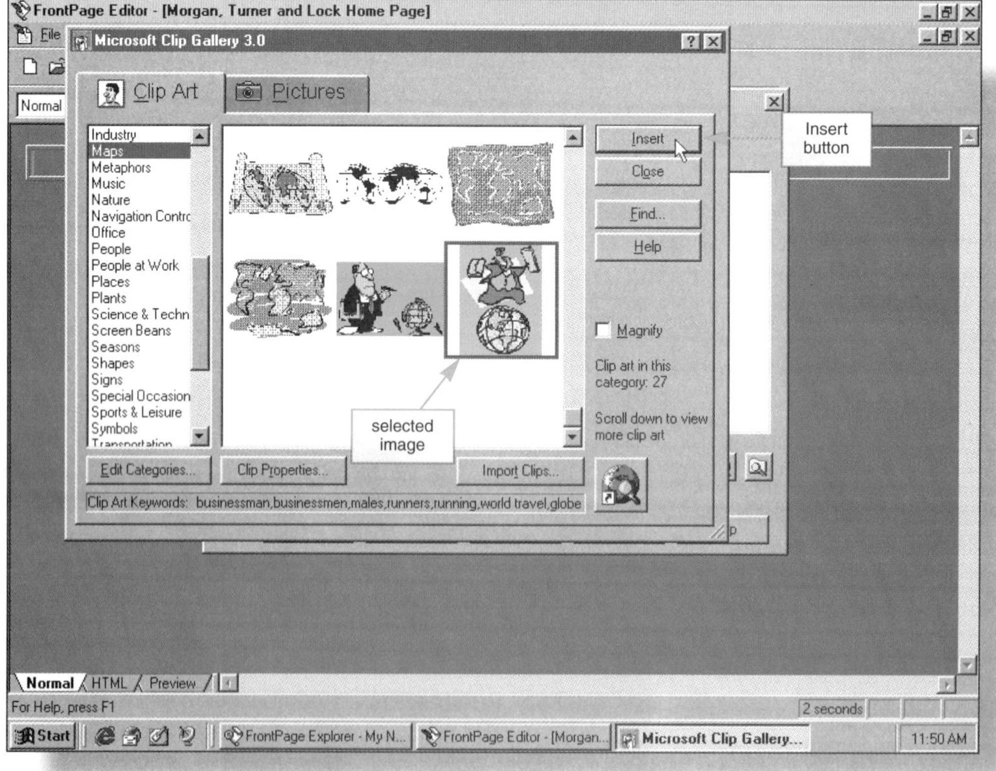

FIGURE 2-26

Click the Insert button.

The clip art image is inserted into the leftmost cell of the table (Figure 2-27).

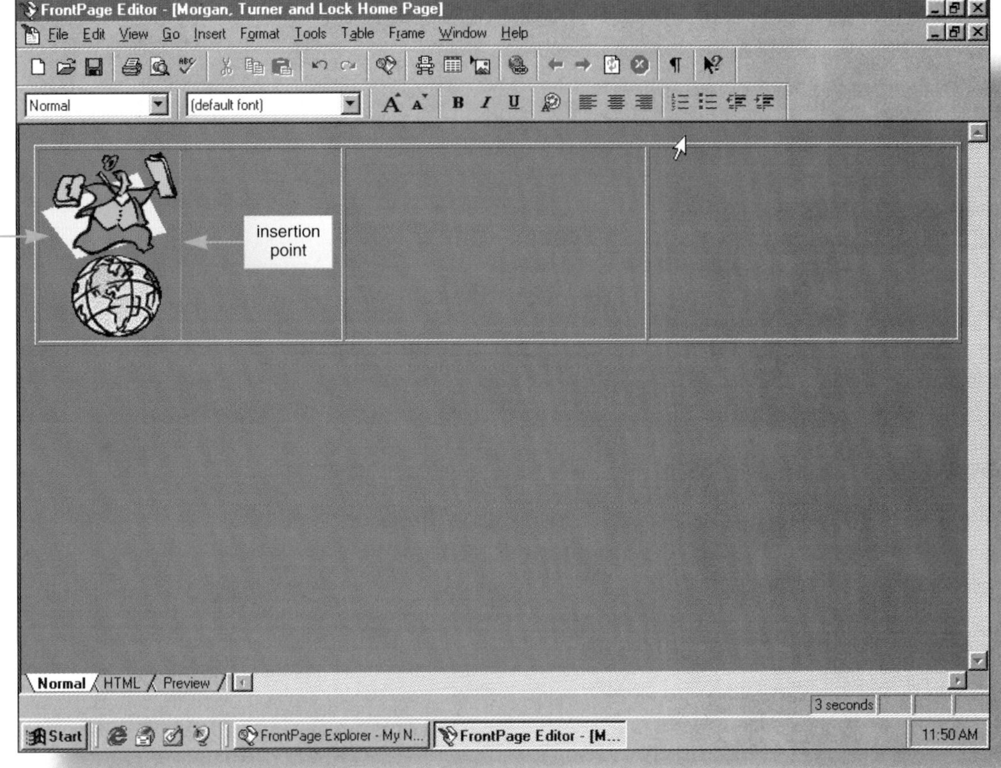

FIGURE 2-27

1. On Insert menu click Clip Art
2. Press ALT+I, C

As you can see in Figure 2-26, many categories of clip art are available. Each category has a varying number of images. Some of the same clip art images will appear in several categories. For example, the man and globe image you inserted in the left table cell on the Web page also can be found in the Travel category.

Copying and Pasting an Image on a Web Page

One of the features of Windows applications is the capability of copying information from one Windows application and inserting it in another Windows application. You can cut or copy portions of a Web page to a temporary storage area in computer memory, called the **Clipboard**, and then paste the contents of the Clipboard to other areas of the Web page. **Copy** and **cut and paste** are useful when you want to move an item to another location or have the same item appearing several times in various places throughout the Web page. The man and globe clip art image you just inserted is to be inserted again; this time in the rightmost cell of the table.

You can, of course, insert the clip art image using the steps you performed previously for inserting an image. Or you can copy the image to the Clipboard and then paste the image from the Clipboard to the Web page at the location of the insertion point. In this instance, the copy and paste operation would be more efficient, because you would have to maneuver through several windows to get the image from the Microsoft Clip Gallery. Perform the steps on the next page to copy and then paste the man and globe image to another location on the Web page.

Copying and Pasting in a Web Page

You can copy text and objects from other Windows applications into the FrontPage Editor. Text pasted from Microsoft Word will retain its formatting when pasted in the FrontPage Editor.

To Copy and Paste an Image on a Web Page

Click the clip art image to select it.

The image is selected (Figure 2-28). A selected image has eight small boxes, called ***handles****, surrounding it.*

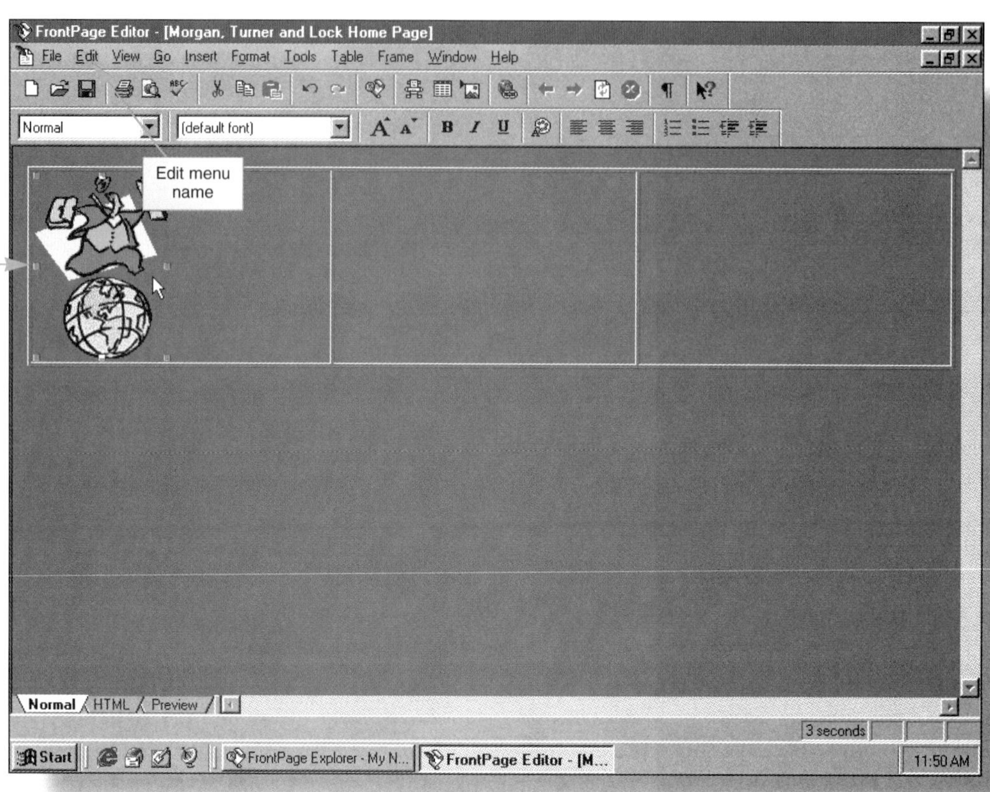

FIGURE 2-28

2 Click Edit on the menu bar and then point to Copy (Figure 2-29).

The ***Copy command*** *copies a selected item to the Clipboard.*

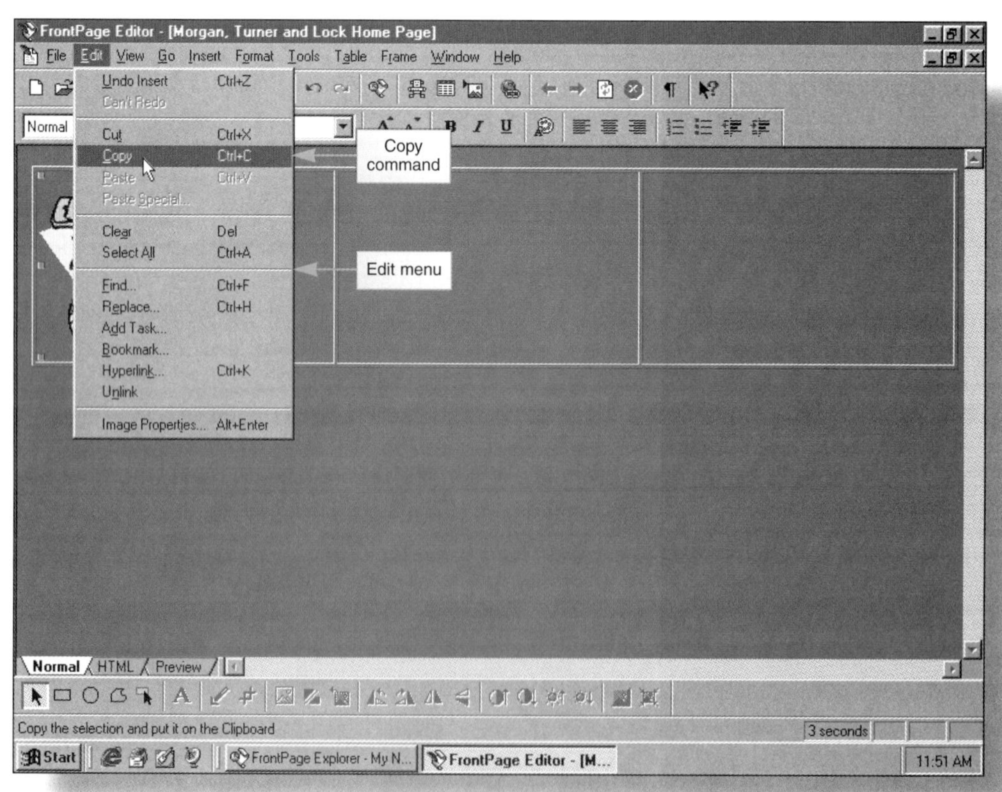

FIGURE 2-29

3 Click Copy and then click the rightmost cell of the table to position the insertion point. Click Edit on the menu bar and then point to Paste (Figure 2-30).

The man and globe image is copied to the Clipboard. The **Paste command** *inserts the contents of the Clipboard at the location of the insertion point.*

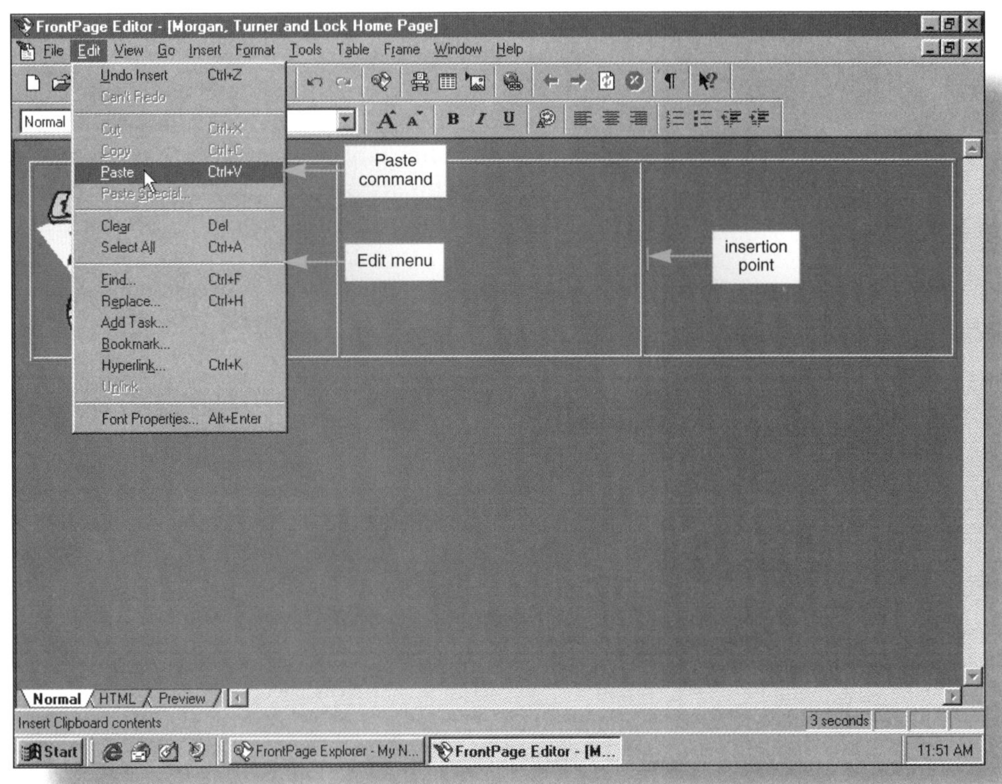

FIGURE 2-30

Click Paste.

The man and globe image on the Clipboard is copied to the rightmost table cell (Figure 2-31).

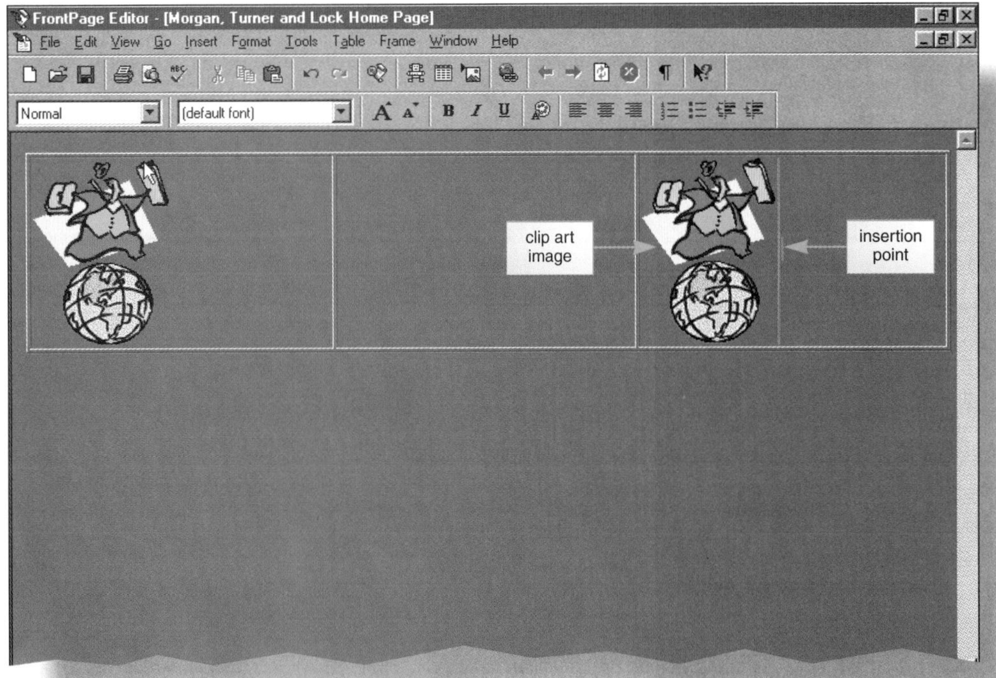

FIGURE 2-31

1. Press ALT+E, C to copy, press ALT+E, P to paste
2. Press CTRL+C to copy, press CTRL+P to paste

You can copy text or an entire table, and then paste it in a similar fashion. Although the contents of the Clipboard can be inserted into other Windows applications, some objects will not display as you would expect. Because other Windows applications do not understand HTML, they will not make an accurate copy of the one row, three column table if you were to try pasting it. You can, however, copy or cut and paste the clip art images and any text into other Windows applications. You will loose any special formatting applied to the text, however. This again, is because of the problem with translating HTML.

More About

Controlling Spacing

Some Web page developers create small, one-color transparent GIF images of various sizes and insert them wherever special spacing needs arise. Because they are transparent, they are invisible, but they still take up space on the page.

Using Tables to Control Spacing on a Web Page

One advantage of using tables is that they allow you to control the arrangement of items on the Web page. You can arrange, or **align**, the current text or image to the left within a table cell, to the right within a table cell, or centered in the table cell. The default alignment for newly inserted items is left-aligned.

The FrontPage Editor provides three alignment buttons on the Format toolbar. The **Align Left button** aligns an item to the left margin of the page or table cell. The **Align Right button** aligns items to the right margin of the page or table cell. The **Center button** centers items on the page or in a table cell. You simply select the paragraph or graphic by clicking it, and then click the appropriate alignment button on the Format toolbar.

To demonstrate how to align items on a Web page, you will select the clip art image you inserted in the rightmost cell and right-align it in the cell, resulting in the positioning of the clip art image to the right margin of the Web page. This alignment allows more room for the company name, which will be entered in the center cell. Perform the following steps to align an item on a Web page.

Steps To Align Items on the Web Page

1 Click the clip art image in the rightmost cell to select it. Point to the Align Right button on the Format toolbar.

The clip art image is selected (Figure 2-32). The handles surrounding the clip art image indicate it is selected.

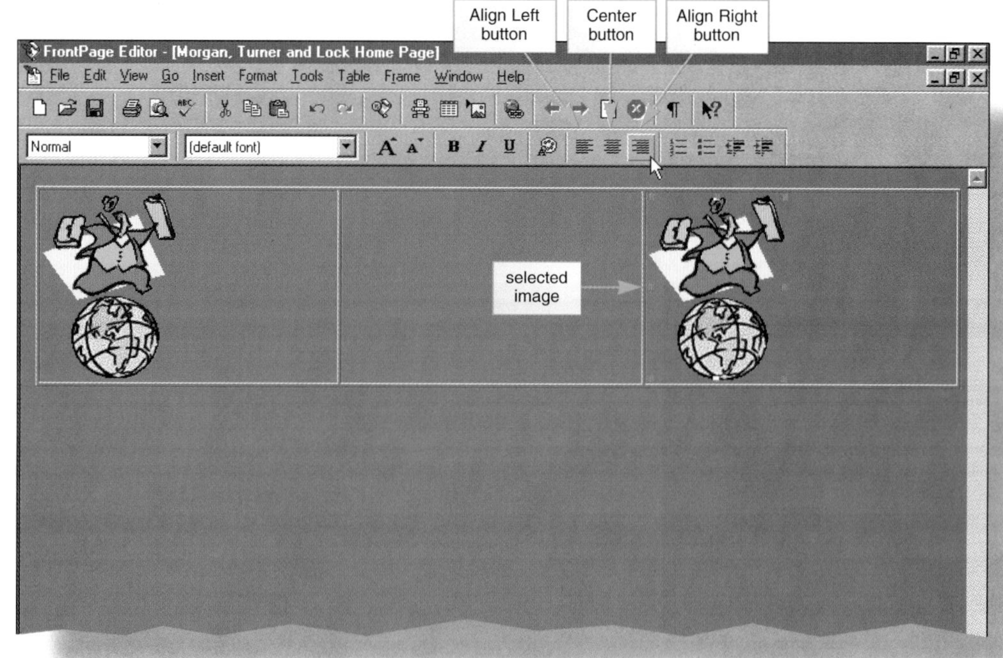

FIGURE 2-32

2 Click the Align Right button on the Format toolbar.

The clip art image is aligned to the right margin of the table cell (Figure 2-33). The ***align right indicator*** *displays in the table cell to denote that the image has been aligned to the right, and the Align Right button on the Format toolbar is recessed.*

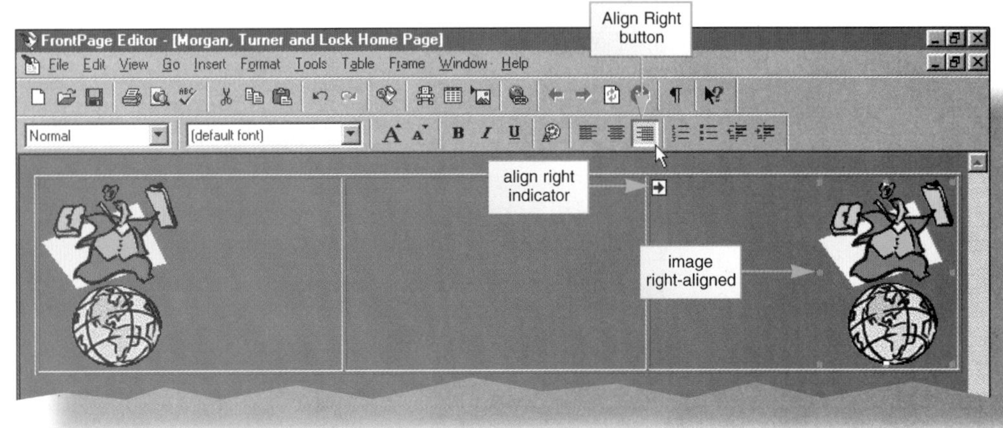

FIGURE 2-33

The image is right-aligned in the rightmost table cell on the Web page. The align right indicator in the table cell will not display when viewing the page in a browser. In later steps you will be using the Center button to center headings, text, and other items on the Web page.

Adjusting Table Borders

Table Borders

You can adjust the width, style, and color of table borders, giving the table a three-dimensional look.

Another useful feature of tables is the ability to move the outside borders of a table and the borders between individual cells, thus providing added flexibility in controlling spacing on the Web page.

You can adjust the borders of the table to control vertical and horizontal spacing. The bottom border can be dragged up or down to control vertical spacing. The left border can be dragged right or left to control horizontal spacing. The borders between cells also can be moved to control spacing within the table.

As shown in Figure 2-33, the clip art images do not consume all the space in their respective cells. You can adjust the borders between the cells to reduce the space in the two outside cells and increase the space in the center cell, thus providing more room for the company name. Perform the following steps to adjust the borders of table cells.

To Adjust Table Cell Borders

1 Point to the cell border between the second and third cell.

The mouse pointer changes to a double-headed arrow (Figure 2-34).

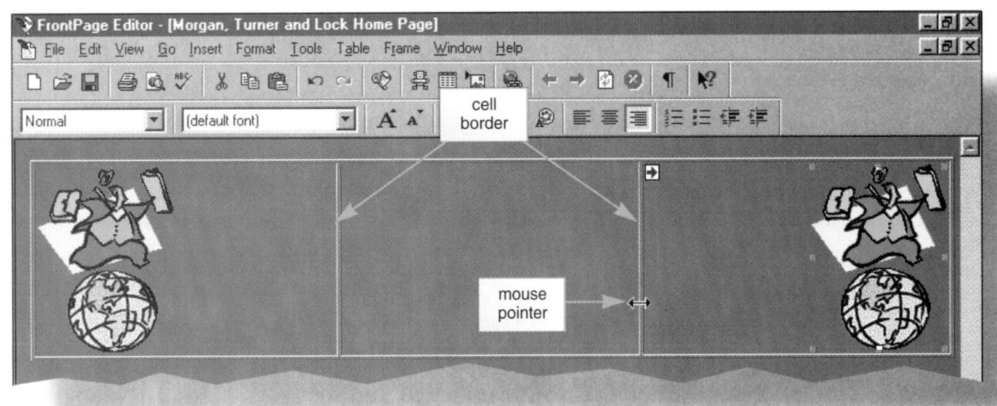

FIGURE 2-34

2 Drag the cell border right to the left edge of the clip art image.

The cell border moves to the right (Figure 2-35).

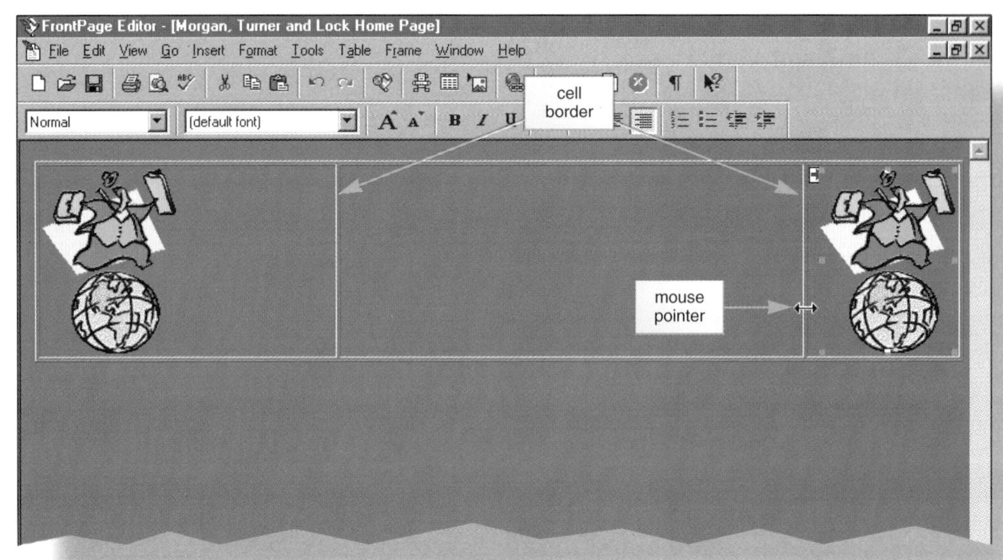

FIGURE 2-35

3 Point to the cell border between the first and second cell. Drag the cell border left to the right edge of the clip art image.

The cell border moves to the left (Figure 2-36).

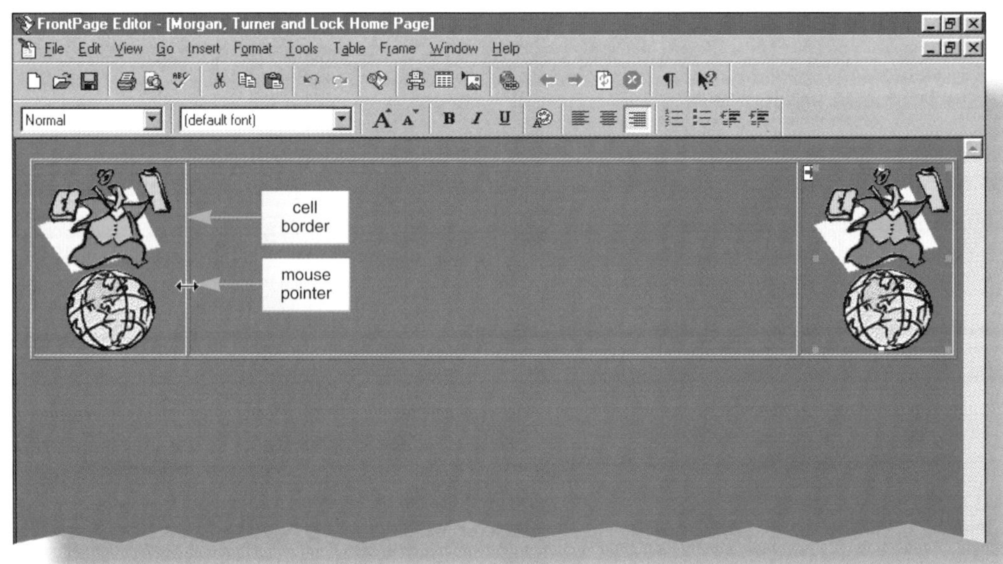

FIGURE 2-36

1. Right-click cell, click Cell Properties on shortcut menu, enter width

Moving the cell to occupy the minimum width for the images allows more space in the center cell for the Morgan, Turner and Lock company name. You should have inserted the images in the table cells before adjusting the cell borders, so you can see just how much space is available. Adjusting table and cell borders is a powerful way of controlling spacing on a Web page.

Tables and the individual cells are surrounded by a default table border. You can adjust the properties of the border, such as the width, color, and use of a 3-D shadow. When using a table for spacing purposes, you most likely will not want the table borders to be seen. You can turn off the border display using the **Table Properties command** on the Table menu. Perform the following steps to turn off the table border.

To Turn Off the Table Border

1 If necessary, click in one of the three cells of the table. Click Table on the menu bar and then point to Table Properties.

The Table menu displays (Figure 2-37). It contains commands to manage tables. The Table Properties command allows you to specify table border information.

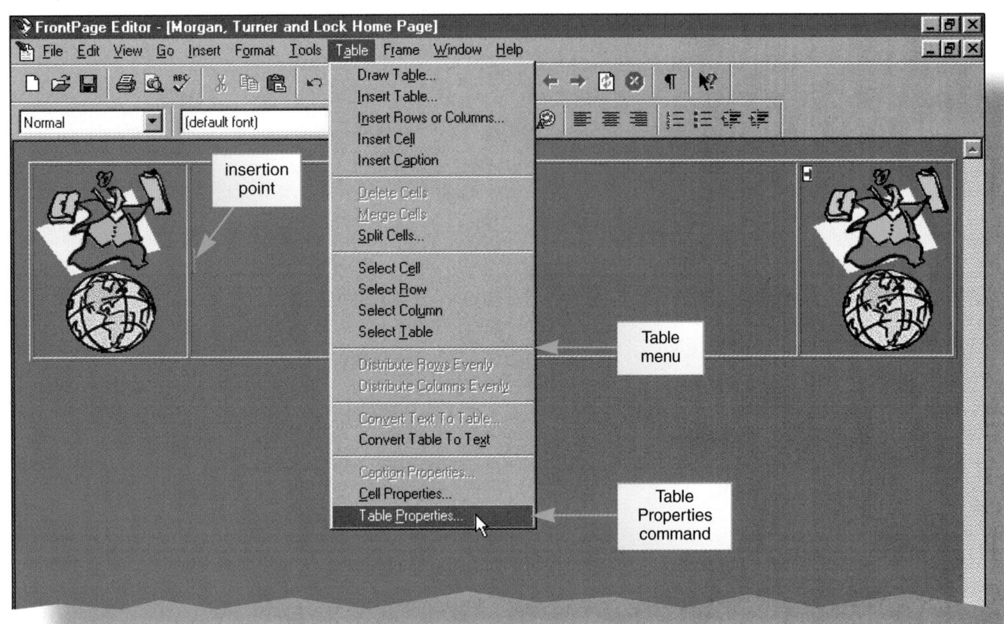

FIGURE 2-37

2 Click Table Properties.

The Table Properties dialog box displays (Figure 2-38). Options in this dialog box allow you to control various aspects of the table border and table background. The **Border Size box** *allows you to control how wide the table border will be in pixels. A* **pixel**, *short for* **picture element**, *is the smallest addressable element on your computer screen. The default border size is one pixel.*

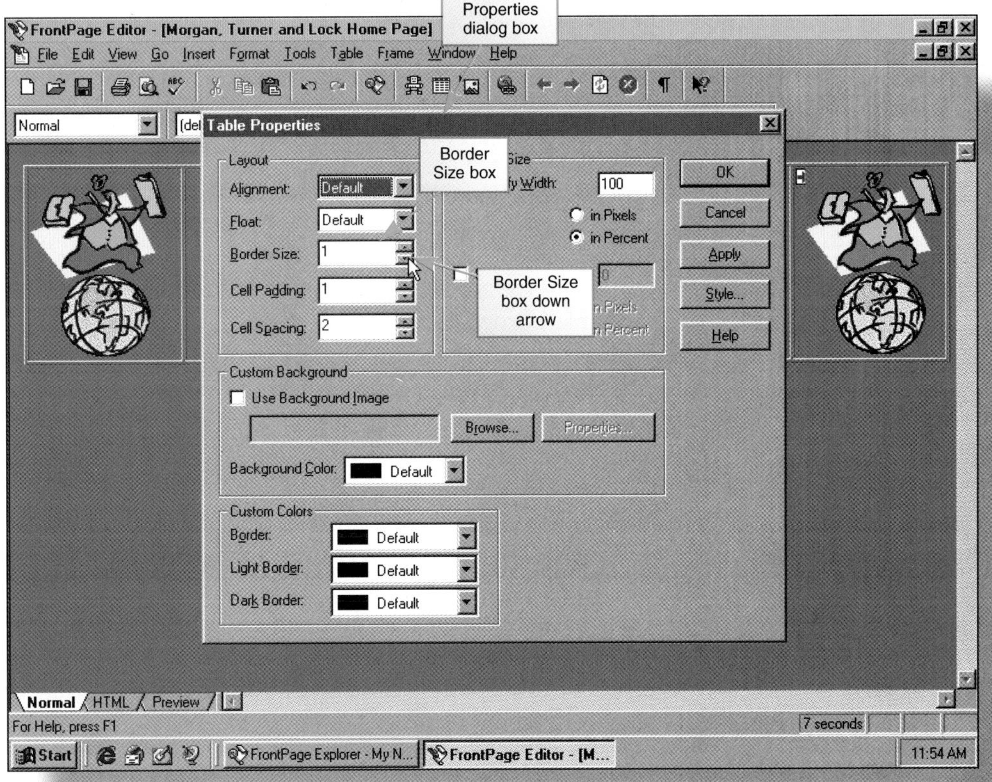

FIGURE 2-38

3 **Click the Border Size box down arrow until zero (0) displays in the box.**

Zero (0) displays in the Border Size box indicating that no visible border will appear around the table cells (Figure 2-39).

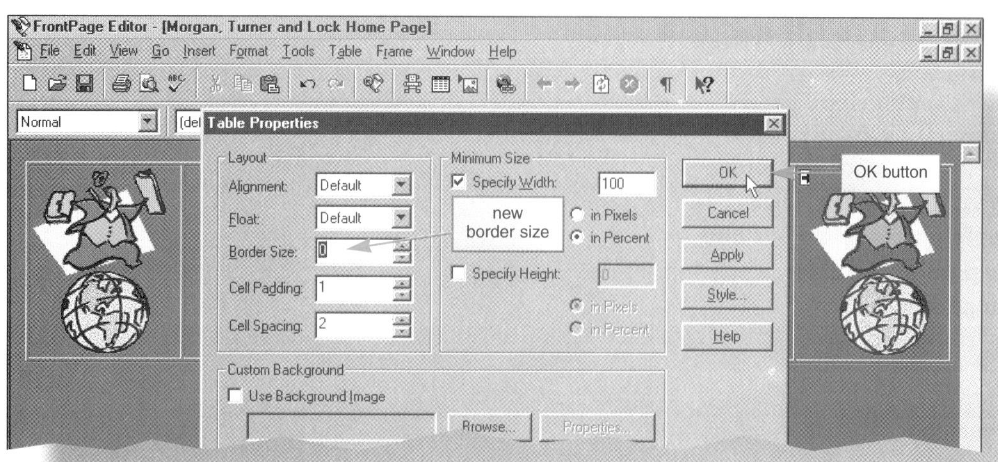

FIGURE 2-39

4 **Click the OK button.**

The table border is replaced with dashed lines (Figure 2-40). These lines show you where the cell borders are and also indicate that no visible border will appear when the Web page displays in a browser.

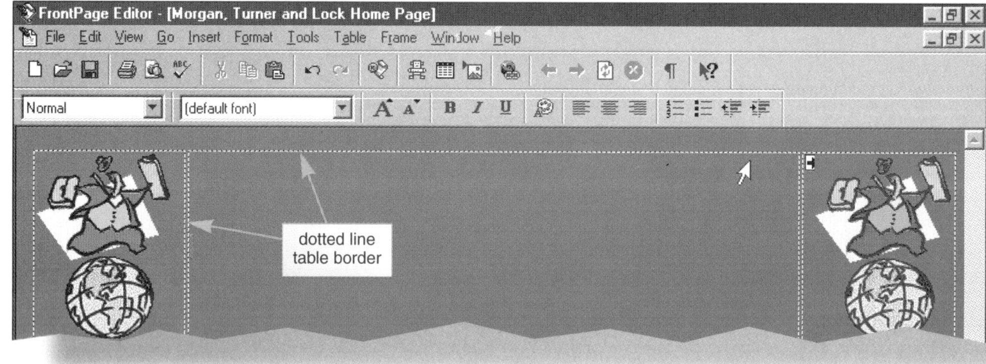

FIGURE 2-40

Other Ways

1. Right-click table, click Table Properties on shortcut menu
2. Press ALT+A, P

You have adjusted the borders around table cells and turned off the display of the table border. Recall from Project 1 that the FrontPage Editor includes a Table toolbar (Figure 1-19 on page FP 1.22) with buttons for frequently used table functions such as adding columns and rows, and adjusting table properties. Now that the size of the center cell has been adjusted, you can insert the heading for the Web page.

Inserting a Heading in a Web Page

Text on a Web page can take many forms, such as a heading, ordered and unordered lists, menus, and normal text. To this text, you can apply special formatting such as different fonts, colors, and sizes. You use the Format toolbar for the more frequently used formatting options.

The process of entering text using the FrontPage Editor has several steps. You might skip one or more of the steps, depending on the current settings. The first step is to select a text style. The **Change Style box** on the Format toolbar contains styles such as lists, menu items, headings, and normal text.

After selecting a style, you will select a font type for the text. A **font** is another name for character set. Some commonly used fonts are Courier, Helvetica, and Arial. You change the font using the **Change Font box** on the Format toolbar.

Then, you select a color for the text. The default color is black. A text color that complements the background color or image you have chosen is preferred so your text does not fade in and out as it moves across a background image or pattern. You do not want to make it hard to read your page because of poor color selection. To change the color of text, use the **Text Color button** on the Format toolbar. Forty-eight basic colors are available and room for 16 custom colors to be mixed.

The Format toolbar contains many text formatting options. The **Increase Text Size button** and the **Decrease Text Size button** allow you to increase or decrease the size of the characters in your text. Using the **Bold**, **Italic**, and **Underline** buttons, you can format certain text in bold, italic, or underlined.

The Morgan, Turner and Lock company name, which will be placed in the center table cell, consists of Heading 1 as its style, Arial as its font, and yellow for the font color. The heading also is centered in the cell. Perform the following steps to set the style, font type and color, and then insert the company name in the center cell.

Formatting Text

Changing the formatting of any text already on the Web page can be accomplished by dragging through the text and then applying different format settings.

To Add a Heading to a Web Page

1 Click the center table cell to position the insertion point.

The insertion point displays in the center table cell (Figure 2-41).

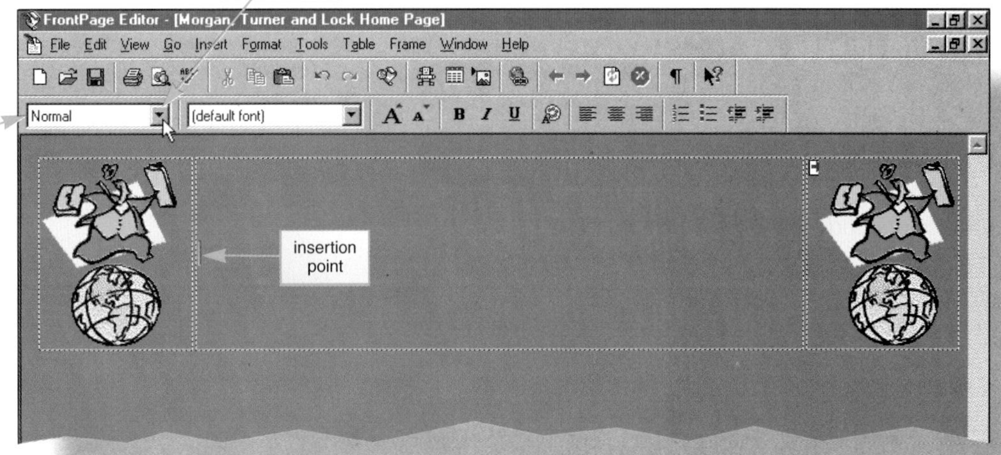

FIGURE 2-41

2 Click the Change Style box arrow. Point to Heading 1.

The Change Style list box displays (Figure 2-42). Heading 1 represents the largest available heading size.

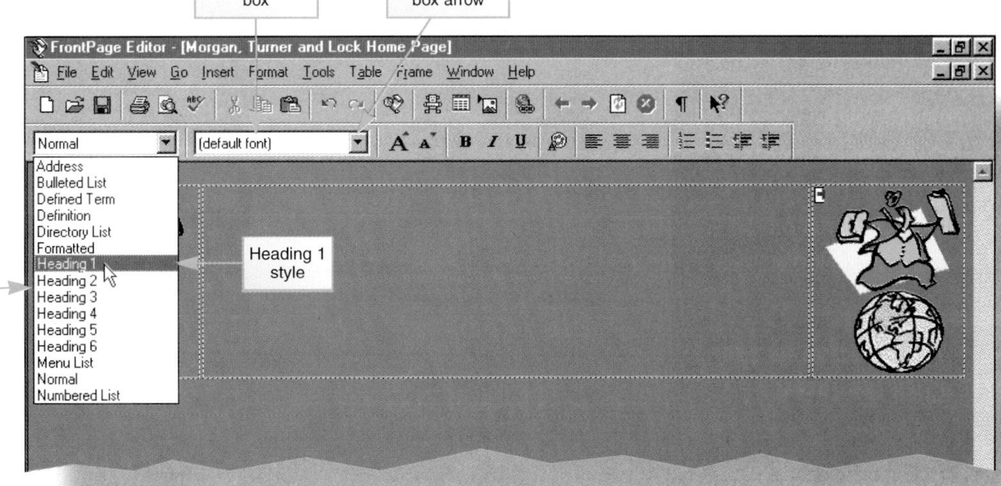

FIGURE 2-42

3 Click Heading 1. Click the Change Font box arrow. Point to Arial.

Heading 1 becomes the text style and the Change Font list box displays (Figure 2-43). It contains a list of fonts available for use when developing Web pages.

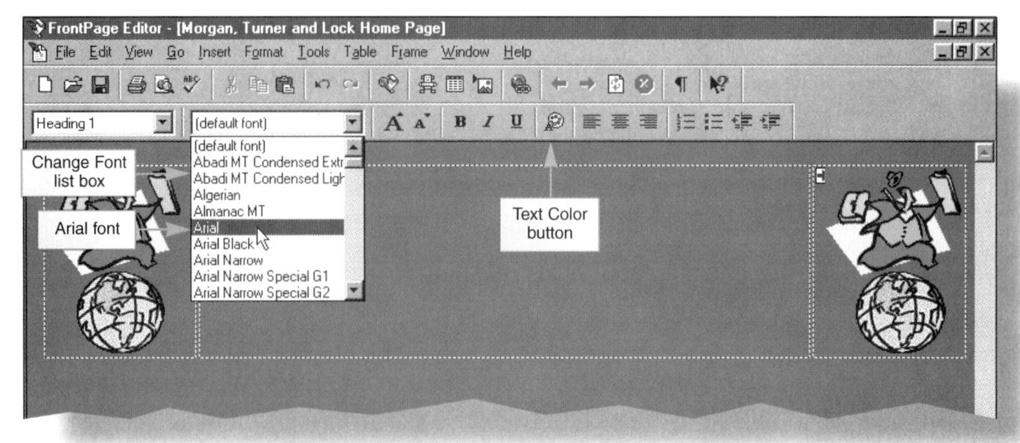

FIGURE 2-43

4 Click Arial. Click the Text Color button on the Format toolbar.

The Color dialog box displays (Figure 2-44). The dialog box contains 48 default colors and an area for 16 custom colors.

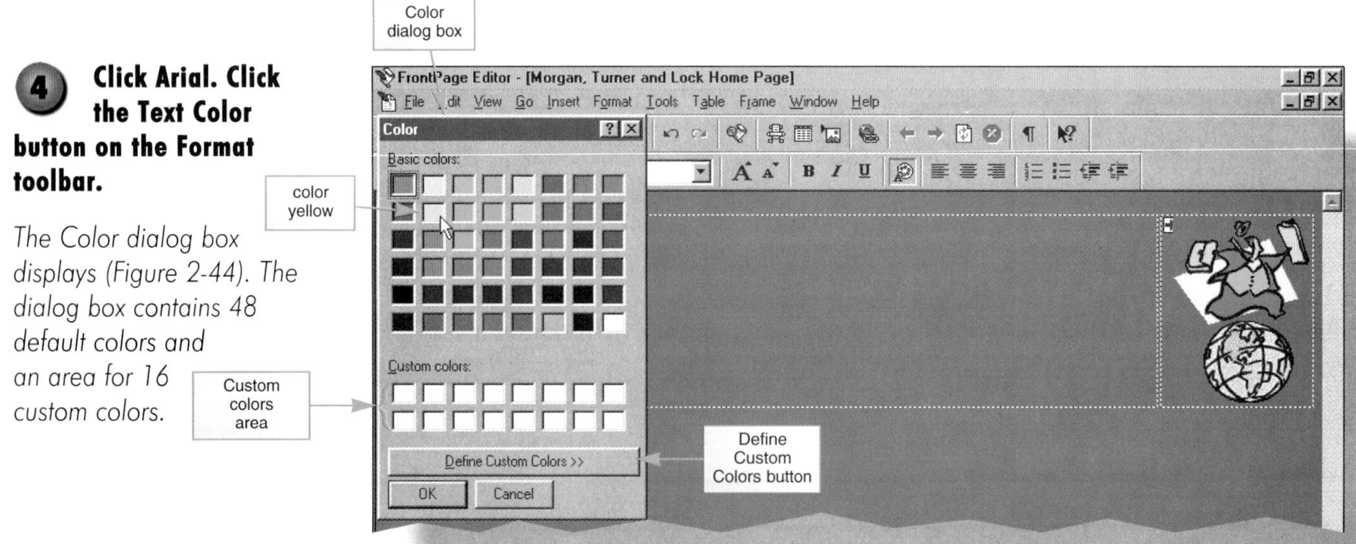

FIGURE 2-44

5 Click the color yellow (row 2, column 2) as shown in Figure 2-45.

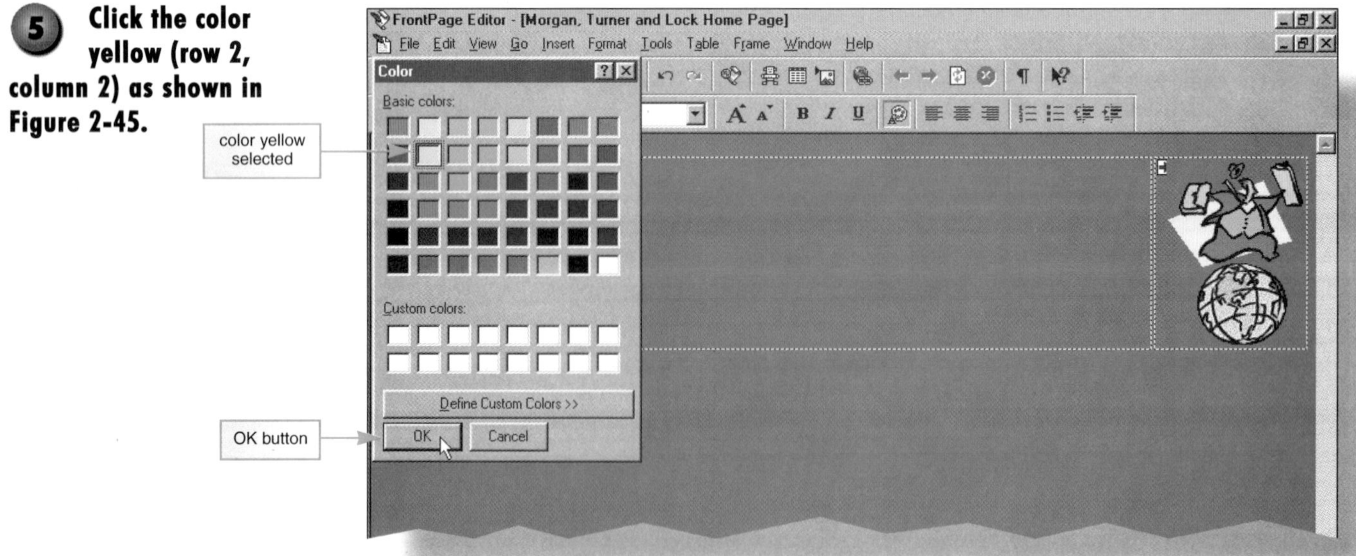

FIGURE 2-45

Click the OK button. Type `Morgan, Turner and Lock Attorneys at Law` **in the middle cell of the table. Click the Center button on the Format toolbar.**

The text displays centered in the middle table cell with a style of Heading 1, in Arial font and in the color yellow (Figure 2-46).

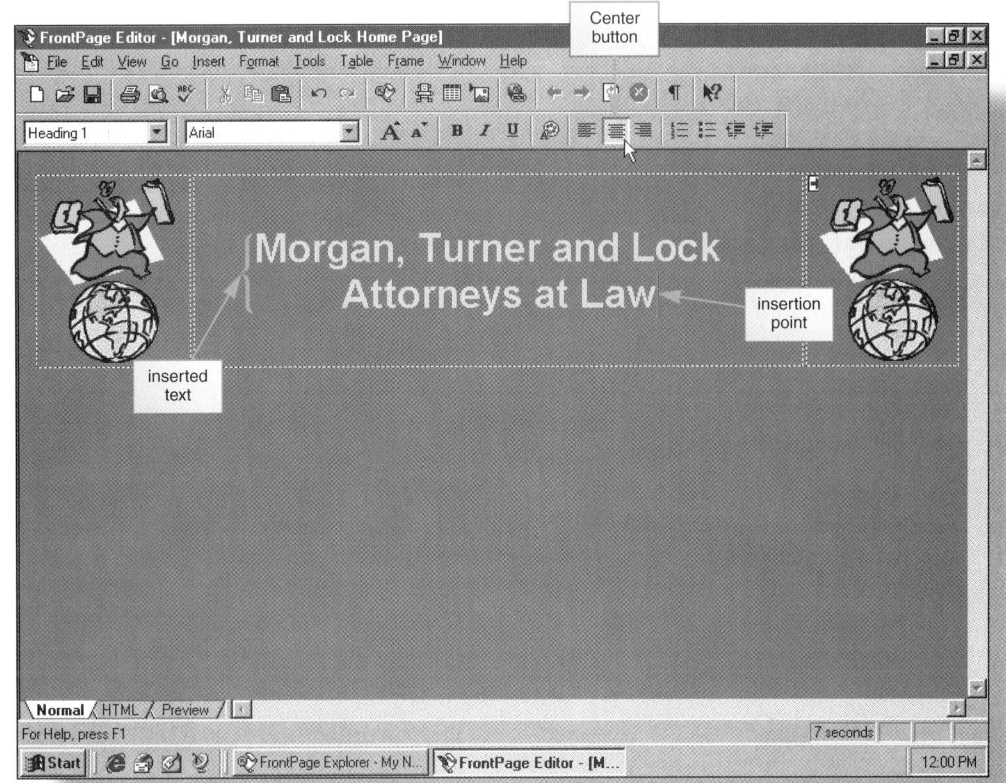

FIGURE 2-46

Other Ways

1. Highlight text, right-click text, click Font Properties on shortcut menu
2. Highlight text, press ALT+ENTER

Because it is the part of the page that first-time viewers initially see in their browsers, it is important to format the header of the Web page so it is appealing and draws further interest. The body of the Web page keeps the viewer's attention when it is verbalized and formatted appropriately. It is customary to separate logical sections of Web pages, such as the header and body, using dividing elements called horizontal rules.

Inserting a Horizontal Rule

The use of elements such as a horizontal rule can add a special look to your pages, as well as provide the viewer with visual clues concerning the location of information on the Web page. Horizontal rules are used to break up the page into sections, and separate elements on the page. A **horizontal rule** is a small, thin line that goes across the entire Web page.

You will use a horizontal rule to separate the header section of the Web page from the body. The steps on the next page insert a horizontal rule below the table containing the clip art images and company name.

More About

Text

If the text formatting in the FrontPage Editor simply does not give the effect you desire, try creating an image of the specially formatted text using a graphics program and then insert the image in the Web page.

To Add a Horizontal Rule to a Web Page

1 Click below the table to position the insertion point, click Insert on the menu bar, and then point to Horizontal Line.

The Insert menu displays and the Horizontal Line command is highlighted (Figure 2-47). The ***Insert menu*** *contains commands to insert various elements in the current Web page.*

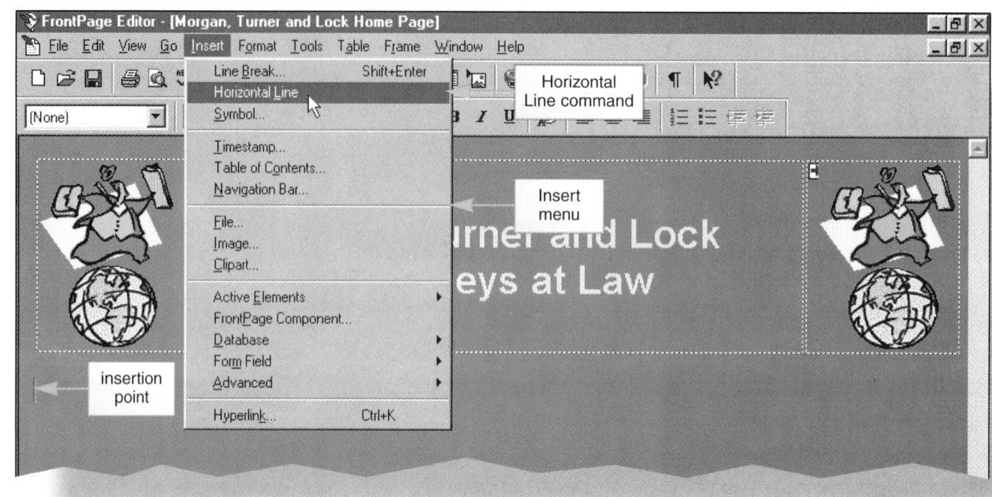

FIGURE 2-47

2 Click Horizontal Line.

The horizontal rule displays below the table (Figure 2-48).

FIGURE 2-48

Other Ways

1. Press ALT+I, L

You can adjust the properties of the horizontal rule, such as the thickness and length, by right-clicking the horizontal rule and then clicking Horizontal Line properties on the shortcut menu. The alignment of the horizontal rule can be controlled using the Align Left, Center, and Align Right buttons on the Format toolbar.

Adding Normal Text to a Web Page

Notice in Figure 2-48 that the style and font reverted to the default values. This occurs whenever you move the insertion point with the mouse or arrow keys. You need to set the style, font, and color again in preparation for entering more text.

The steps for adding normal text are similar to the steps you used previously to add the heading: set the style, set the font, and set the color. The following steps will add all the normal text that will display on the Web page.

To Add Normal Text to a Web Page

1 Click anywhere below the horizontal rule to position the insertion point and then click the Change Style box arrow. Click Normal. Click the Change Font box arrow and then click Arial. Click the Text Color button and then click the color yellow (row 2, column 2). Click the OK button.

The Change Style box indicates Normal style and the Change Font box indicates Arial (Figure 2-49). The new text entered from this point will reflect these formatting attributes.

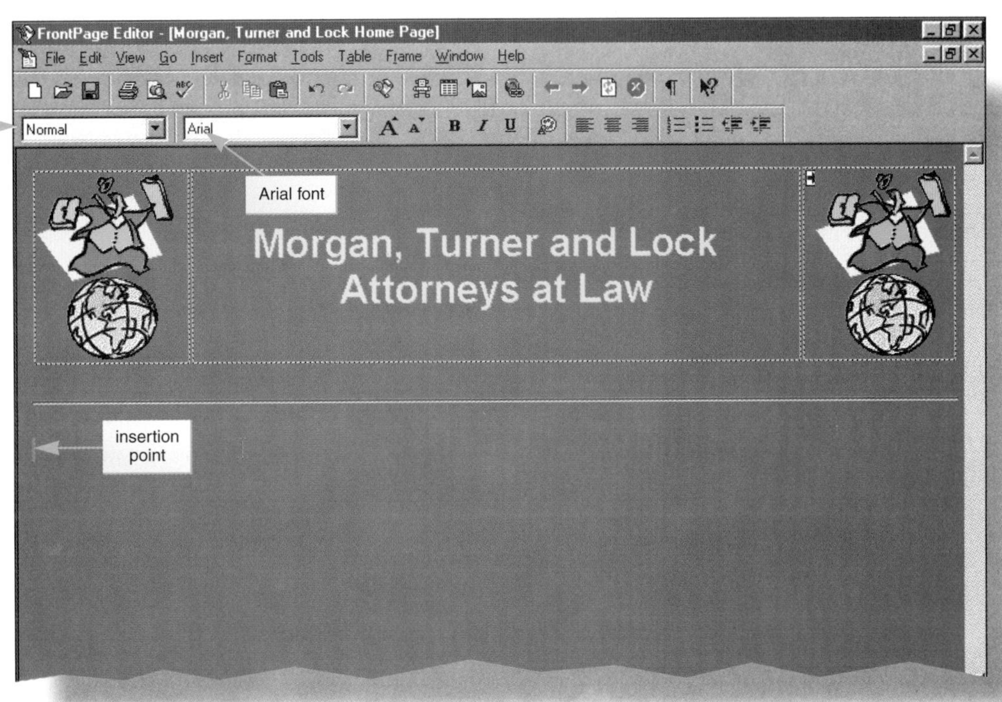

FIGURE 2-49

2 Type `Welcome to our Web site` **as the first line of text. Click the Center button on the Format toolbar.**

The yellow text displays centered on the Web page in the Arial font (Figure 2-50).

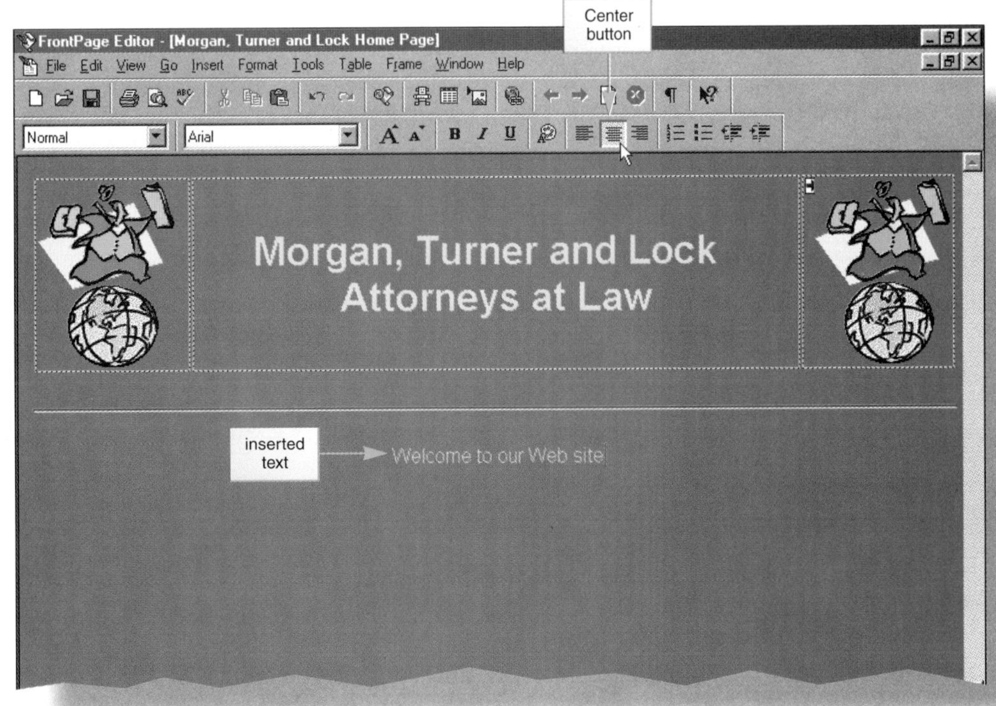

FIGURE 2-50

3 **Press the ENTER key to insert a new paragraph and then type** `We provide legal services to individuals, corporations and government entities world-wide. Browse through our services. Meet our people. Fill out our survey to see if we can help you.`

The text displays centered on the Web page (Figure 2-51). Notice the style, font, color, and alignment settings are preserved. This is because you have not repositioned the insertion point using the mouse or arrow keys.

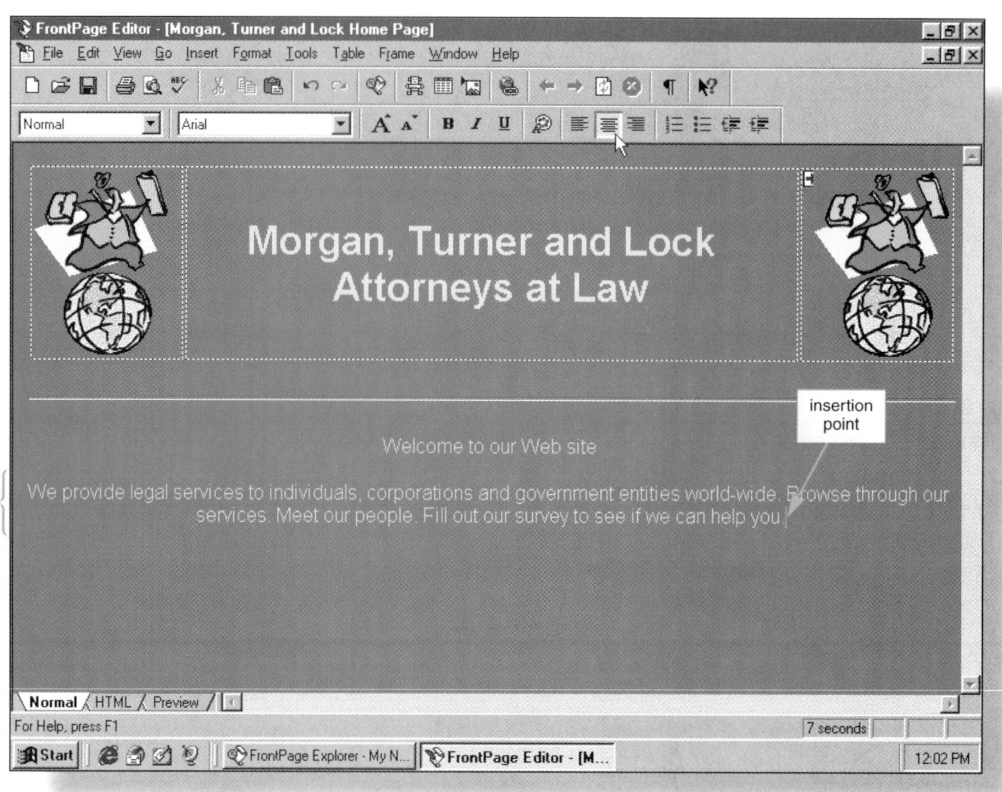

FIGURE 2-51

4 **Press the ENTER key to insert a new paragraph and then type** `Serving the public for 89 years` **as the new text.**

The text displays centered on the Web page (Figure 2-52).

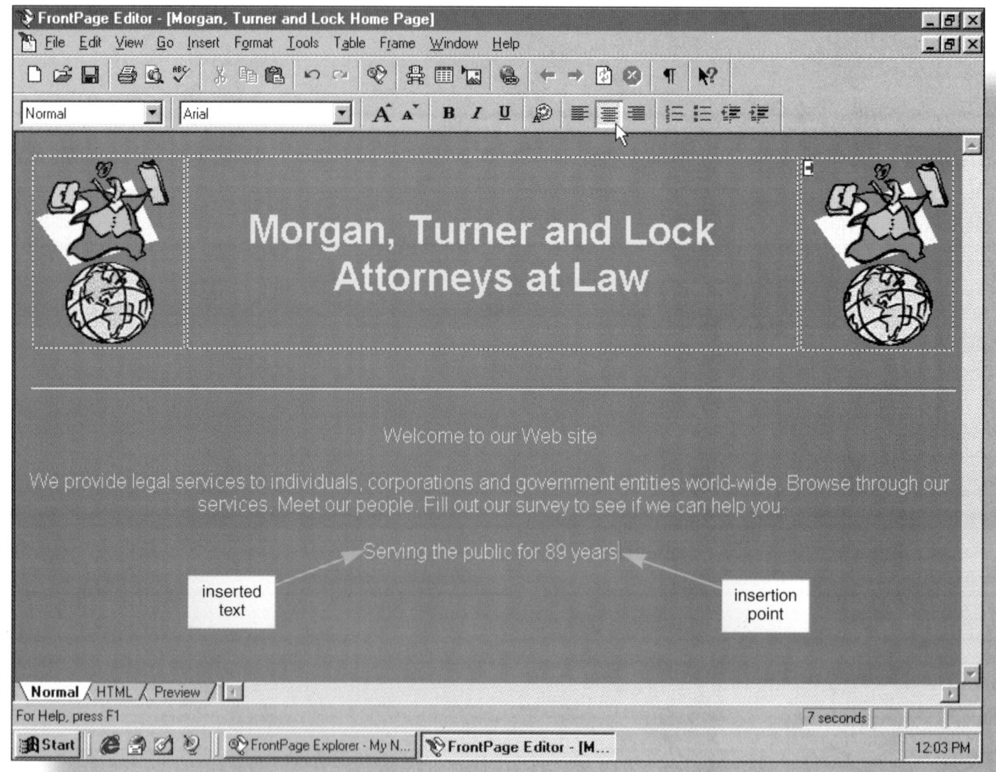

FIGURE 2-52

5 **Press the ENTER key to insert a new paragraph. Click the Change Style box arrow, click Heading 4 and then type** `Services    People    Survey` **separating the first two words with four spaces each.**

The text displays centered with a style of Heading 4 (Figure 2-53). These words will serve as hyperlinks to other pages in the FrontPage web. The style was changed to Heading 4 to make the text slightly larger that normal text.

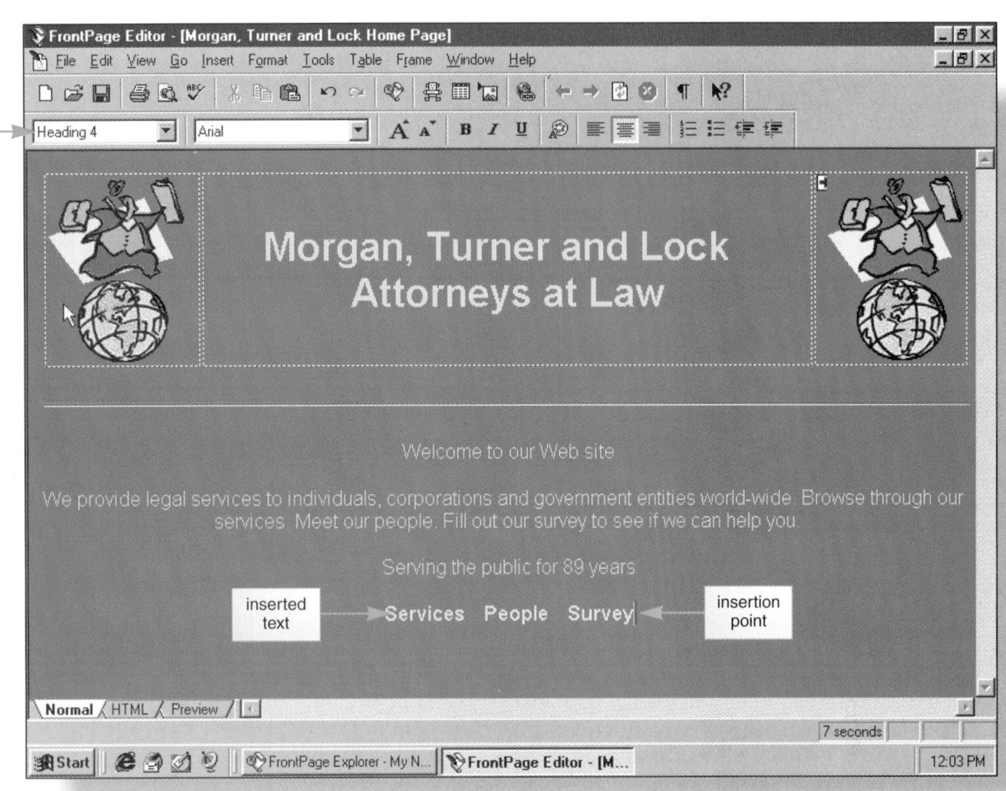

FIGURE 2-53

6 **Press the ENTER key to insert a new paragraph. Click the Change Style box arrow, click Normal, and then type** `Contact us at webmaster@www.mtl.com` **as the new text.**

The text displays centered with a style of Normal (Figure 2-54). It is customary to display e-mail addresses formatted in italic text to differentiate them further from the rest of the text.

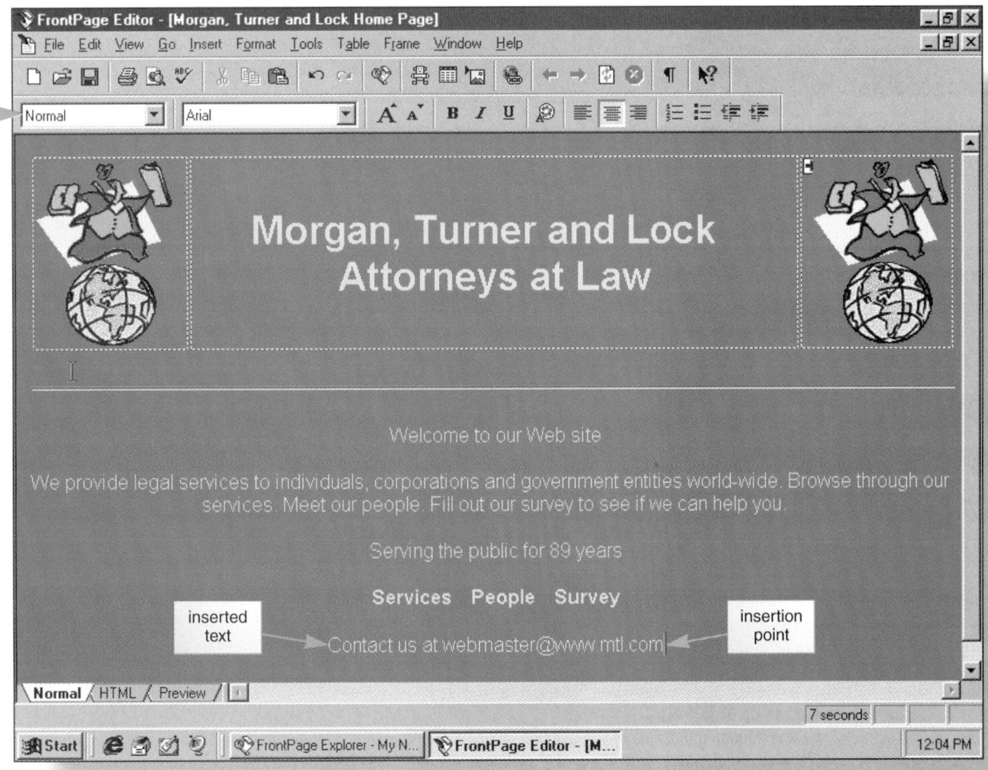

FIGURE 2-54

7 Drag through the webmaster@www.mtl.com text to select it.

The selected text is highlighted (Figure 2-55).

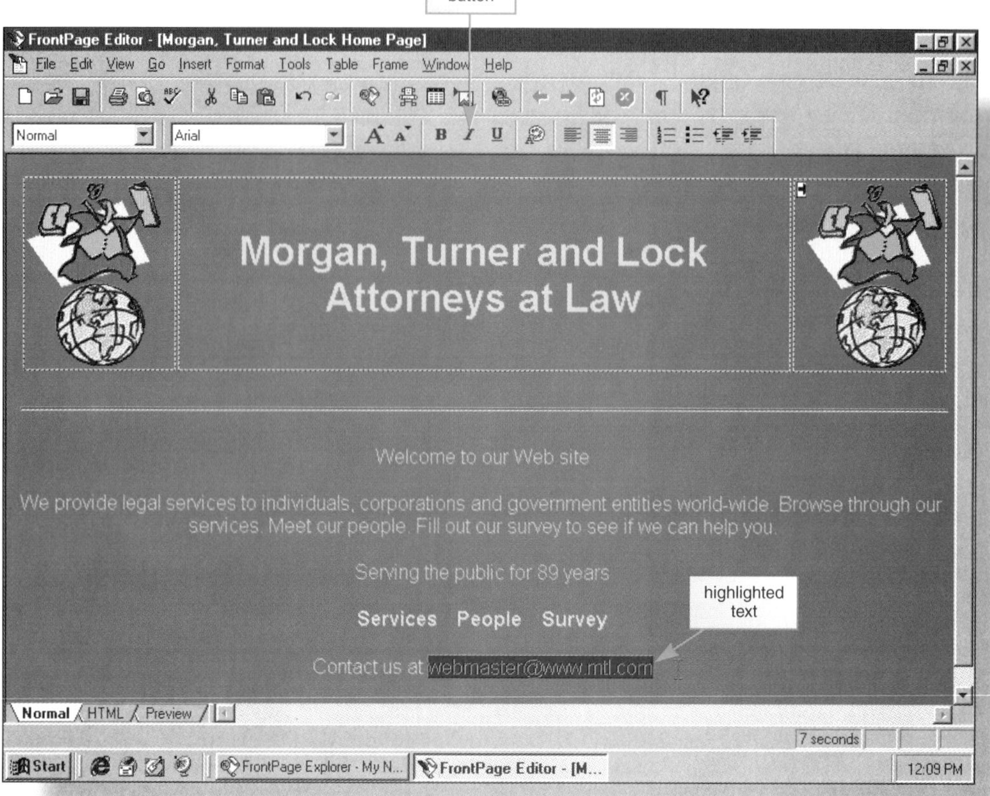

FIGURE 2-55

8 Click the Italic button on the Format toolbar.

The selected text is changed to italic (Figure 2-56).

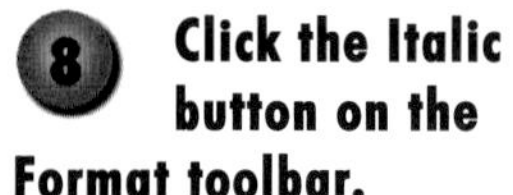

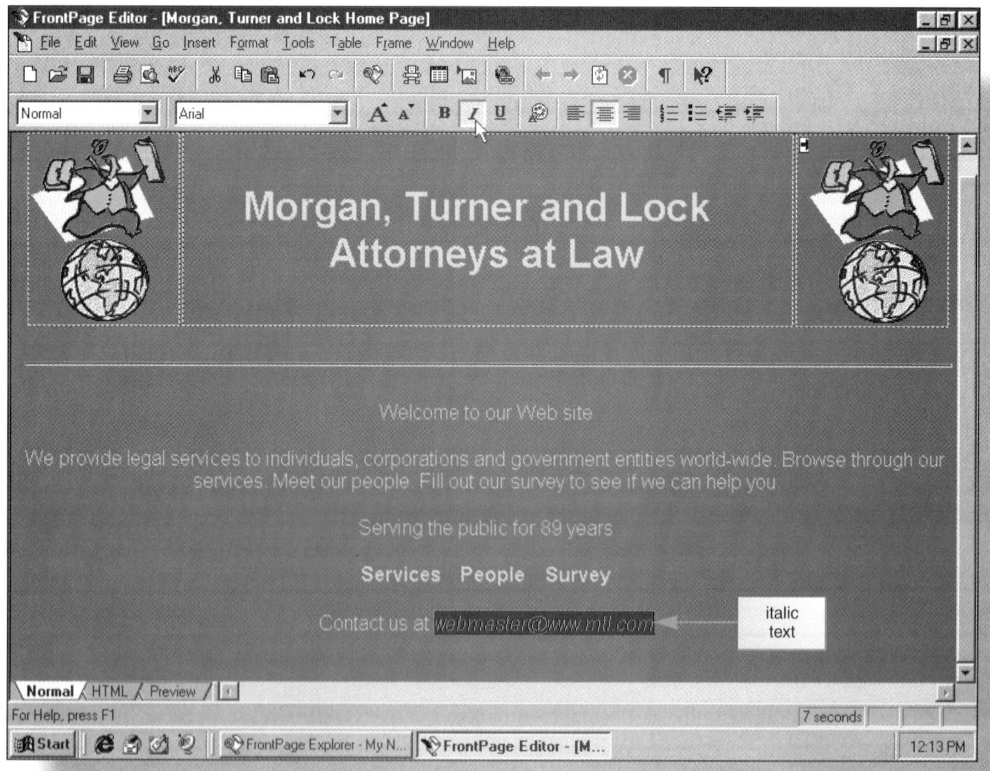

FIGURE 2-56

Other Ways

1. On the Format menu click Font Properties
2. Highlight text, right-click text, click Font Properties on shortcut menu
3. Highlight text, press ALT+ENTER

You can see from the previous steps that the Format toolbar is very useful when entering text. You can change styles, fonts, color, and other properties very quickly as you move through the body of the Web page.

Using an Image as a Horizontal Rule

With the insertion of the e-mail contact information, you actually have entered both the body and the footer of the Web page. The footer of the page begins with the Services People Survey line. Another horizontal rule is appropriate between the body and the footer to distinguish the two sections.

Instead of inserting the ordinary horizontal rule, however, you will use an inline image as a divider. Perform the following steps to insert a clip art image as a horizontal rule.

To Insert an Image as a Horizontal Rule

1 Click the end of the line, Serving the public for 89 years, to position the insertion point at the end of that line.

The insertion point displays at the end of the line (Figure 2-57).

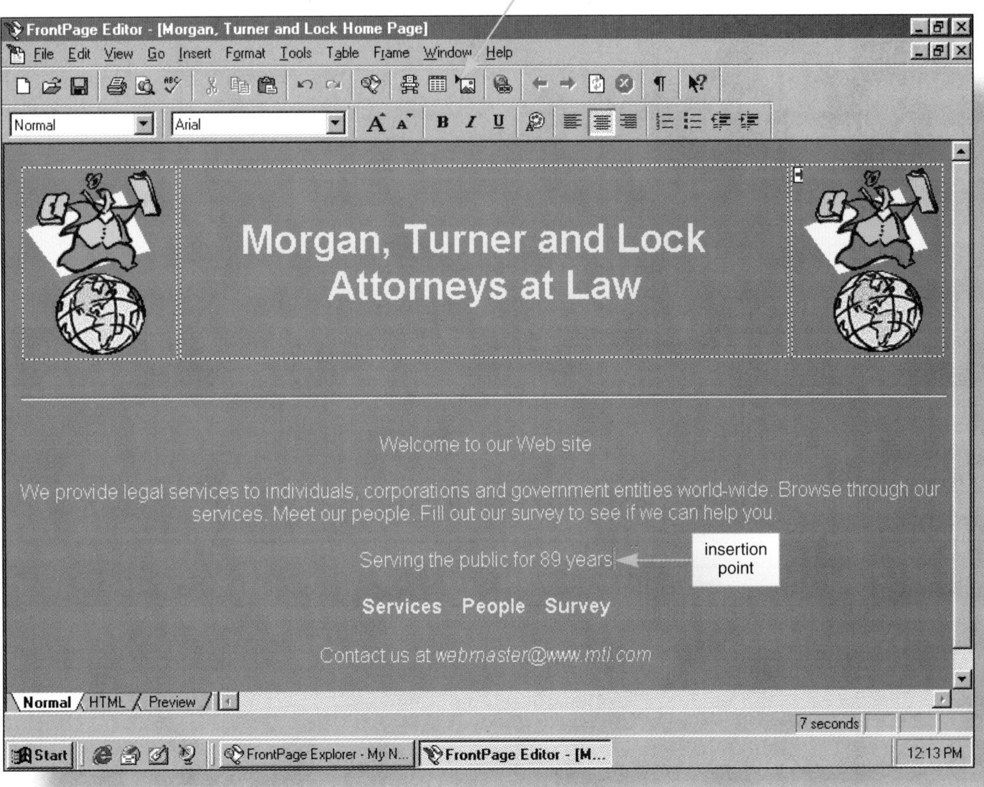

FIGURE 2-57

2 **Press the ENTER key to insert a new paragraph. Click the Insert Image button on the Standard toolbar.**

The Image dialog box displays (Figure 2-58).

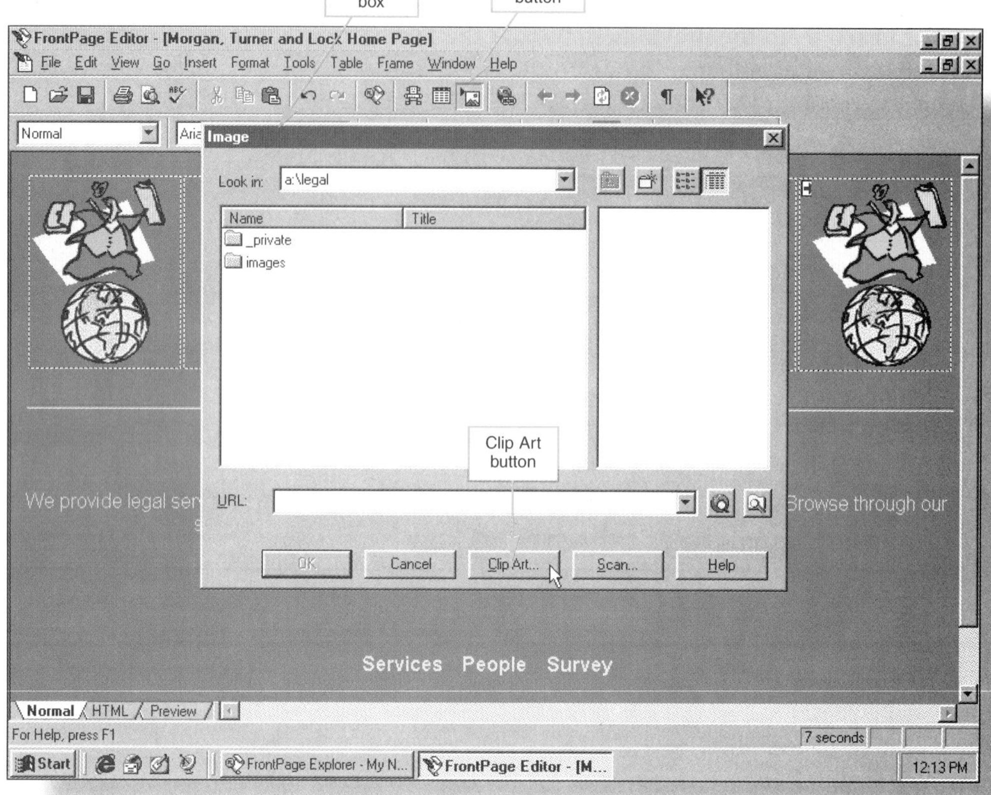

FIGURE 2-58

3 **Click the Clip Art button. Scroll to the bottom of the categories list box until the Web Dividers category displays. Click Web Dividers.**

The Microsoft Clip Gallery 3.0 dialog box displays with samples of available Web dividers (Figure 2-59).

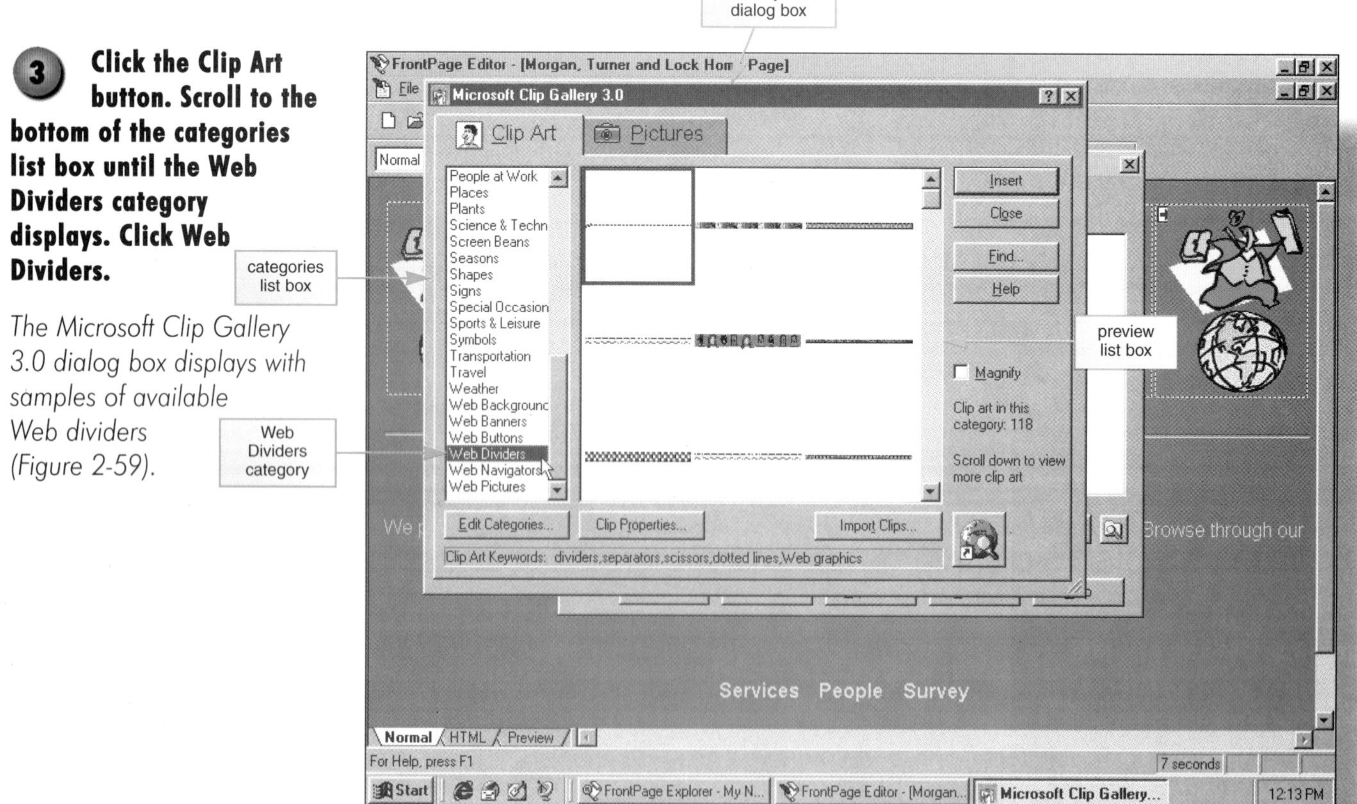

FIGURE 2-59

4 Scroll through the preview list box until the fifteenth row or any other row of dividers that interests you displays (Figure 2-60).

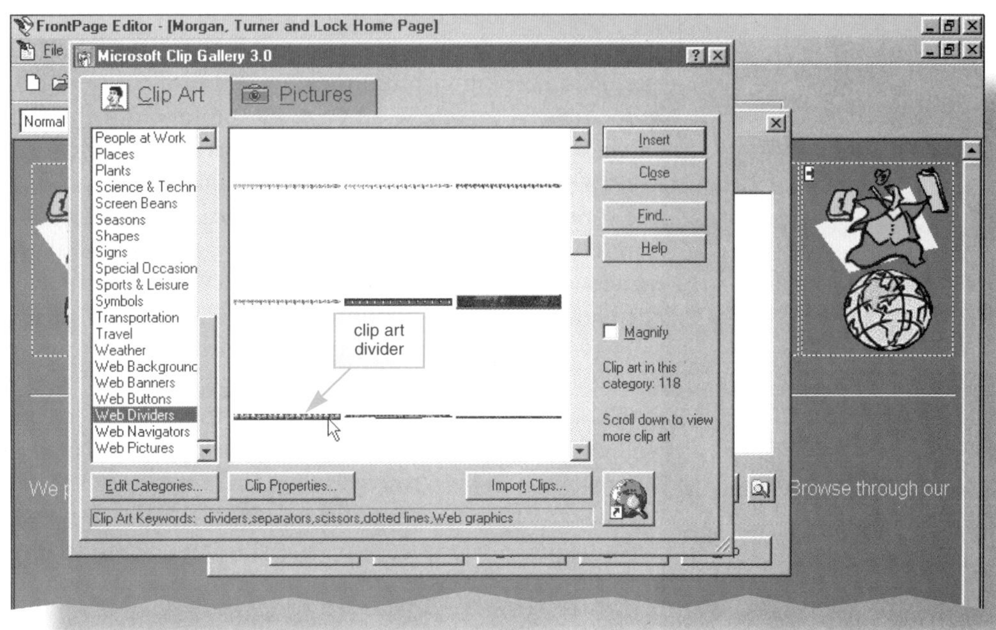

FIGURE 2-60

5 Double-click the first divider in the fifteenth row or any other divider.

The divider displays in the Web page at the location of the insertion point below the line of text, Serving the public for 89 years (Figure 2-61).

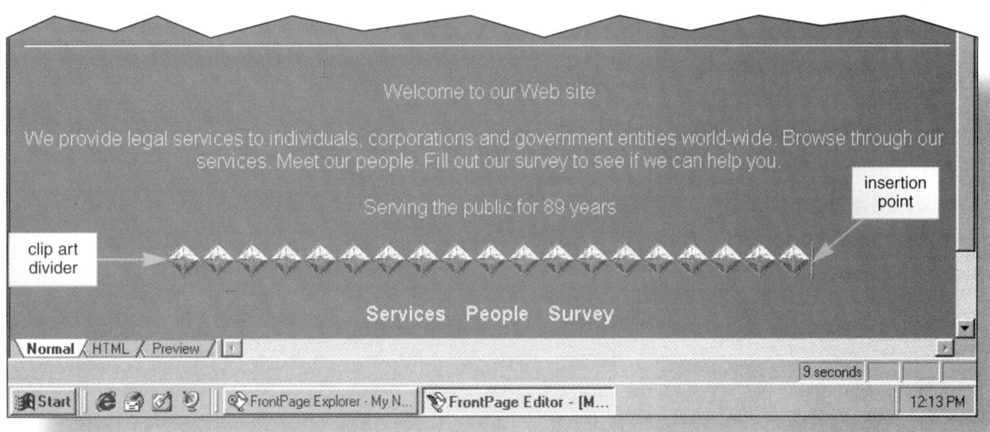

FIGURE 2-61

1. On Insert menu click Clip Art
2. Press ALT+I, C

FrontPage comes complete with a wide selection of colorful dividers, buttons and other images designed specifically for use on Web pages. It is worthwhile to spend some time browsing through the clip art selections to see what is available.

Creating Hyperlinks

The World Wide Web consists of millions of diverse documents. All of these documents are brought together through the use of **hyperlinks**. You navigate the Web by clicking hyperlinks on the Web page. Hyperlinks are crucial for Web page development – the Web would not exist without them. Good Web sites have useful hyperlinks to local pages within the site, and hyperlinks to other related sites on the World Wide Web.

Hyperlinks

In the past, all text hyperlinks were underlined and specially colored. Today, it is possible to create text hyperlinks that are any color and are not underlined. This, sometimes, makes it difficult to identify them on a Web page.

A well-designed Web page has multiple hyperlinks written in such a way as to produce an easy-to-use, easy-to-read Web document. The Web page should be designed keeping in mind the choice and placement of hyperlinks. Referring to the guidelines in Table 2-1 on page FP 2.6, avoid using the *click here* notation, unless no other way to create the hyperlink exists.

Use appropriately worded hyperlink text to produce a natural association within the topic. For example, if you were creating a series of Web pages on whales and wanted to include a hyperlink to a page about whale flippers, you might include a sentence on the Web page that reads, Whales maneuver using their *flippers* to steer through the water. The word, flippers, would be set up as the hyperlink to the flippers Web page. Avoid this type of wording, To see information about whale flippers, *click here.*

The first step in creating a hyperlink is to select the text or image that the viewer will click as the hyperlink on the Web page. The next step is to provide the URL of the resource to be retrieved when the hyperlink is clicked. Several hyperlinks appear on the Morgan, Turner and Lock Home page: one e-mail hyperlink and six hyperlinks to other Web pages in the FrontPage web. Perform the following steps to add hyperlinks to the Morgan, Turner and Lock Home page.

To Insert a Hyperlink in a Web Page

1 Drag through the webmaster@www.mtl.com e-mail address to select it. Point to the Create or Edit Hyperlink button on the Standard toolbar (Figure 2-62).

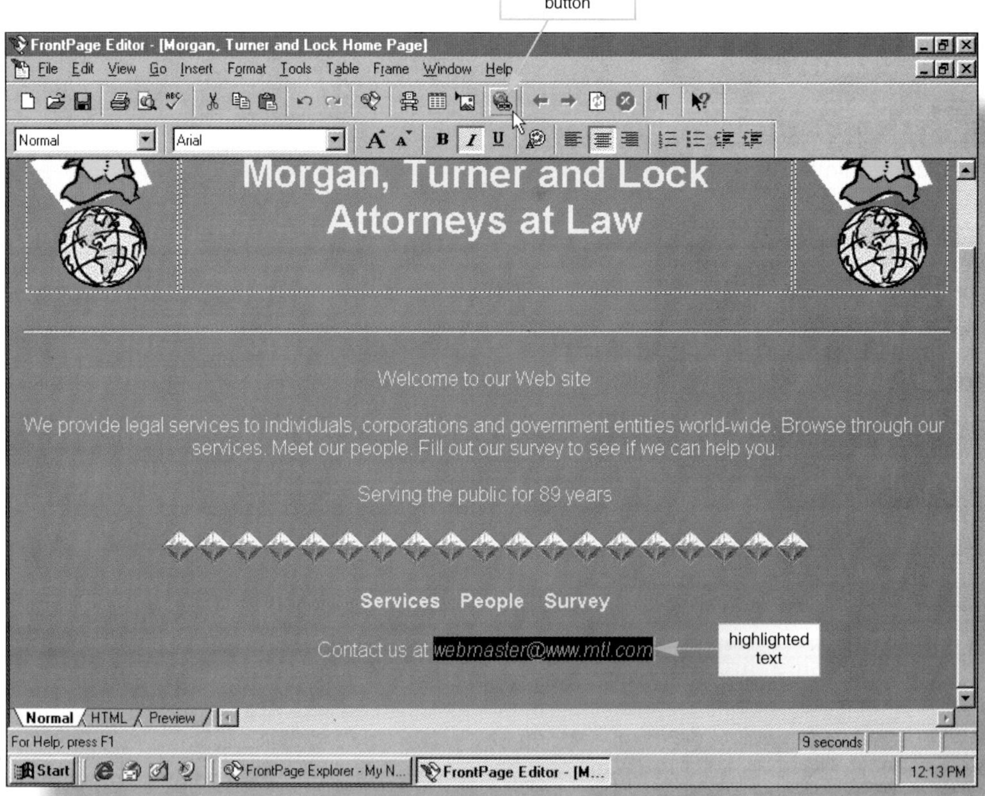

FIGURE 2-62

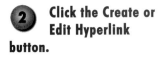

2 Click the Create or Edit Hyperlink button.

The Create Hyperlink dialog box displays (Figure 2-63).

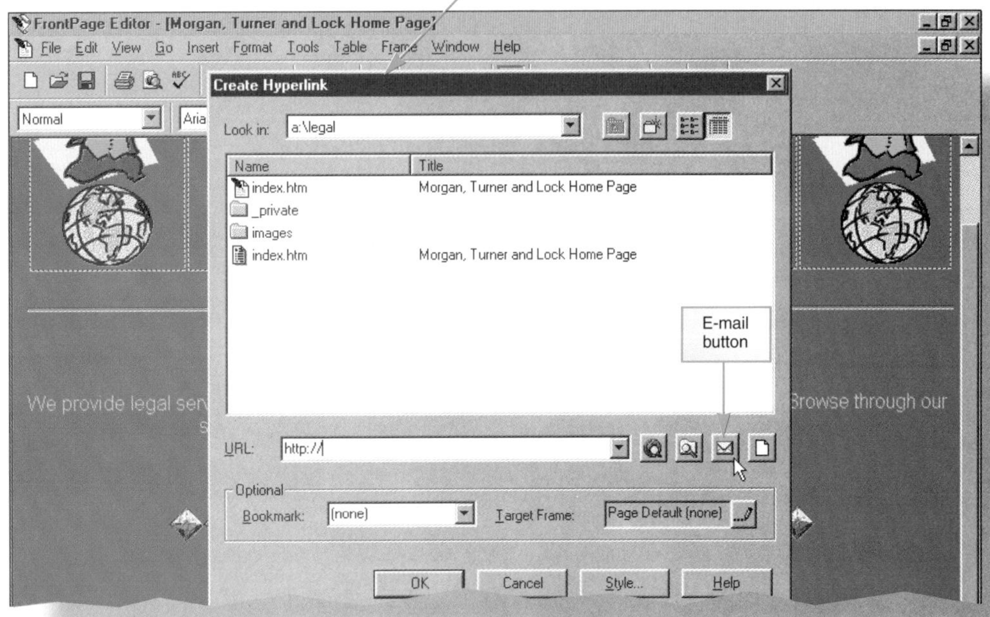

FIGURE 2-63

3 Click the E-Mail button.

The Create E-mail Hyperlink dialog box displays (Figure 2-64).

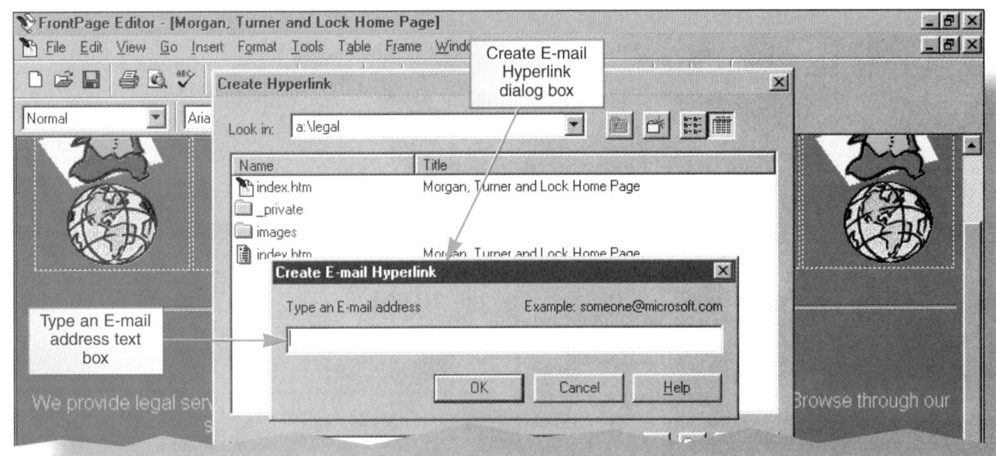

FIGURE 2-64

4 Type `webmaster@www.mtl.com` **in the Type an E-mail address text box.**

The text displays in the text box (Figure 2-65).

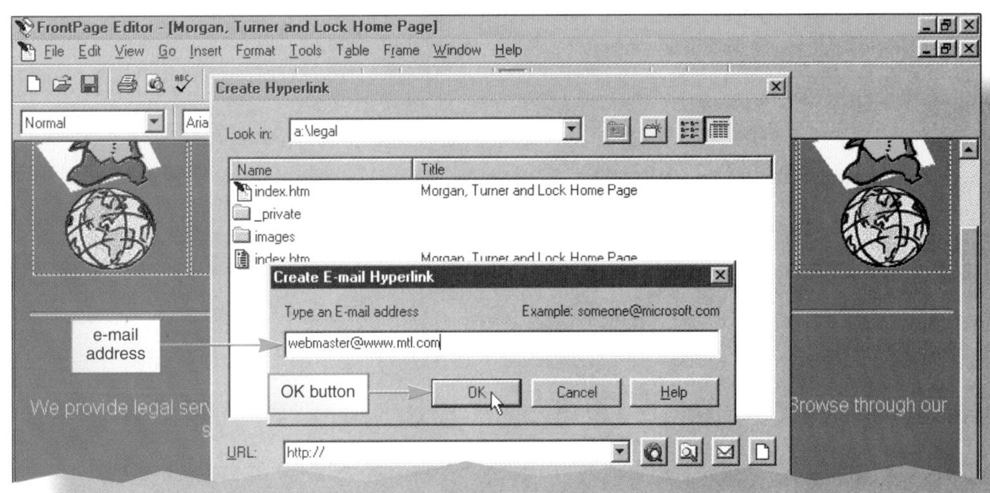

FIGURE 2-65

5 Click the OK button in the Create E-mail Hyperlink dialog box.

The e-mail URL displays in the URL text box (Figure 2-66).

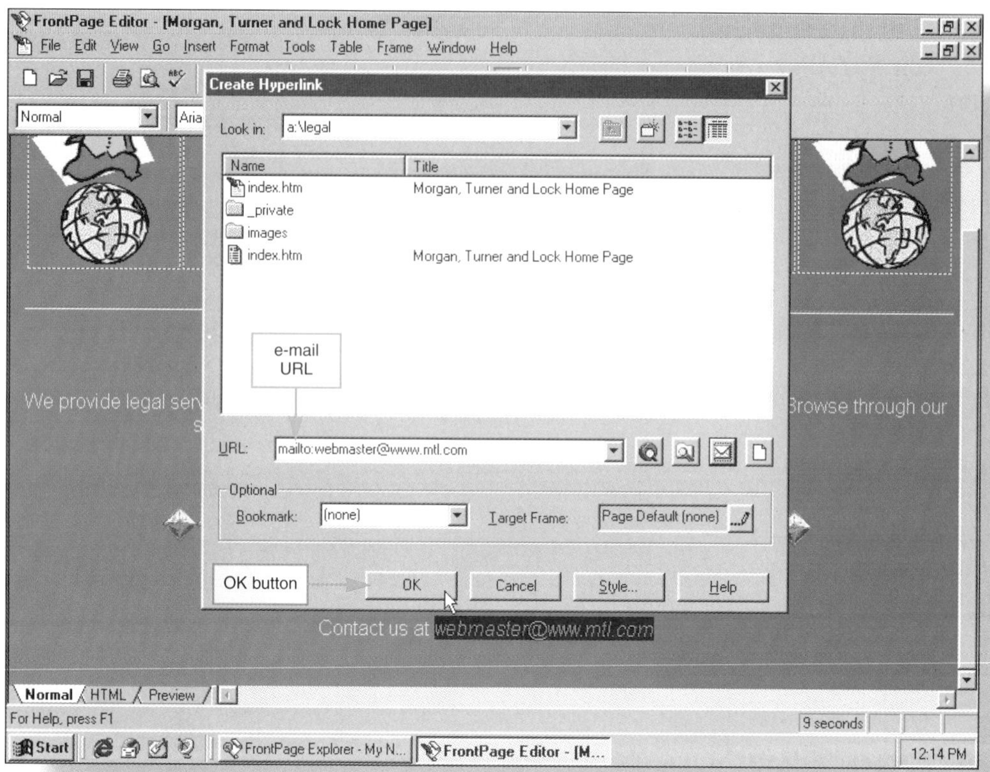

FIGURE 2-66

6 Click the OK button. Position the mouse pointer over the webmaster@www.mtl.com text.

The e-mail URL displays on the status bar at the bottom of the screen when the mouse pointer is positioned over the e-mail hyperlink (Figure 2-67).

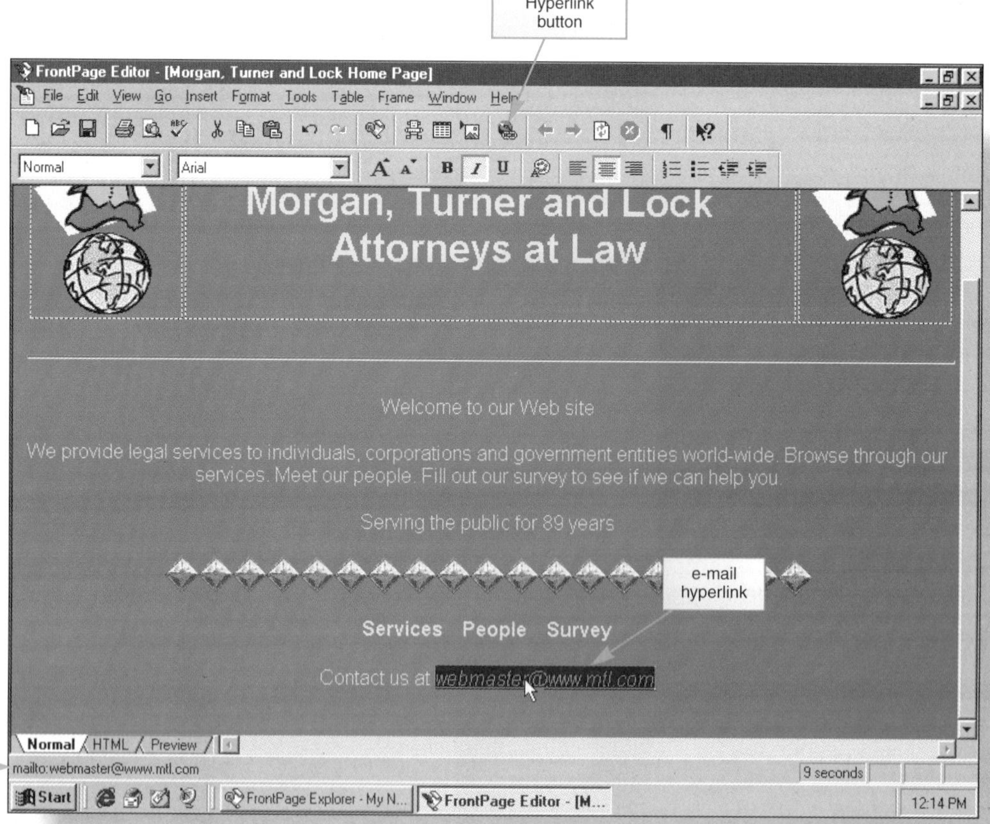

FIGURE 2-67

7 **Drag through the word, Services, below the divider, and then click the Create or Edit Hyperlink button on the Standard toolbar.**

The Create Hyperlink dialog box displays (Figure 2-68).

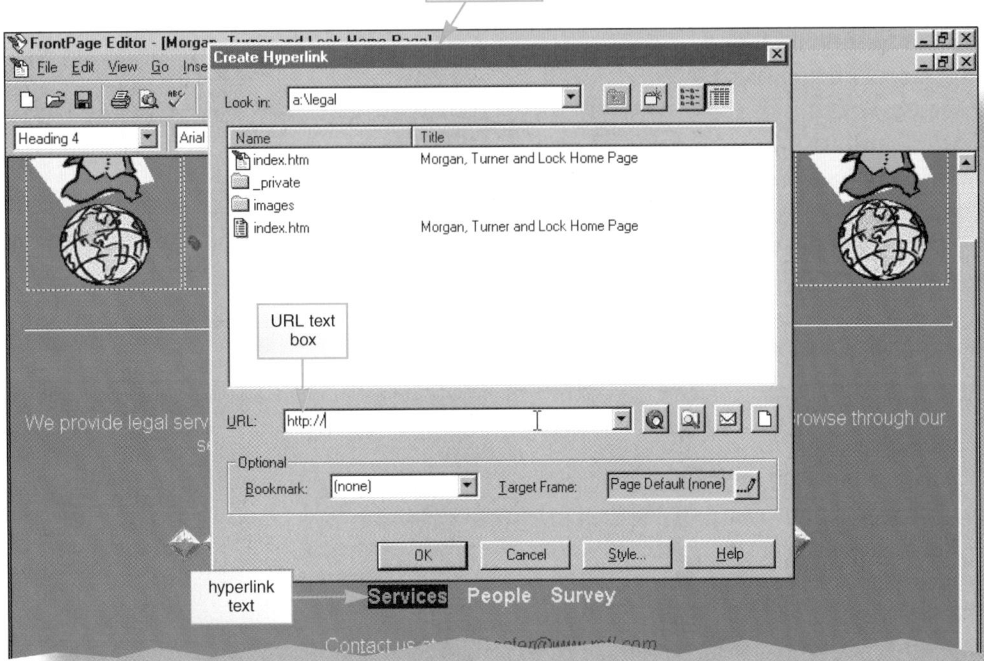

FIGURE 2-68

8 **Double-click the URL text box and then type** `services.htm` **in the text box.**

The services.htm text replaces the http:// text (Figure 2-69).

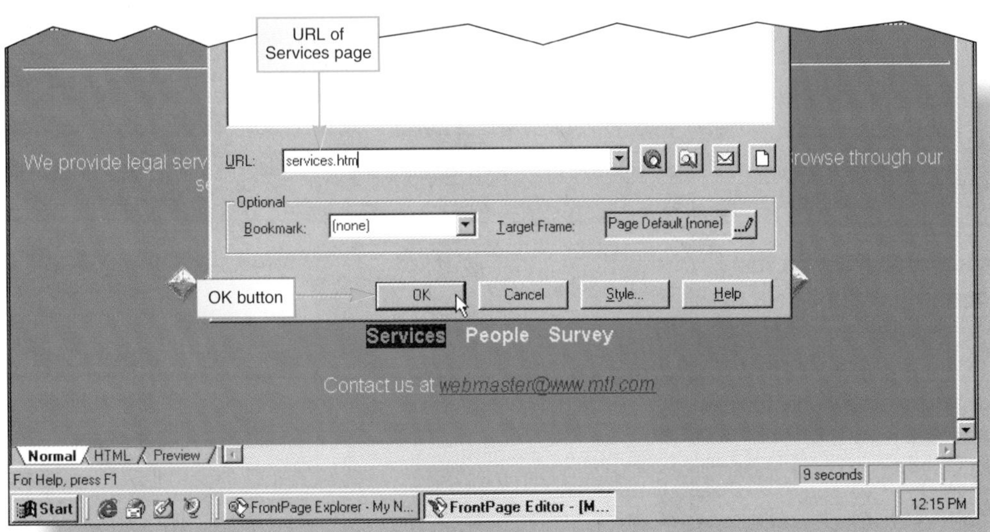

FIGURE 2-69

9 **Click the OK button. Position the mouse pointer over the Services hyperlink text.**

The services.htm URL displays on the status bar when the mouse pointer is positioned over the Services hyperlink text (Figure 2-70).

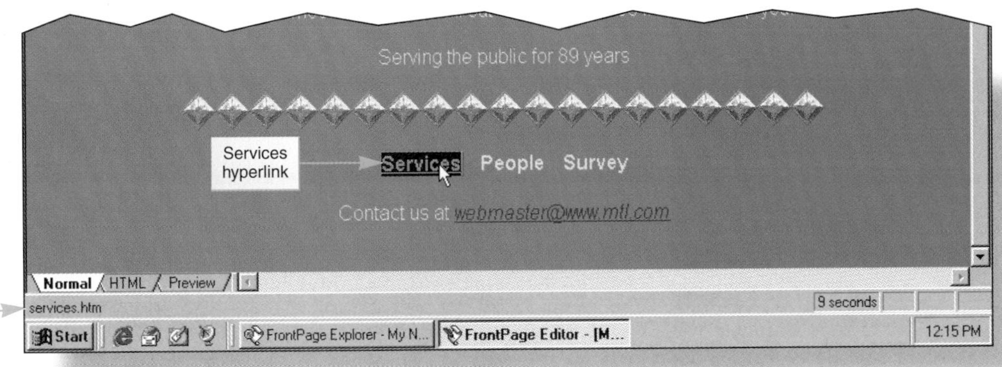

FIGURE 2-70

10 Drag through the word, People, click the Create or Edit Hyperlink button on the Standard toolbar, double-click the URL text box, type `people.htm` **in the text box, click the OK button, and then position the mouse pointer over the People hyperlink.**

The people.htm URL displays on the status bar when the mouse pointer is positioned over the People hyperlink text (Figure 2-71).

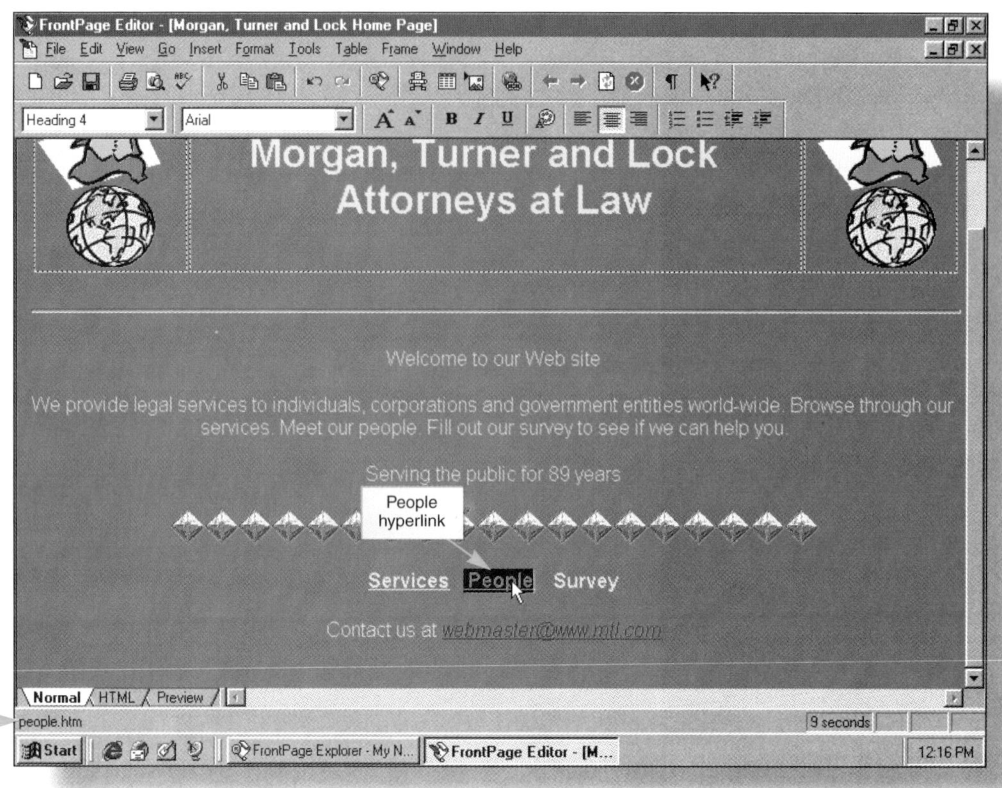

FIGURE 2-71

11 Drag through the word, Survey, click the Create or Edit Hyperlink button on the Standard toolbar, double-click the URL text box, type `survey.htm` **in the text box, click the OK button, and then position the mouse pointer over the Survey hyperlink.**

The survey.htm URL displays on the status bar when the mouse pointer is positioned over the Survey hyperlink text (Figure 2-72).

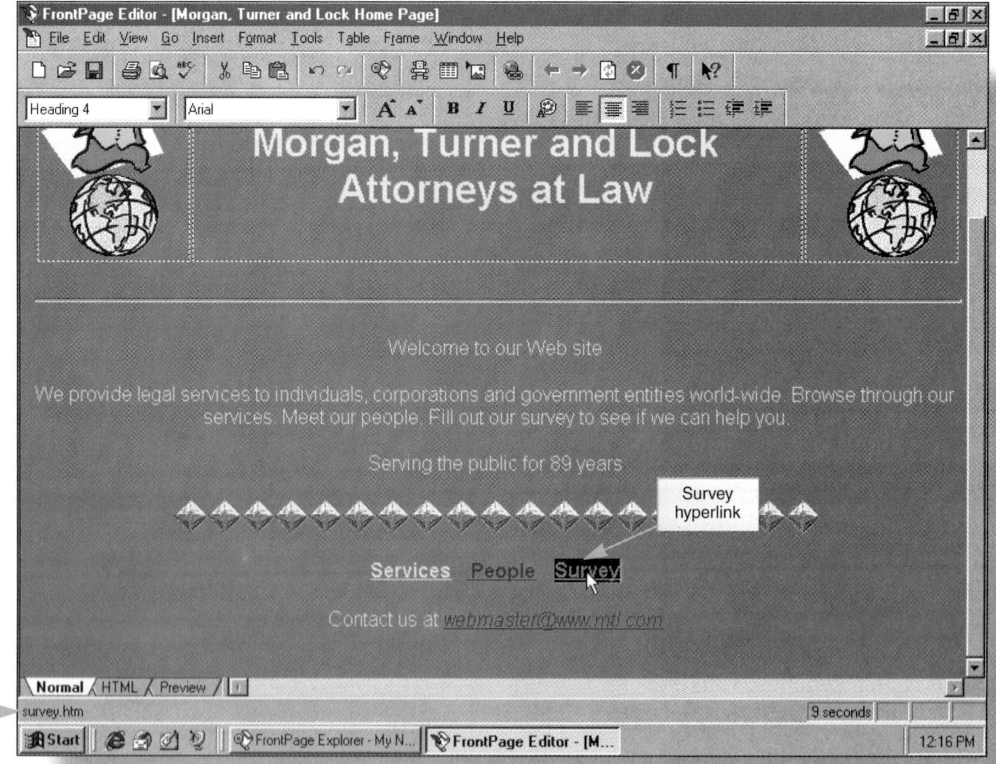

FIGURE 2-72

12 **In the sentence, Browse through our services, drag through the word, services, click the Create or Edit Hyperlink button on the Standard toolbar, double-click the URL text box, type** `services.htm` **in the text box, click the OK button, and then position the mouse pointer over the word, services.**

The services.htm URL displays on the status bar when the mouse pointer is positioned over the services hyperlink text (Figure 2-73).

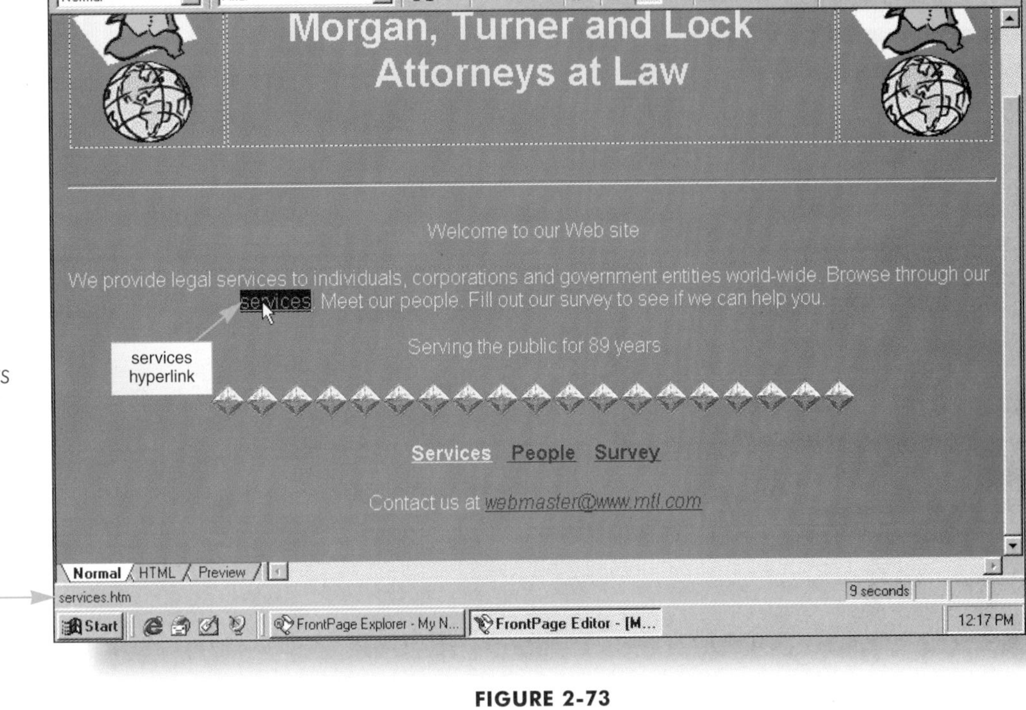

FIGURE 2-73

13 **In the sentence, Meet our people, drag through the word, people, click the Create or Edit Hyperlink button on the Standard toolbar, double-click the URL text box, type** `people.htm` **in the text box, click the OK button, and then position the mouse pointer over the word, people.**

The people.htm URL displays on the status bar when the mouse pointer is positioned over the people hyperlink text (Figure 2-74).

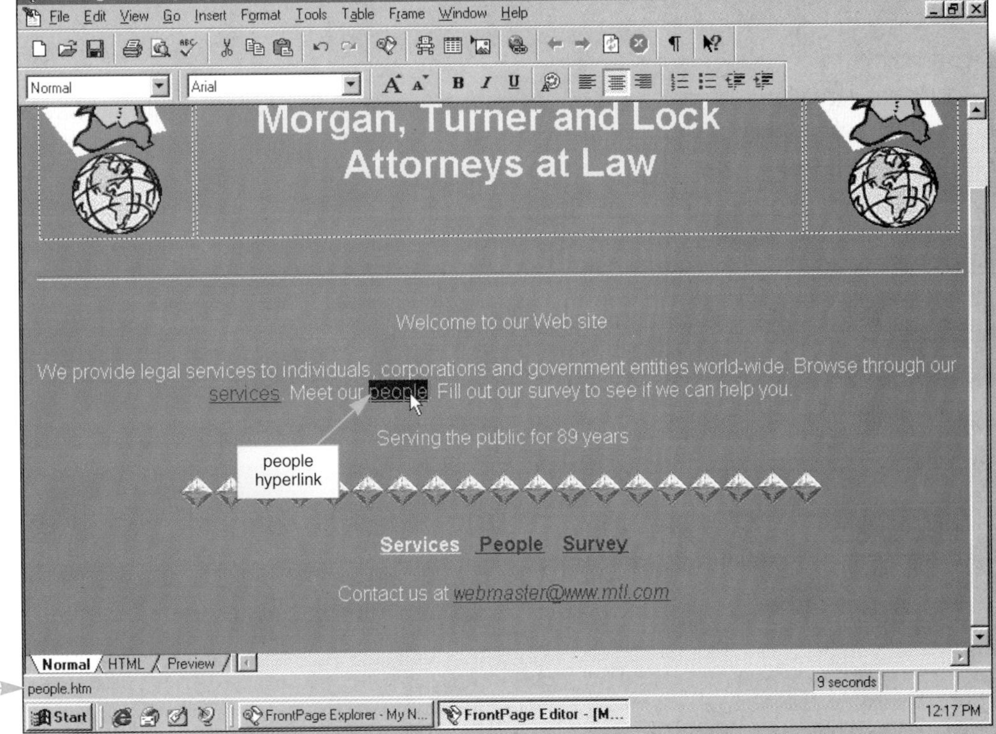

FIGURE 2-74

14 **In the sentence, Fill out our survey, drag through the word, survey, click the Create or Edit Hyperlink button on the Standard toolbar, double-click the URL text box, type** survey.htm **in the text box, click the OK button, and then position the mouse pointer over the word, survey.**

The survey.htm URL displays on the status bar when the mouse pointer is positioned over the survey hyperlink text (Figure 2-75).

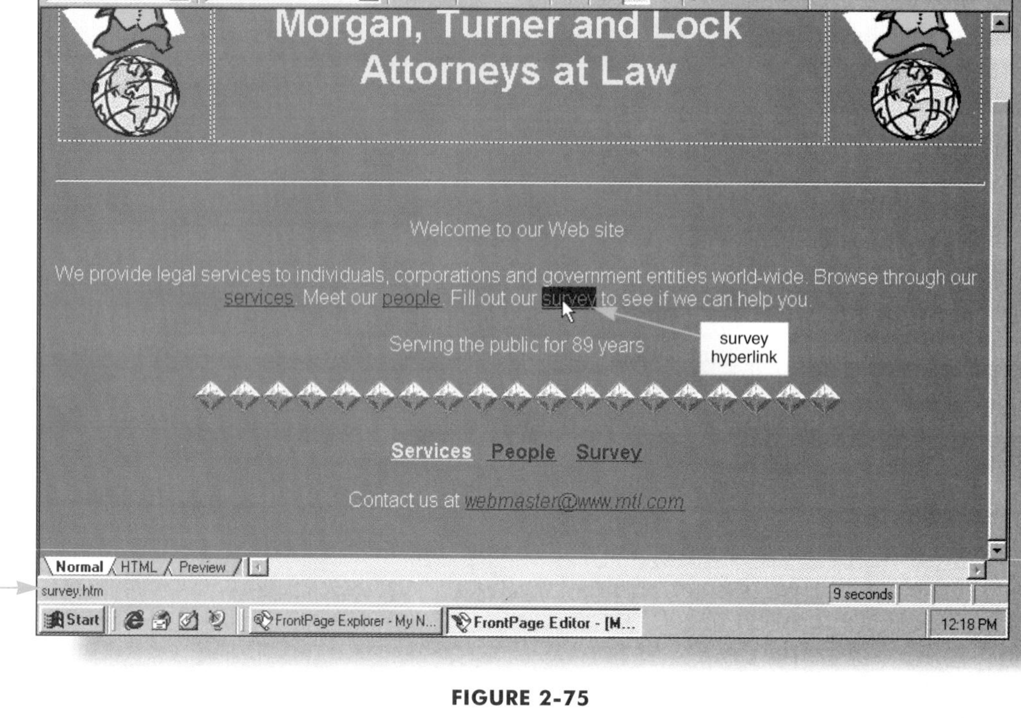

FIGURE 2-75

Other Ways

1. Highlight text, press ALT+I, K
2. Highlight text, press CTRL+K

More About

Hyperlinks

If you have many hyperlinks to place on a Web page, consider using a bulleted list to organize them. Use descriptive text for the hyperlinks.

Two sets of hyperlinks were created for each linked page: services.htm, people.htm, and survey.htm. The set of hyperlinks in the footer at the bottom of the page allow repeat visitors quick access to all the important hyperlinks in this web. Knowledgeable viewers will not have to search through all the items on the Web page to find the desired hyperlink.

The hyperlinks embedded within the text in the body of the Web page were chosen carefully from the available wording to avoid using the *click here* types of labels and allow the transparent flow from one document to the next. These elements are important to preserve good design on the Web page. The content of the linked resource is explained within the context of the sentence. First-time viewers have access to, and can click an interesting hyperlink as soon as they encounter it.

Previewing and Printing a Web Page

In Project 1, you printed the Web page without previewing it on the screen. By previewing the Web page, you can see exactly how it will look without generating a printout, or hard copy. Previewing a Web page using the Print Preview command on the File menu can save time, paper, and the frustration of waiting for a printout only to discover it is not what you want.

You also can print the Web page while in Print Preview. Perform the following steps to preview and then print the Morgan, Turner and Lock Web page.

To Preview a Web Page

1 **Ready the printer according to the printer instructions. Click File on the menu bar and then point to Print Preview (Figure 2-76).**

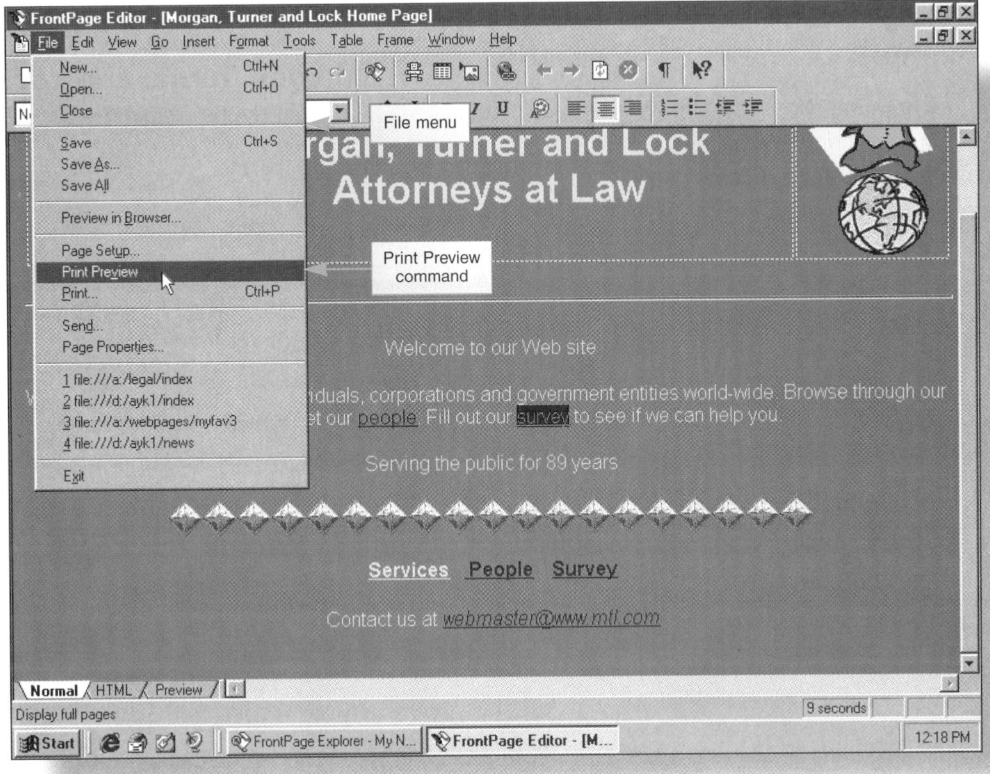

FIGURE 2-76

2 **Click Print Preview.**

FrontPage displays a preview of the Web page in the preview pane and the mouse pointer changes to a magnifying glass (Figure 2-77).

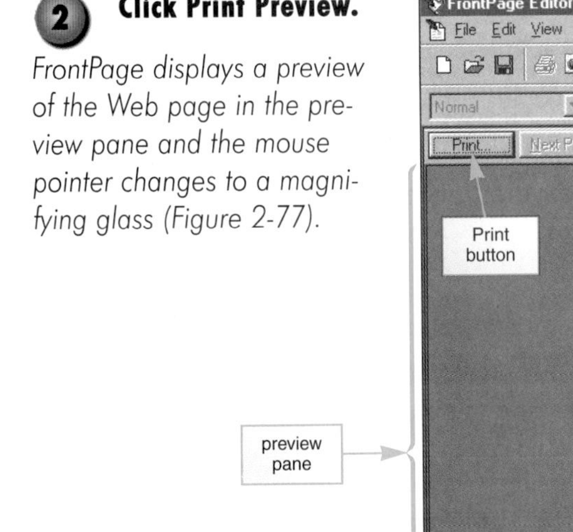

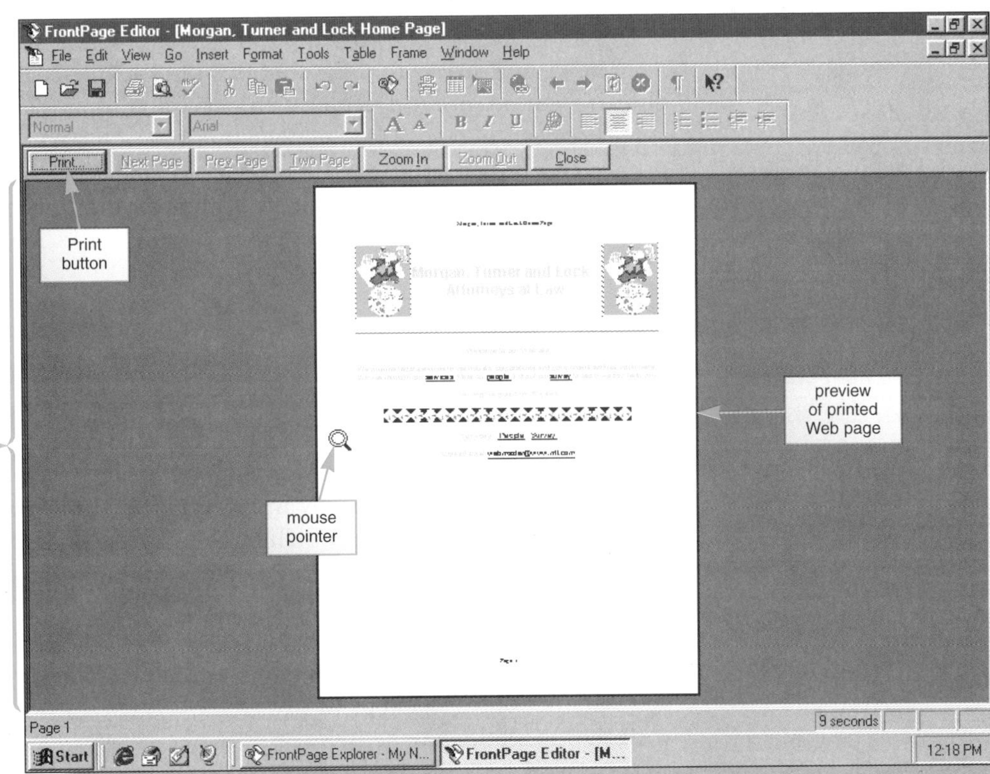

FIGURE 2-77

3 **Click the Print button on the Print Preview toolbar. Click the OK button in the Print dialog box.**

The preview pane closes and the Web page prints. When the printing operation is complete, retrieve the printout (Figure 2-78).

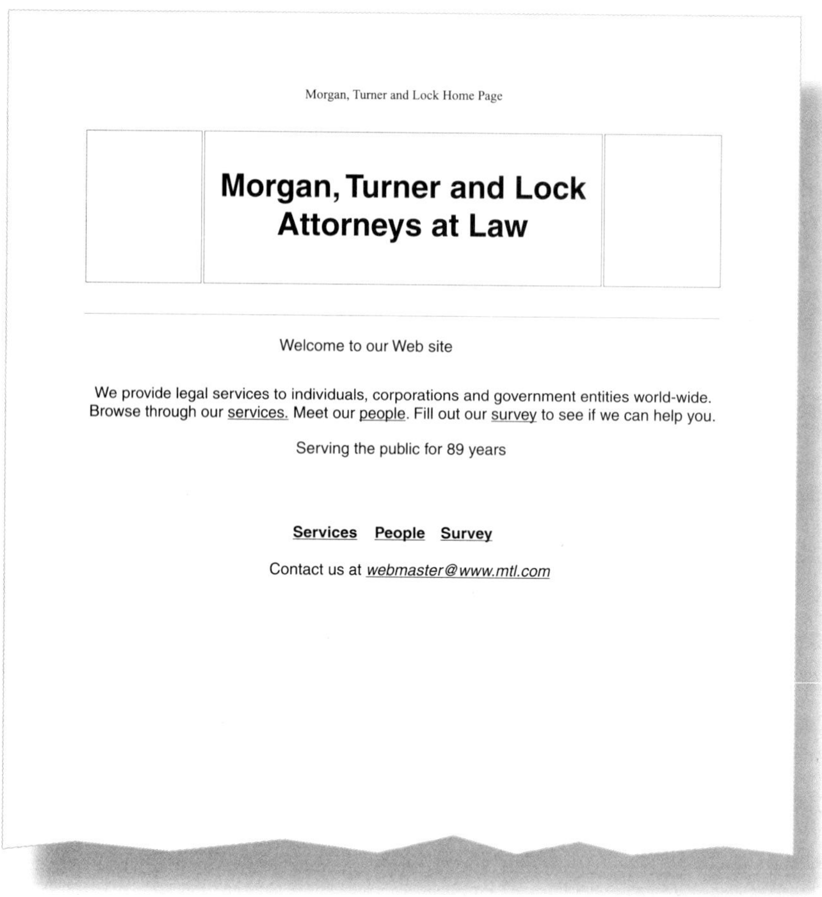

FIGURE 2-78

Other Ways

1. Press ALT+F, V

The Print Preview toolbar contains buttons to scroll through a multipage printout, to zoom in and out of the Web page, and to close the preview pane. You can use Print Preview to determine the page number of a particular page in a multipage printout, and then print only that page. This allows you to print only that section of a long Web page you are working on, thus saving time and paper.

More About

Saving Web Pages

The FrontPage Editor does not prompt for a file name when saving. You can choose a different file name by using the Save As command on the File menu.

Saving the Web Page

Once you have finished editing the Web page you should save it on disk. With the Morgan, Turner and Lock Home page, the save operation consists of saving the HTML and the clip art images for the Web page. The clip art images you inserted in earlier steps were not physically inserted in the Home page. The FrontPage Editor placed HTML instructions to include the clip art image files using an <img src=> tag. This tag has a reference to the file name containing the clip art image, but it still must be saved with the Web page.

When the Web page is saved, it contains only the HTML tags referencing the file. The FrontPage Editor will save the image files in the web folders on drive A as well. Perform the following steps to save the Morgan, Turner and Lock Home page, along with the embedded image files.

To Save a Web Page

1 Click the Save button on the Standard toolbar.

The Save Embedded Files dialog box displays (Figure 2-79). This dialog box shows the file names of the clip art images you inserted in the Web page.

2 Click the OK button.

The Morgan, Turner and Lock Home page and the clip art image files are saved on the floppy disk in drive A.

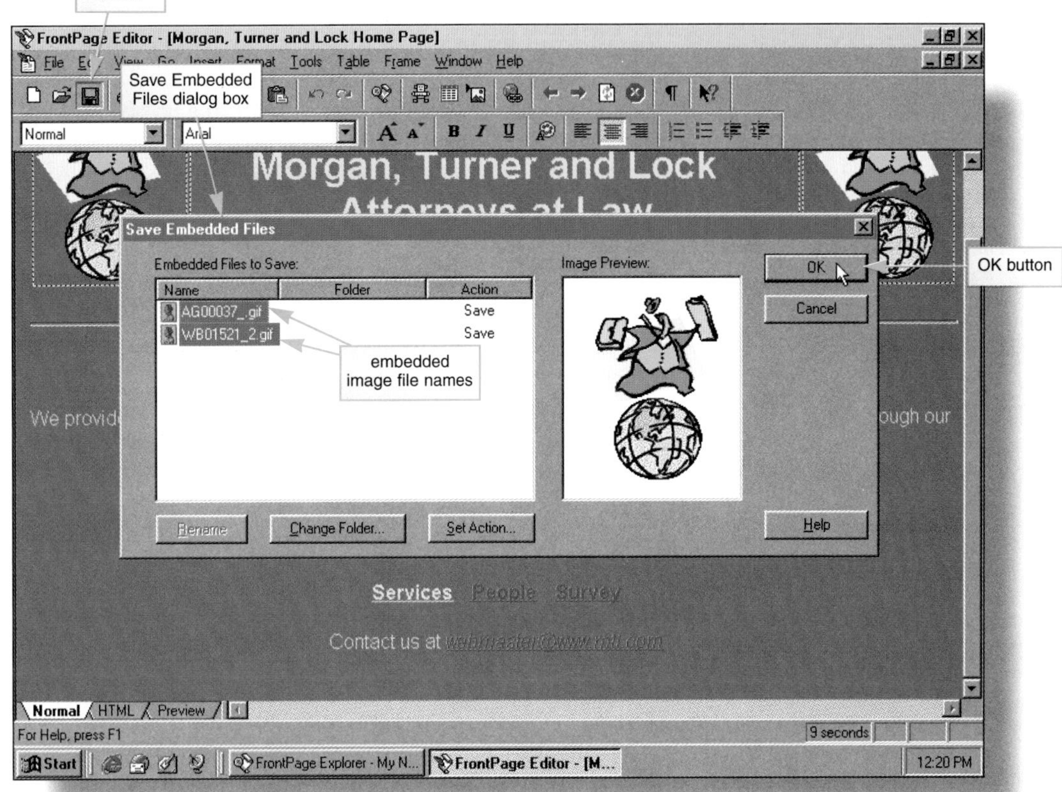

FIGURE 2-79

Other Ways

1. On File menu click Save
2. Press ALT+F, S
3. Press CTRL+S

It is important that the clip art images are saved as part of the FrontPage Web. These image files must be available when publishing the FrontPage web to a Web server. If you do not save them, and then publish the FrontPage web, those <img src=> tags will be broken because the files referenced by the tags will not be on the Web server. Then, the Web page will not display properly.

Quitting the FrontPage Editor

Once the Web page is saved, you can quit the FrontPage Editor. The step to quit is summarized below.

TO QUIT THE MICROSOFT FRONTPAGE EDITOR

Click the Close button on the FrontPage Editor title bar.

The FrontPage Editor window closes and the FrontPage Explorer window displays.

Publishing

If you are given a specific folder on the Web server to publish your web, create subfolders below the top-level folder. Publishing individual Webs in their own folders eases the management of the files and folders that make up each web.

Publishing the Web Page

Recall from Project 1 that publishing a Web page is the process of sending copies of Web pages, image files, multimedia files, and any other files and folders to a Web server where they then become available to the World Wide Web. With FrontPage, you can publish your Web by clicking a single button.

You can publish the Morgan, Turner and Lock Home page using the steps listed below. The People, Services, and Survey Web pages in the Morgan, Turner and Lock FrontPage web do not yet exist, however, and those are indicated as hyperlinks on the Home page to other Web pages.

If you publish the Home page, individuals viewing the Home page will encounter errors if they click any hyperlink except the e-mail hyperlink. This might cause viewers to get a bad impression of the company. Therefore, it is best to wait until all the other pages in the web on which you are working are completed before publishing the Web. The following steps summarize how to publish the Morgan, Turner and Lock web. As discussed in Project 1 on page FP 1.7, be sure to substitute your own URL, or an error will occur. If you do not know what URL to use, ask your instructor.

To Publish the FrontPage Web

1 Click the Publish button on the Standard toolbar. If the Microsoft Web Publishing Wizard dialog box displays, click the Cancel button.

The Publish dialog box displays (Figure 2-80).

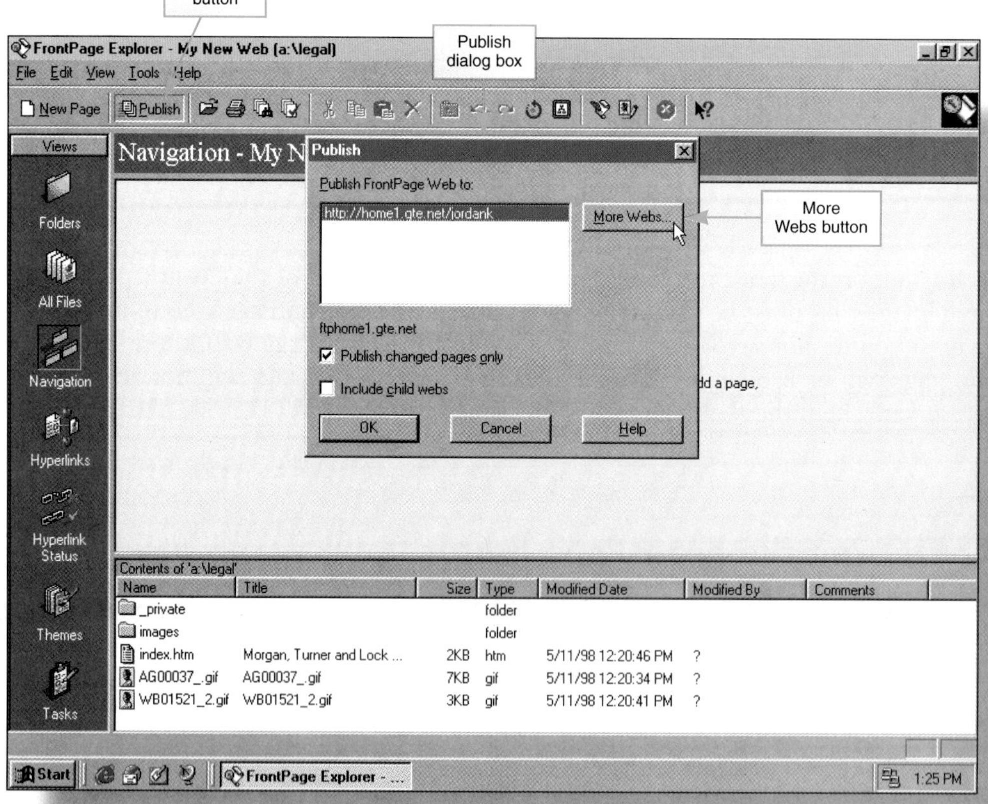

FIGURE 2-80

2 **Click the More Webs button.**

The Publish FrontPage Web dialog box displays (Figure 2-81).

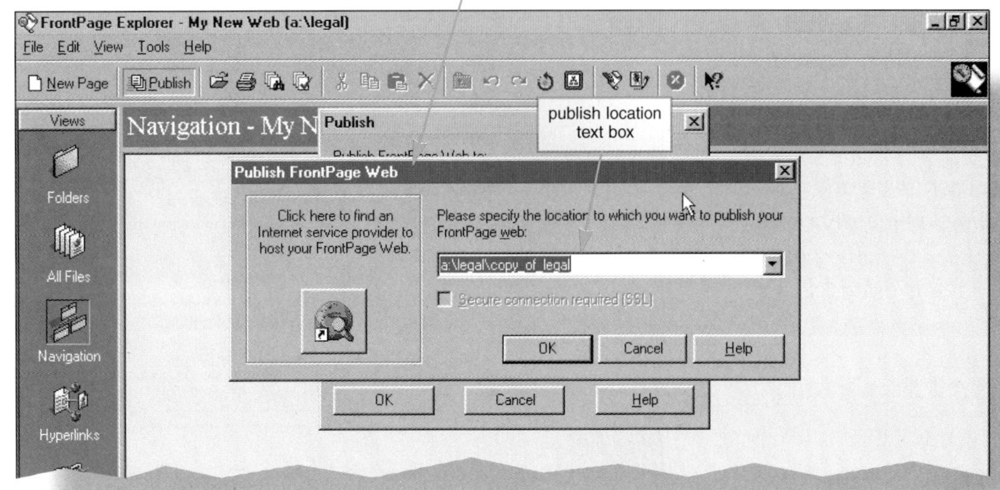

FIGURE 2-81

3 **Type** `http://home1.gte.net/jordank/legal` **in the publish location text box (substitute your own URL or an error will occur).**

The destination URL displays in the text box (Figure 2-82).

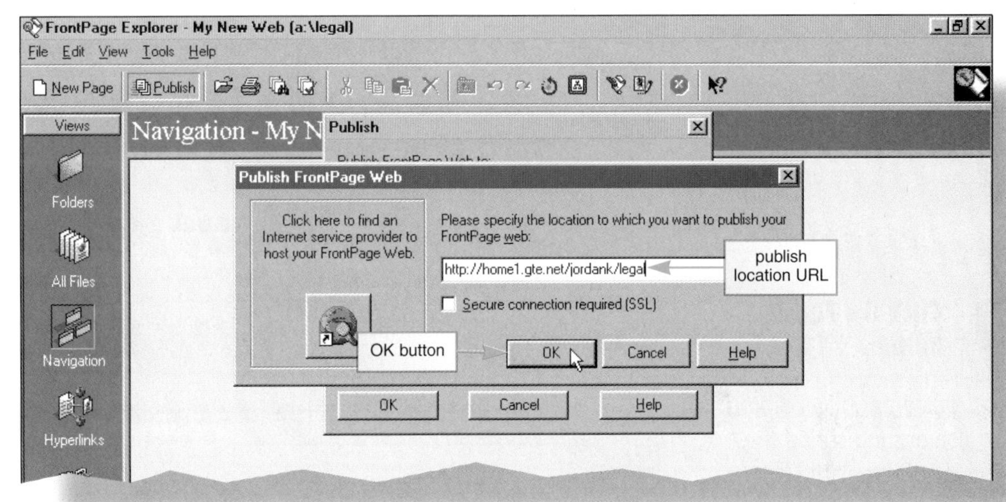

FIGURE 2-82

4 **Click the OK button in the FrontPage Web dialog box. Type** `ftphome1.gte.net` **in the FTP Server Name text box (substitute your own FTP server name or an error will occur). Type** `legal` **in the Directory Path text box.**

The Microsoft Web Publishing Wizard dialog box displays (Figure 2-83). The FTP server name and folder name display in the text boxes.

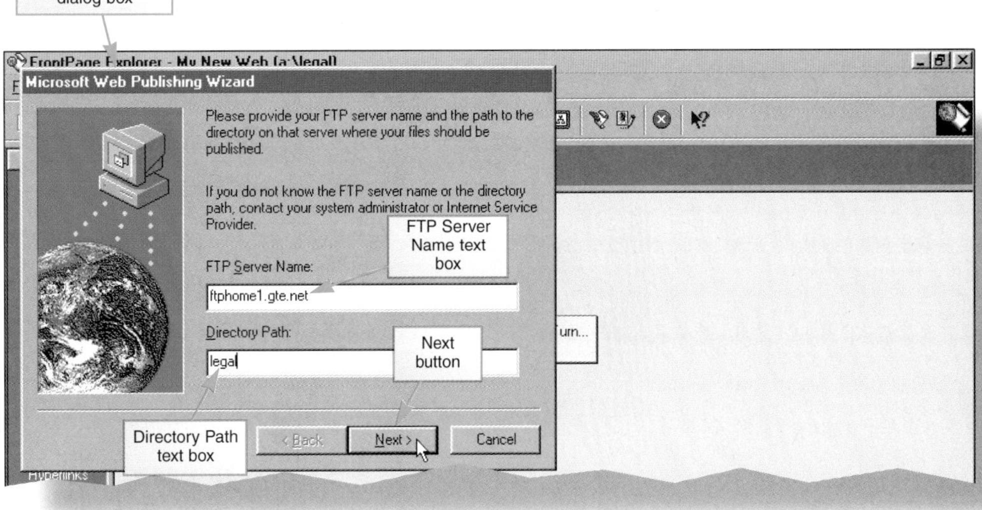

FIGURE 2-83

5 **Click the Next button. Type your FTP user name and password in the text boxes.**

The user name and password display in the text boxes (Figure 2-84). The password displays as asterisks.

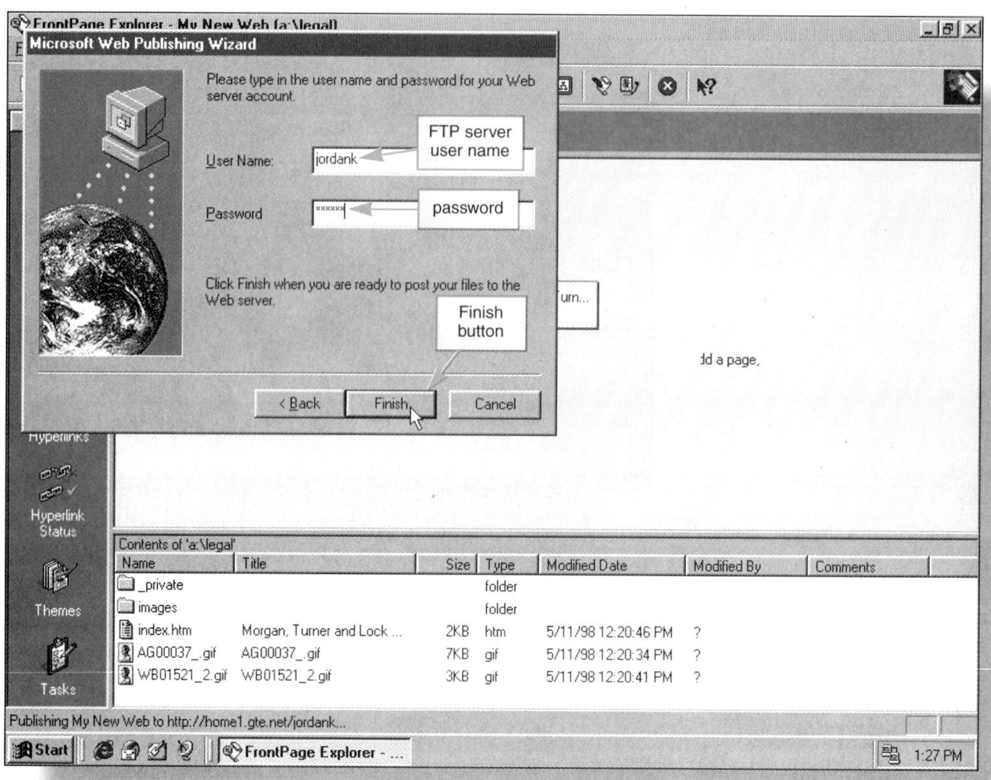

FIGURE 2-84

6 **Click the Finish button.**

The Transferring Files dialog box displays indicating the status of the transfer (Figure 2-85). When the transfer is complete, the dialog box closes and the FrontPage Explorer window redisplays.

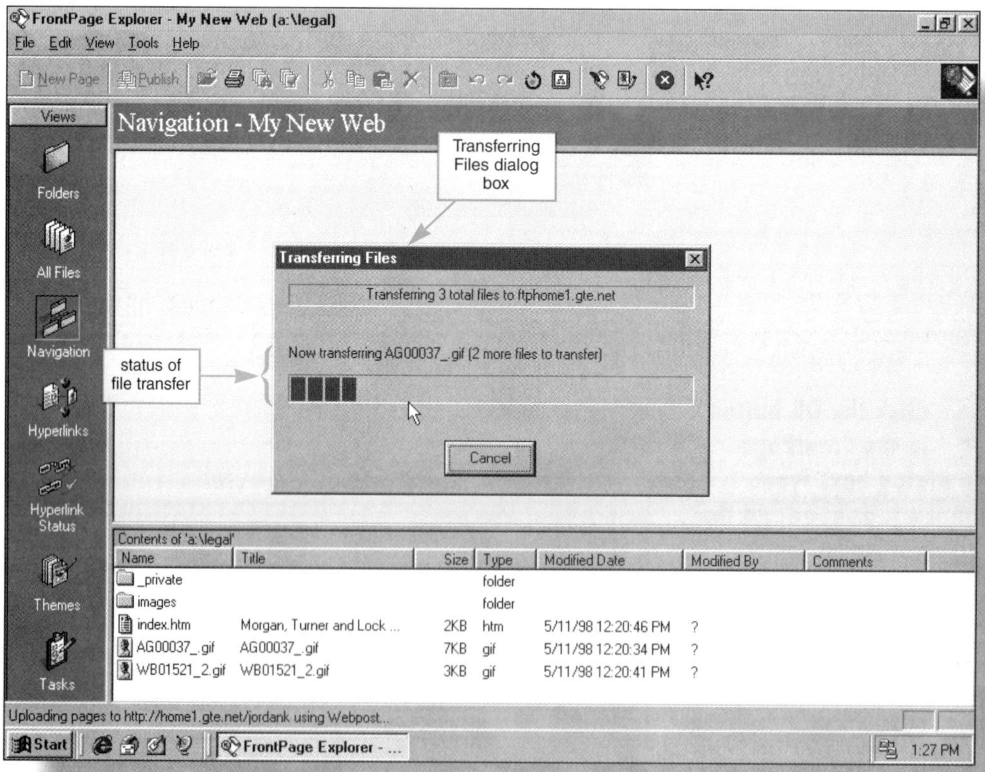

FIGURE 2-85

You now can view the Morgan, Turner and Lock Home page by entering http://home1.gte.net/jordank/legal in any browser and then pressing the ENTER key.

Quitting Microsoft FrontPage

When you have published the Morgan, Turner and Lock web, you can quit Microsoft FrontPage. The step for quitting is summarized below.

TO QUIT MICROSOFT FRONTPAGE

If necessary, click the Close button on the FrontPage Editor title bar. Click the Close button on the FrontPage Explorer title bar.

The FrontPage Explorer window closes and the Windows desktop displays.

Project Summary

The partners of the Morgan, Turner and Lock law firm are happy with the Web page you developed. In creating the Home page, you gained knowledge of HTML basics and Microsoft FrontPage. Project 2 introduced you to essential Web page development. You learned about good design criteria. With these tools, you created a new, one-page web providing your own original content, and then you changed the background of the Web page. You inserted a table and adjusted the table properties. Using appropriate images, you inserted clip art to enhance the appearance of the Web page. Then, you added text and learned how to change formats such as style, font size, color, and alignment. Next, you inserted horizontal rules. You learned how to select items carefully for use as hyperlinks, and then you previewed your Web page before printing. Finally, you saved a Web page along with the embedded image files.

What You Should Know

Having completed this project, you now should be able to perform the following tasks:

- Add a Heading to a Web Page *(FP 2.31)*
- Add a Horizontal Rule to a Web Page *(FP 2.34)*
- Add Normal Text to a Web Page *(FP 2.35)*
- Adjust Table Cell Borders *(FP 2.27)*
- Align Items on the Web Page *(FP 2.26)*
- Change the Background Color *(FP 2.14)*
- Change the Title of a Web Page *(FP 2.12)*
- Copy and Paste an Image on a Web Page *(FP 2.24)*
- Create a New One-page Web *(FP 2.9)*
- Edit the Web Page *(FP 2.14)*
- Insert a Clip Art Image in a Web Page *(FP 2.21)*
- Insert a Hyperlink in a Web Page *(FP 2.42)*
- Insert a Table in a Web Page *(FP 2.18)*
- Insert an Image as a Horizontal Rule *(FP 2.39)*
- Preview a Web Page *(FP 2.49)*
- Publish the FrontPage Web *(FP 2.52)*
- Quit Microsoft FrontPage *(FP 2.55)*
- Quit the Microsoft FrontPage Editor *(FP 2.51)*
- Save a Web Page *(FP 2.51)*
- Start FrontPage 98 *(FP 2.9)*
- Turn Off the Table Border *(FP 2.29)*

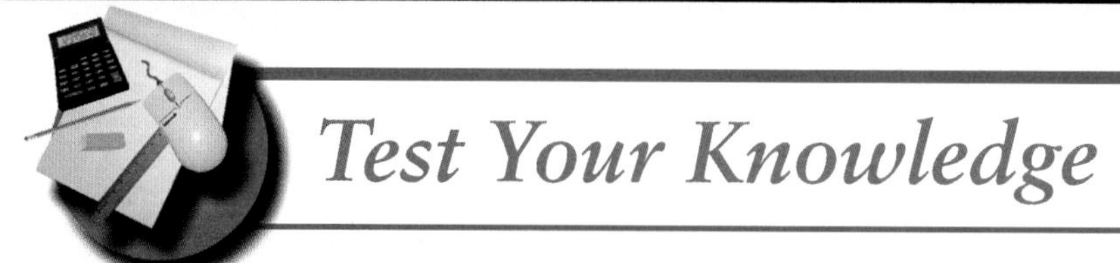

Test Your Knowledge

1 True/False

Instructions: Circle T if the statement is true or F if the statement is false.

T F 1. Two phases to Web page development are design and implementation.
T F 2. A typical Web page is composed of three sections: a header, the body, and a trailer.
T F 3. You can change the title of a Web page by right-clicking the title in the FrontPage Editor title bar.
T F 4. The background of a Web page can be a solid color, an image, or a pattern.
T F 5. You use HTML tables to arrange information that only looks best in rows and columns.
T F 6. FrontPage comes with a library of ready-to-use images, called snip art.
T F 7. The Clipboard is a temporary storage area in the computer's memory.
T F 8. You can apply special formatting such as different fonts, colors, and sizes to images on a Web page.
T F 9. Tables are crucial to Web page development – the Web would not exist without them.
T F 10. By previewing a Web page, you can see exactly how it will look without generating a printout, or hard copy.

2 Multiple Choice

Instructions: Circle the correct response.

1. __________ can contain rules, guidelines, tips, and templates that assist in creating Web pages.
   a. HTML browsers
   b. Web guides
   c. Style guides
   d. HTML standards
2. You can change the title of a Web page by right-clicking the __________.
   a. page icon
   b. title bar
   c. Web page background
   d. title HTML
3. The background of a Web page can be a(n) __________.
   a. solid color
   b. image
   c. pattern
   d. all of the above
4. The intersection of a row and column in a table is called a(n) __________.
   a. intersection
   b. cell
   c. element
   d. entry

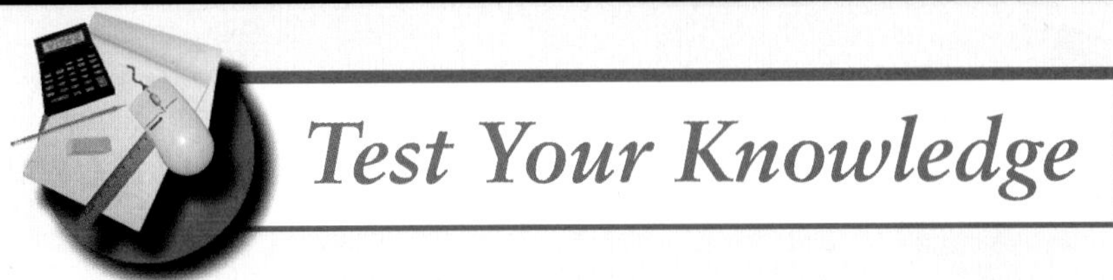

Test Your Knowledge

5. With the Undo and Redo buttons, you can reverse or apply the last __________ changes.
   a. 5
   b. 10
   c. 20
   d. 30
6. The __________ of tables can be adjusted to control spacing on the Web page.
   a. number of columns
   b. number of rows
   c. depth
   d. borders
7. Text on a Web page can take the form of __________.
   a. normal text
   b. menus
   c. unordered lists
   d. all of the above
8. __________ are used to break up the Web page into sections.
   a. Headings
   b. Horizontal rules
   c. Tables
   d. Blank spaces
9. By previewing a Web page, you can see exactly how it will look without __________.
   a. publishing the Web
   b. generating a printout
   c. implementing the Web page design
   d. editing the Web page
10. FrontPage places HTML instructions to include the image files using a(n) __________.
    a. <img src=> tag
    b. <clip art=> tag
    c. <src img=> tag
    d. <image=> tag

3 Understanding the Format Toolbar

Instructions: In Figure 2-86 on the next page, arrows point to several buttons on the Format toolbar. In the spaces provided, briefly explain the purpose of each button.

(continued)

Understanding the Format Toolbar *(continued)*

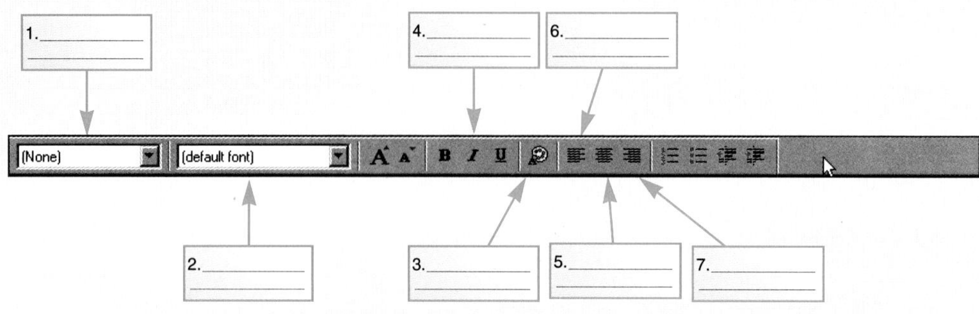

FIGURE 2-86

4 Understanding Good Web Page Design Criteria

Instructions: Listed below are criteria for good Web page design. In the spaces provided, write at least two guidelines for each item that, if followed, would improve a typical Web page design.

1. Authentication ______________________________
2. Aesthetics ______________________________
3. Performance ______________________________
4. Consistency ______________________________
5. Validity ______________________________
6. Images ______________________________
7. Hyperlinks ______________________________
8. External Files ______________________________

1 Using FrontPage Help

Instructions: Start FrontPage 98 and perform the following tasks with a computer.

1. Click the Cancel button in the Getting Started dialog box.
2. Click Help on the menu bar and then click Microsoft FrontPage Help.
3. On the Contents sheet, double-click the Using FrontPage book and then double-click the Working With Tables book (Figure 2-87).

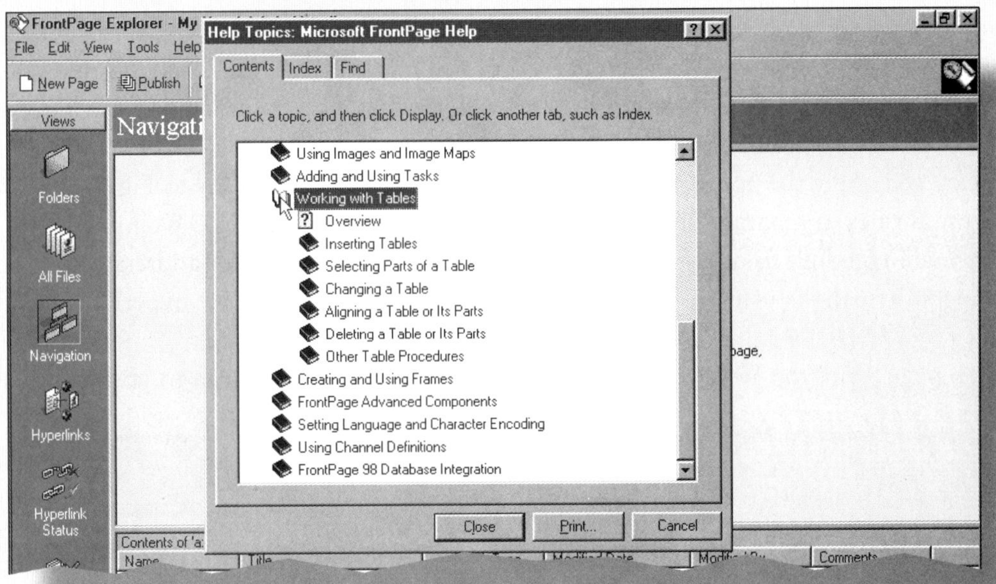

FIGURE 2-87

4. Read through the Help information on tables to find out how to set the background color of a table.
5. Write a brief explanation of how to set the background color of an HTML table, and hand it in to your instructor.

2 Using FrontPage Online Help

Instructions: Start FrontPage 98 and perform the following tasks with a computer.

1. Click the Cancel button in the Getting Started dialog box.
2. Click Help on the menu bar and click Microsoft on the Web.
3. On the FrontPage 98 Home Page – Microsoft Internet Explorer, click the Solutions & Resources hyperlink.
4. On the Solutions & Resources Web page, select one of the topics and explore the pages.
5. Write a brief report of what you found, including items such as hyperlinks to other resources, downloadable files, images, or software, and tips and techniques.

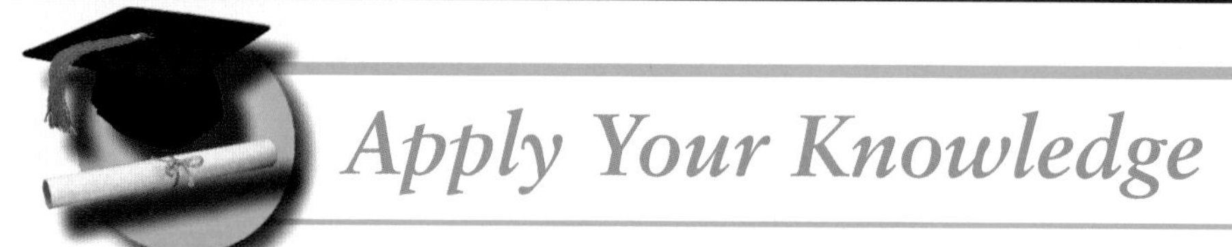

1 Creating a Web Page

Instructions: The See-Food Restaurant Home page is shown in Figure 2-88 as it would appear in a Web browser. Perform the following activities to create the See-Food Restaurant Home page.

1. Start FrontPage and create a new one-page web.
2. Change the title of the Home page to *See-Food Restaurant Home Page*.
3. Edit the Home page.
4. Select an appropriate background color for the Web page.
5. Insert a one row, two column table in the Web page.
6. Insert a clip art image with an appropriate seafood or restaurant theme into the left table cell.
7. Adjust the table properties so the table border does not show and the middle border is adjacent to the right side of the clip art image inserted in step 6.
8. Insert the text, and apply the appropriate formatting so the text looks similar to Figure 2-88. Select appropriate horizontal rules to separate the header and footer from the body of the Web page.
9. Create the e-mail hyperlink using webchef@www.see-food.com as the e-mail address.
10. Create the menu hyperlinks using menu.htm for the URL. Create the delivery hyperlinks using delivery.htm as the URL.
11. Save the Web page. Print the Web page, write your name on it, and hand it in to your instructor.

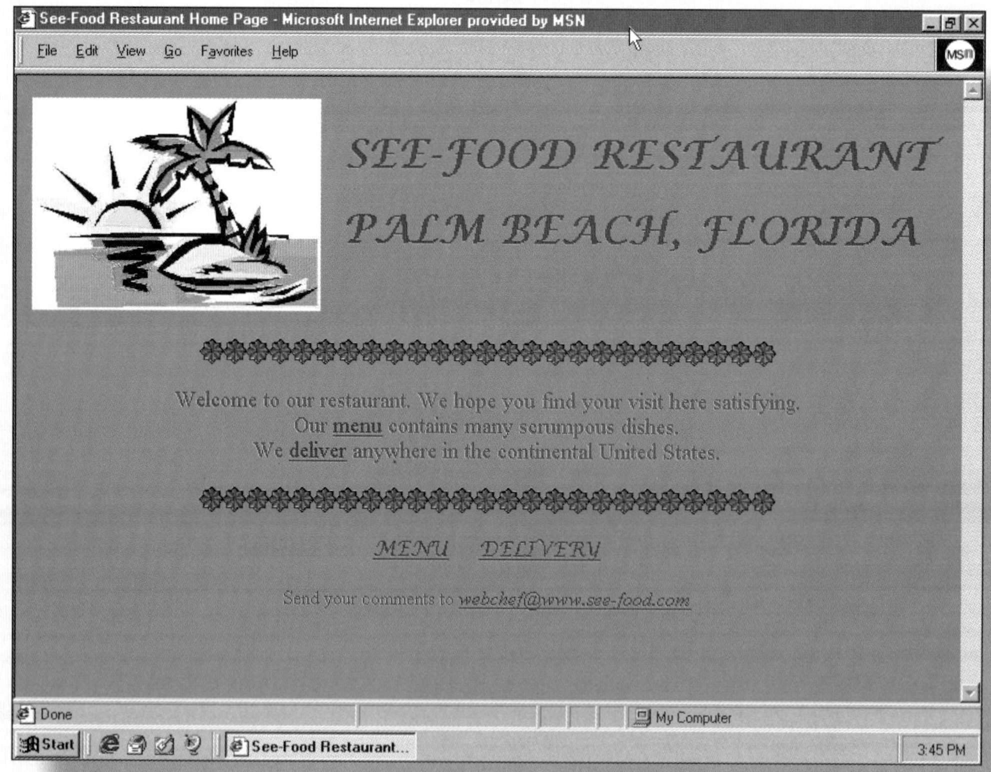

FIGURE 2-88

In the Lab

1 Creating a Table

Instructions: Start FrontPage 98 and perform the following steps with a computer.

1. Create a new one-page web. Edit the Home page.
2. Set the style to Heading 1. Type `Table 1` and then center the heading.
3. Insert a six-row, four-column table in the Web page.
4. Using the following data, populate the table cells with the proper text.

	EASTERN REGION	CENTRAL REGION	WESTERN REGION
January	2345.44	1120.33	1436.33
February	5400.00	1923.23	1212.33
March	2343.22	1232.10	1124.54
April	2345.60	1750.50	1656.35
May	5453.33	1654.90	1910.50

5. Adjust the borders to tighten up any unused space within the cells, and then center the table in the Web page. (*Hint*: Use the Table Properties dialog box.)
6. Print the Web page, write your name on it, and hand it in to your instructor.

2 Using a Pattern as a Web Page Background

Instructions: Start FrontPage 98 and perform the following steps with a computer.

1. Create a new one-page web.
2. In the FrontPage Editor, click Format on the menu bar and then click Background.
3. If necessary, click the Background tab when the Page Properties dialog box displays. Click Specify Background and Colors and then click Background Image.
4. Click the Browse button and then click the Clip Art button.
5. Scroll down to the bottom of the categories list box until Web Backgrounds displays. Click Web Backgrounds.
6. Browse through the available backgrounds until you find one you like. Double-click the sample background image.
7. Click the OK button. The background pattern you selected should display in the FrontPage Editor (Figure 2-89 on the next page).
8. Click the HTML tab to display the HTML source, and then click the Print button on the Standard toolbar.
9. Write your name on the printout, circle the body HTML tag containing the background parameter, and hand it in to your instructor.

(continued)

Using a Pattern as a Web Page Background (continued)

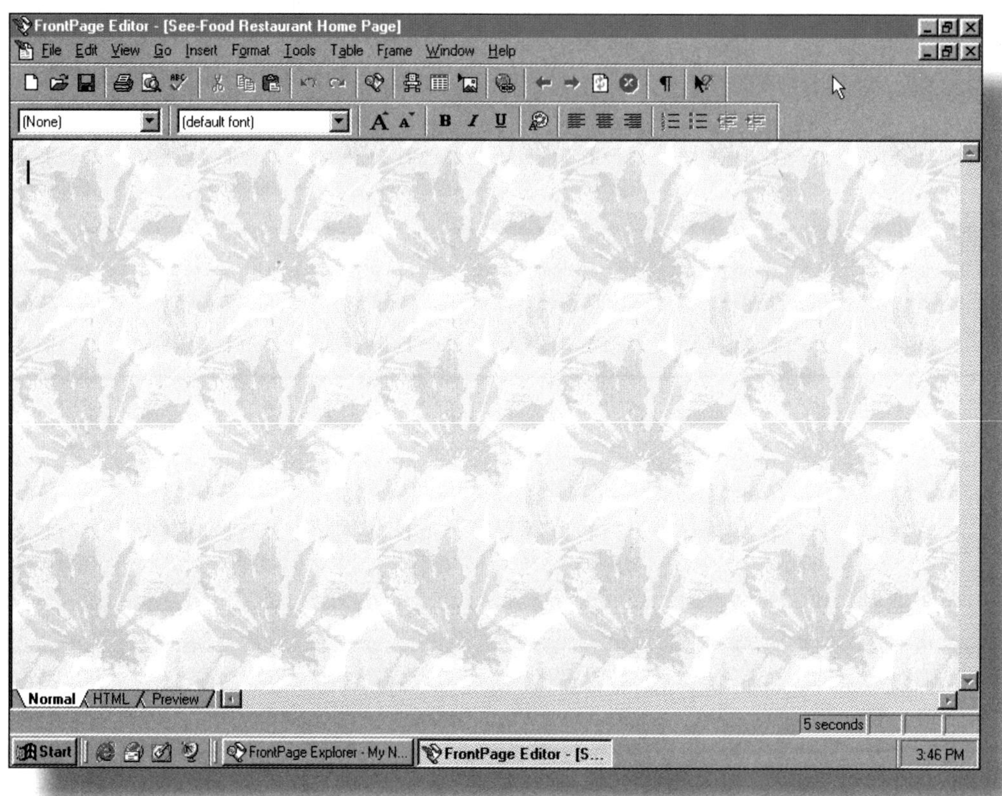

FIGURE 2-89

3 Formatting Text

Instructions: Start FrontPage 98 and perform the following steps with a computer.

1. Create a new one-page web.
2. Enter the following text. Be sure to carry out the formatting indicated by each line (Figure 2-90).
```
This line has a style of Heading 1.
This line is normal, italic text.
This line is Times New Roman, normal blue text.
This line is right-aligned, normal text.
This line is centered and has a style of Heading 4.
```
3. Click the HTML tab to display the HTML source and then print the Web page.
4. Write your name on the printout and hand it in to your instructor.

In the Lab

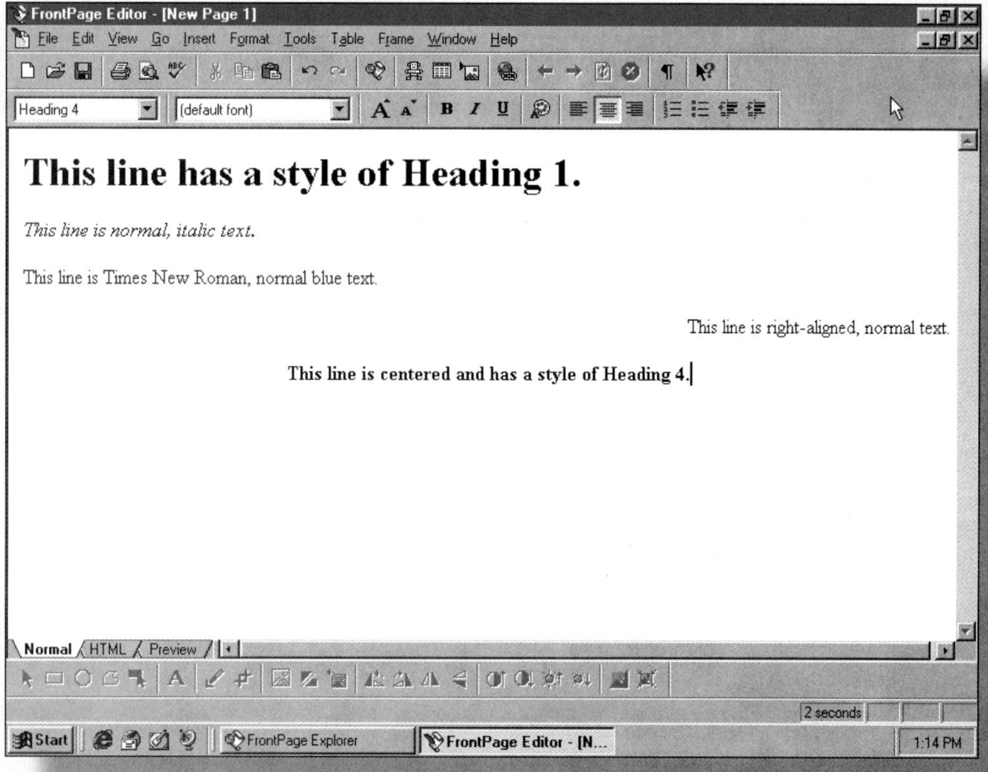
FrontPage Editor - [New Page 1]
This line has a style of Heading 1.
This line is normal, italic text.
This line is Times New Roman, normal blue text.
This line is right-aligned, normal text.
This line is centered and has a style of Heading 4.

FIGURE 2-90

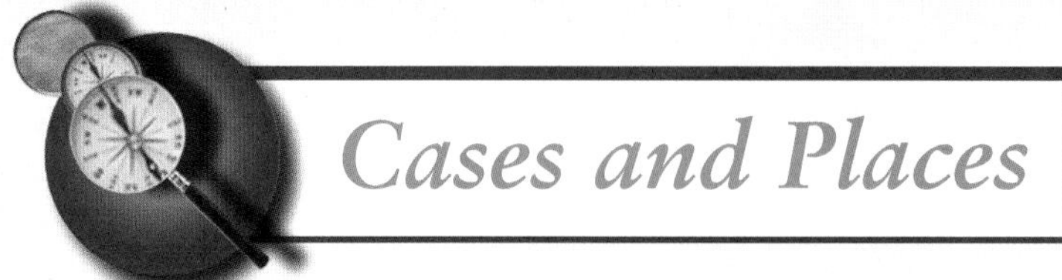

Cases and Places

The difficulty of these case studies varies:
▶ are the least difficult; ▶▶ are more difficult; and ▶▶▶ are the most difficult.

1 ▶ You want to create your own personal Web page of clip art images, arranged in a table. Use one of the Web search engines to find sources of free Web page clip art. Copy and paste at least nine clip art images onto your own page. Add a header and footer to the page. Publish the page if you have access to a Web server.

2 ▶ Many companies that offer Web-related products and services sponsor awards programs for the *best* Web pages. Search for one of these award-winning pages or *Best of the Web* sites. Print one of the award-winning pages. On the back of the printout, list the good design criteria that you think won it the award.

3 ▶ Many companies that offer Web-related products and services sponsor awards programs for the *worst* Web pages. Search for one of these *Worst of the Web* sites. Print one of the worst pages. On the back of the printout, write a list of the good design criteria that you think would improve the page.

4 ▶▶ Many sites on the World Wide Web offer libraries of images such as buttons, dividers, and background patterns for use with Web pages. Using the Web search engine of your choice, search for four or five sites that have such libraries of images. Print one page from each site containing samples of the images.

5 ▶▶ Many times, the information that will be placed in a table on a Web page already exists in some type of electronic format – a text document or a spreadsheet. FrontPage has facilities for loading data into a table on a Web page. Using FrontPage Help, find out how to convert existing text into a table.

6 ▶▶▶ You are starting a business and want to create a Home page introducing your business and its services. Create a Home page for your business that incorporates tables, clip art images, background, and text, without violating any of the good design criteria. Publish the page if you have access to a Web server.

7 ▶▶▶ Find a local business or organization that does not have a Web page. Research information about that organization. Build a Home page for that organization.

Microsoft FrontPage 98

Using Graphics and Images in Web Page Design

OBJECTIVES

You will have mastered the material in this project when you can:

- Add a new page to a FrontPage web
- Set up a background image
- Display the Image toolbar
- Washout an image
- Copy and paste from another Web page
- Insert an image from the World Wide Web into a Web page
- Resize an image
- Make a color in an image transparent
- Create an image map
- Add a hotspot to an image map
- Highlight hotspots
- Specify targets of an image map hotspot
- Insert a JPEG image on a Web page
- Create a thumbnail image
- Display the hyperlinks in a FrontPage web

World Wide Web Marketing

on the Electronic Silk Road

Traveling from one exciting Web site to the next can make you feel like a merchant-explorer in a new online world. Every site leads to countless new ones, all brimming with the riches of information, ideas, knowledge, and news. In today's fast-paced World Wide Web, the word is *marketing*. Web sites are used to attract and keep customers interested, providing a new route for communication and commerce.

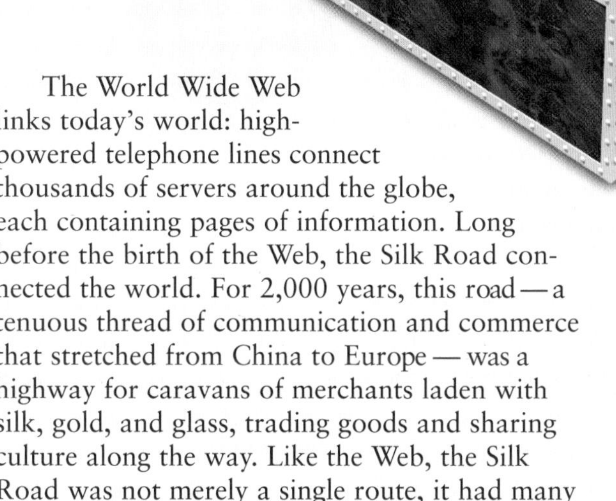

The World Wide Web links today's world: high-powered telephone lines connect thousands of servers around the globe, each containing pages of information. Long before the birth of the Web, the Silk Road connected the world. For 2,000 years, this road — a tenuous thread of communication and commerce that stretched from China to Europe — was a highway for caravans of merchants laden with silk, gold, and glass, trading goods and sharing culture along the way. Like the Web, the Silk Road was not merely a single route, it had many different branches that connected different towns.

Tim Berners-Lee, the father of the Web, was the first to travel the hyperlinks of the Web. While working at CERN, the European Particle Physics Laboratory in Switzerland in the 1980s, Berners-Lee wrote a program called Enquire, which stored information using random associations and used hypertext to move around the Internet. In 1989, Berners-Lee proposed the Web, and travel on the Web was underway.

Today, all you need is a modem, an Internet service provider, and a Web browser, and you are ready to explore this electronic Silk Road. Your Web browser is your golden tablet, providing passage between linked sites all over the world.

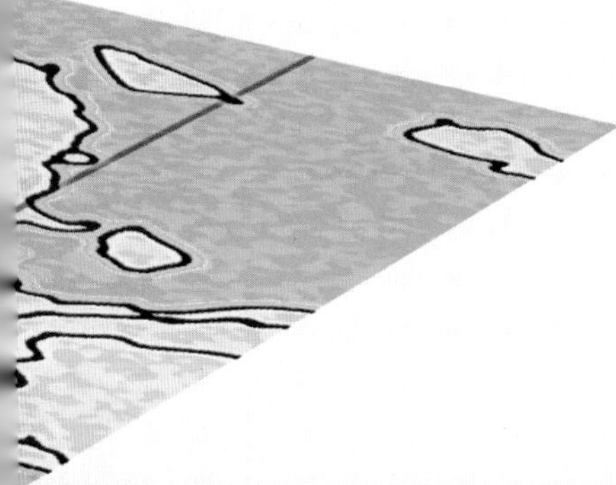

Browsing the World Wide Web is the Silk Road to learning essential Web site design. Looking at other's work, you quickly can recognize good and bad practices. The successful Web site must be innovative and effective to stand out. One way to achieve this effect is to use images and graphics in your Web page design. In good Web pages, images are not simply shown, they are integrated to furnish information, display pictures of goods and services, and permit navigation.

In this project, you will learn about the types of images used on the Web and master the graphics editing options necessary to include these images in your FrontPage web. FrontPage allows you to access the World Wide Web and select interesting and pertinent themes and backgrounds to add appeal to your pages. You will create a thumbnail image that points your viewers to a larger image of the same picture. Then, you can apply special formatting to images and manipulate the images using the Image toolbar. The Image toolbar contains buttons that perform actions such as rotating the image, adding text to an image, increasing or decreasing the brightness or contrast, or adding beveled edges. All of these elements ensure your success in developing a Web site that attracts and influences those browsing the Web and gets you noticed.

Like the Silk Road, you can experience the wealth of the Web. In your Web travels, you can gather the richness of ideas, insight, and design that only browsing the Web can provide.

Microsoft FrontPage 98

Using Graphics and Images in Web Page Design

CASE PERSPECTIVE

In the fast-paced World Wide Web of today, the word is, *marketing*. Web sites are used to attract and keep customers interested. The successful Web site must be innovative and effective in order to stand out from the crowd. One way to accomplish this is by using images and graphics. Mastering the graphics techniques used on the Web is indispensable for the successful Web page developer.

In Project 2, you began Web page development as a part-time assistant at the Morgan, Turner and Lock law firm. Continuing your work on its Web site in this project, you will use graphics and images to build the additional pages. The Web site consists of the Home page created in Project 2 and a small number of pages that introduce the firm and its people, describe the services available, and provide a means of obtaining some preliminary information from potential clients. Your current task is to design and develop a Web page that contains a list of services the firm wants to advertise, while effectively using images wherever possible.

Introduction

In the early stages of the Web, graphics were seldom used. Today, graphical images are an integral part of most Web pages. It would be difficult to find a Web site that does not make extensive use of images.

Good Web pages do not just show images, they integrate them and use them effectively. Images on Web pages are used to provide information, serve as decoration, display pictures of products or artistic works, and provide navigation.

Because images, graphics, and animation now are used so widely, it is important to take the time to learn about the types of images used on the Web and master the graphics editing options necessary to include these objects in your Web pages. You need to know the characteristics, advantages, and disadvantages of each type of image file so you will know the best type of image to use for a particular situation.

Project 2 introduces you to using images and how to apply special formatting to them. You will apply a tiled background to a Web page, create a transparent GIF image, create an image map, and create a thumbnail image. The Web page you will create in this project is the next page in the web for Morgan, Turner and Lock, the Services page, as shown in Figure 3-1. You created hyperlinks to this page from the Morgan, Turner and Lock Home page. Before you begin creating the Web page, you should familiarize yourself with some important concepts and definitions.

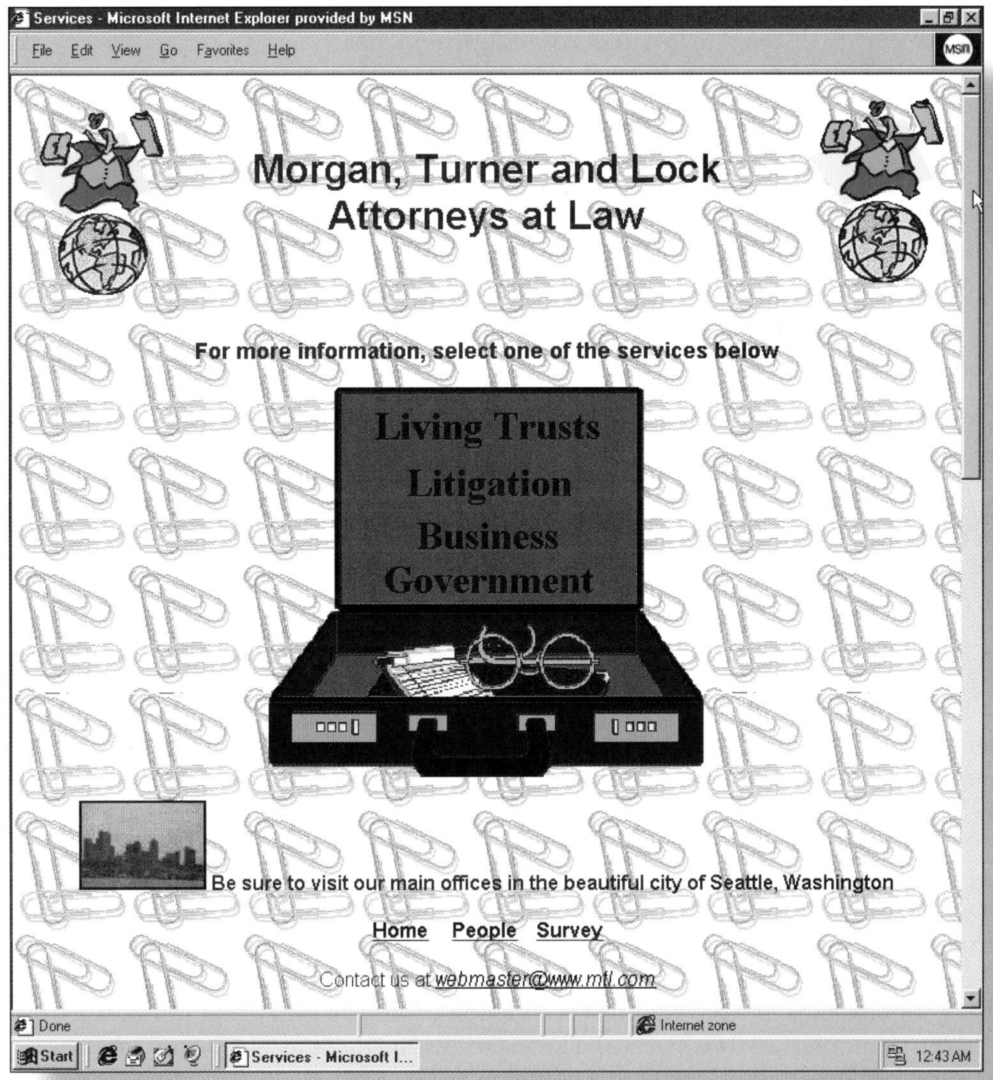

FIGURE 3-1

Image File Formats

Many different formats are used to represent images on computers. Table 3-1 on the next page shows some of the various image file formats. Numerous graphics editors and tools are available that allow you to create and edit images. For example, you can create your own custom buttons, bullets, dividers, and background images. FrontPage supports two types of image file formats: GIF and JPEG.

Table 3-1

IMAGE FILE TYPE	DESCRIPTION
BMP	Windows bitmap file format – device-independent format, introduced with Windows 3.0 and increasingly supported by Windows applications.
EPS	Encapsulated postscript file format – an extension of the Postscript file graphics format developed by Adobe systems.
GIF	Graphic Interchange Format file format – a popular graphics exchange format used by the CompuServe Information Service and other online graphics sources. GIF is a licensed product for developers of commercial, for-profit software; however, for the nonprofit personal home page, a license agreement is not required.
JPEG	Joint Photographic Expert Group file format – used for true color 24-bit photographic images scanned or digitized from films.
PCX	Paintbrush file format – used in Windows Paintbrush and other paint programs and supported by many desktop publishing and graphics programs.
PNG	Portable Network Graphics file format – a file format for the lossless, portable, well-compressed storage of raster images.
RAS	Sun Raster file format – the raster image file format developed by Sun Microsystems, Inc.
TGA	Targa file format – a photo-realistic image format designed for systems with a Truevision display adapter.
TIF	Tagged Image File format – supported by many desktop publishing programs.
WMF	Windows Metafile format – a vector graphics format used mostly for word processing clip art.

Regardless of the file type, an image is displayed on a monitor screen using small points of color called pixels. A **pixel**, or **picture element**, is the smallest addressable point on the screen. An image is formed on the screen by displaying pixels of different color. The combined group of different-colored pixels makes up the image. The **image file** contains the information needed to determine the color for each pixel used to display the image.

The **bit resolution** of an image refers to the number of bits of stored information per pixel. With an **8-bit image**, 8 bits of information are stored for each pixel. Using the binary numbering system, you can represent up to 256 numbers using 8 bits. Thus, an 8-bit image can have a maximum of 256 colors, with each number representing a different color.

A **24-bit image** can have up to 16.7 million colors. These types of images have near-photographic quality. Each pixel consumes four times as much storage as a pixel in an 8-bit image, however, resulting in a larger file size for an image with the same number of pixels.

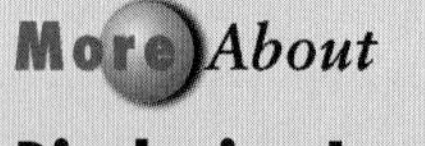

Displaying Images

Current computers allow you to specify the number of bits of color your computer will display. If the number is smaller than the bit resolution of an image, the image will not display properly. Right-click the desktop to see the current setting for your computer monitor.

GIF Image Files

GIF stands for **Graphic Interchange Format.** GIF files use 8-bit resolution and support up to 256 colors. GIF files support indexed color image types, line art, and grayscale images.

Special types of GIF files, called **animated GIFs**, contain a series of images that are displayed in rapid succession, giving the appearance of movement. Special animated GIF editors are available to combine the series of images and set the display timing.

A **transparency index** exists in the GIF89a format. This allows you to specify a transparent color, which causes the background of the Web page to display through the color that has been set as transparent.

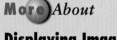

If you are using line art, icons, or images such as company logos, make sure they are in the GIF89a format. You then will be able to take advantage of the transparency features.

JPEG Image Files

JPEG stands for **Joint Photographic Expert Group**. The advantage to using JPEG files is the high-color resolution. JPEG supports 24-bit resolution, providing up to 16.7 million possible colors. If you are including photographic images in your Web page, they must use JPEG format because of the support for full color.

When you insert an image that is not in GIF or JPEG format, FrontPage automatically converts it to the GIF format if the image has 8 bits of color or less. The image is converted automatically to JPEG format if the image has more than 8 bits of color.

With FrontPage, you can import image files into the current FrontPage web, insert images in Web pages, align images with text, and create and edit image maps. The editing commands in the FrontPage Editor allow you to change the appearance of the image. You can crop, rotate, and resize an image. In addition, you can change its brightness and contrast, make it black and white, or give the image beveled edges.

FrontPage can work with graphics editing programs such as the **Microsoft Clip Gallery**, which is a tool for previewing and managing clip art, pictures, sounds, video clips, and animation. The Microsoft Clip Gallery comes with a collection of clip art and pictures you can insert into your Web pages. You used Microsoft Clip Gallery to create the Morgan, Turner and Lock Home page in Project 2.

Designing the Web Page

The marketing director at Morgan, Turner and Lock is looking for a Web page that lists several services that the law firm wants to advertise, with hyperlinks to more information concerning each service. In addition, it wants to identify Seattle, Washington as the location of its main offices. You worked on a design for the Services page in Project 2. After a second meeting with the marketing director, the design shown in Figure 3-2 has been approved.

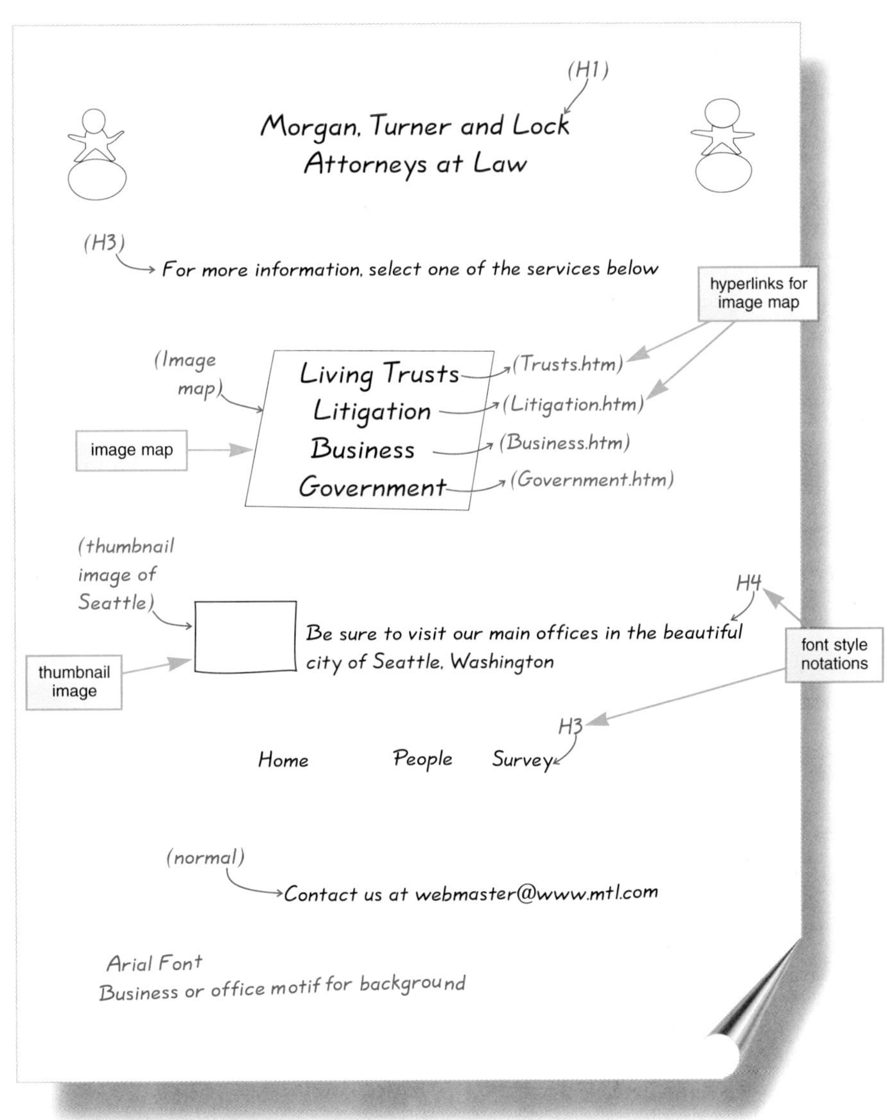

FIGURE 3-2

The page shown in Figure 3-2 on the previous page contains the heading and images used with the Home page. Using these design criteria provides a consistent look to the pages making up the Morgan, Turner and Lock web. The same footer is used with a change to one of the hyperlinks. Instead of a hyperlink to the Services page (see Figure 2-1 on page FP 2.5), the hyperlink will point back to the Home page. This will provide proper navigation among the various pages within the FrontPage web.

The list of services is represented by a special graphic called an image map. Image maps will be discussed later in the project. The small image shown in Figure 3-2 is called a **thumbnail image**, which is a hyperlink to a larger version of the same picture. An image representing an office theme will be used for the background of the Web page.

As shown in Figure 3-2, the design document specifies any special formatting requirements, such as color, text size, and alignment. With the design of the page completed, you now can implement the design using Microsoft FrontPage 98.

Importing Images

You can import an image simply by dragging the image from another Windows application to the Navigation, Folders or All Files view.

Adding a New Web Page to an Existing FrontPage Web

In the preceding projects, you created a new FrontPage web using templates. The templates already contained several Web pages and you did not have to add any additional pages.

With increased experience in designing and developing new FrontPage webs, you may find that templates are not always easily adaptable to the desired result. Therefore, you can use your own creativity to enhance new pages added to the current web. Project 3 demonstrates how to add a new Web page to an existing FrontPage web and embellish it with graphics and images. First, start FrontPage 98 using the following steps summarized below.

TO START FRONTPAGE 98

 Click the Start button on the taskbar. Point to Programs on the Start menu.

 Click Microsoft FrontPage on the Programs submenu.

The FrontPage Explorer window opens and the Getting Started dialog box displays.

Opening an Existing FrontPage Web

Before you can add a new Web page, perform the following steps to open the Morgan, Turner and Lock FrontPage web created in Project 2. If you did not complete Project 2, see your instructor for a copy.

To Open an Existing FrontPage Web

1 Insert the floppy disk containing the Morgan, Turner and Lock web. Click Open an Existing FrontPage Web. Click My New Web (disk). Point to the OK button.

The Getting Started dialog box displays as shown in Figure 3-3.

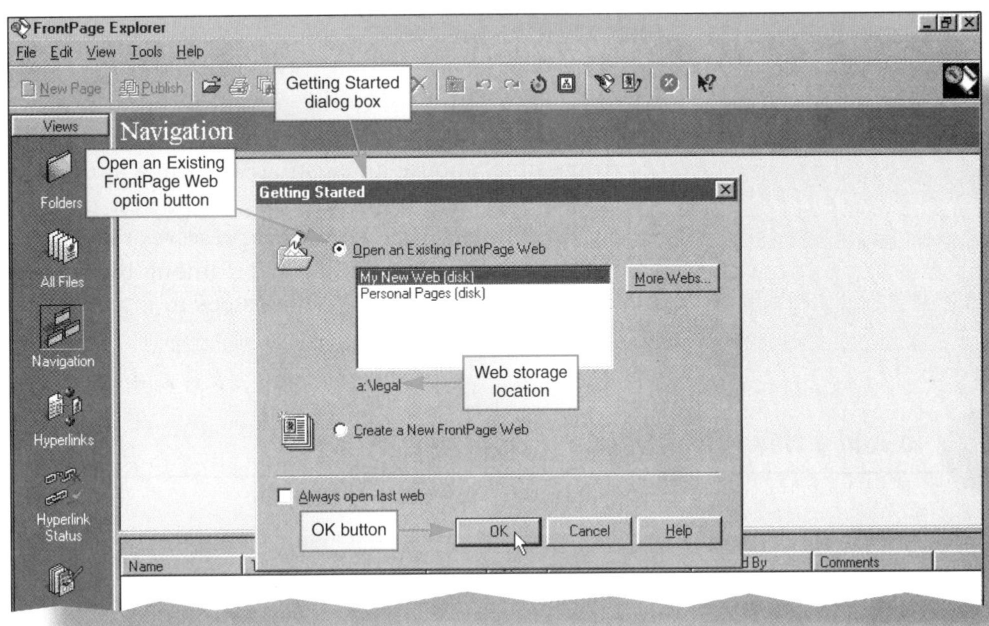

FIGURE 3-3

2 Click the OK button.

The FrontPage Explorer window displays in Folders view, listing the files and folders for the FrontPage web (Figure 3-4).

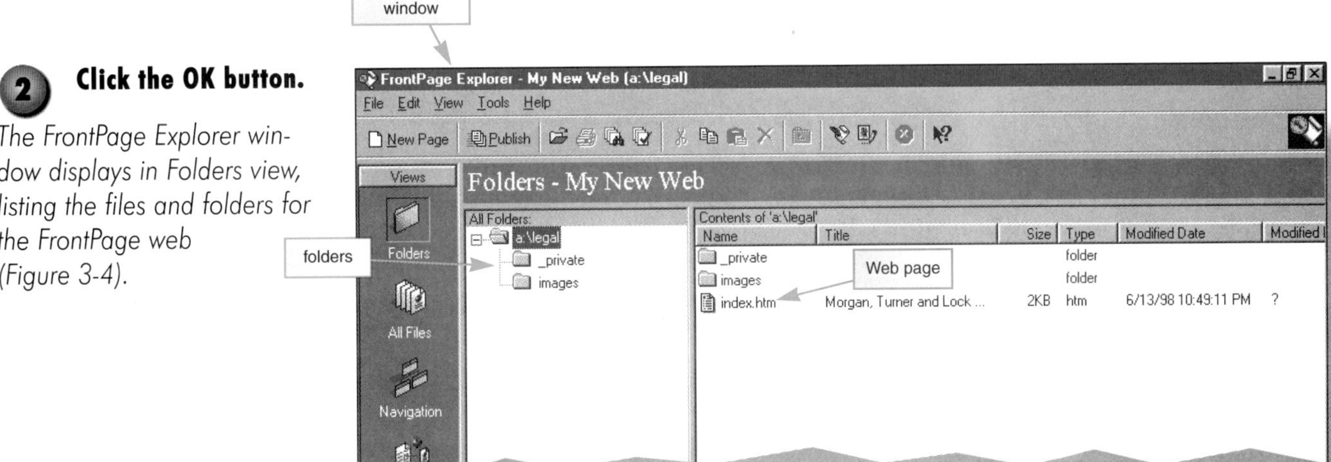

FIGURE 3-4

The Getting Started dialog box contains all of the available FrontPage webs created thus far, and displays them in the Existing FrontPage Web list box. The Morgan, Turner and Lock web is listed on the floppy disk in drive A.

You can access other webs on Web servers by clicking the **More Webs button** in the Getting Started dialog box. This allows you to manage webs and Web pages that are being viewed actively by World Wide Web users. With the Morgan, Turner and Lock web open in the FrontPage Explorer, you now can add a new Web page.

Adding a New Web Page to a FrontPage Web

In previous projects, you used templates consisting of one or more pre-existing Web pages. As you develop customized webs, you will add new Web pages to the web when the need arises.

The FrontPage Explorer toolbar contains the **New Page button** that you can use to add a new Web page to the current web. First, however, you need to indicate the location of the new page by selecting a page icon in the Navigation pane.

If possible, choose an existing Web page in the Morgan, Turner and Lock web that has a hyperlink to the new page. The new page icon will be inserted as a child below the selected page icon. This preserves the visual relationship in the graphical tree diagram in the Navigation pane among the Web pages that are connected using hyperlinks. Perform the following steps to insert a new page in the current FrontPage web.

Steps To Add a New Web Page to a FrontPage Web

Click the Navigation button on the Views bar. Click the Morgan, Turner and Lock Home Page page icon to select it. Point to the New Page button on the toolbar.

The FrontPage Explorer displays in Navigation view (Figure 3-5).

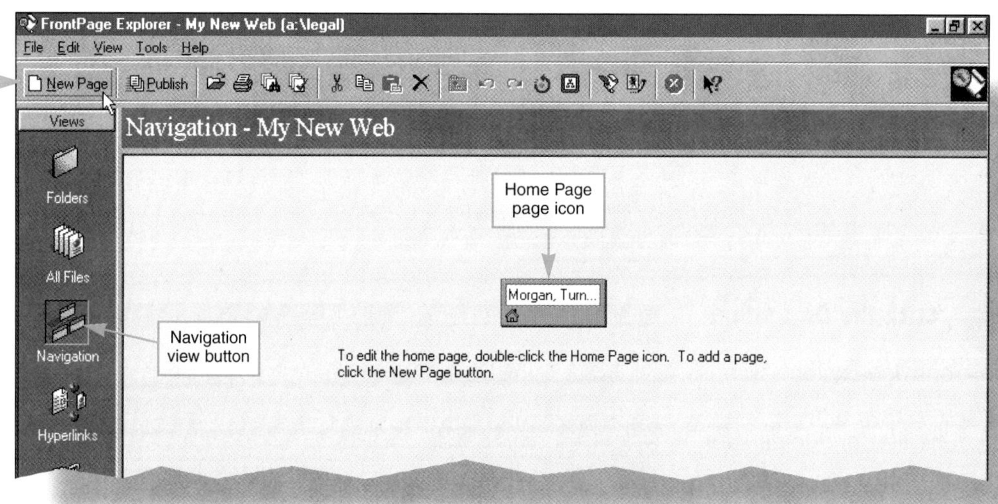

FIGURE 3-5

Click the New Page button.

The FrontPage Explorer dialog box displays asking if you want to add navigation bars to your pages (Figure 3-6).

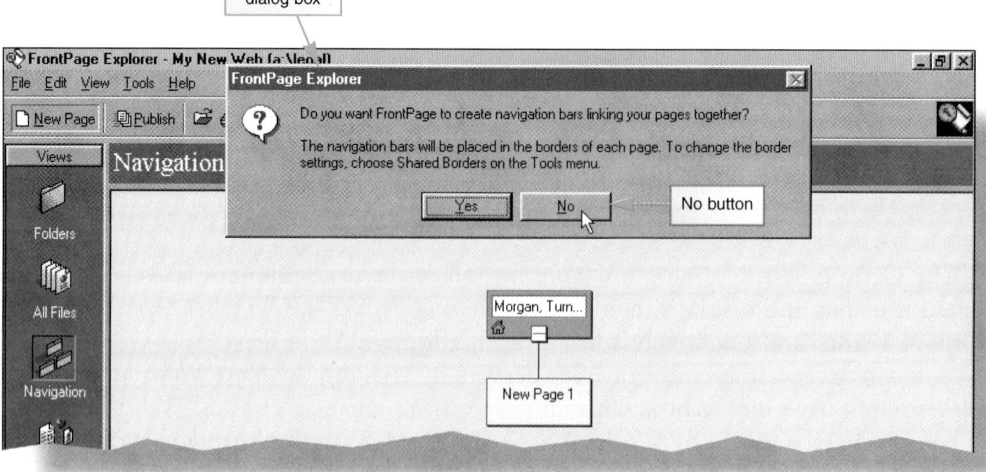

FIGURE 3-6

3 Click the No button.

A new page icon displays in the Navigation pane with a title of New Page 1 (Figure 3-7). The Files pane includes the file name of the new page.

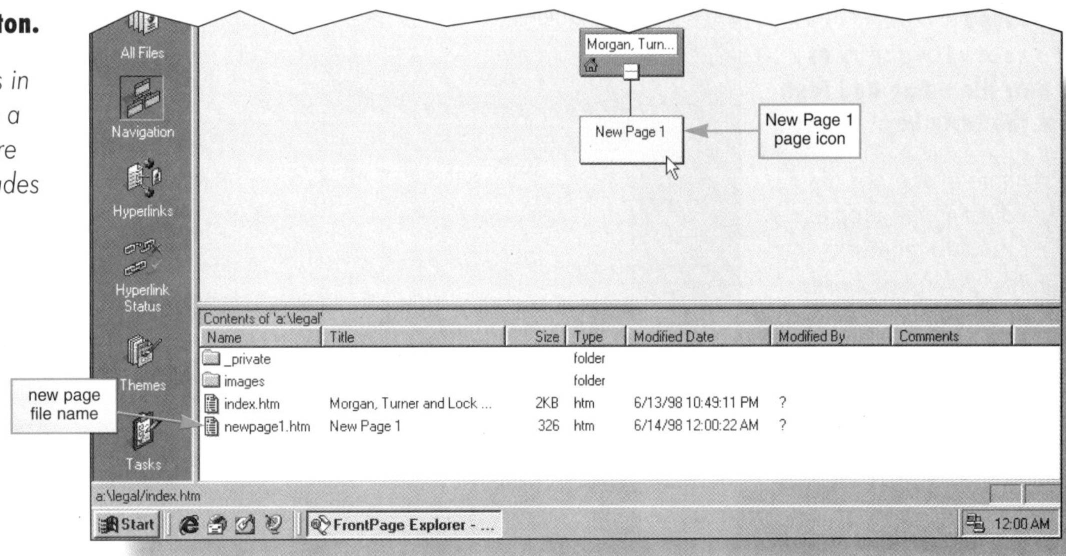

FIGURE 3-7

4 Right-click the New Page 1 page icon. Click Rename on the shortcut menu and then type `Services` **in the edit text box. Press the ENTER key.**

The new title of the Web page, Services, displays in the page icon (Figure 3-8).

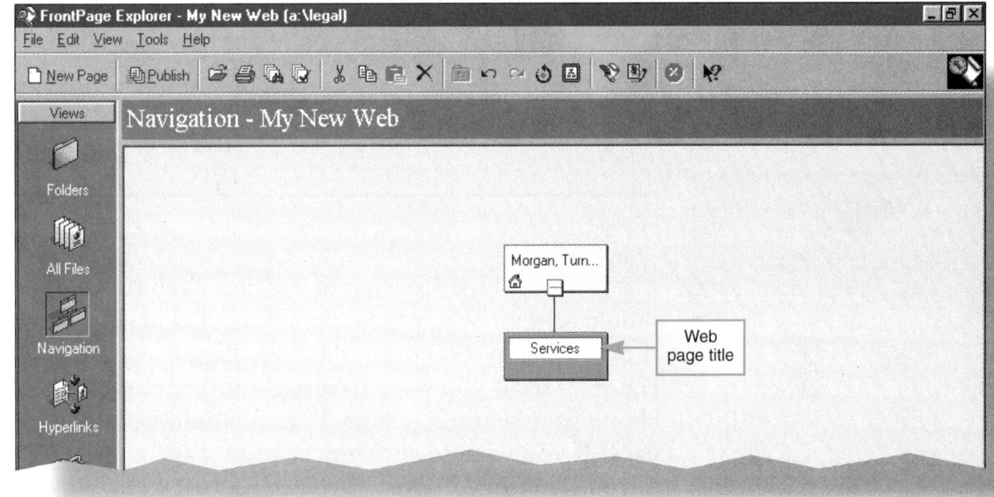

FIGURE 3-8

5 In the Files pane, right-click the file name, newpage1.htm. Click Rename on the shortcut menu.

The newpage1.htm file name is highlighted and an edit text box displays around the file name (Figure 3-9).

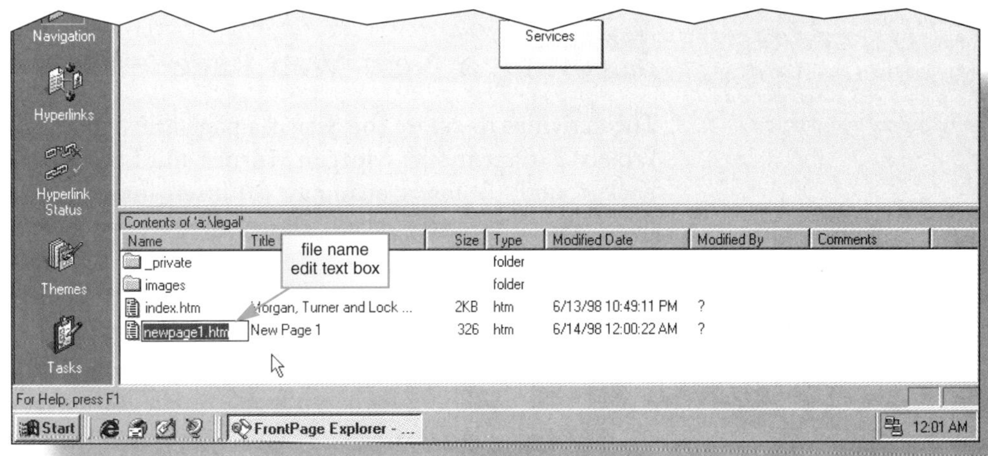

FIGURE 3-9

Type `services.htm` **as the new file name and then press the ENTER key.**

The rename dialog box displays indicating the progress of your rename request. When the dialog box closes, the Files pane reflects the renamed file, services.htm (Figure 3-10).

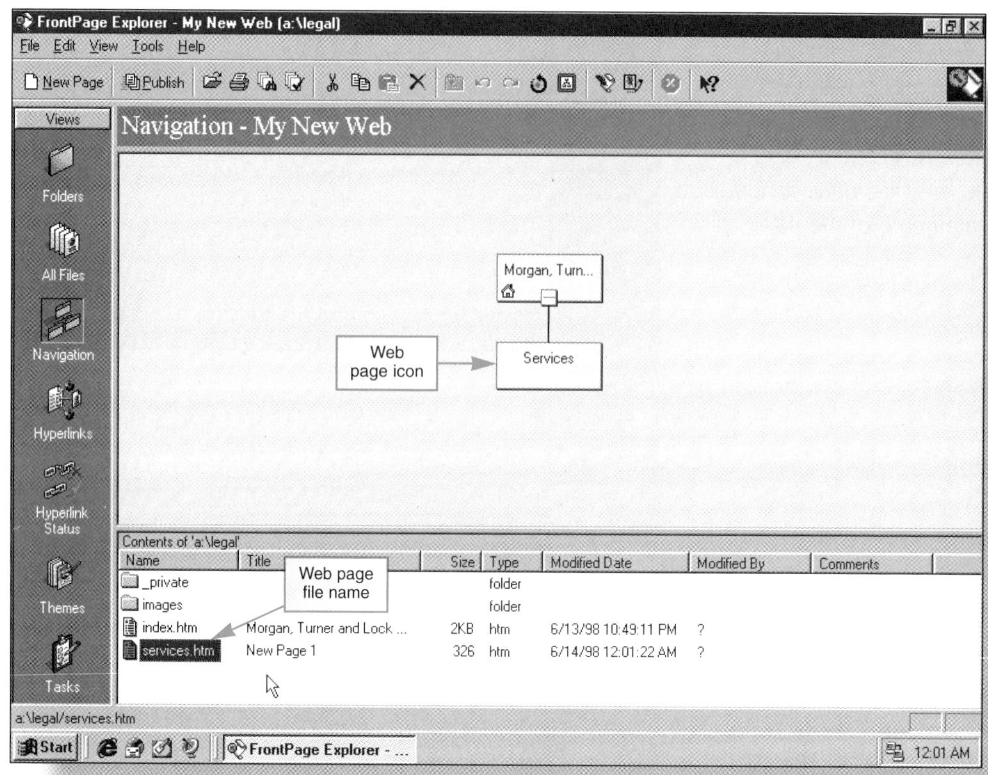

FIGURE 3-10

1. On File menu click New, click Page
2. Press ALT+F, N, P
3. Press CTRL+N

To control the location of the new Web page in the graphical tree diagram, you should select a Web page icon before clicking the New Page button. Because you clicked the top-level page, the New Page 1 page was added just below it, as shown in Figure 3-10. If you were to insert another page with the Morgan, Turner and Lock Home page selected, a New Page 2 would be added on the same level as the Services page. If you were to click the Services page and then click New Page, the New Page 2 would be added below the Services page, creating a three-level graphical tree diagram.

More About

Navigation View

You can move the page icons in Navigation view by dragging them to a new location. This allows you to reorganize the graphical tree diagram.

Editing a New Web Page

The activities to create the Services page are similar to the steps you followed in Project 2 to create the Morgan, Turner and Lock Home page: (1) select the page background; (2) insert headings; (3) insert images; (4) insert text; (5) establish hyperlinks; and (6) test the page. Perform the following steps to start the FrontPage Editor and edit the Services page.

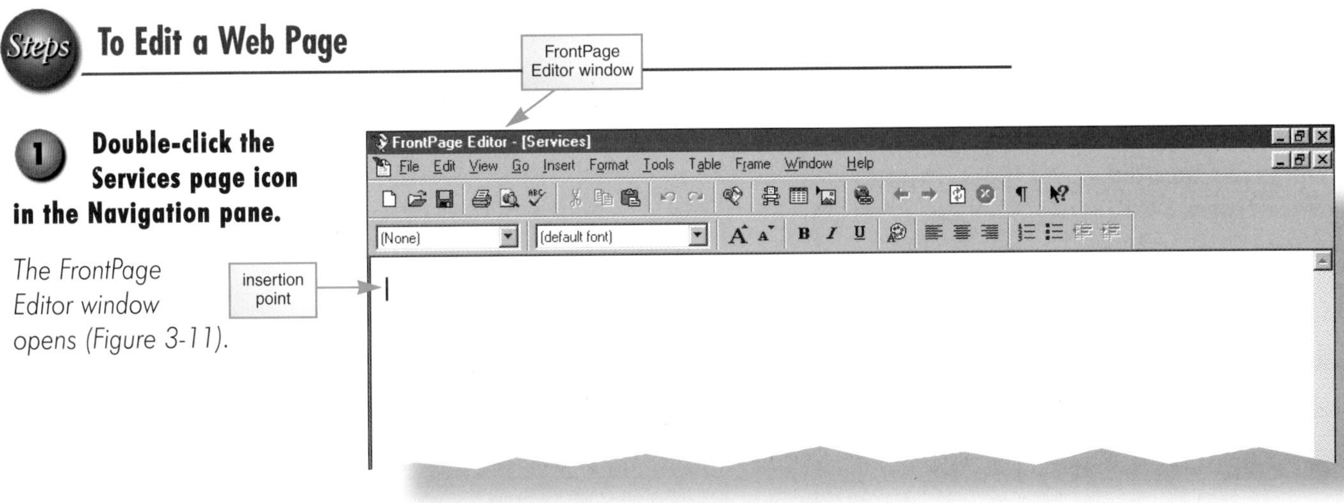

To Edit a Web Page

1 Double-click the Services page icon in the Navigation pane.

The FrontPage Editor window opens (Figure 3-11).

FIGURE 3-11

Other Ways

1. Right-click file name, click Open

Once the Services page is open, you can start the design shown in Figure 3-2 on page FP 3.7. The design makes extensive use of graphics. You will, however, be able to take advantage of the image handling capabilities provided with FrontPage to accomplish all the graphical effects.

The Image Toolbar

The FrontPage Editor has features for manipulating images within a Web page. The **Image toolbar** contains a set of buttons that perform actions such as rotating the image and changing the brightness and contrast. The buttons on the Image toolbar may be active or inactive, depending on the type of image and its context.

The Image toolbar can be hidden or displayed, depending on the setting on the View menu. You can display the Image toolbar by following these steps.

To Display the Image Toolbar

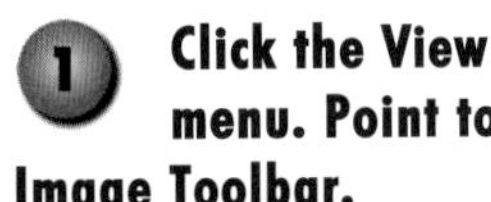

1 Click the View menu. Point to Image Toolbar.

The View menu displays (Figure 3-12). Visible toolbars are indicated with a check mark.

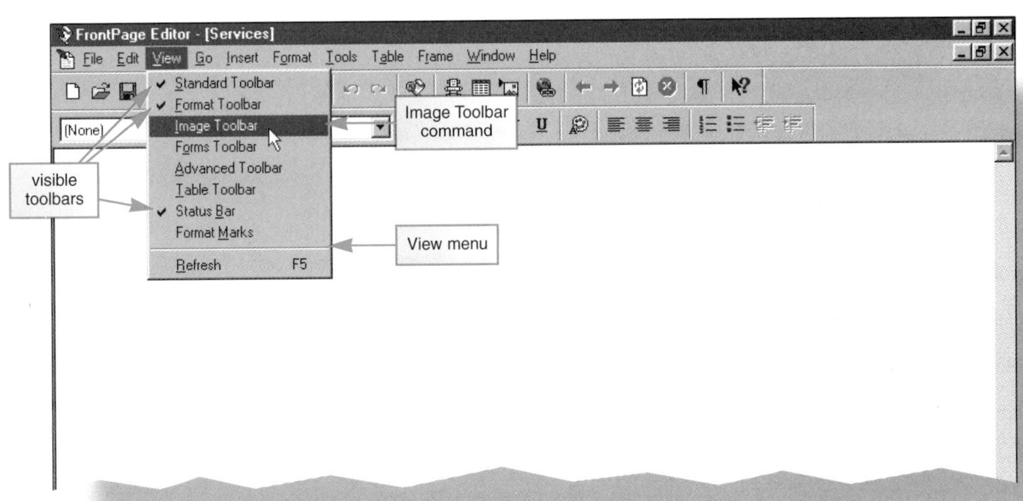

FIGURE 3-12

2 If Image Toolbar is not checked, click Image Toolbar. If necessary, drag the Image toolbar to the position shown in Figure 3-13.

The Image toolbar displays in the FrontPage Editor window (Figure 3-13).

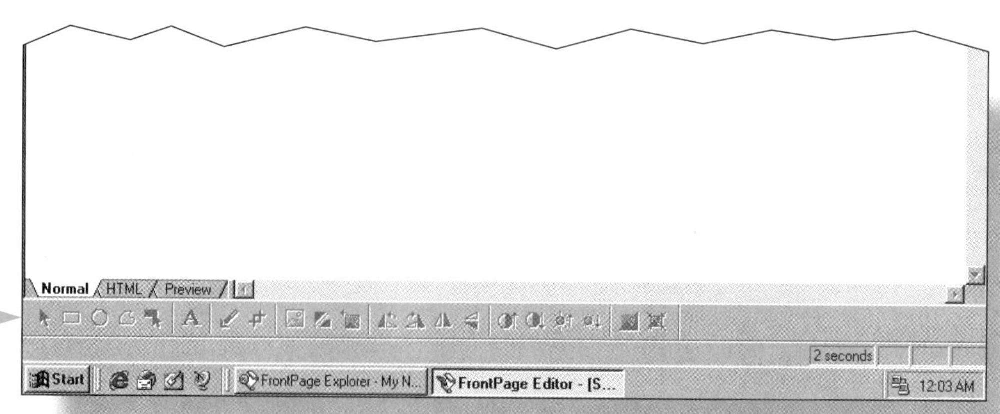

FIGURE 3-13

Other Ways

1. Press ALT+V, I

Table 3-2 shows the buttons on the Image toolbar and a brief explanation of their purpose. Each button will be discussed further as it is used in the Project.

Table 3-2

BUTTON	BUTTON NAME	PURPOSE	BUTTON	BUTTON NAME	PURPOSE
	Select	Selects a hotspot on an image map		Rotate Left	Rotates an image to the left
	Rectangle	Draws a rectangular hotspot		Rotate Right	Rotates an image to the right
	Circle	Draws a circular hotspot		Reverse	Reverses an image (rotates it 180 degrees)
	Polygon	Draws a polygonal hotspot		Flip	Flips an image horizontally
	Highlight Hotspots	Highlights hotspots		More Contrast	Increases the contrast of an image
A	Text	Adds text to an image		Less Contrast	Decreases the contrast of an image
	Make Transparent	Makes a color transparent		More Brightness	Increases the brightness of an image
	Crop	Crops an image		Less Brightness	Decreases the brightness of an image
	Washout	Washes out an image		Bevel	Adds a bevel effect to an image's edges
	Black and White	Converts an image to black and white		Resample	Resamples an image (changes the file size)
	Restore	Restores an image from a disk file			

FrontPage will not allow you to edit the image directly. You need a separate image editor program to perform that activity. You can, however, indicate an image editor program to start automatically when you double-click an image. The **Options command** on the Tools menu of the FrontPage Explorer includes a **Configure Editors sheet** on which you can identify an image editor program.

Setting a Background Image

The **background** of a Web page refers to the color or texture behind every object on the Web page. The default background is white. In Project 1, the background was specified as part of the theme that you applied to the web using the Themes view. In Project 2, you selected a color from a palette of available colors to use as the background.

FrontPage also allows you to specify a URL that points to an image file that is **tiled**, or repeated, across and down, to create the background of the Web page. This process is similar to the wallpaper on your Windows desktop. You can specify an image file name within the current FrontPage web or the URL of any image file on the World Wide Web.

Morgan, Turner and Lock wants an office theme such as push pins or paper clips for the background of its Web page. The following steps demonstrate how to display an image on the World Wide Web, obtain a copy of the image file, and then use it as the tiled background for a Web page.

Background Images

Not all images make good tiled backgrounds because of their size and shapes. The edges of the image must flow smoothly from one copy to another in order to present a seamless background.

To Set a Background Image

1 **Click Format on the menu bar and then point to Background (Figure 3-14).**

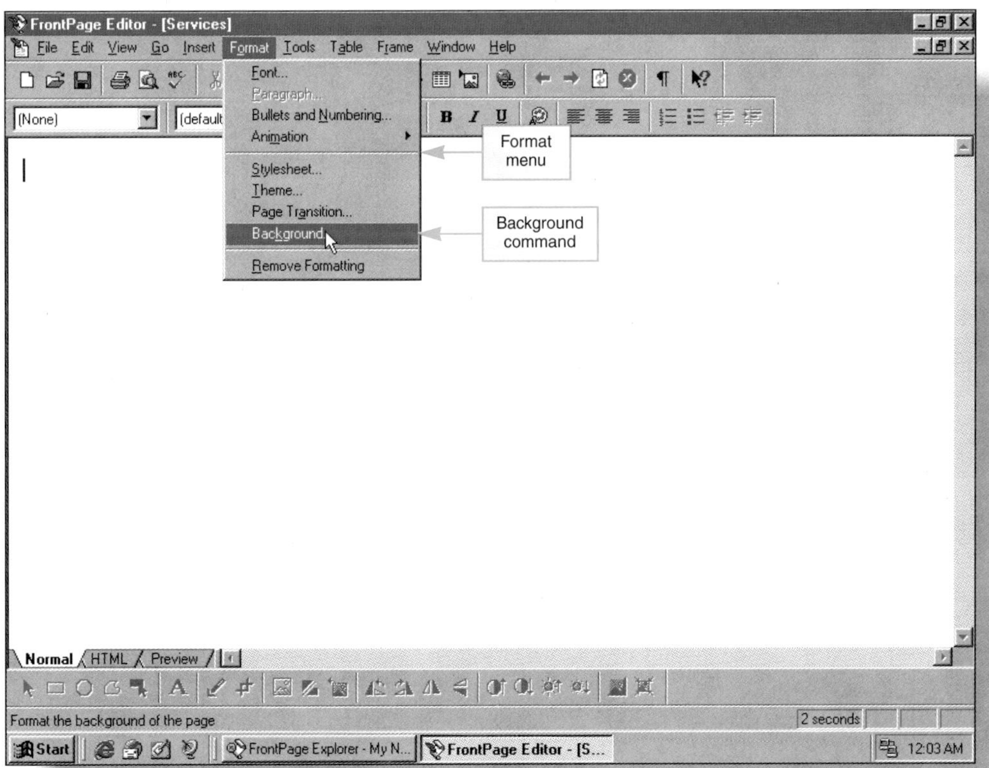

FIGURE 3-14

Click Background.

The Page Properties dialog box displays (Figure 3-15). The dialog box indicates that the color white is the current background color.

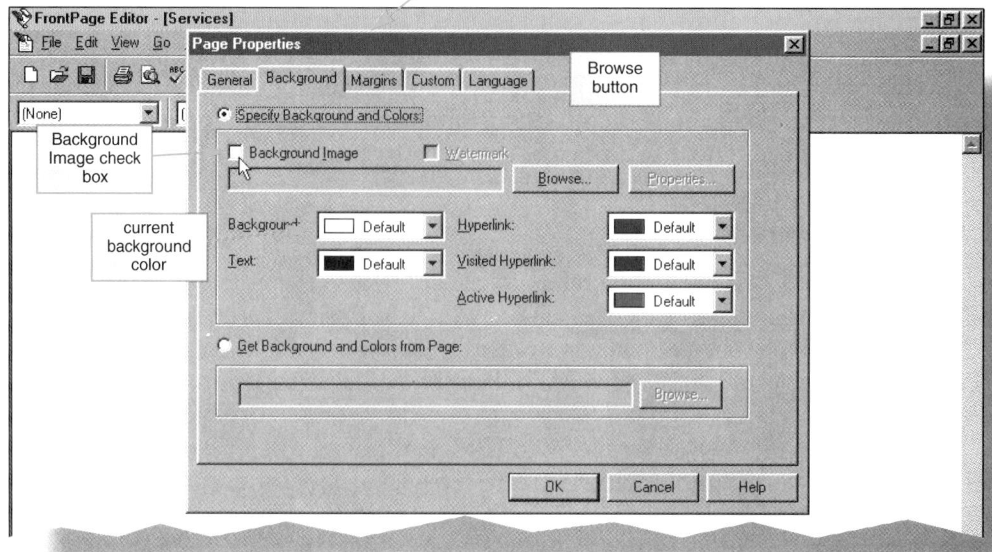

FIGURE 3-15

Click Background Image and then point to the Browse button.

The Background Image text box no longer appears dimmed and contains an insertion point (Figure 3-16). You can type a file name or URL in the text box, or click the Browse button to search for the file name or URL.

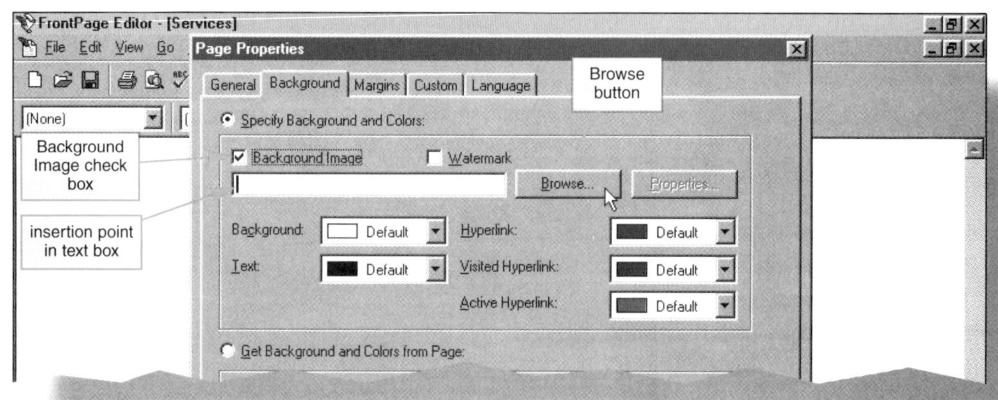

FIGURE 3-16

Click the Browse button.

The Select Background Image box displays (Figure 3-17). You can select images stored on your computer or from the World Wide Web.

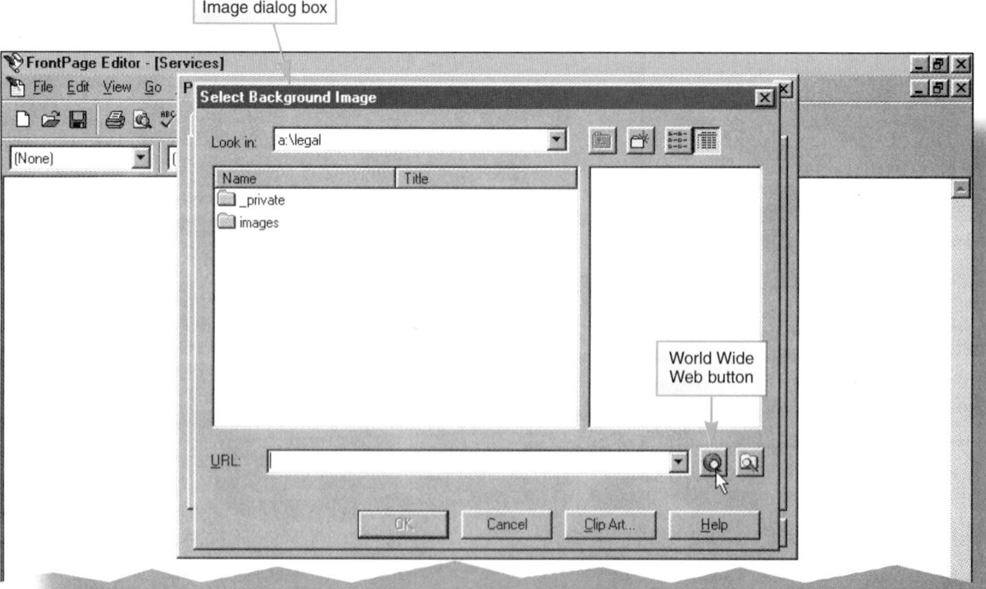

FIGURE 3-17

Click the World Wide Web button.

The Create FrontPage Link – Microsoft Internet Explorer window opens with instructions for continuing (Figure 3-18). Microsoft has a Web site containing images available for Web development that are free to use.

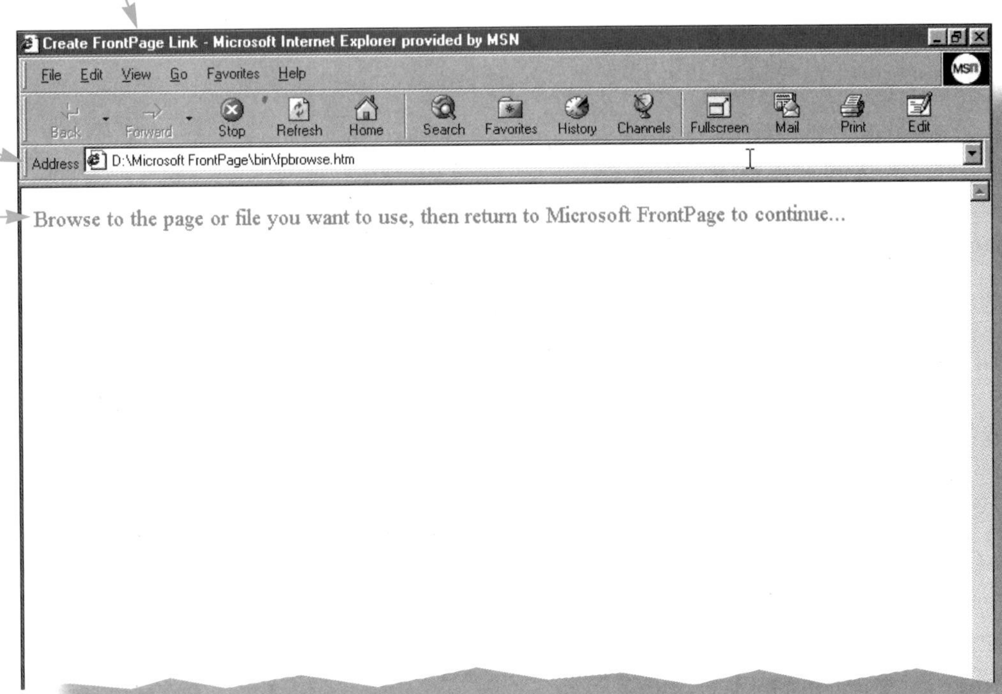

FIGURE 3-18

Click the Address bar. Type `www.microsoft.com/gallery/images/default.asp` **and then press the ENTER key.**

The SBN Workshop window opens and the Images Web page displays (Figure 3-19). The SBN Workshop contains a library of free icons, buttons, arrows, dividers, and other images available for use with Web pages.

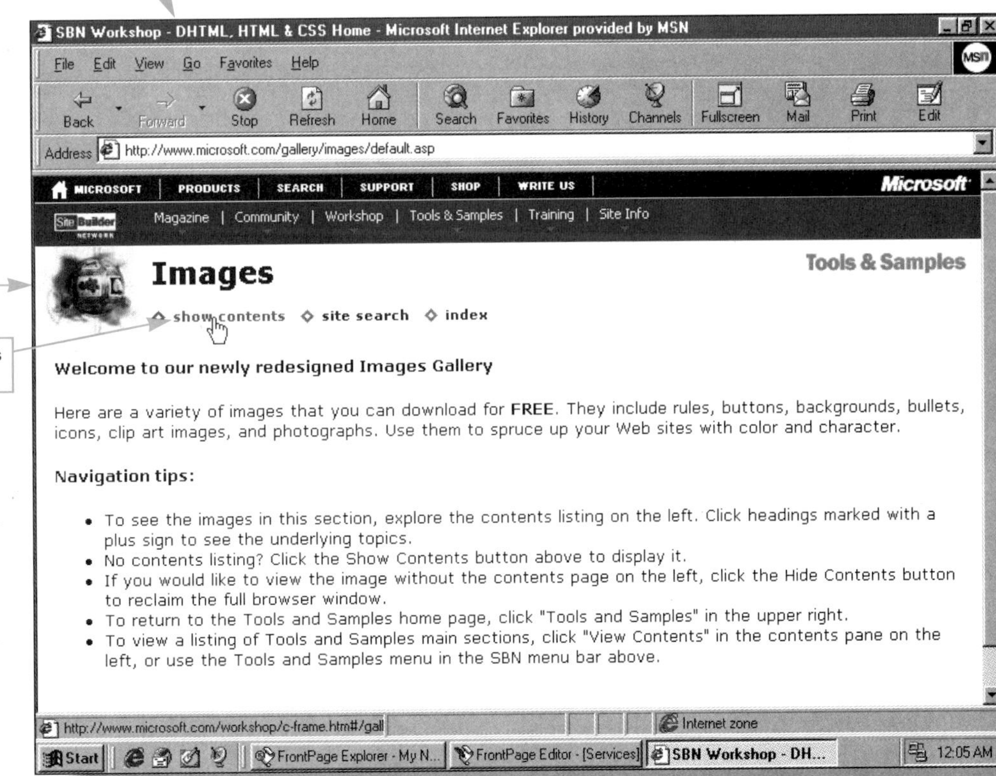

FIGURE 3-19

7 Click the show contents hyperlink. In the Tools & Samples frame, click the Clip Art: Business category and then click the Paper Clips hyperlink.

The Paper Clips image displays in the Web page (Figure 3-20). The image should be saved to your FrontPage web so you can use it as the background image.

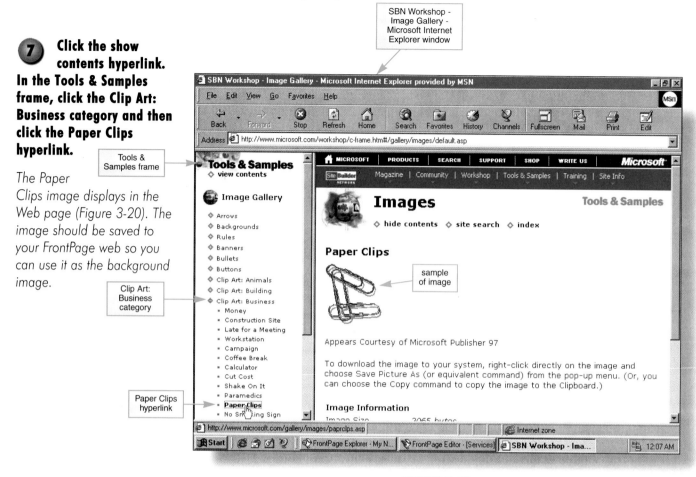

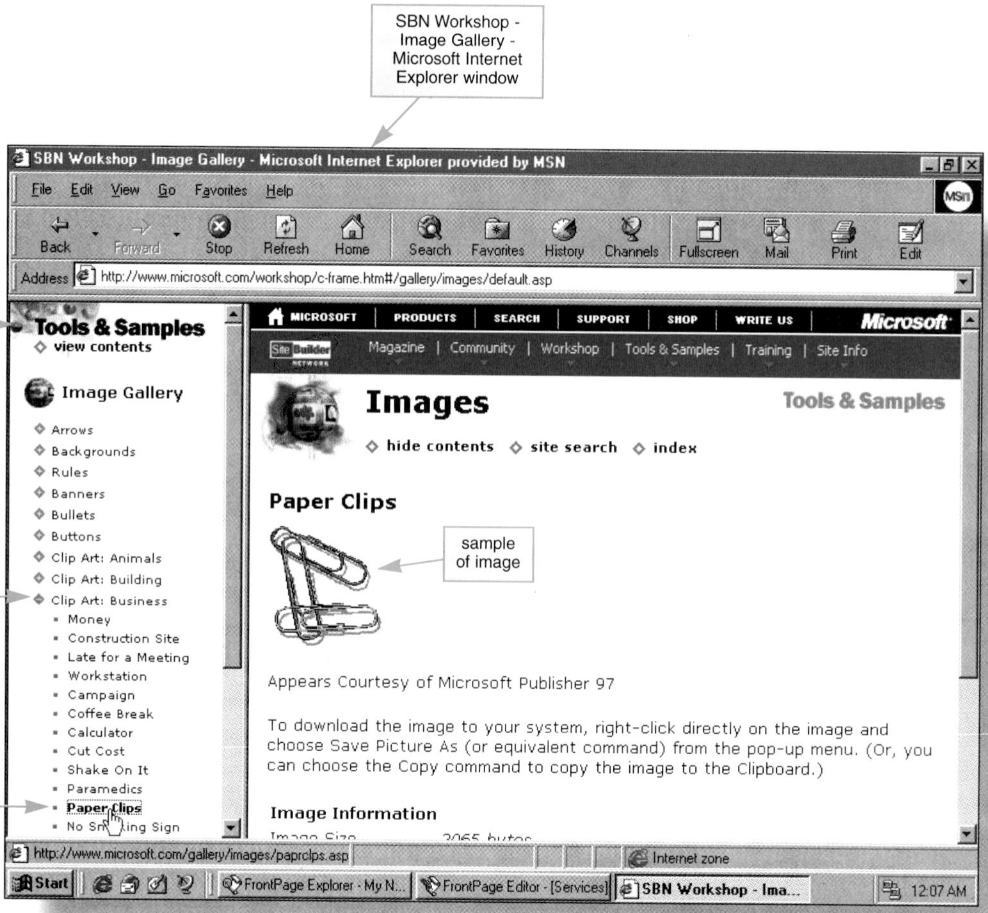

SBN Workshop - Image Gallery - Microsoft Internet Explorer window

Tools & Samples frame

Clip Art: Business category

Paper Clips hyperlink

sample of image

FIGURE 3-20

Right-click the paper clips image.

A shortcut menu displays (Figure 3-21). The Save Picture As command will save the image file on your computer.

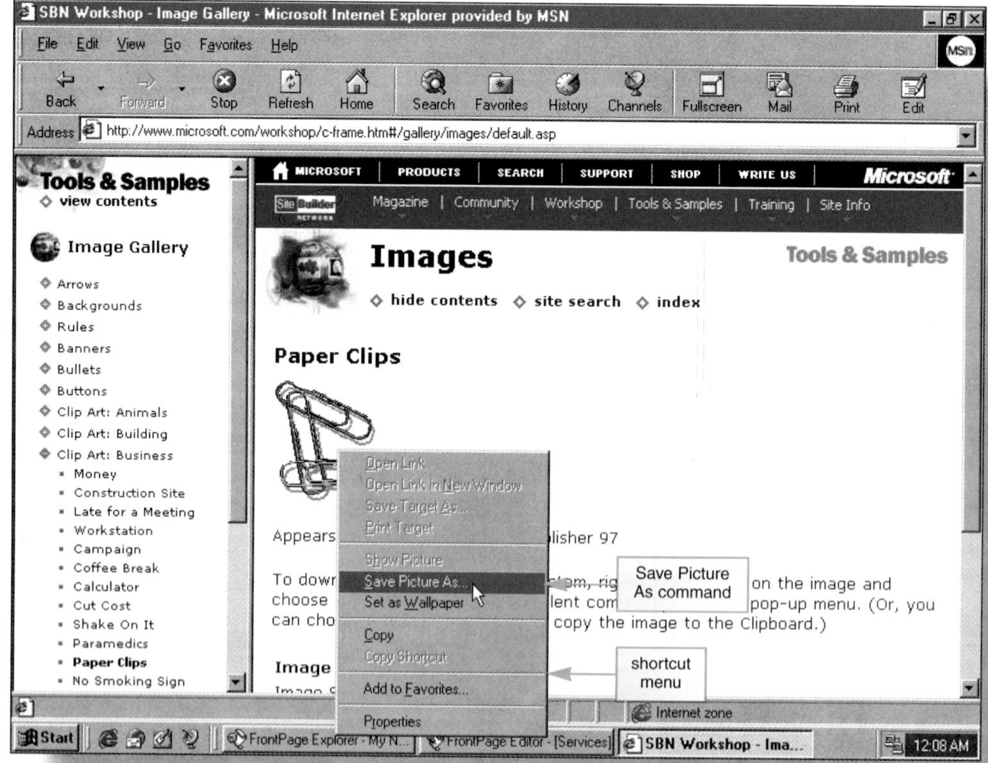

FIGURE 3-21

9 **Click Save Picture As.**

The Save Picture dialog box displays (Figure 3-22).

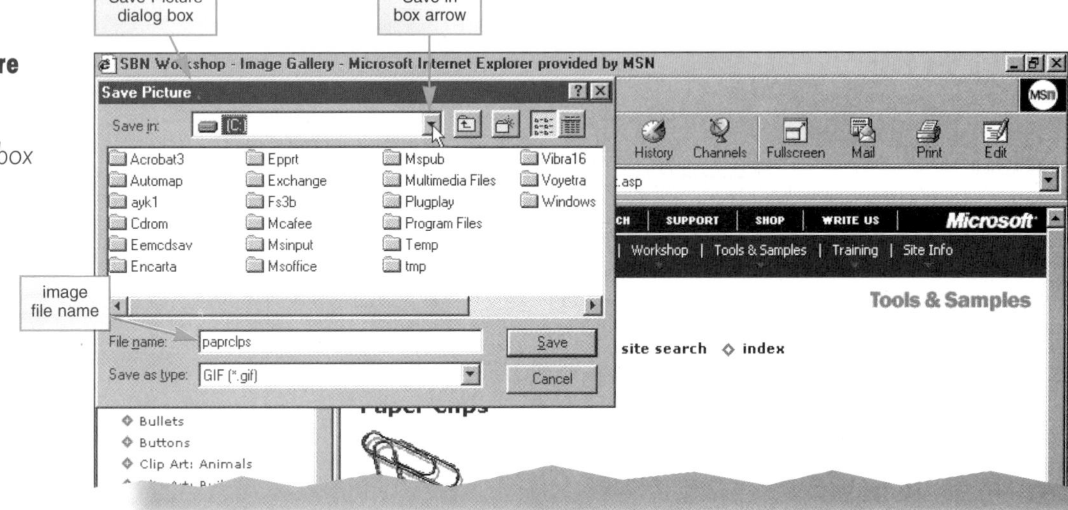

FIGURE 3-22

10 **Click the Save in box arrow and then click 3½ Floppy (A:).**

The list of files on drive A displays (Figure 3-23). Recall that the Morgan, Turner and Lock Web pages are located in the legal folder on drive A.

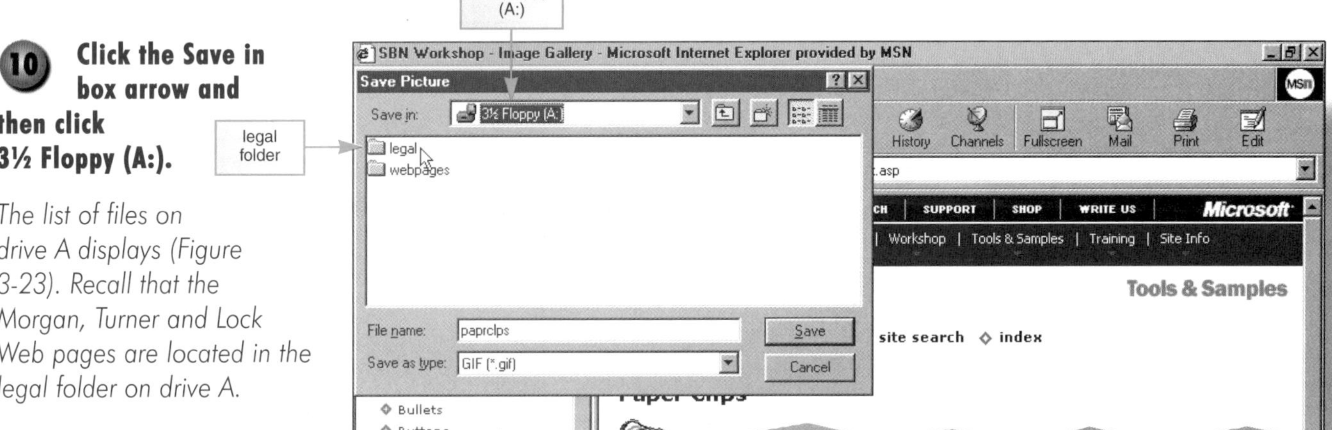

FIGURE 3-23

11 **Double-click the legal folder. Double-click the images folder.**

The list of files in the images folder on drive A displays (Figure 3-24). The Paper Clips image will be saved in a file called paprclps.gif in the images folder on drive A.

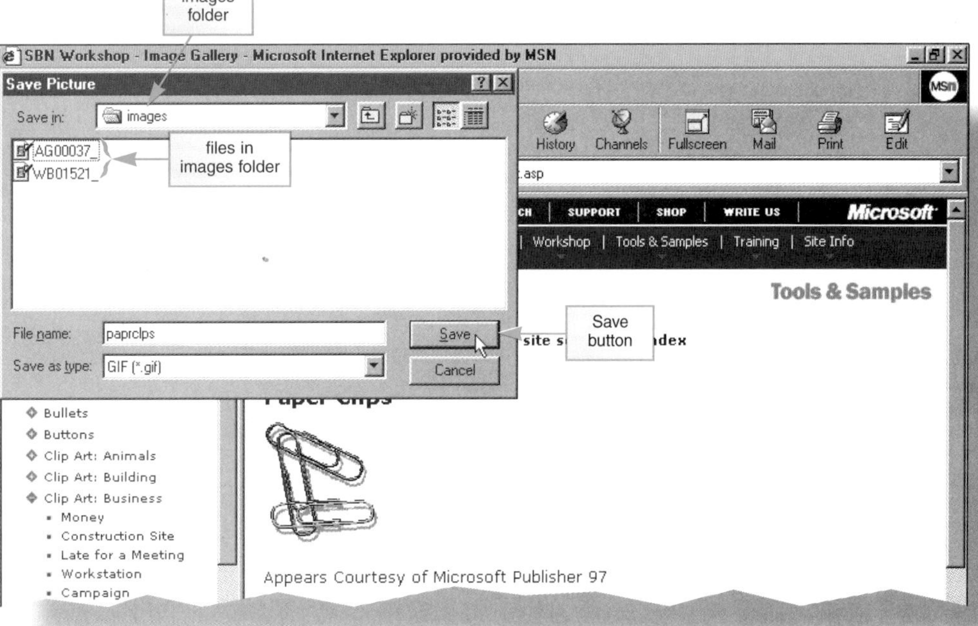

FIGURE 3-24

12 **Click the Save button. Click the FrontPage Editor button on the taskbar.**

The file is saved on the floppy disk in drive A, and the Select Background Image dialog box in the FrontPage Editor displays.

13 **Double-click the images folder in the files list box.**

The box displays a list of files in the images folder on drive A (Figure 3-25).

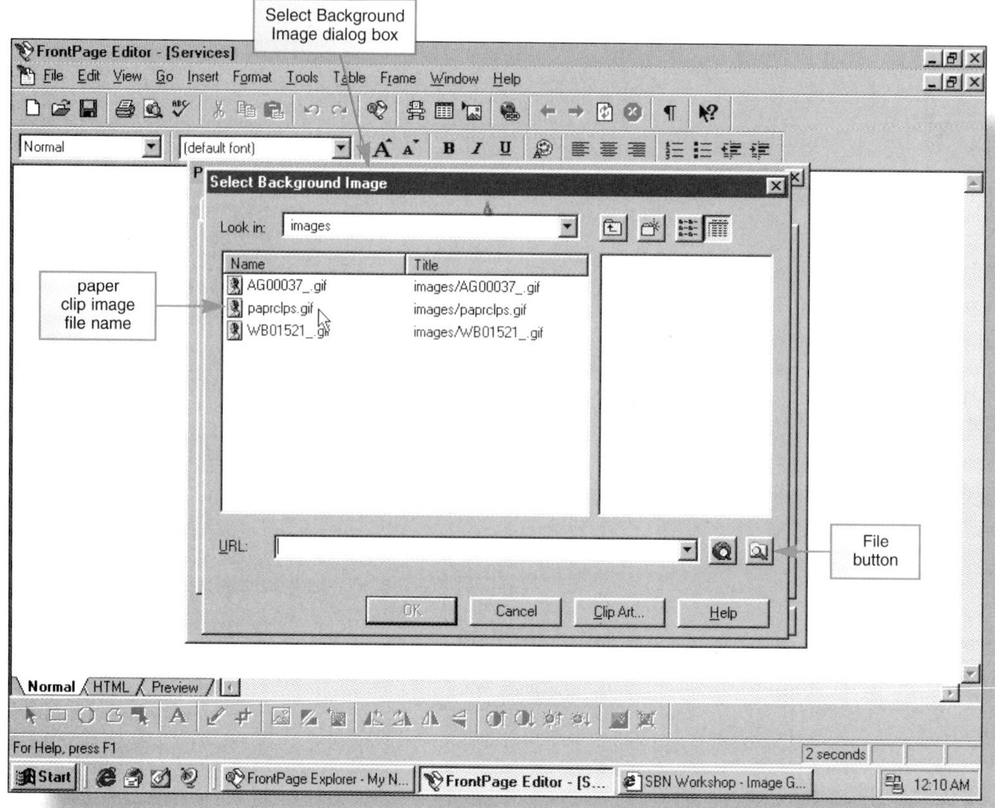

FIGURE 3-25

14 **Click paprclps to select it and then point to the OK button.**

The paprclps file name is selected (Figure 3-26).

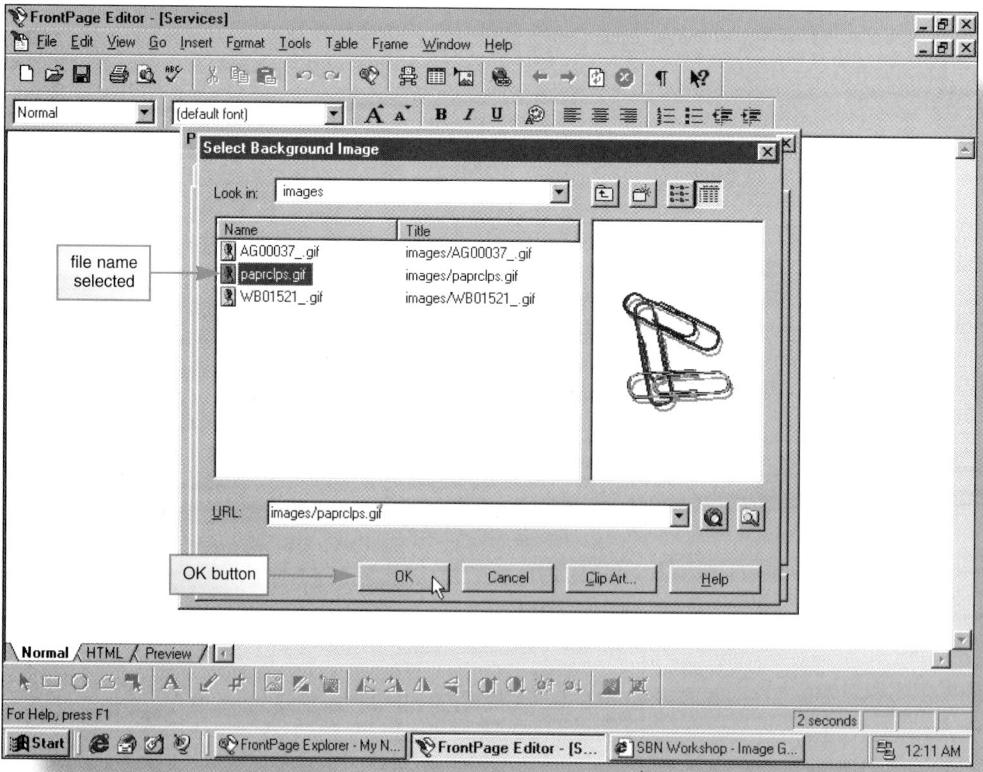

FIGURE 3-26

15 Click the OK button in the Select Background Image box.

The path to the paprclps.gif file displays in the Background Image text box (Figure 3-27).

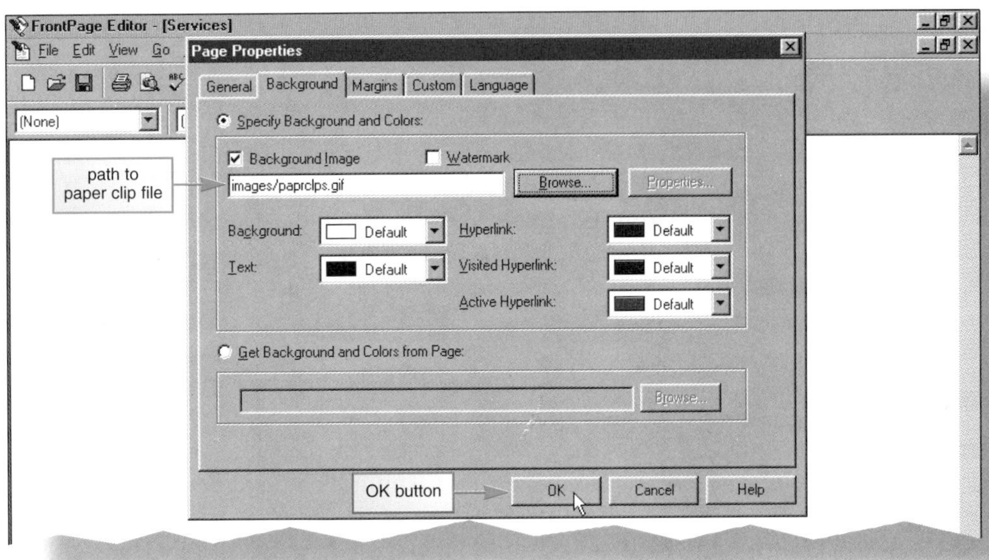

FIGURE 3-27

16 Click the OK button in the Page Properties dialog box.

The FrontPage Editor window displays with the paper clips image tiled across and down the page (Figure 3-28).

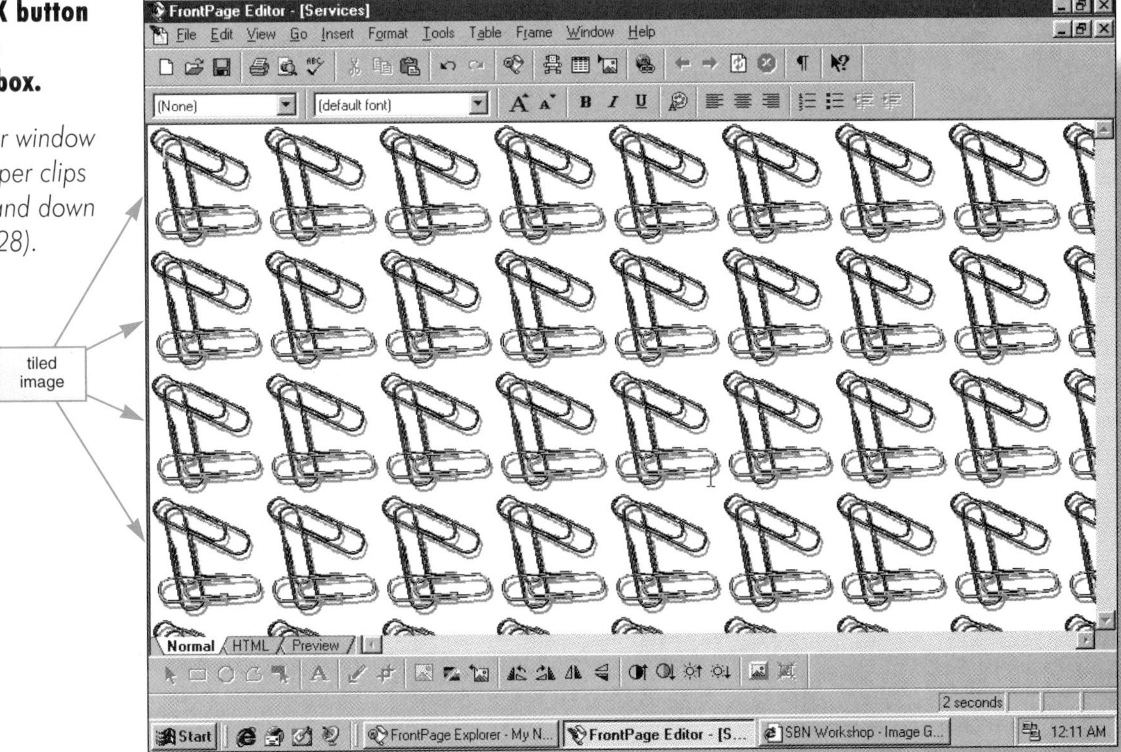

FIGURE 3-28

1. Press ALT+K, O, I, B

The paper clips image has been tiled, or repeated, across and down the Web page. Not all images lend themselves to tiling. Trial and error is the best way to determine whether or not an image would make a good background.

You should consider carefully whether to download or simply point to images on the World Wide Web. Each choice poses problems. You must obtain permission before using an image or graphic that belongs to someone else. If you use a URL that points to an image on another Web server computer on the World Wide Web, someone could remove or rename the image file, or the Web server could be taken out of service. If this happens, your Web page background no longer will be available. Thus, it is best to save the image on your computer.

The current color scheme of the tiled paper clip background is too bright and could interfere with the text to be placed on the Web page. Using the Washout button on the Image toolbar will soften the colors of an image. The next section illustrates how to achieve this effect.

Washing Out Images

Be careful before permanently changing an image used on the Web. Many Web sites share image files to conserve disk space. If you change an image file and then publish it on the Web, other Web pages that use that image could be affected.

Washing Out an Image

Softening the colors of the paper clip background increases the ease with which the text can be read by users accessing the Services page. The **Washout button** creates a low-contrast, see-through version of an image with a *washed out* appearance.

Applying the washout effect to an image permanently alters its look. You will have to make a copy of the original image file if you need a version that does not have washout applied.

To apply the washout effect to an image on the current page, select the image by clicking it and then click the Washout button. To apply the washout effect to the background image on the current page, click the Washout button when no images are selected. Perform the following steps to apply the washout effect to the paper clip background.

To Washout an Image

1 Point to the Washout button on the Image toolbar (Figure 3-29).

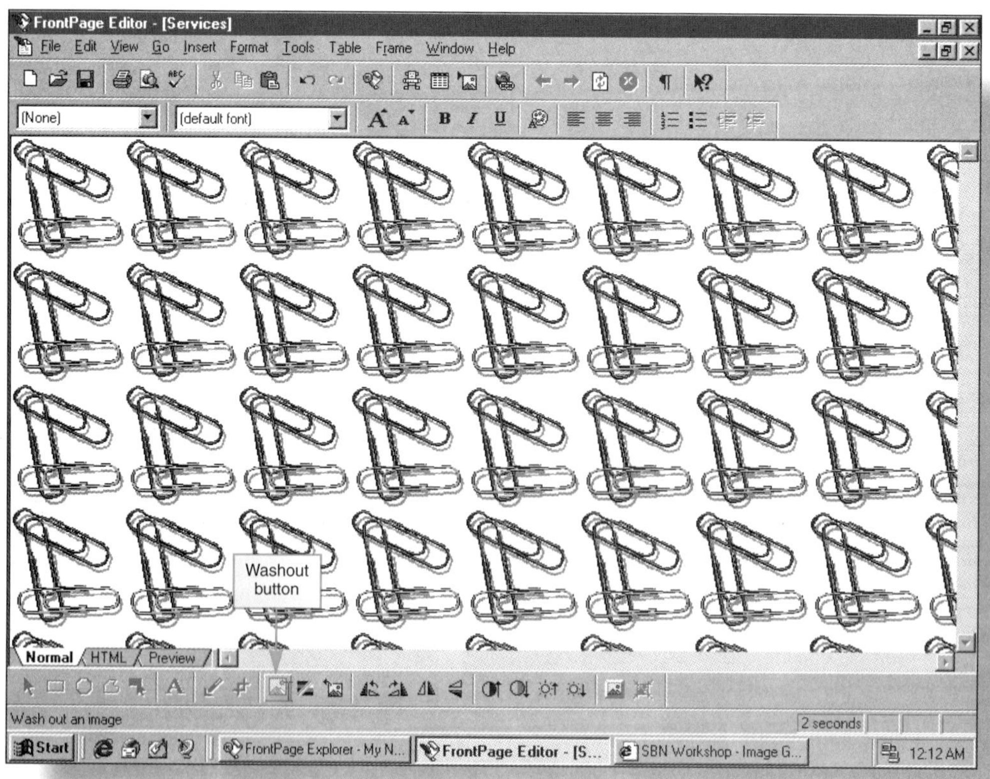

FIGURE 3-29

Click the Washout button.

The paper clips background image becomes transparent (Figure 3-30).

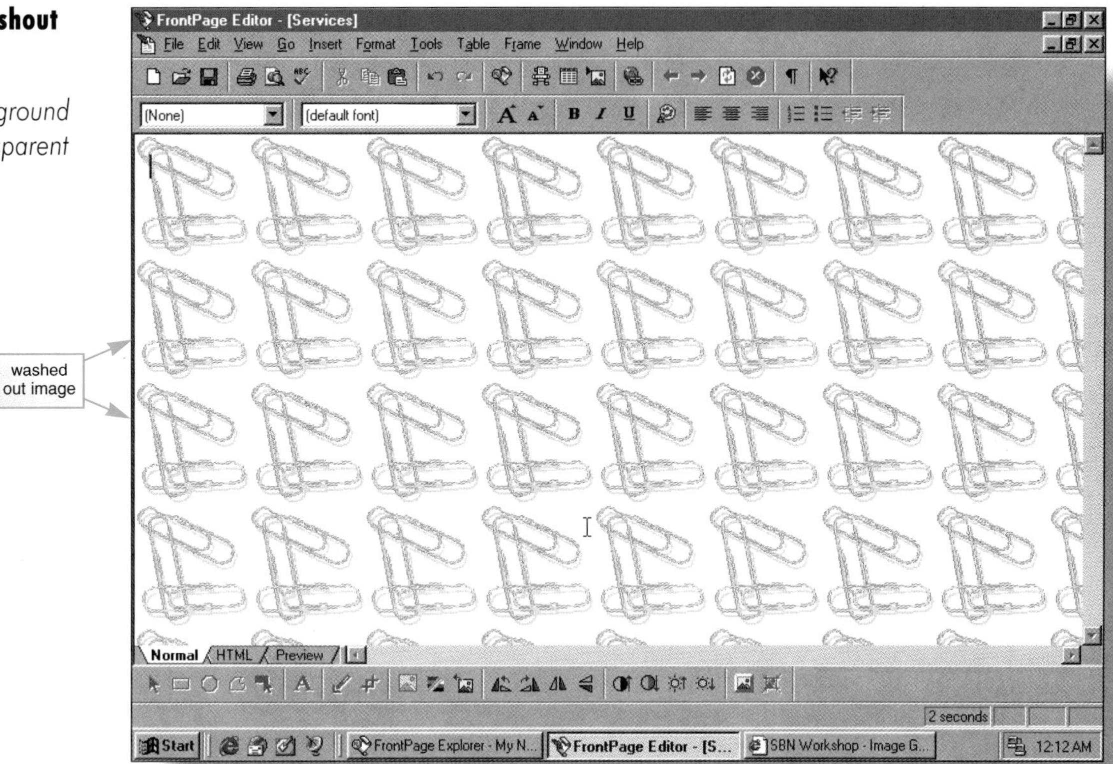

FIGURE 3-30

Applying the washout effect to the paper clips background eliminates the problem of bright colors interfering with the text that will be inserted on the Web page.

With the background applied, you can begin inserting other objects on the Web page. One important criterion for developing pages in a web is that related pages have a similar look. As another page in the Morgan, Turner and Lock web, you want to insert a Web page heading that is similar to the one on the Home page.

It is not necessary to duplicate the steps used in Project 2 to achieve this. You simply can copy the Web page heading from the Home page using familiar copy and paste procedures.

Copying Objects from Another Web Page

In the FrontPage Editor, the procedure to copy objects consists of opening the target Web page, opening the source Web page, selecting the objects to be copied, placing them on the Clipboard, and pasting them in the target Web page. The target Web page already is open. To complete the procedure, you now must open the source Web page, select the object or objects to be copied, copy the selected objects to the Clipboard, open the target Web page, and then paste the contents of the Clipboard into the Web page. The steps on the next page illustrate how to copy the three-cell table containing the Morgan, Turner and Lock Home page heading and paste it in the Services Web page.

Copying and Pasting

You can copy images into a Web page by dragging the image from another Windows application to the FrontPage Editor window.

To Copy and Paste Objects from Another Web Page

1 Click the Open button on the Standard toolbar.

The Open dialog box displays (Figure 3-31). It contains the list of files and folders that make up the Morgan, Turner and Lock web.

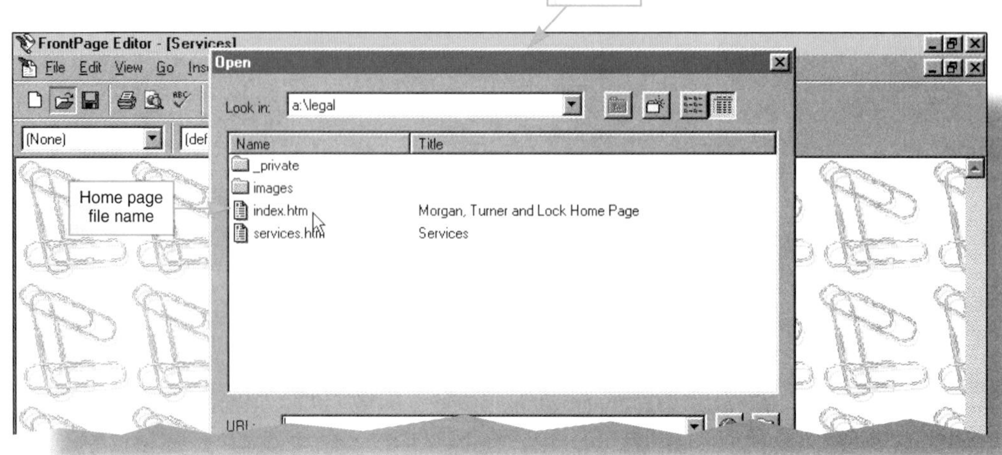

FIGURE 3-31

2 Click index.htm to select it.

The file name, index.htm, is selected (Figure 3-32).

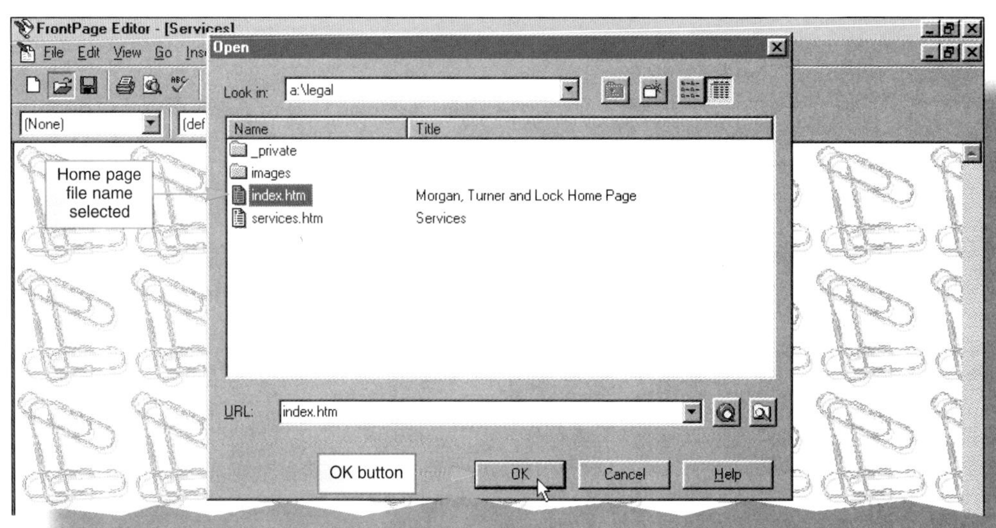

FIGURE 3-32

3 Click the OK button.

The Morgan, Turner and Lock Home Page displays in the FrontPage Editor window (Figure 3-33).

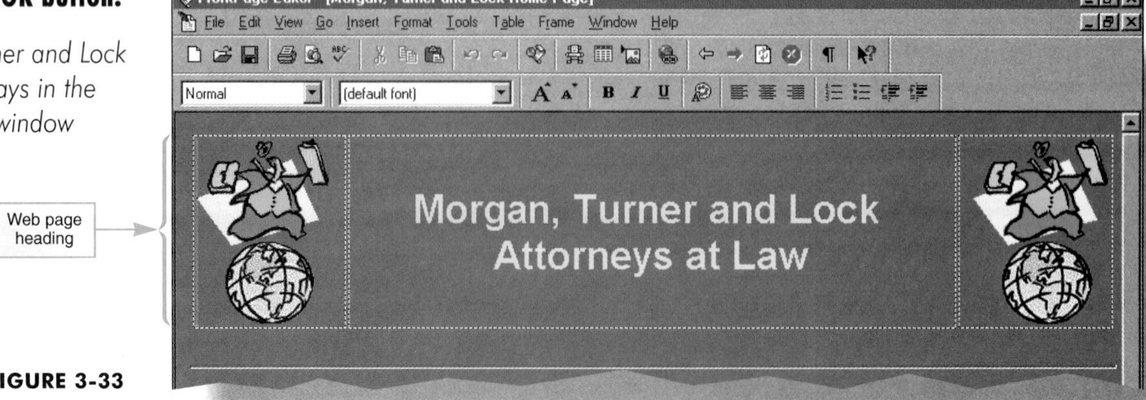

FIGURE 3-33

4 **Drag through the three-cell table containing the two clip art images and the Morgan, Turner and Lock Attorneys at Law heading to select it. Click Edit on the menu bar and then point to Copy.**

The two images and the heading are highlighted, and the Edit menu displays (Figure 3-34).

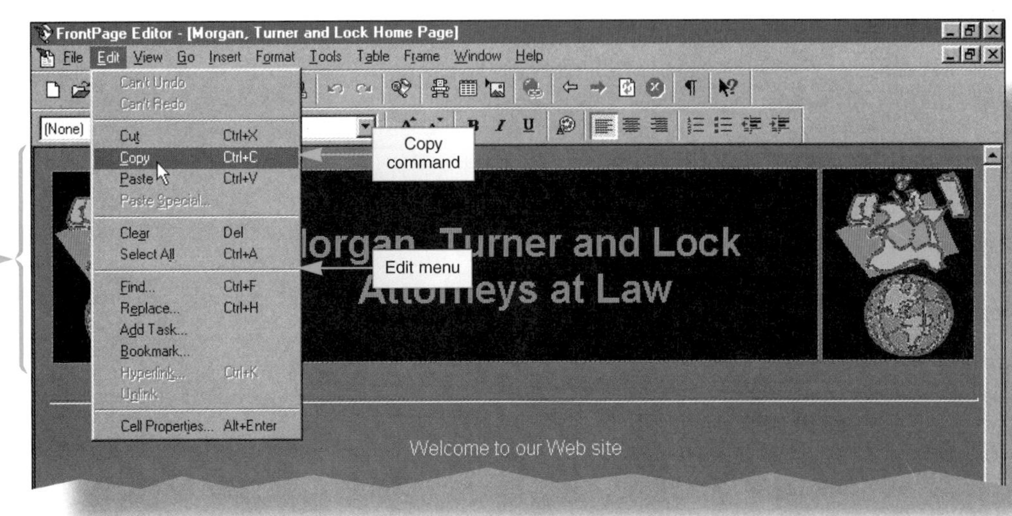

FIGURE 3-34

5 **Click Copy. Click Window on the menu bar and then point to Services.**

The selected images and text are copied to the Windows Clipboard, and the Window menu displays (Figure 3-35).

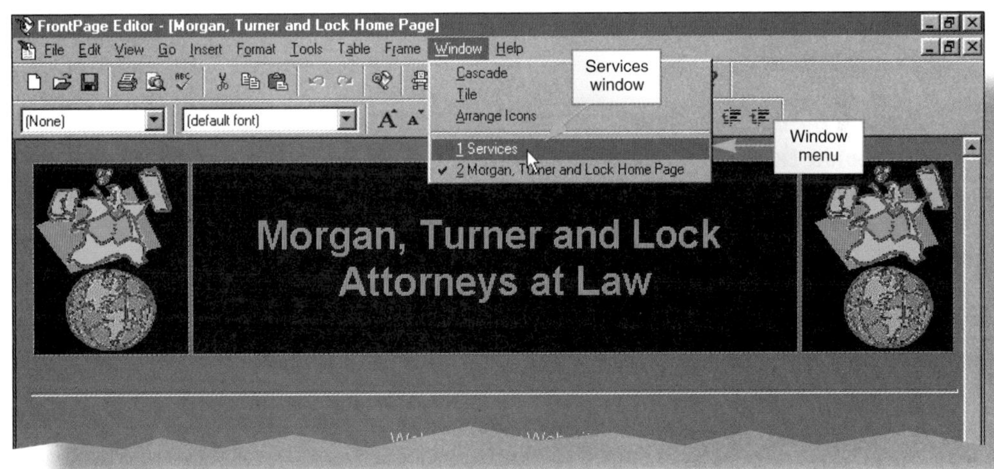

FIGURE 3-35

6 **Click Services. Click Edit on the menu bar and then click Paste.**

The Services page displays, and the table containing the clip art images and the text heading is inserted in the current Web page (Figure 3-36). Because the heading text color is incompatible with the background image, it barely is visible. The text color needs to be changed so it becomes easier to view.

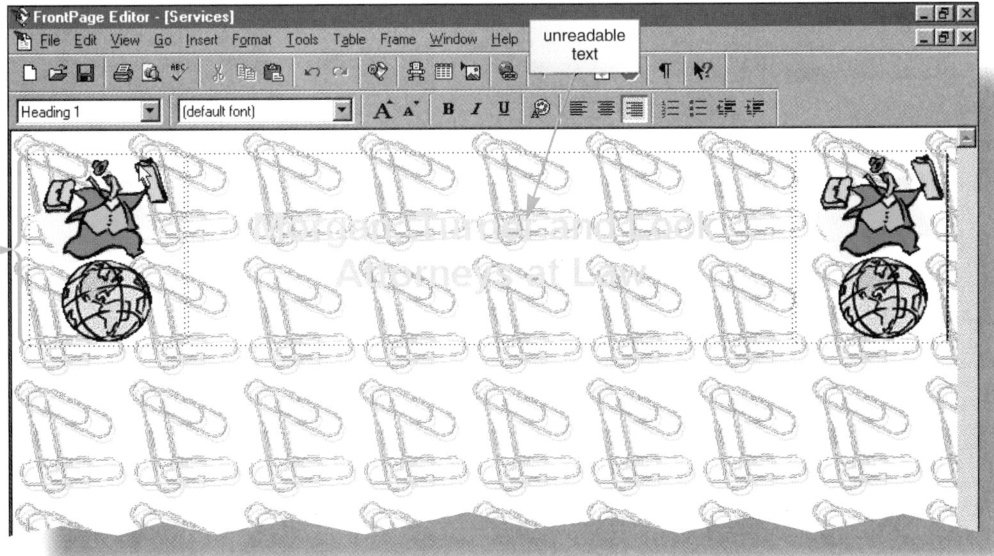

FIGURE 3-36

7 Drag through the heading text to select it. Click the Text Color button on the Format toolbar to display the Color dialog box. Click the color black (row 6, column 1) to select it.

The heading text is highlighted and the Color dialog box displays with the color black selected (Figure 3-37).

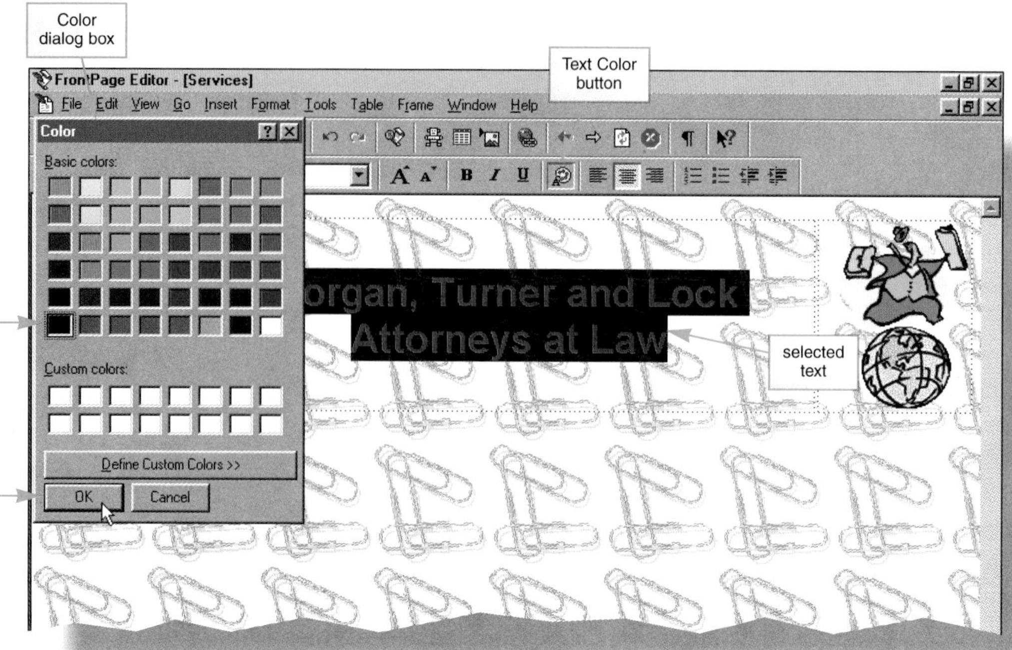

FIGURE 3-37

8 Click the OK button. Click below the table to deselect the text.

The text displays using the new color black (Figure 3-38).

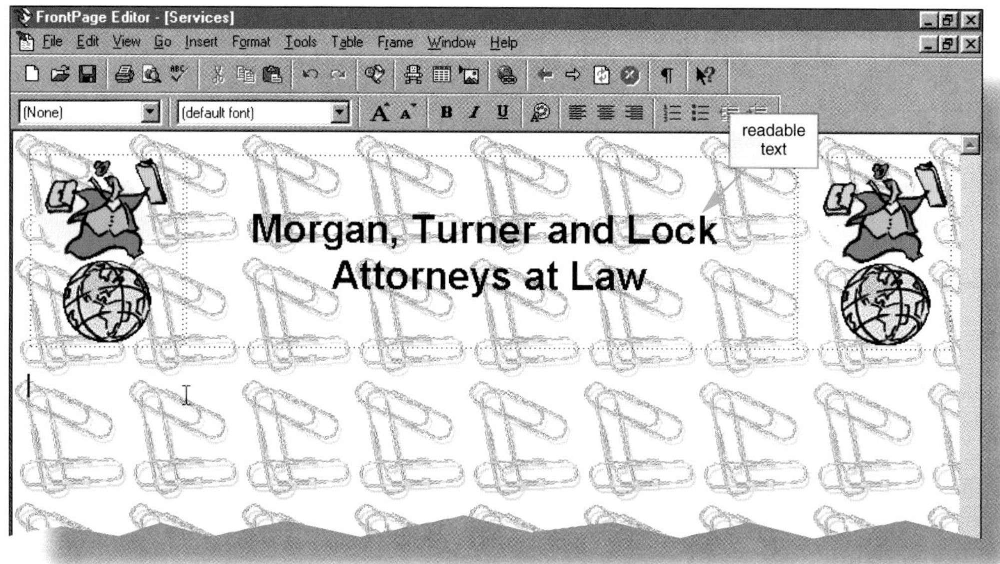

FIGURE 3-38

Other Ways

1. Press ALT+E, C; press ALT+E, V
2. Right-click object, click Copy; right-click, click Paste

As you can see in Figure 3-36 on the previous page, not every combination of text and background colors results in an easy-to-read, aesthetically pleasing Web page. You might have to experiment with several color combinations before deciding on one with the qualities you want.

Adding Text to the Web Page

Now that a text color has been chosen that works well with the paper clips background, the remaining text can be added to the Web page. Perform the following steps to add text to the Web page.

To Add Text to a Web Page

1 Click below the table containing the heading to position the insertion point. Click the Change Style box arrow on the Format toolbar and then click Heading 3. Click the Change Font box arrow on the Format toolbar and then click Arial. Click the Text Color button on the Format toolbar and then click the color black (row 6, column 1). Click the OK button.

The current style is Heading 3 and the current font is Arial (Figure 3-39). The insertion point is positioned below the heading (the three-cell table).

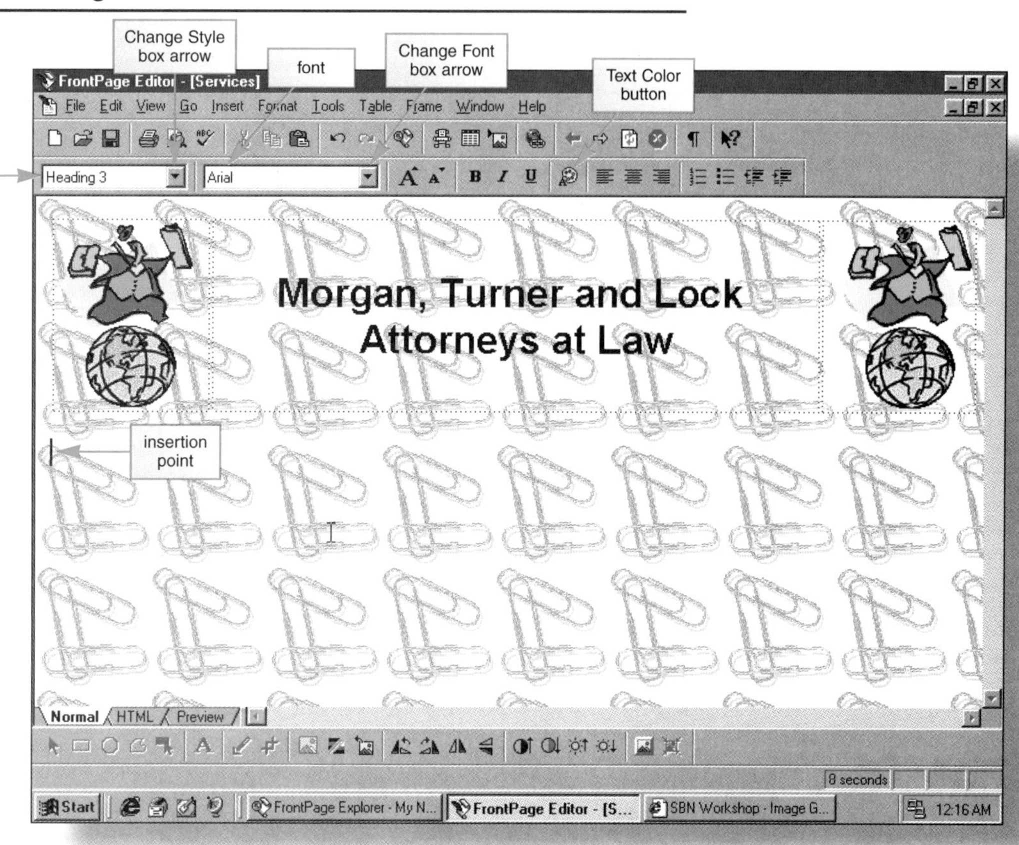

FIGURE 3-39

2 Type `For more information, select one of the services below` **and then click the Center button on the Format toolbar.**

The text displays centered in the Web page (Figure 3-40).

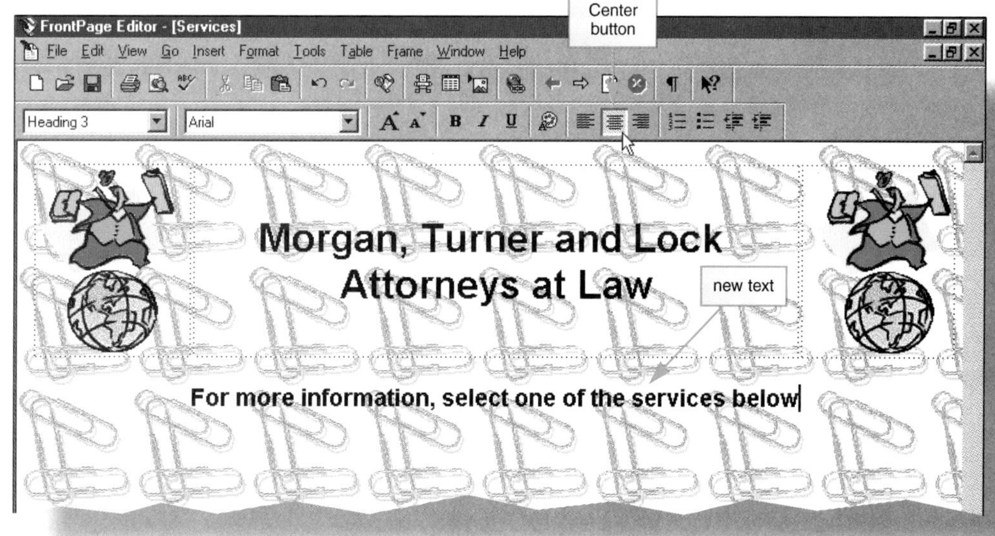

FIGURE 3-40

The Heading 3 style produces text that is larger than normal text, and Arial font is the font used in the Morgan, Turner and Lock Home page.

Obtaining Images

You can browse the Web and select any image to insert in your Web page. Be sure you have permission to use the image before placing it in your FrontPage web. Some images on the Web are copyrighted.

Inserting an Image from the World Wide Web in the Web Page

In Project 2, you inserted clip art images on the Web page. These images were included along with FrontPage 98 for use in Web page development. Using Windows Paint or other graphics editing programs, you can create your own images. Collections of images on CD-ROM also are available for purchase. A number of Web sites on the World Wide Web offer free collections of images to the public for use in Web page development.

It is possible to use any image you find on the World Wide Web in your Web pages. Before you use an image, button, divider, or other item, however, be sure you have permission to use it, or that you see a notice indicating the image is provided free, before you include it in your Web pages.

Microsoft has a Web site, called the Site Builder Network (SBN), which is devoted to Web page development. It contains free libraries of images, sounds, animations, and other items that can be used in Web page development. The URL for the Site Builder Network Image Gallery is www.microsoft.com/gallery/images/default.asp. You already used this site to obtain the paper clip background image. The following steps show how to return to the Site Builder Network Web site and insert one of the available images on a Web page.

To Insert an Image from the World Wide Web

1 Press the ENTER key to position the insertion point. Click the Insert Image button on the Standard toolbar. Point to the World Wide Web button.

The Image dialog box displays (Figure 3-41).

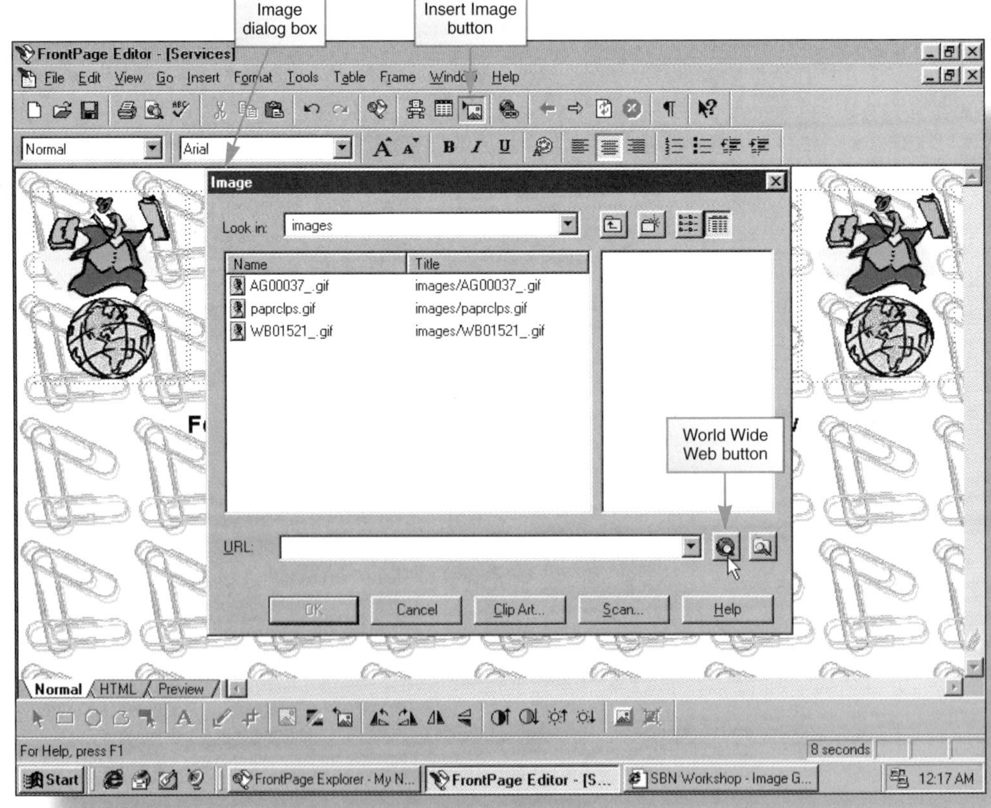

FIGURE 3-41

2 Click the World Wide Web button. If necessary, click the Address bar and then type `www.microsoft.com/gallery/images/default.asp`**. Press the ENTER key, click the show contents hyperlink, and then click the Clip Art: Business category.**

The SBN Workshop Web page displays in the Internet Explorer window (Figure 3-42). It contains links to files containing images, sounds, tools, and other Web development materials.

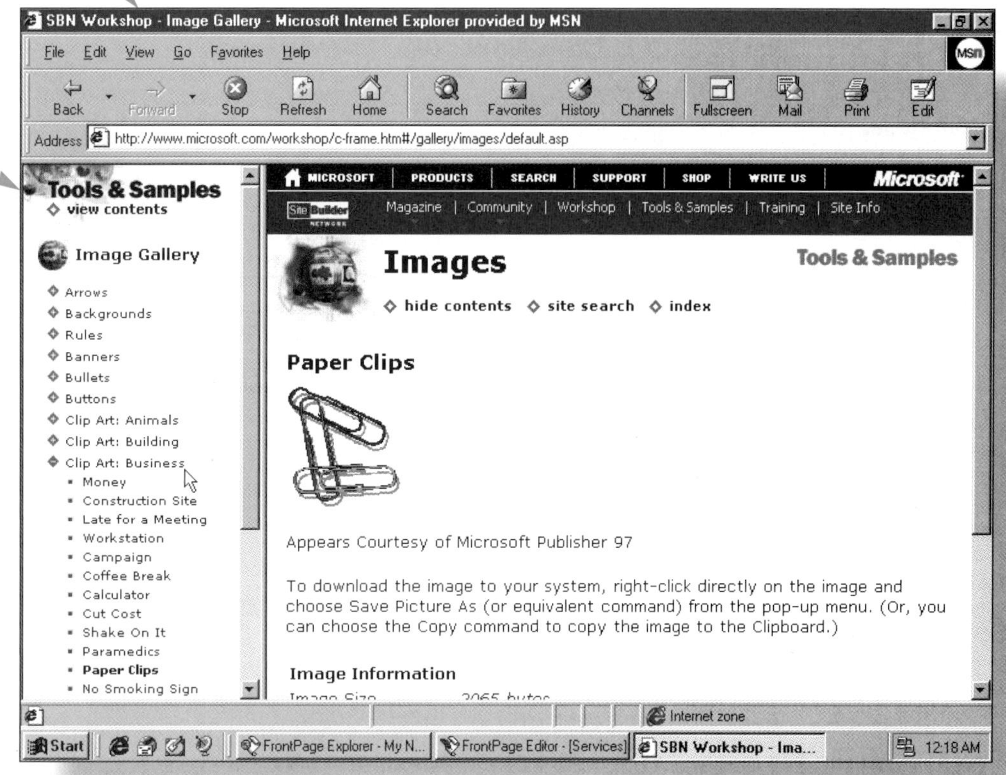

FIGURE 3-42

3 Scroll down the list of available image files until the Open Briefcase hyperlink displays. Click the Open Briefcase hyperlink.

A sample of the image displays in the Web page (Figure 3-43). To use the image in your FrontPage web, you will save a copy of the image to the images folder in the Morgan, Turner and Lock web.

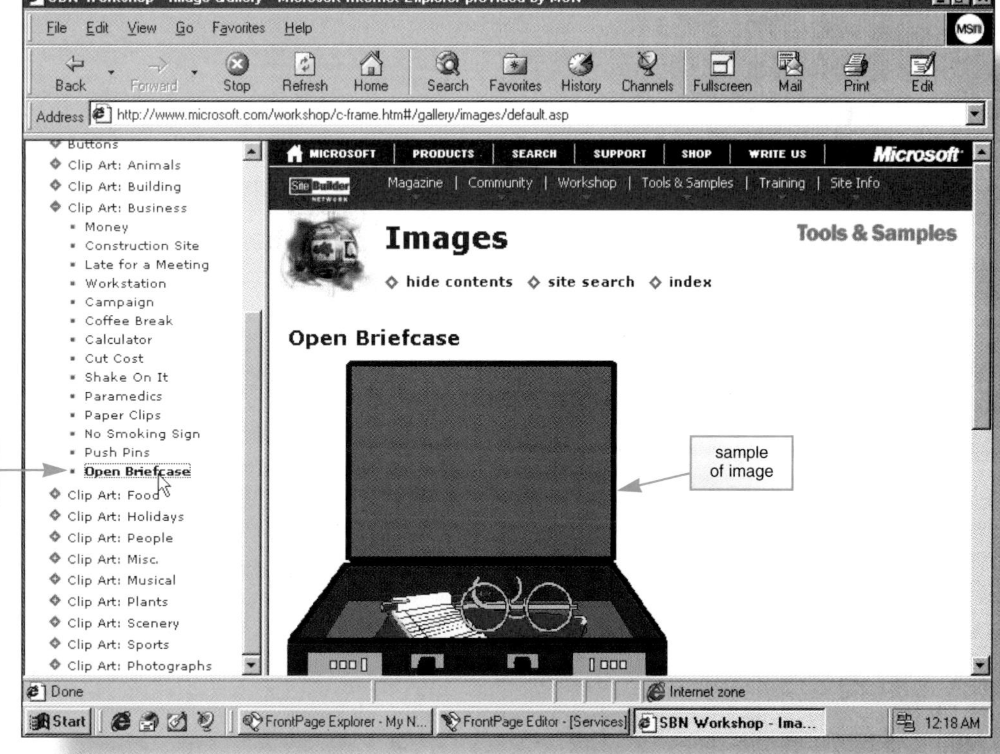

FIGURE 3-43

4 Right-click the sample image. Click Save Picture As on the shortcut menu.

The Save Picture dialog box displays (Figure 3-44). The list of files and folders stored on the floppy disk display.

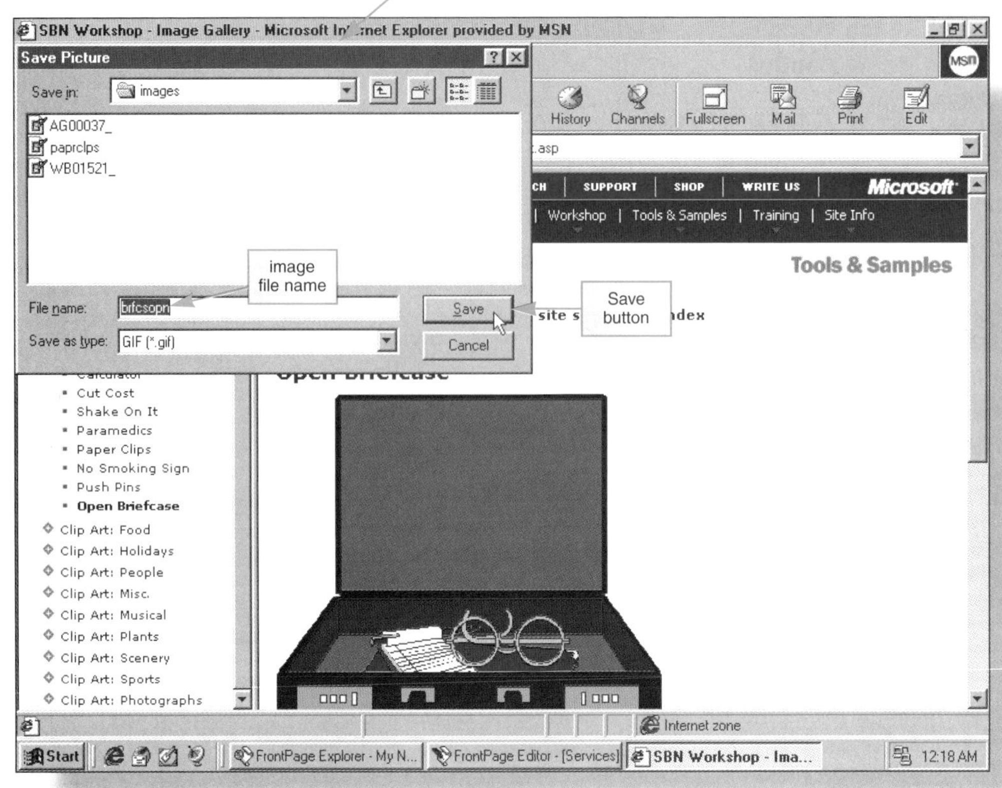

FIGURE 3-44

5 Click the Save in box arrow. Click 3½ Floppy (A:). Double-click legal. Double-click images. Click the Save button.

The file is transferred to your computer using the file name brfcsopn.gif.

6 Click the FrontPage Editor button on the taskbar. Click the File button in the Image dialog box. If necessary, click the Save in box arrow, click 3½ Floppy (A:), double-click legal, double-click images. Click brfcsopn.

The Select File dialog box displays (Figure 3-45). The file name, brfcsopn, is selected.

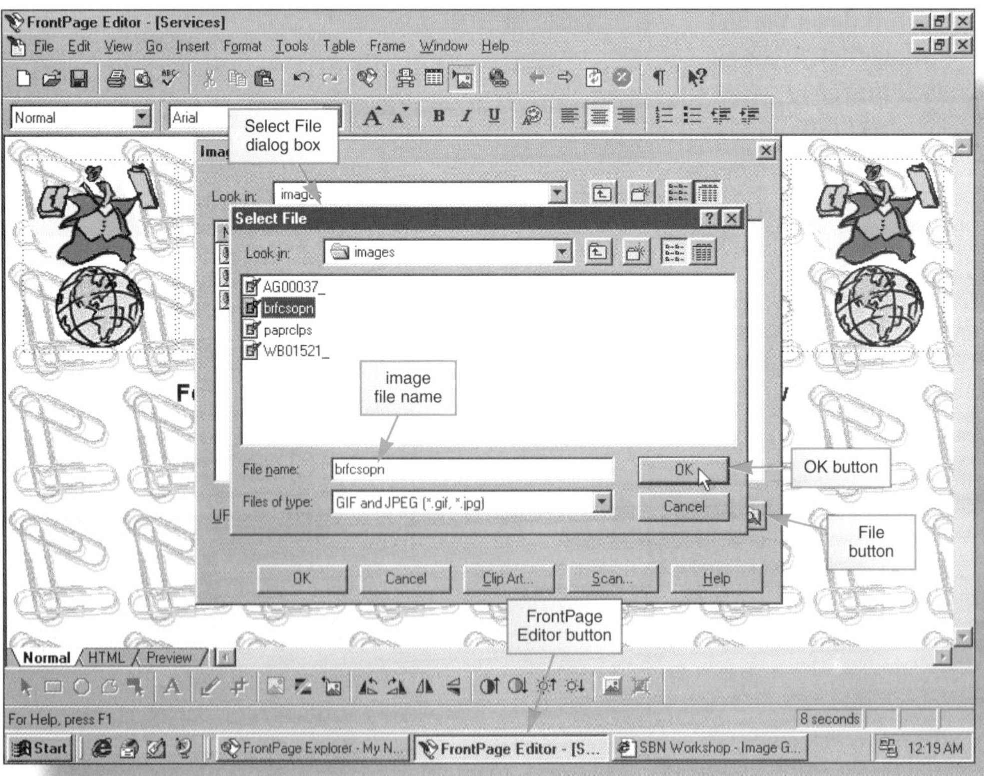

FIGURE 3-45

7 Click the OK button in the Select File dialog box. Scroll down the Services Web page.

The open briefcase image displays in the Services Web page (Figure 3-46).

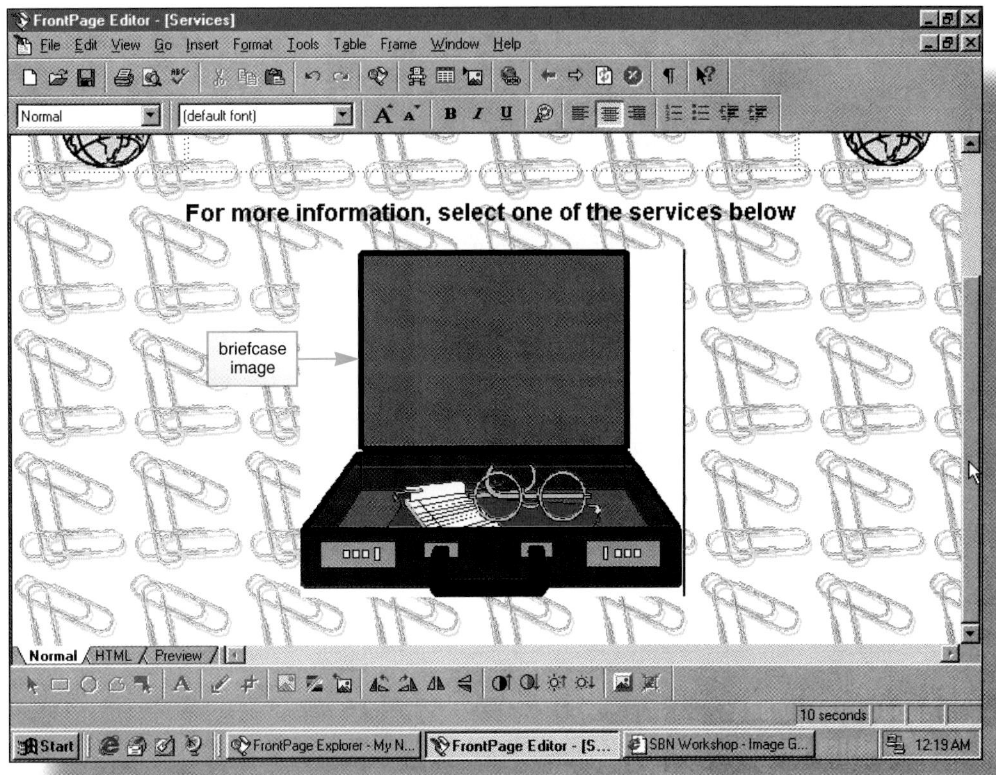

FIGURE 3-46

Other Ways

1. On Insert menu click Image
2. Press ALT+I, I

Using this technique, you can obtain copies of neat buttons, dividers, background patterns, pictures, and animations that are available on the World Wide Web, provided you have permission to use them. Saving the images that you find on the World Wide Web into the images folder in the current FrontPage web ensures that all of the images will be in one place, and always will be available so your Web pages display properly.

You might want to do all your browsing and image saving at one time, placing several images in the images folder, so you do not have to interrupt your Web page development to search for just the right image. Some images are very large, so be sure you have sufficient space on the disk where you will be storing them.

Once you have the image inserted on the Web page, you can begin to use the image editing facilities of the FrontPage Editor to customize the image to fit in your Web page design.

More About

The Image Folder

Keep separate Image folders for each FrontPage web. This ensures you do not accidentally overlay an image file that is used in some other web that has the same file name.

Resizing a Clip Art Image

Sometimes an image you want to use is too small or too large to fit within the space you have set aside for it in your Web page design. You can resize an image, shrinking or stretching it, by selecting the image and dragging its handles until it becomes the desired size.

Resizing an image does not automatically change the size of the image file. It changes only the HTML tags for the image, so the browser actually does the shrinking or stretching when the image is displayed. This is an advantage for small images that you have stretched to a larger size. The small image file takes less time to load than if the file contained the image at its larger size.

Resampling an Image

Because resampling stores a new copy of the image in the image file, you might want to make a backup copy of the original image file, in case you save an unwanted change accidentally. You can retrieve a fresh copy from the backup and continue with your development.

Conversely, for images you have made smaller, the file still contains the image at its original size, and it still must be loaded even though the browser displays a smaller version of the image. To take advantage of the download performance brought on by a smaller image, you must resample the image. **Resampling** an image stores the image in the file at its new size.

The briefcase image will be the image map. It will contain four hyperlinks to the services you listed during the Web page design (see Figure 3-1 on page FP 3.5). Currently, the image is small in relation to the rest of the Web page; too much space exists on the left and right sides. Without resizing the image, it might be difficult to fit the four hyperlinks in the top half of the briefcase in a manner that is easy for the user to read and to use.

In this case, you must resize the image to make it larger by selecting the image and dragging the handles to the desired size. Normally, you would not resample an image that has been made larger for the reasons discussed previously. It is necessary to resample the briefcase image later in the project, however, and then save the changes. Perform the following steps to resize the briefcase image.

To Resize a Clip Art Image

1 Click the briefcase image to select it. Point to the handle in the lower-right corner of the image.

The image is selected, and the mouse pointer changes to a double-headed arrow (Figure 3-47).

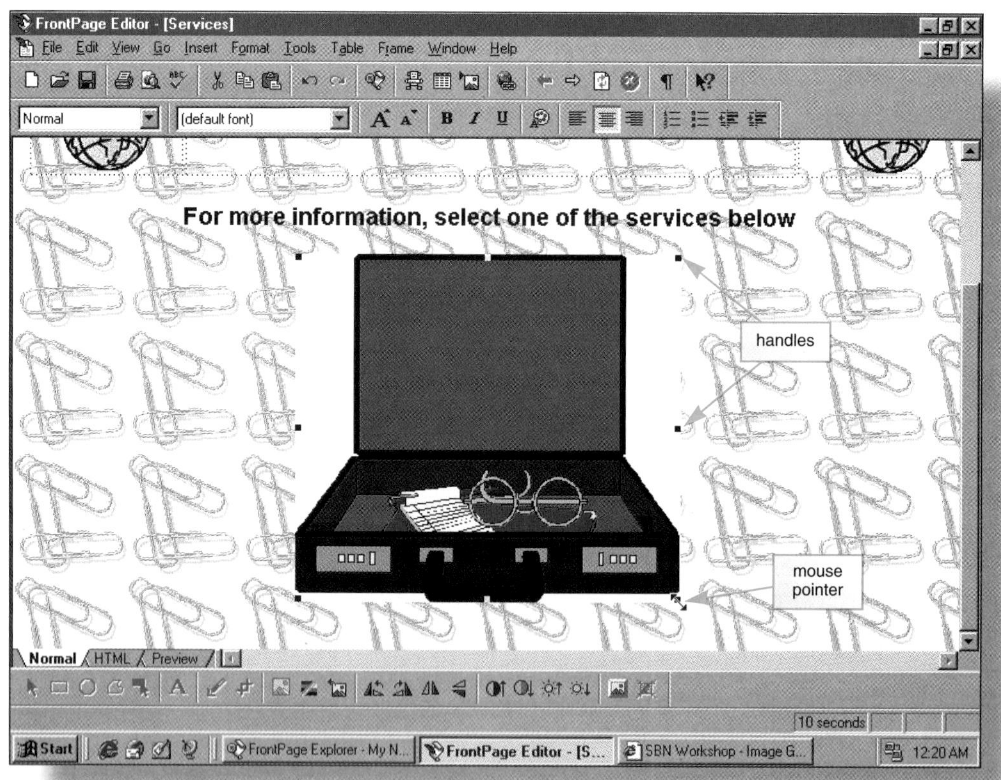

FIGURE 3-47

2 Drag the handle down and to the right to increase the size of the image.

A box displays indicating the new size of the clip art image (Figure 3-48).

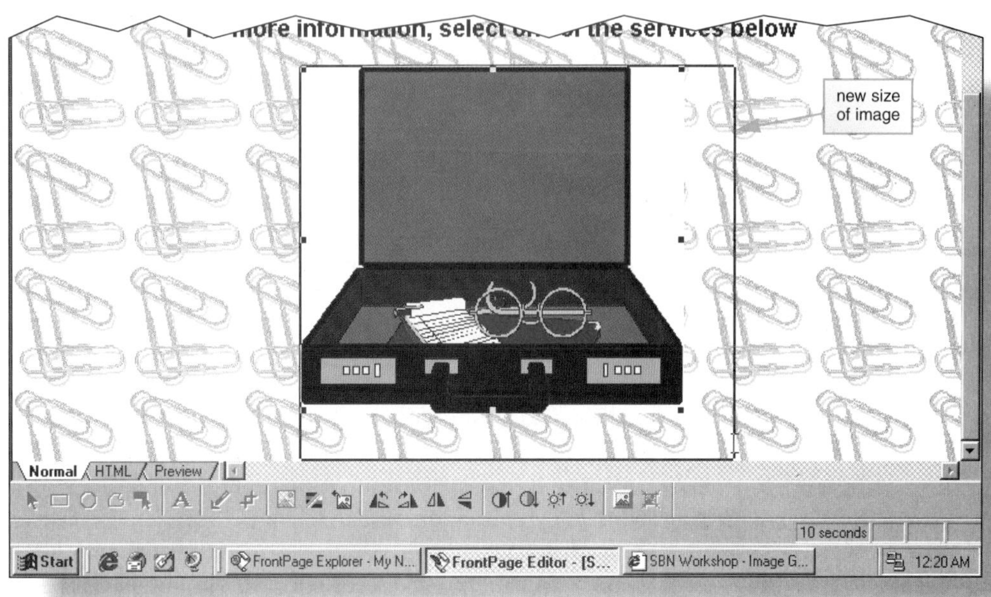

FIGURE 3-48

3 Release the handle.

The resized clip art image redisplays (Figure 3-49).

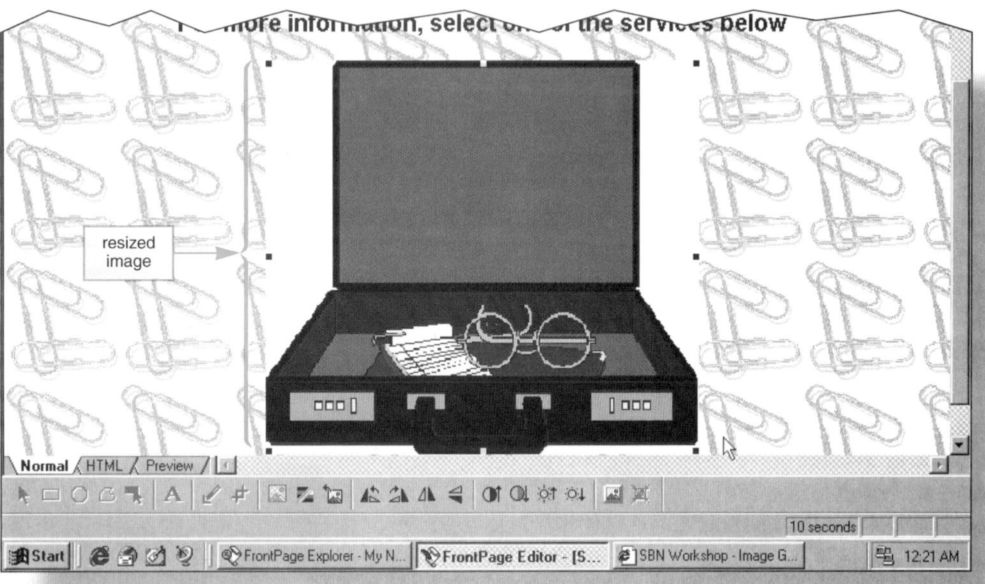

FIGURE 3-49

Notice the box that displays while dragging the handles moves both horizontally and vertically at the same time. This happens because the FrontPage Editor is preserving the horizontal to vertical ratio of the image, so you do not end up with a distorted image. This prevents you from stretching the image in only one direction, so you avoid an image that is extremely tall and very skinny or that looks flat.

The larger image can be made permanent by clicking the Resample button on the Image toolbar. You can return the image to the original size currently stored in the image file by clicking the **Restore button** on the Image toolbar.

The briefcase image in its current state presents a minor problem combined with the paper clip background. Although the briefcase has irregular edges, the image actually is box-shaped. Notice in Figure 3-50 that the white space on the left and right sides of the briefcase obscure the paper clip background. Using a technique that will make the white color of the briefcase image transparent, you can eliminate this problem.

Transparent Images

GIF images that are animated will not allow you to select a transparent color. An animated GIF image consists of several images that are displayed in rapid succession.

Creating a Transparent Image

A **transparent image** sometimes is referred to as a **floating image** because it appears to *float* on the Web page. To make an image transparent, you select one of the colors in the image to be the transparent color. The **transparent color** is replaced by the background color or image of the page.

An image can have only one transparent color. If you select another transparent color, the first transparent color reverts to its original color. Use the **Make Transparent button** on the Image toolbar to make a selected color transparent. When you click the Make Transparent button, the mouse pointer changes to the **Make Transparent pointer**. You then click a color on the image to make it transparent.

To make an image transparent, it must be in the GIF file format. FrontPage will ask you if you want to convert a JPEG image to GIF format if you try to make a JPEG image transparent. Because GIF only supports up to 256 colors, you may lose some image quality by converting from JPEG to GIF.

The procedure for making a transparent image is to select the image and then choose the transparent color using the Make Transparent pointer. For the change to take affect immediately, you must resample the image. Resampling an image changes the file size of the image. To make the color white around the sides of the briefcase image the transparent color so the paper clip background shows through and resample the briefcase image, perform the following steps.

To Create a Transparent Image

1 Click the briefcase clip art image to select it. Point to the Make Transparent button on the Image toolbar.

The briefcase image is selected (Figure 3-50).

FIGURE 3-50

2 Click the Make Transparent button and then point to the color white in the briefcase image.

The mouse pointer changes to the Make Transparent pointer (Figure 3-51).

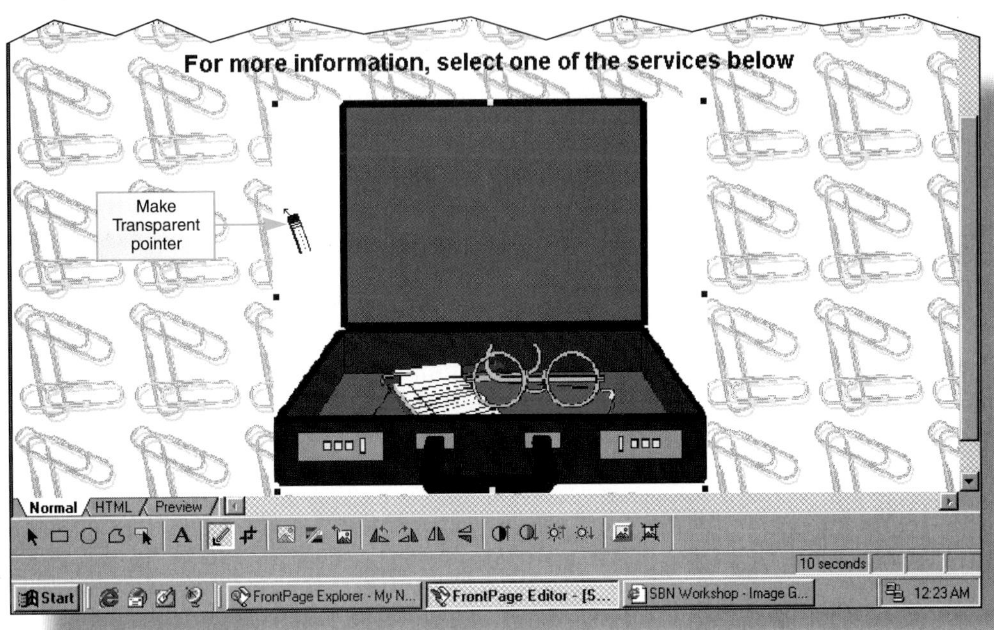

FIGURE 3-51

3 Click the color white in the briefcase image.

The Make Transparent pointer is restored to the normal block arrow pointer. You must resample the image for the changes to take effect.

4 Click the Resample button on the Image toolbar.

The color white becomes transparent, and is replaced by the paper clip background (Figure 3-52).

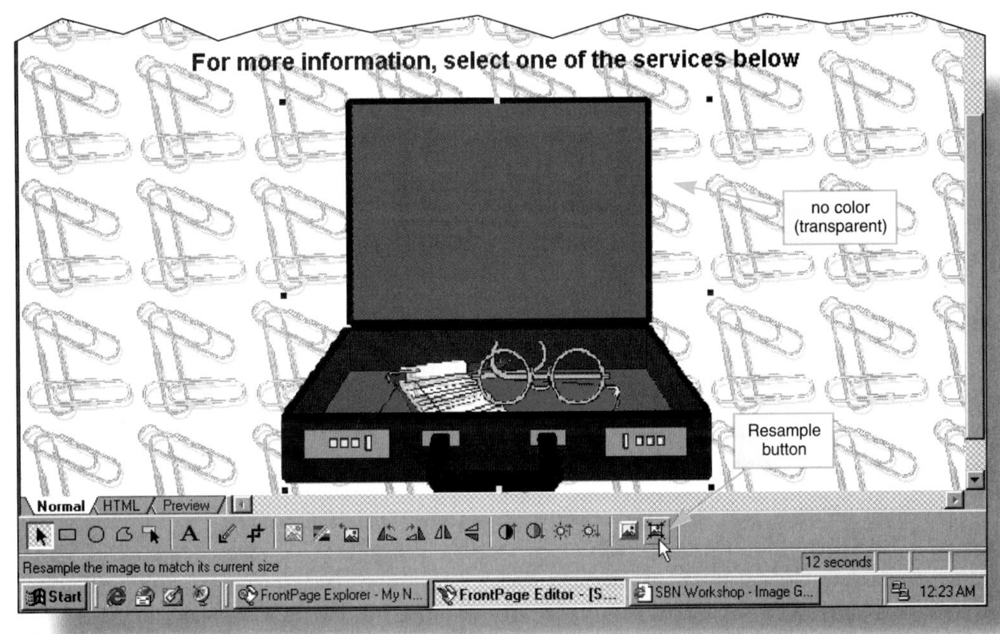

FIGURE 3-52

You must take care when selecting a color to be transparent. If the color appears in other sections of the image, it will become transparent in the other sections as well, and might have an unexpected or undesirable effect. If you look closely in Figure 3-52 at the pad of paper inside the briefcase, you will see the paper clip background showing.

In this case, it is not significant because you have to look very carefully to see it. You could run into problems, however, if for example, you have a purple background and an image containing a face. If you make white the transparent color, it could result in a face with purple eyes and purple teeth.

Image Map Styles

To change the image map style, click Web Settings on the Tools menu, and then select Image Map in the Style list box in the Advanced tab of the FrontPage Web Settings dialog box.

Image Maps

The purpose of the briefcase image is to serve as an image map. **Image maps** are special graphic images containing areas called hotspots. A **hotspot** is a specially designated portion of the image that is set up as a hyperlink. Clicking one of the hotspots is the same as clicking a regular text hyperlink. The hotspot lets you jump to the URL that is defined for that region of the image.

Image maps bring new ways to create interactive Web pages. They provide an alternative to plain text hyperlinks. A well-designed image map gives the viewer clues about the destination of each hyperlink. For example, an art gallery might have an image containing a diagram of the various rooms in which different types of art are exhibited. Clicking a room displays another Web page containing images of related works of art. A college or university could have an image containing a map of the campus with hotspots defined for each building. Clicking a building would display another Web page describing the building.

When creating an image map, you want to use a motif or metaphor for your images. For example, a campus map of different buildings might be used for obtaining navigation assistance. A bookshelf with books listing different topics might be used in a help desk application.

Defining Hotspots

To create an image map, you first decide on an image to use. Then, you define the hotspots on the image, and finally, you assign URLs to each hotspot.

Hotspots can be circles, rectangles, or irregularly shaped areas called polygons. You designate hotspots using the hotspot buttons on the toolbar. For example, when you click the Rectangle button, the mouse pointer changes to a pencil pointer. You would click and hold one corner of the desired rectangle, drag to the opposite corner, and then release the mouse button. The Create Hyperlink dialog box automatically opens so you can type the target URL that will be assigned to the hotspot. You also can add text to an image and then create hotspots using the text.

The top half of the briefcase image has a large empty area on which you will add text descriptions of services being advertised by Morgan, Turner and Lock. You will then will make hotspots using the text descriptions. Perform the following steps to add hotspots to the image, making it an image map.

To Add a Hotspot to an Image Map

1 If necessary, click the briefcase image to select it, and then click the Text button on the Image toolbar.

A resizable text box displays in the briefcase image (Figure 3-53).

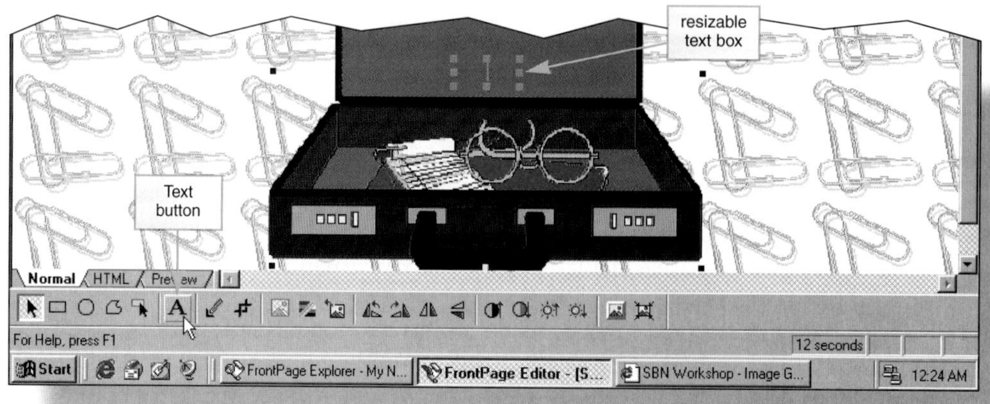

FIGURE 3-53

2 **Type** `Living Trusts` **in the text box.**

The text displays in the text box (Figure 3-54).

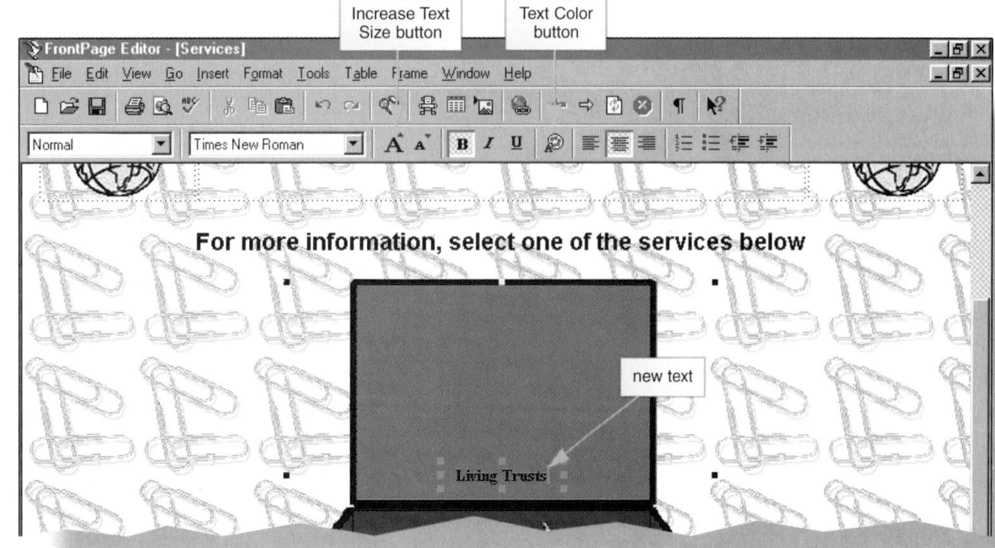

FIGURE 3-54

3 **Click the Text Color button on the Format toolbar. When the Color dialog box displays, click the color blue (row 4, column 5) and then click the OK button. Click the Increase Text Size button on the Format toolbar four times.**

The text color changes to blue, and the size of the text increases in the text box (Figure 3-55). The text is too large to display in the text box, so the size of the text box will have to be increased.

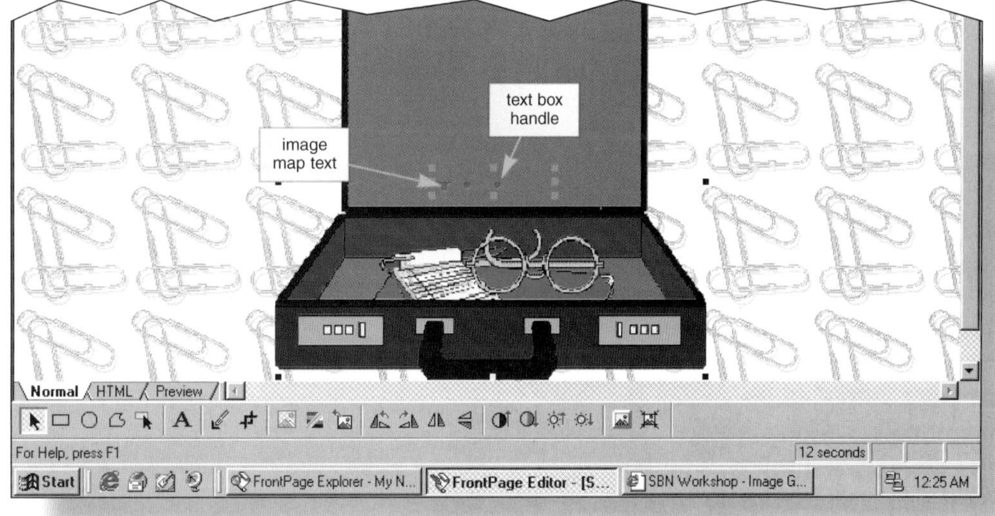

FIGURE 3-55

4 **Drag the text box handles to span the width of the briefcase top and approximately one quarter of the height of the briefcase top.**

The size of the text box increases and the blue text displays (Figure 3-56). The size should allow you to define four hotspots.

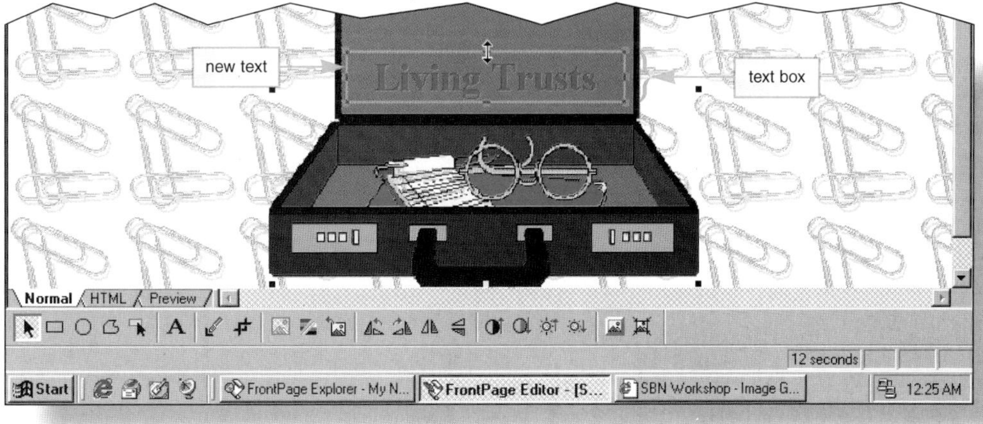

FIGURE 3-56

5 **Click outside of the text box to deselect it. Drag the text box to the top portion of the top of the briefcase image.**

The hotspot displays at the top of the image (Figure 3-57).

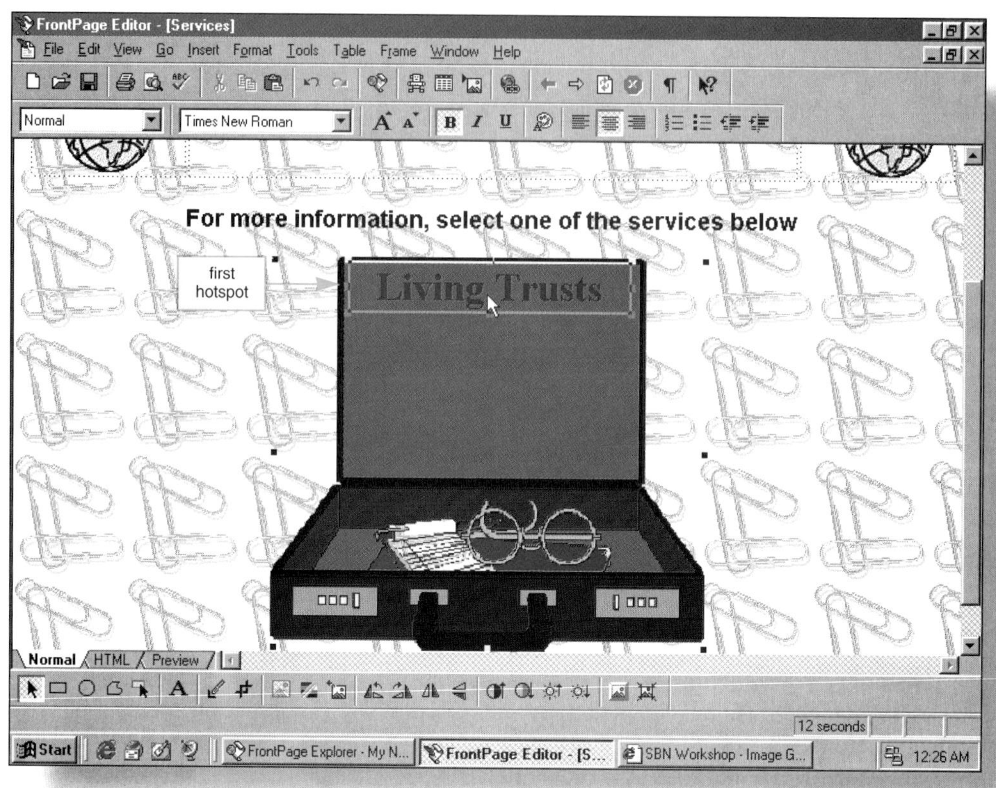

FIGURE 3-57

6 **Click the Text button on the Image toolbar. Type** `Litigation` **in the text box. Click the Text Color button on the Format toolbar. When the Color dialog box displays, click the color blue (row 4, column 5) and then click the OK button. Click the Increase Text Size button on the Format toolbar four times. Resize the text box to approximately the same size as the first text box. Click outside of the text box to deselect it. Drag the text box below the Living Trusts hotspot.**

The hotspot displays below the Living Trusts hotspot (Figure 3-58).

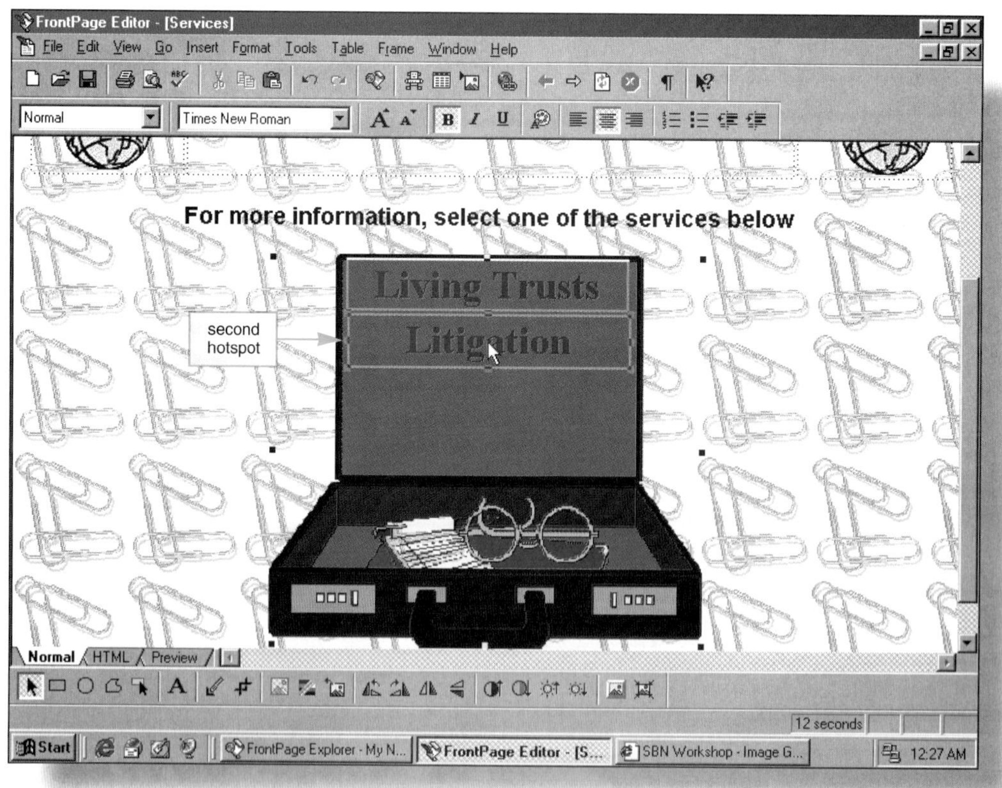

FIGURE 3-58

7 **Click the Text button on the Image toolbar. Type** `Business` **in the text box. Click the Text Color button on the Format toolbar. When the Color dialog box displays, click the color blue (row 4, column 5) and then click the OK button. Click the Increase Text Size button on the Format toolbar four times. Resize the text box to approximately the same size as the previous two text boxes. Click outside of the text box to deselect it. Drag the text box below the Litigation hotspot.**

The hotspot displays below the Litigation hotspot (Figure 3-59).

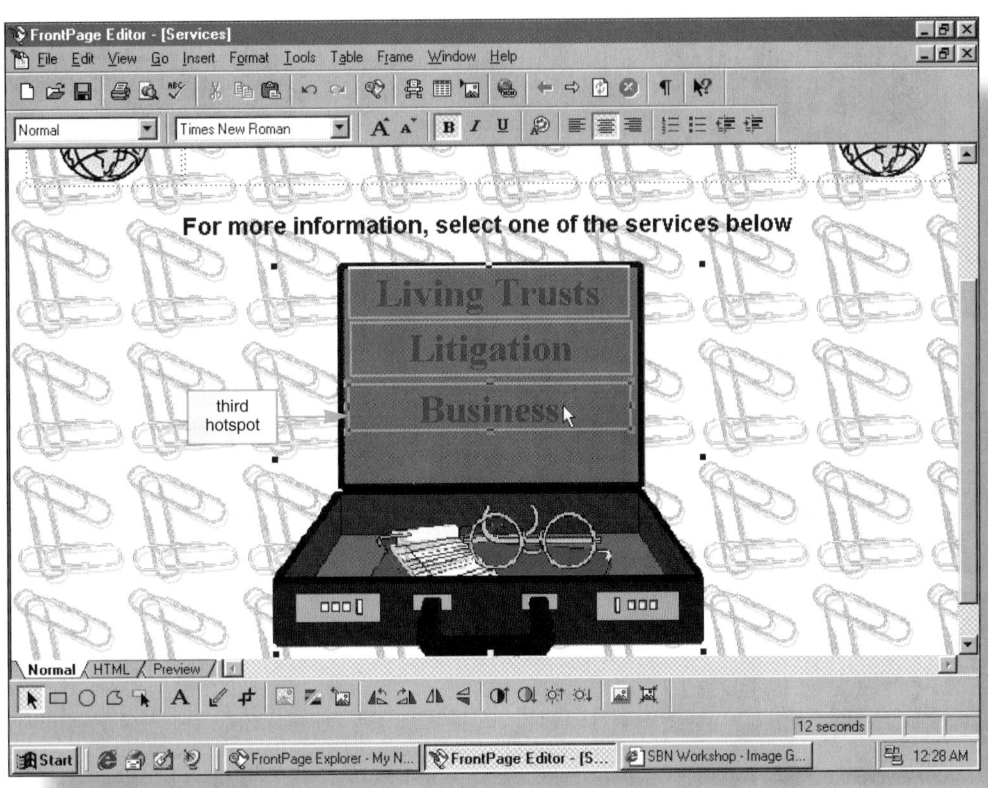

FIGURE 3-59

8 **Click the Text button on the Image toolbar. Type** `Government` **in the text box. Click the Text Color button on the Format toolbar. When the Color dialog box displays, click the color blue (row 4, column 5) and then click the OK button. Click the Increase Text Size button on the Format toolbar four times. Resize the text box to approximately the same size as the other three text boxes. Click outside of the text box to deselect it. Drag the text box below the Business hotspot.**

The hotspot displays below the Business hotspot (Figure 3-60).

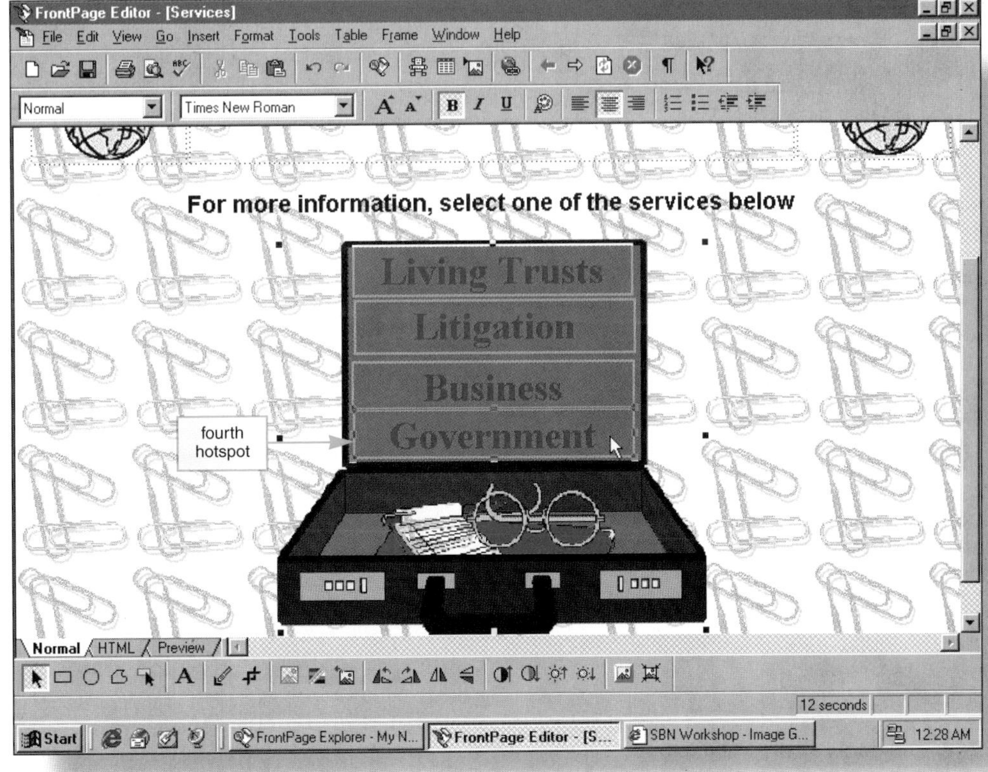

FIGURE 3-60

You have successfully created hotspots on an image map. When creating hotspots using the circle, rectangle, or polygon buttons on the Image toolbar, the Create Hyperlink dialog box automatically displays as soon as you release the mouse button after drawing the hotspot using the pencil pointer. This did not happen when you inserted the text in the previous steps because you could add text to an image without making the text a hotspot. You must add the target URLs to text hotspots manually.

Adding Image Map Targets

Once the text hotspots are defined, assigning the target URLs is the same as setting up a regular hyperlink. Perform the following steps to assign target URLs to the text hotspots in the briefcase image map.

To Specify the Target of an Image Map Hotspot

1 Double-click the Living Trusts hotspot.

The Create Hyperlink dialog box displays (Figure 3-61).

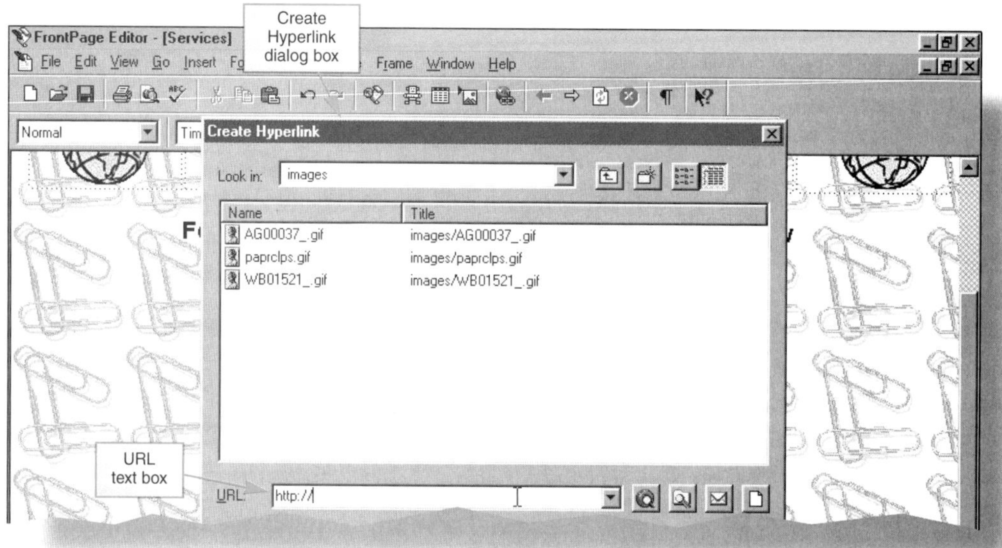

FIGURE 3-61

2 Double-click the URL text box and then type `trusts.htm` **in the text box.**

The file name displays in the URL text box (Figure 3-62).

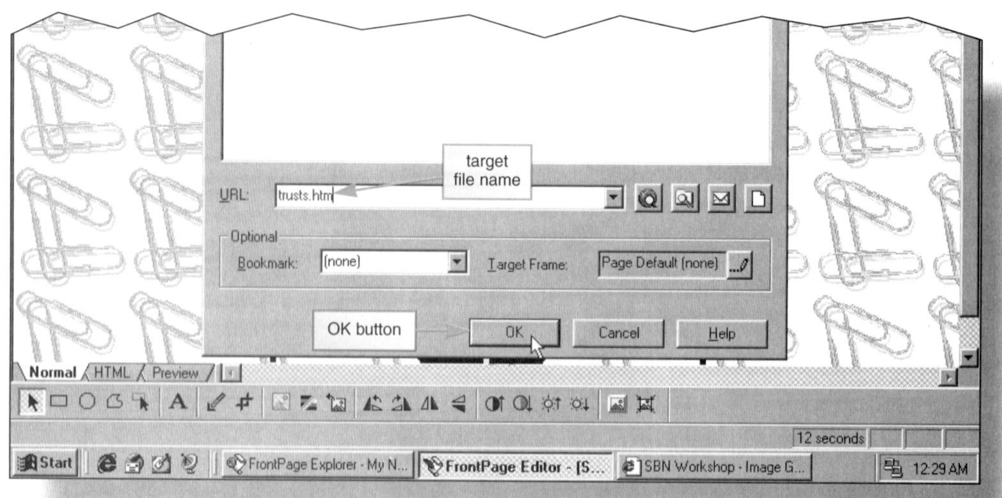

FIGURE 3-62

3 **Click the OK button and then point to the Living Trusts hotspot.**

The target URL of the hyperlink displays on the status bar (Figure 3-63).

FIGURE 3-63

4 **Double-click the Litigation hotspot. Double-click the URL text box and then type** `litigation.htm` **in the text box. Click the OK button and then point to the Litigation hotspot.**

The target URL of the hyperlink displays on the status bar (Figure 3-64).

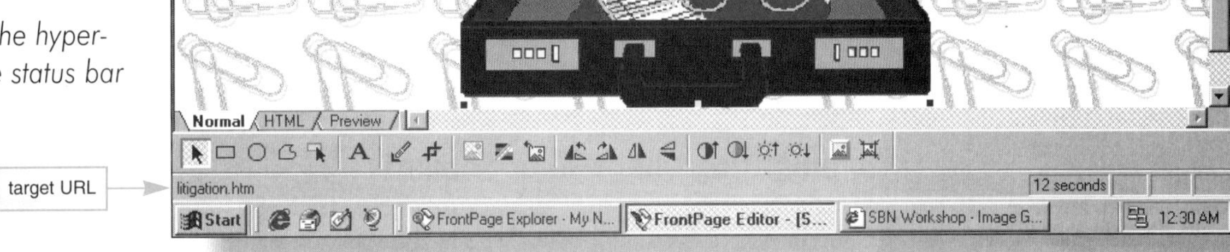

FIGURE 3-64

5 **Double-click the Business hotspot. Double-click the URL text box and then type** `business.htm` **in the text box. Click the OK button and then point to the Business hotspot.**

The target URL of the hyperlink displays on the status bar (Figure 3-65).

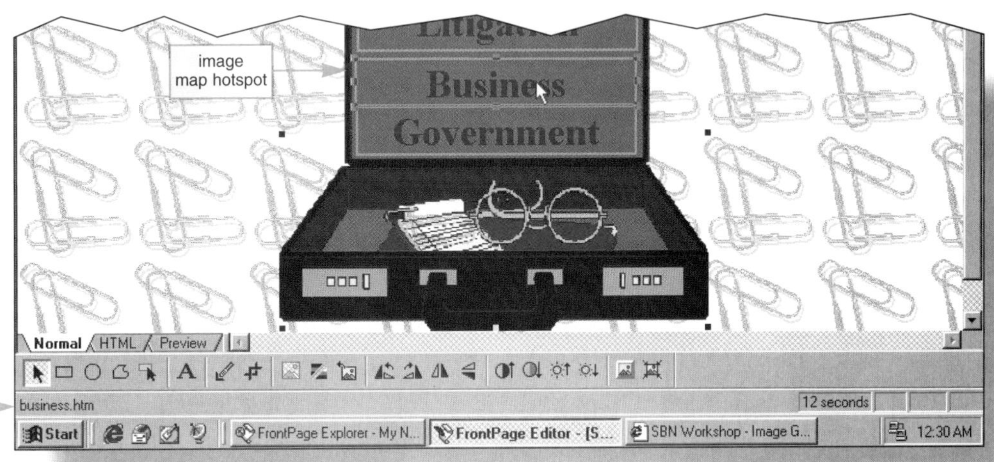

FIGURE 3-65

6 **Double-click the Government hotspot. Double-click the URL text box and then type** `government.htm` **in the text box. Click the OK button and then point to the Government hotspot.**

The target URL of the hyperlink displays on the status bar (Figure 3-66).

target URL

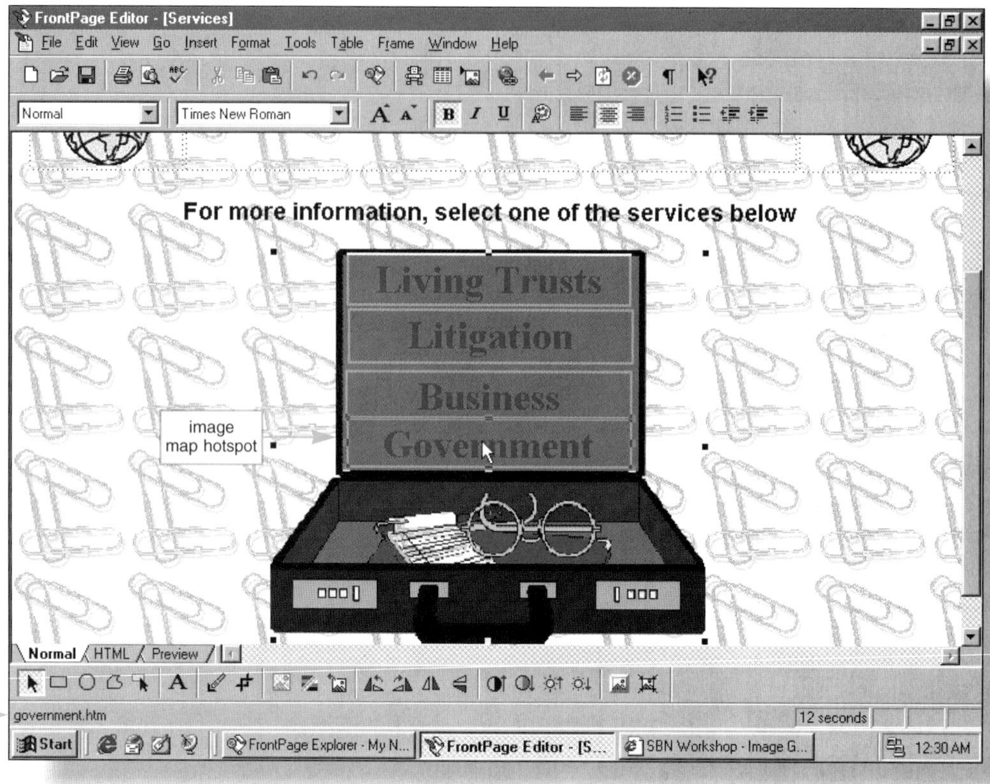

FIGURE 3-66

1. On Edit menu click Image Hotspot Properties
2. Right-click hotspot, click Image Hotspot Properties
3. Press ALT+ENTER

More About

Image Map Hotspots

You can set a default hyperlink for any area on the image map that does not have a hotspot defined. Click the General tab in the Image Properties dialog box.

Image maps are an excellent way to present links visually in an intuitive and user-friendly fashion. Creating your own image maps is not hard to do, but requires some careful preparation.

Highlighting Image Map Hotspots

The hotspots on the briefcase image map are easy to see because you added text descriptions to the image map. Some image maps will not have any text or image features associated with hotspots. Locating the hotspot outlines can be difficult in these instances.

The Image toolbar includes the **Highlight Hotspots button** that toggles between displaying hotspots only and displaying the image and the hotspot. Perform the following steps to highlight the hotspots on the briefcase image map.

To Highlight Hotspots

1 **Click the Highlight Hotspots button on the Image toolbar.**

The image becomes white, and the hotspots are revealed with black outlines (Figure 3-67). In this view, you easily can see the hotspots.

2 **Click the Highlight Hotspots button.**

The briefcase image redisplays.

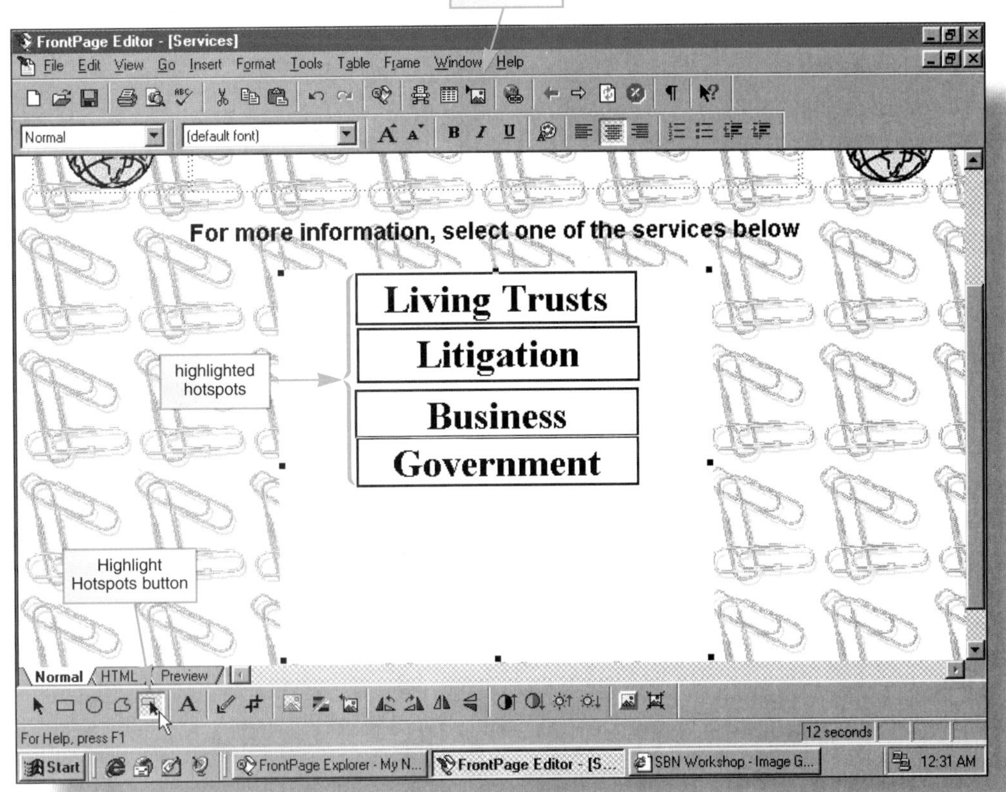

FIGURE 3-67

The Highlight Hotspots button is useful when image features make it difficult to see the hotspot outlines that are superimposed on the image.

Inserting Photographs on a Web Page

Although GIF images allow you to create effects such as animation and image maps, they are not a good choice for photographic-quality color images because of their 256 color limitation.

You must use JPEG images to achieve photographic-quality color images. Inserting a JPEG image uses the same steps as inserting a GIF image. Perform the steps on the next page to insert an image of the skyline of Seattle, Washington on the Web page.

Photographic Images

Take care when using photographic images with 24-bit color. Not everyone on the Web has a monitor and display adapter that supports 24-bit color. Try changing your Windows color setting to a lower-bit resolution and displaying the Web page to see how the images look.

To Insert a JPEG Image on a Web Page

1 **Click the background to the right of the briefcase image to position the insertion point and then press the ENTER key. Click the Insert Image button on the Standard toolbar. When the Image dialog box displays, click the World Wide Web button. If necessary, click the Address bar. Type** `www.microsoft.com/gallery/images/default.asp` **and then press the ENTER key. In the Internet Explorer window, click the show contents hyperlink and then click the Clip Art: Photographs category. Scroll down the list of images until the Seattle hyperlink displays. Click the Seattle hyperlink.**

Clip Art: Photographs category

sample image

Seattle hyperlink

FIGURE 3-68

A sample of a JPEG image of the city of Seattle displays (Figure 3-68).

2 **Right-click the image. Click Save Picture As on the shortcut menu. Click the Save in box arrow. Click 3½ Floppy (A:). Double-click legal. Double-click Images. Click the Save button in the Save Picture dialog box. Click the FrontPage Editor button on the taskbar. Click the File button in the Images dialog box. Click seattle to select it. Click the OK button in the Select File dialog box. Scroll down the Web page to display the image.**

FIGURE 3-69

The JPEG image of the Seattle skyline displays centered in the Web page (Figure 3-69).

JPEG images can be quite large and can take a long time to load, especially if the Web page contains several. Creating a thumbnail version of a JPEG image can speed up the time it takes to load the Web page.

Creating a Thumbnail Image

A **thumbnail image** is a smaller version of an image that has been set up as a hyperlink to the full-sized image file. When you create a thumbnail image, a small version of the image is created and stored in a file. The full-sized version of the image is replaced by the small version of the image on the Web page. The small version of the image then is set up as a hyperlink to the full-sized image. When you click the thumbnail image, the full-sized version of the file is loaded in your browser.

You use the **AutoThumbnail command** on the Tools menu to create a thumbnail image. Perform the following steps to create a thumbnail image for the picture of Seattle.

Thumbnail Images

Thumbnail images are useful for business Web sites when displaying products for sale. Potential customers can display the large size image of only those products in which they are interested.

To Create a Thumbnail Image

1 Click the Seattle image to select it. Click Tools on the menu bar.

The Seattle image is selected, and the Tools menu displays (Figure 3-70). The AutoThumbnail command transforms an image into a thumbnail hyperlink.

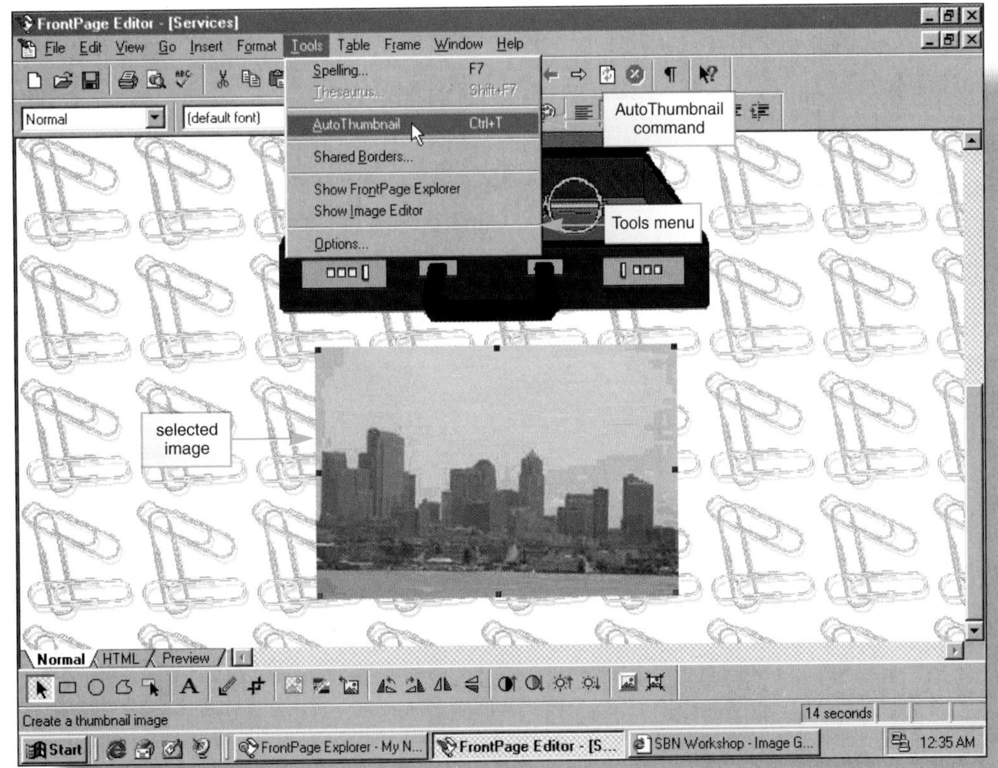

FIGURE 3-70

2 Click AutoThumbnail. Point to the thumbnail image of Seattle.

The thumbnail image of Seattle displays and the URL of the full-size Seattle image displays on the status bar (Figure 3-71).

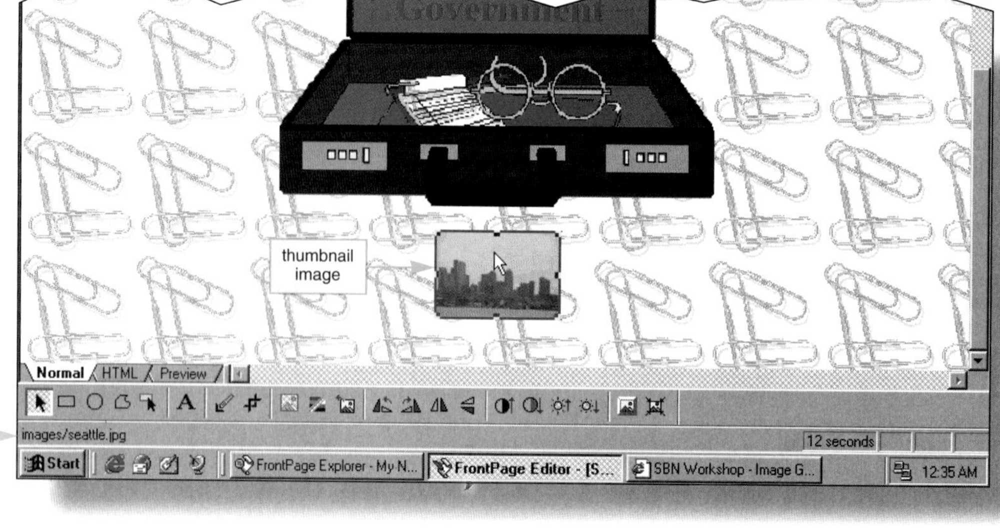

FIGURE 3-71

3 Press the RIGHT ARROW key to position the insertion point to the right of the thumbnail image. Click the Change Style box arrow on the Format toolbar and then click Heading 4. Click the Change Font box arrow on the Format toolbar and then click Arial. Click the Text Color button and then click the color black. Type `Be sure to visit our main offices in the beautiful city of Seattle, Washington` **to the right of the thumbnail image.**

Appropriate descriptive text displays to the right of the thumbnail image (Figure 3-72).

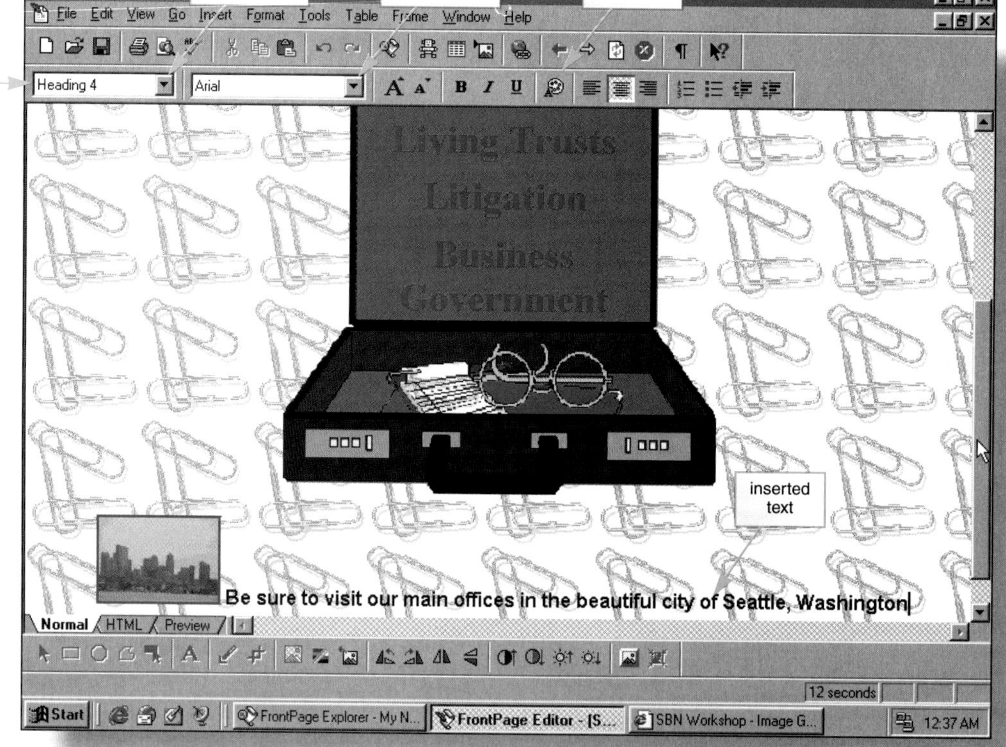

FIGURE 3-72

Other Ways

1. Press ALT+T, A
2. Press CTRL+T

You have successfully created a thumbnail image for a JPEG file. When a user clicks the image, the full-sized version of the picture of Seattle will display.

The Web page is almost complete. The only remaining objects to be inserted are in the Web page footer. The footer can be copied from the Morgan, Turner and Lock Home page and then customized for the Services page. Perform the following steps to copy the footer from the Home page and then change the navigation hyperlinks.

To Copy and Paste the Web Page Footer

1 **Scroll down and then click below the thumbnail image to position the insertion point. Click Window on the menu bar and then click Morgan, Turner and Lock Home Page. Scroll down to the bottom of the Web page. Drag through the last two lines on the Home page containing the navigation hyperlinks. Click Edit on the menu bar and then point to Copy.**

The Morgan, Turner and Lock Home page displays with the last two lines highlighted (Figure 3-73).

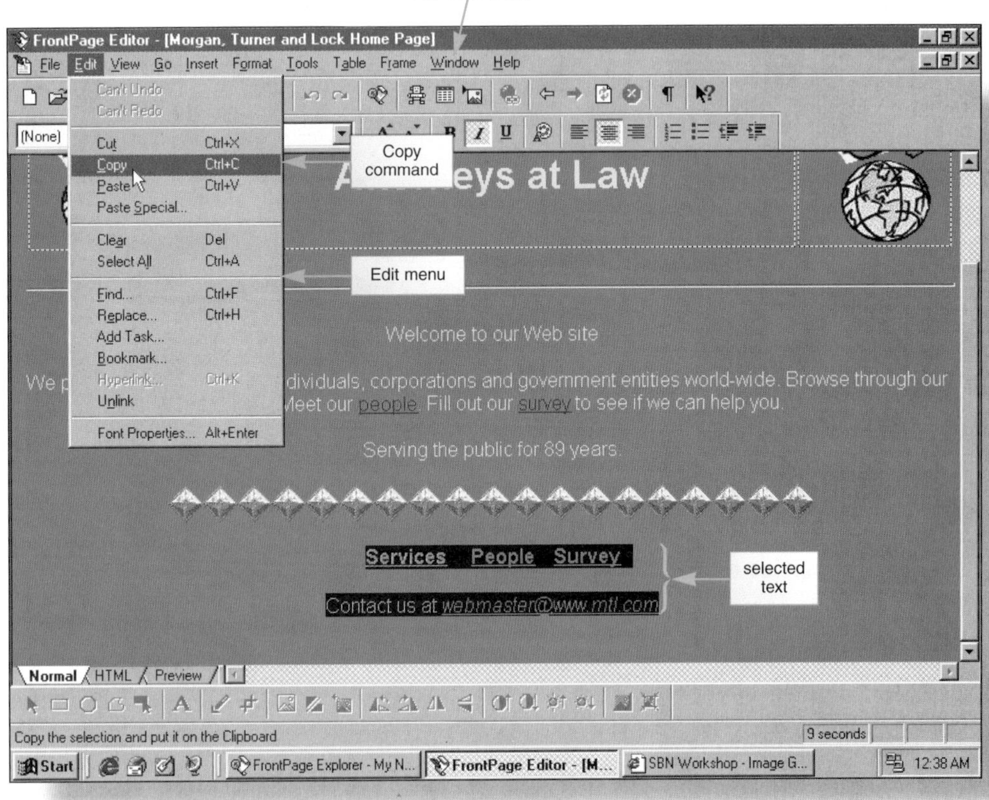

FIGURE 3-73

2 **Click Copy. Click Window on the menu bar and then click Services. On the Edit menu, click Paste.**

The two lines of text are pasted from the Clipboard into the Web page (Figure 3-74).

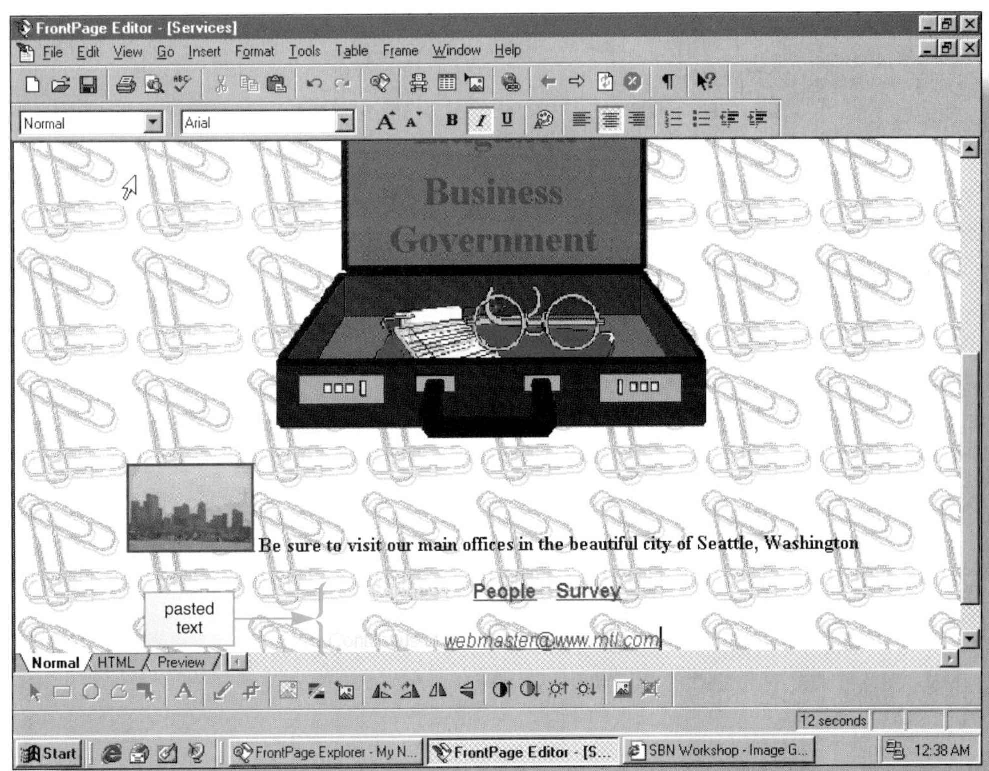

FIGURE 3-74

3 **Drag through the two lines of text to select them. Click the Text Color button on the Format toolbar. When the Color dialog box displays, click the color black. Click the OK button.**

The text color changes to black.

4 **Click above the text to deselect it. Drag through the Services hyperlink to select it. Type** Home **and then right-click the Home hyperlink. Point to Hyperlink Properties on the shortcut menu.**

The Services text is replaced with the word, Home, and a shortcut menu displays (Figure 3-75).

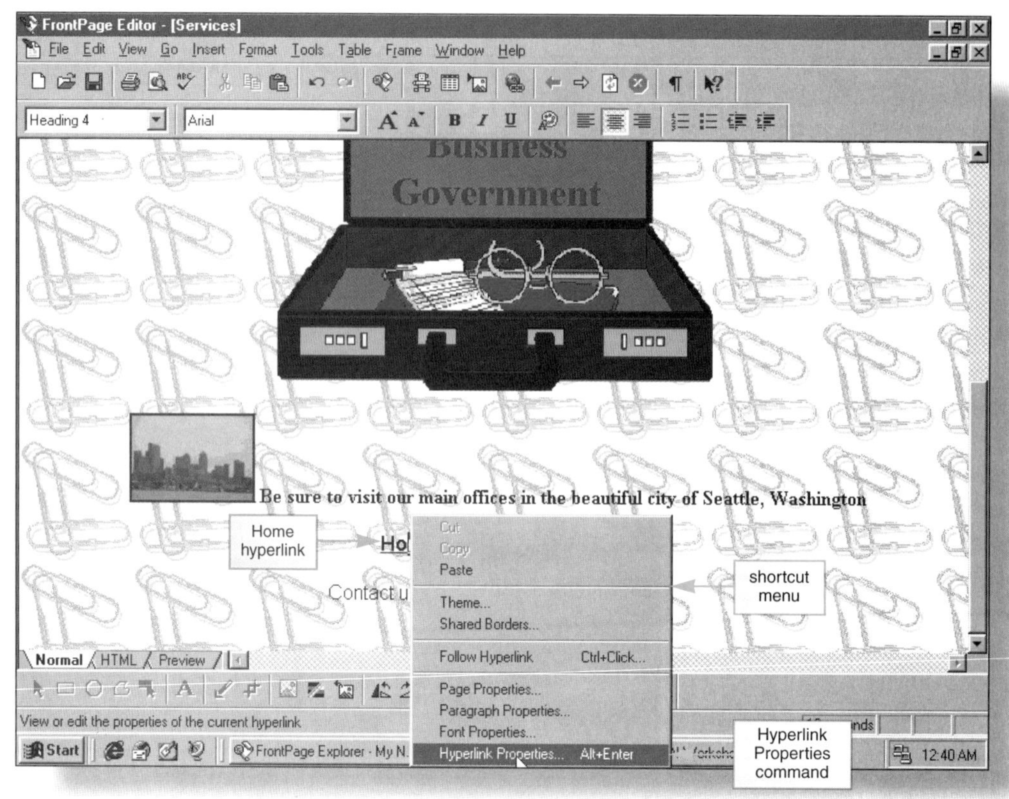

FIGURE 3-75

5 **Click Hyperlink Properties.**

The Edit Hyperlink dialog box displays (Figure 3-76).

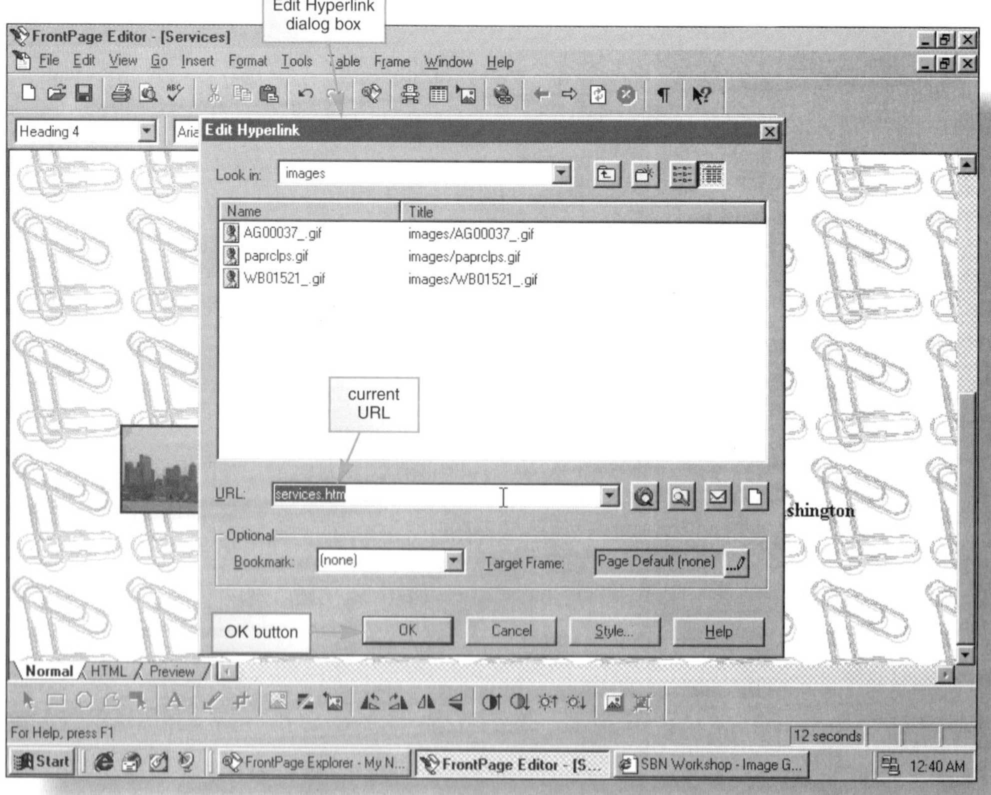

FIGURE 3-76

6 Double-click the URL text box. Type `index.htm` **and then click the OK button. Point to the Home hyperlink.**

The target URL, index.htm, displays on the status bar (Figure 3-77).

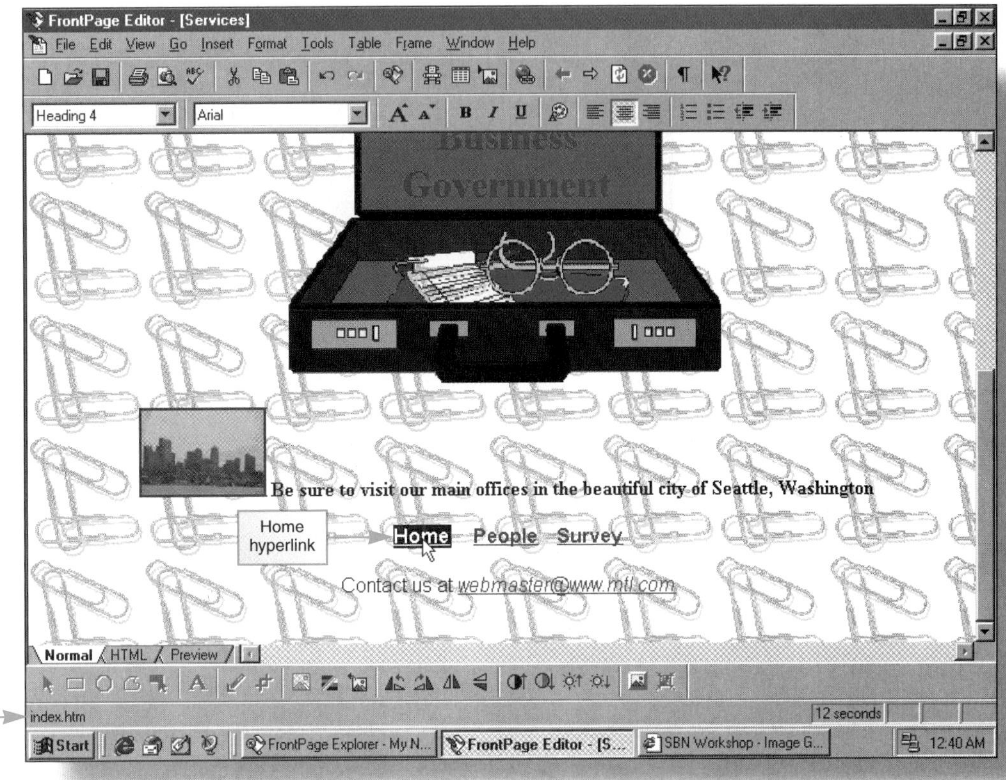

FIGURE 3-77

With the addition of the footer, the Web page is complete. You now can save the Web page on disk.

Saving the Web Page

Once you have finished editing the Web page you should save it on disk. As with the Morgan, Turner and Lock Home page, the save operation will consist of more than just saving the HTML for the Web page. The images you inserted in earlier steps also will be saved in the folders on drive A. Perform the following steps to save the Services page, along with any embedded image files.

TO SAVE THE WEB PAGE

1. Click the Save button on the Standard toolbar.
2. Click the OK button to save the embedded images along with the Web page.

The Save Embedded Files dialog box displays as shown in Figure 3-78 on the next page, after you click the Save button. When you click the OK button, the Web page and embedded images are saved on disk, and the FrontPage window redisplays.

Other Ways

1. On File menu click Save
2. Press ALT+F, S
3. Press CTRL+S

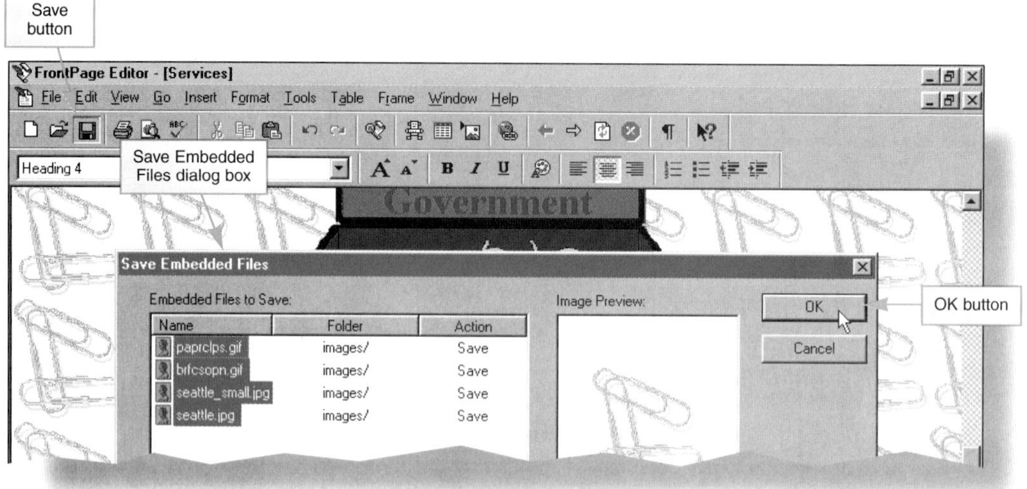

FIGURE 3-78

Saving Images

Be sure to remove from the images folder any unused image files you imported or downloaded from the Web. Image files take up disk space on the development computer as well as the Web server.

It is important that the images be saved as part of the FrontPage web. These image files must be available when publishing the FrontPage web to a Web server. If you did not save them and then published the FrontPage web, the <img src=> tags would be broken because the files referenced by the tags would not be on the Web server, and therefore, the Web page would not display properly.

Printing the Web Page

Once the Web page has been saved on a floppy disk, you can print it. Perform the following steps to print the Services page.

To Print the Web Page

1 Ready the Printer. Click the Print button on the Standard toolbar.

The Print dialog box displays (Figure 3-79).

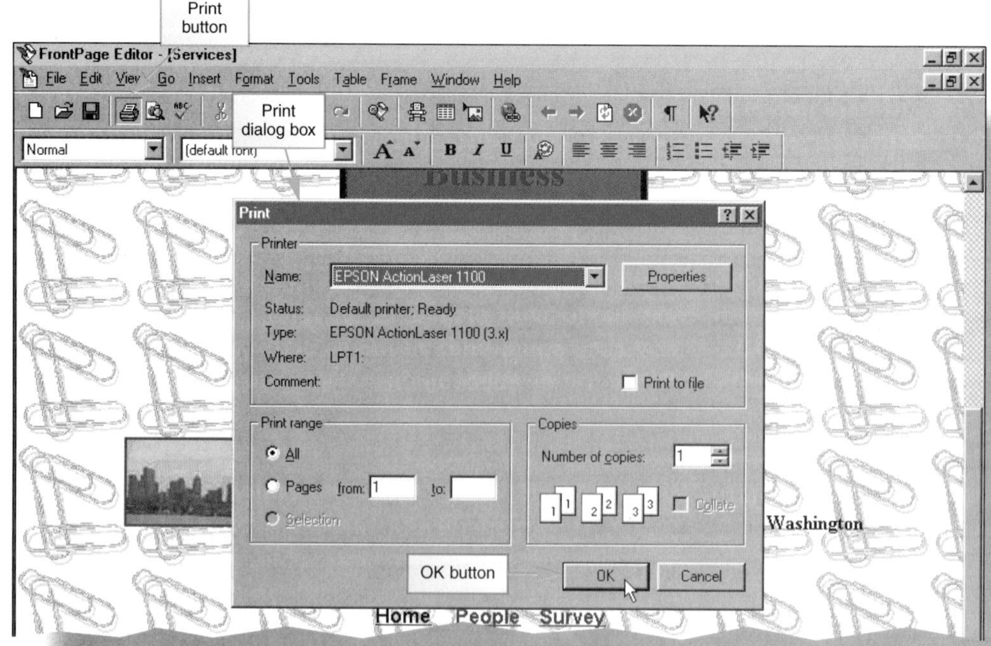

FIGURE 3-79

Click the OK button.

When the printer stops, retrieve the printout (Figure 3-80).

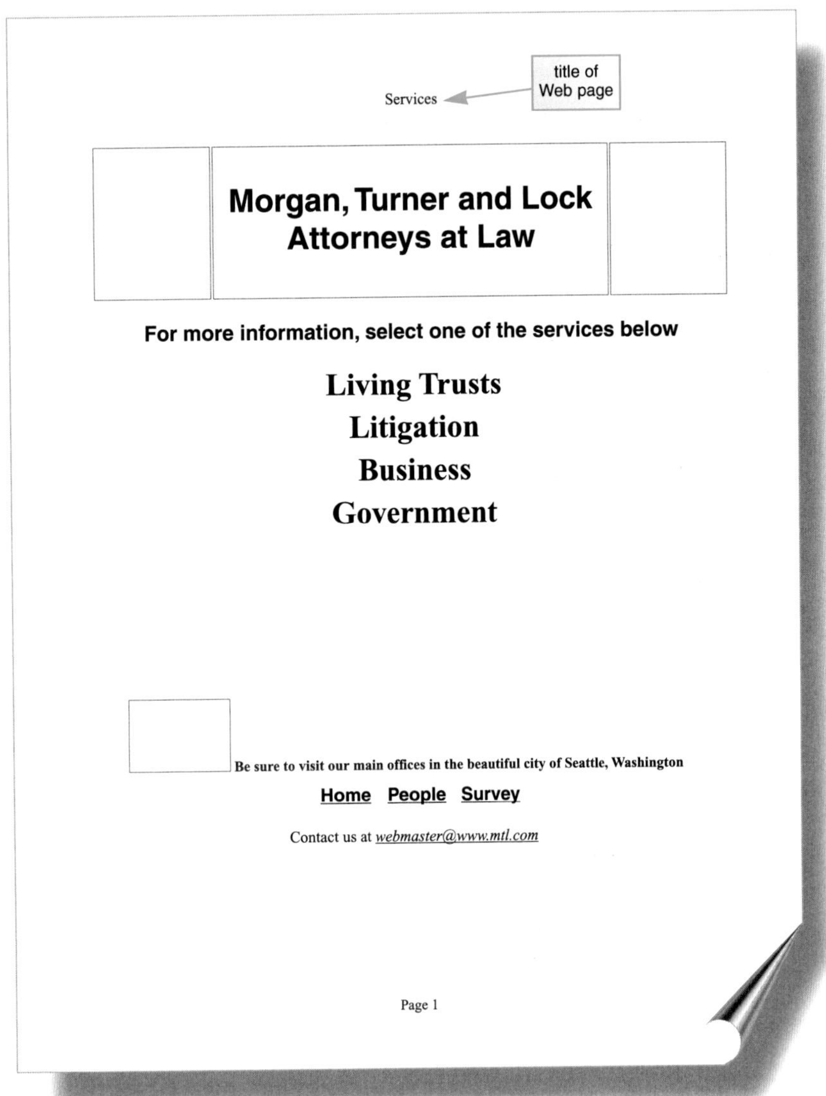

FIGURE 3-80

Other Ways

1. On File menu click Print
2. Press ALT+F, P
3. Press CTRL+P

Quitting the FrontPage Editor

Once the Web page is saved, you can quit FrontPage Editor. The steps are summarized below.

TO QUIT MICROSOFT FRONTPAGE EDITOR

Click the Close button on the FrontPage Editor title bar.

If necessary, click the Close button on the Internet Explorer title bar.

The FrontPage Editor window closes and the FrontPage Explorer window displays.

Other Ways

1. On File menu click Exit
2. Press ALT+F, X

Displaying the Hyperlinks in a FrontPage Web

Recall in Project 2 during the construction of the Morgan, Turner and Lock Home page, you created links to three other Web pages. The file names of the three pages are services.htm, people.htm, and survey.htm. You will have completed the services.htm file by completing the activities in this project. The other two hyperlinks point to files that do not yet exist, however. You added four new hyperlinks in the image map in this project. These hyperlinks that point to nonexistent files are referred to as **broken hyperlinks**.

Several reasons exist for encountering broken hyperlinks. The file that is the target of the hyperlink could have been deleted, renamed, moved to another folder or moved to another Web server. The Web server on which the file resides could have its Internet address changed, could be out of service for some period of time, or be taken permanently out of service.

Keeping track of these broken hyperlinks in the Morgan, Turner and Lock web is simple, because only six broken links exist. When developing very large webs, with many files and hyperlinks, however, it would be very difficult to try to remember which hyperlinks are broken.

The **Hyperlinks view** in the FrontPage Explorer alleviates this problem. It will display in a graphical format the Web pages and their hyperlinks, and indicate which hyperlinks are broken. Perform the following steps to display the Hyperlinks view and determine the broken hyperlinks in the Morgan, Turner and Lock web.

Hyperlinks View

If Hyperlinks view reveals a misspelled hyperlink, you can load the page in the FrontPage Editor by double-clicking the page icon in Hyperlink view and then quickly correct the hyperlink.

Steps To Display the Hyperlinks in the Current FrontPage Web

1 Click the Hyperlinks button on the Views bar.

The FrontPage Explorer displays in Hyperlinks view (Figure 3-81).

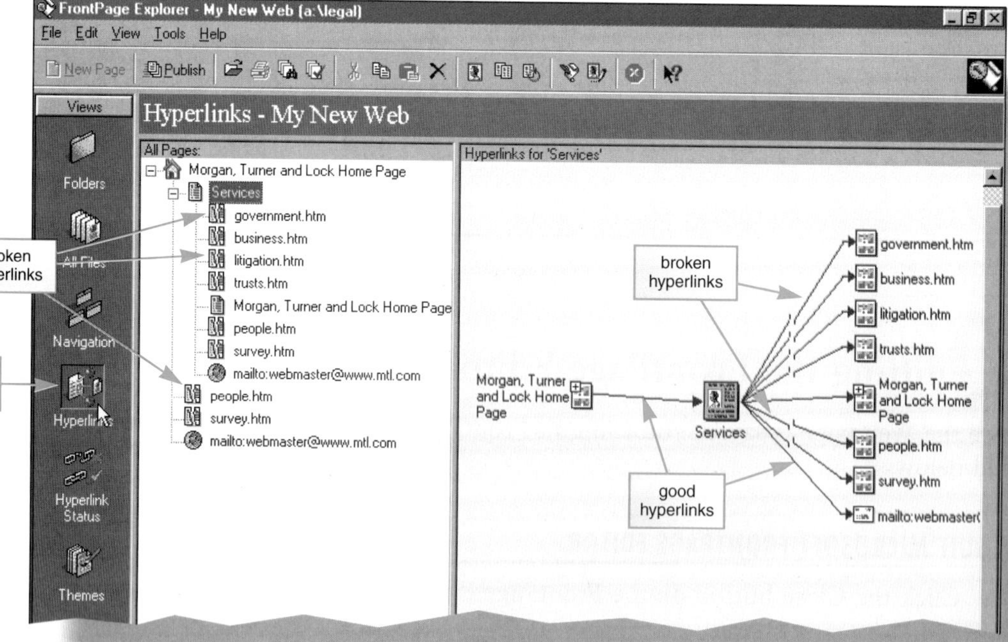

FIGURE 3-81

1. On View menu click Hyperlinks
2. Press ALT+V, H

The Hyperlinks view displays a graphical diagram of the hyperlinks in the current FrontPage web starting with the top-level page. In this web it is the Morgan, Turner and Lock Home page, which displays in the All Pages pane shown in Figure 3-81. One hyperlink exists from the Home page to the Services page. The Services page contains eight hyperlinks, six of which are broken. You can select another page in the web to view its hyperlinks by clicking the page icon in the graphical diagram.

Notice in the All Pages pane of the Hyperlinks view shown in Figure 3-81 that six page icons seem broken in half. These represent broken hyperlinks in the Home page and the Services page. You can use the Hyperlinks view to verify quickly which links, if any, are broken in the current FrontPage web.

More About

Hyperlink Status

Be aware that if you choose to check the status of all the hyperlinks in the current Web, it could take a significant length of time. FrontPage not only will look in the current web, but also will look on the World Wide Web following hyperlinks to make sure the targets exist.

Publishing the FrontPage Web

Recall that in Project 2, the Morgan, Turner and Lock web was published on the World Wide Web. You since have added a Web page and the accompanying image files to the FrontPage web. For this new Web page to be available on the World Wide Web, you must publish the Morgan, Turner and Lock web again.

When you publish a FrontPage web that has been published before, FrontPage will install only those parts of the web that are new or that have changed since the last time the web was published. This reduces the amount of data transfer that takes place, which is good for webs with many folders, Web pages, and files.

The following steps summarize how to publish a FrontPage web. As discussed in Project 1 on page FP 1.50, be sure to substitute your own URL or an error will occur. If you do not know what URL to use, ask your instructor.

TO PUBLISH THE FRONTPAGE WEB

1. Click the Publish button on the toolbar. If the Microsoft Web Publishing Wizard dialog box displays, click the Cancel button.
2. Click the More Webs button.
3. Type `http://home1.gte.net/jordank/legal` in the Location text box (substitute your own URL, or an error will occur).
4. Click the OK button in the FrontPage Web dialog box. Type `ftphome1.gte.net` in the FTP Server Name text box (substitute your own FTP server name, or an error will occur). Type `legal` in the Directory Path text box.
5. Click the Next button. Type your FTP user name and password.
6. Click the Finish button.

You now can view the Services page by entering http://home1.gte.net/jordank/legal/services.htm in any browser and pressing the ENTER key. Be sure to test the hyperlink to the Home page and from the Home page to the Services page.

Quitting the FrontPage Explorer

Once you have published the changes to the Morgan, Turner and Lock web, you can quit the FrontPage Explorer. The step to quit is summarized below.

TO QUIT THE FRONTPAGE EXPLORER

 Click the Close button on the title bar.

The Windows desktop displays.

Project Summary

Having completed Project 3, you now are ready to incorporate images and special image formatting in your Web pages. In this project, you learned how to insert a new Web page into a FrontPage web. You learned about image file formats. You created a tiled background from an image file. You created a transparent image. You created an image map and assigned target URLs to the hotspots. You inserted a photographic image in a Web page and created its thumbnail image. Finally, you learned how to display the status of the hyperlinks used in the Web pages of the current FrontPage web.

What You Should Know

Having completed this project, you now should be able to perform the following tasks.

- Add a Hotspot to an Image Map *(FP 3.36)*
- Add a New Web Page to a FrontPage Web *(FP 3.10)*
- Add Text to a Web Page *(FP 3.27)*
- Copy and Paste Objects from Another Web Page *(FP 3.24)*
- Copy and Paste the Web Page Footer *(FP 3.47)*
- Create a Thumbnail Image *(FP 3.45)*
- Create a Transparent Image *(FP 3.34)*
- Display the Hyperlinks in the Current FrontPage Web *(FP 3.52)*
- Display the Image Toolbar *(FP 3.13)*
- Edit a Web Page *(FP 3.13)*
- Highlight Hotspots *(FP 3.43)*
- Insert a JPEG Image on a Web Page *(FP 3.44)*
- Insert an Image from the World Wide Web *(FP 3.28)*
- Open an Existing FrontPage Web *(FP 3.9)*
- Print the Web Page *(FP 3.50)*
- Publish the FrontPage Web *(FP 3.53)*
- Quit the FrontPage Explorer *(FP 3.54)*
- Quit Microsoft FrontPage Editor *(FP 3.51)*
- Resize a Clip Art Image *(FP 3.32)*
- Save the Web Page *(FP 3.49)*
- Set a Background Image *(FP 3.15)*
- Specify the Target of an Image Map Hotspot *(FP 3.40)*
- Start FrontPage 98 *(FP 3.8)*
- Washout an Image *(FP 3.22)*

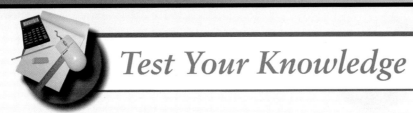

Test Your Knowledge

1 True/False

Instructions: Circle T if the statement is true or F if the statement is false.

T F 1. You do not need to know the characteristics and advantages of each type of image file to use them effectively in Web page development.
T F 2. FrontPage supports ten types of image file formats.
T F 3. An image is formed on the screen by displaying pixels of different colors.
T F 4. GIF images support 256 different colors.
T F 5. JPEG images support 256 different colors.
T F 6. The process of repeating an image across and down the Web page background is called paneling.
T F 7. Resampling a resized image stores the image back in the file at its new size.
T F 8. Image maps are special graphic images that have defined hotspots.
T F 9. Hotspots on an image must be circles or rectangles.
T F 10. A thumbnail image is a smaller version of an image file that has been set up as an image map.

2 Multiple Choice

Instructions: Circle the correct response.

1. FrontPage supports two types of image files, GIF and __________.
   a. BMP
   b. JPEG
   c. EPS
   d. WMF
2. A(n) __________ is the smallest addressable point on the screen.
   a. insertion point
   b. color
   c. period
   d. pixel
3. The __________ file format supports 256 colors.
   a. PIXEL
   b. JPEG
   c. GIF
   d. none of the above
4. The __________ file format supports 16.7 million colors.
   a. PIXEL
   b. JPEG
   c. GIF
   d. none of the above

(continued)

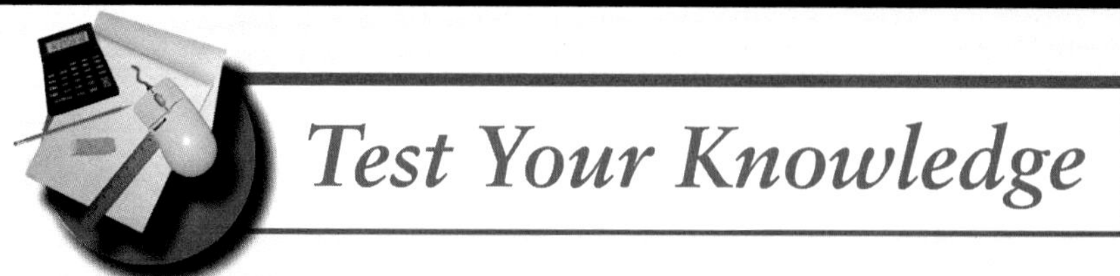

Test Your Knowledge

Multiple Choice *(continued)*

5. The __________ button on the Image toolbar creates a low-contrast, see-through version of an image.
   a. Washout
   b. Transparent
   c. Decrease Contrast
   d. Decrease Brightness
6. A __________ image sometimes is referred to as a floating image because it appears to float on the Web page.
   a. JPEG
   b. hyperlinked
   c. thumbnail
   d. transparent
7. A __________ is a specially designated portion of an image that has been set up as a hyperlink.
   a. hotspot
   b. pixel
   c. thumbnail
   d. handle
8. The __________ is useful when you cannot easily see the hotspots you created.
   a. pencil pointer
   b. Hotspots command
   c. Highlight Hotspots button
   d. Show Hotspots command
9. A __________ is a smaller version of an image that has been set up as a hyperlink to a full-sized image file.
   a. hotspot
   b. fingernail image
   c. transparent GIF
   d. thumbnail image
10. Hyperlinks that point to nonexistent files are referred to as __________.
    a. broken
    b. transparent
    c. thumbnails
    d. washed out

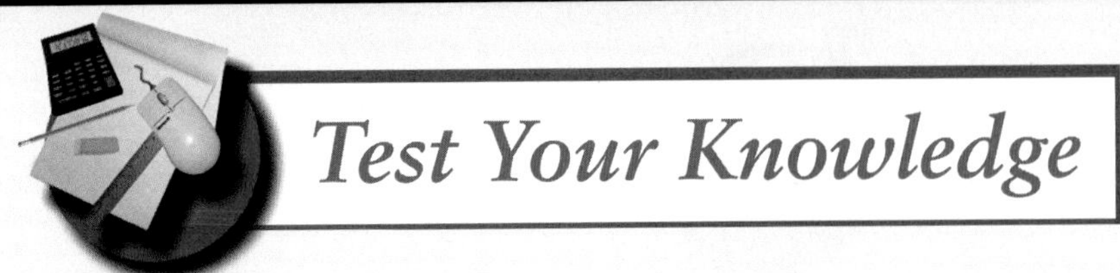

3 Understanding the Image Toolbar

Instructions: In Figure 3-82, arrows point to several buttons on the Image toolbar. In the spaces provided, briefly explain the purpose of each button.

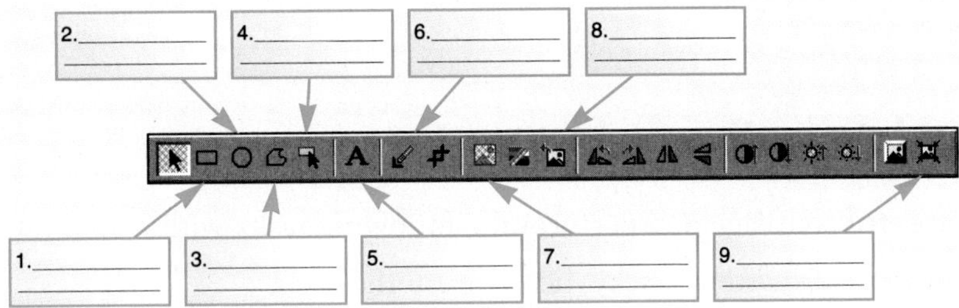

FIGURE 3-82

4 Understanding FrontPage Image Terminology

Instructions: Define the following terms:

TERM	DEFINITION
1. GIF	________
2. JPEG	________
3. pixel	________
4. tiled background	________
5. transparent image	________
6. resampling	________
7. image map	________
8. hotspot	________
9. thumbnail image	________

1 Using the FrontPage Editor Help

Instructions: Another feature of GIF files is that they can be interlaced. Using the FrontPage Editor Help, find and display information on interlaced GIF files. Write a description of interlaced GIF files and how they are used on the Web and hand it in to your instructor.

2 Online Product Information and Support

Instructions: Start Microsoft FrontPage and perform the following tasks with a computer.

1. Click Help on the menu bar and then click Microsoft on the Web.
2. Click the Solutions & Resources hyperlink (Figure 3-83). Click the How to Articles category.
3. Browse through the available articles and find one that involves images.
4. Print the article, write your name on it, and hand it in to your instructor.

FIGURE 3-83

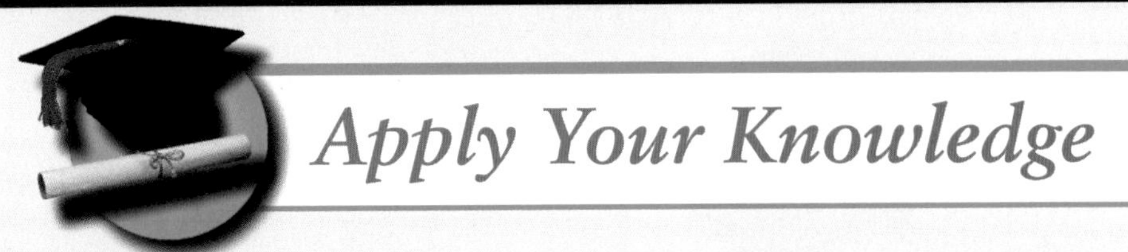

1 Creating a Transparent Image

Instructions: Transparent images appear to *float* on the Web page. This technique is used frequently for clip art images, icons, and corporate logos. Perform the following activities to create a transparent image.

1. Start FrontPage 98.
2. When the Getting Started dialog box displays, click the Cancel button.
3. Click Tools on the menu bar and then click Show FrontPage Editor.
4. Select a background color using the Background command on the Format menu.
5. Click the Insert Image button on the Standard toolbar.
6. Click the World Wide Web button. When the Internet browser window opens, connect to www.microsoft.com/gallery/images/default.asp.
7. Click the show contents hyperlink. Scroll through the list of available images and display a sample of an image that interests you.
8. Insert a formatted floppy disk in drive A. Save the image on the floppy disk in drive A by right-clicking the image and then clicking Save Picture As on the shortcut menu. Write down the name of the file, because you will need to know it for step 10.
9. Click the FrontPage Editor button on the taskbar. When the Image dialog box displays, click the File button. Click the Look in box arrow and then click 3½ Floppy (A:).
10. When Select File dialog box displays, click the file name of the image you saved in step 8 and then click the OK button. Click the OK button in the Image dialog box.
11. Click the image to select it. Click Edit on the menu bar and then click Copy to copy the image to the Clipboard. Click to the right of the image to position the insertion point and then click Paste on the Edit menu. This will insert another copy of the image in the Web page.
12. Click the first image to select it and then click the Make Transparent button on the Image toolbar.
13. Click a color to make it transparent using the Make Transparent pointer. When the dialog box displays asking if you want to change all copies of the image, click the No button. This step will create a side-by-side, before and after comparison of the images (Figure 3-84).
14. Print the Web page, write your name on it, and hand it in to your instructor.

FIGURE 3-84

1 Creating a Tiled Background

Instructions: You can use just about any image to serve as a background for a Web page, although the results sometimes will be surprising. Perform the following steps with a computer.

1. Start FrontPage 98.
2. When the Getting Started dialog box displays, click the Cancel button.
3. Click Tools on the menu bar and then click Show FrontPage Editor.
4. Click Format on the menu bar and then click Background.
5. In the Page Properties dialog box, click Background Image, and then click the Browse button.
6. When the Select Background Image dialog box displays, click the File button. If necessary, click the Look in box arrow and then click the Windows folder on drive C.
7. Click the Files of type box arrow and then click Bitmap (*.bmp).
8. Click one of the background patterns provided with Windows and then click the OK button in the Select File dialog box (Figure 3-85).
9. Click the OK button in the Page Properties dialog box. The bitmap image should become the tiled background of the Web page.
10. FrontPage will convert the bitmap file to another format before saving the Web page on disk. Insert a formatted floppy disk in drive A and then click the Save button on the Standard toolbar. In the Save As File dialog box, click the Save in box arrow, click 3½ Floppy (A:), and click the Save button. The Save Embedded Files dialog box displays. What is the file type of the background image you selected in step 8? Click the OK button to save the files or the Cancel button to cancel the operation.
11. At the top of the Web page, type your name and the answer to the question in step 10. Be sure to select a text color that is readable on the background. Print the Web page, and hand it in to your instructor.

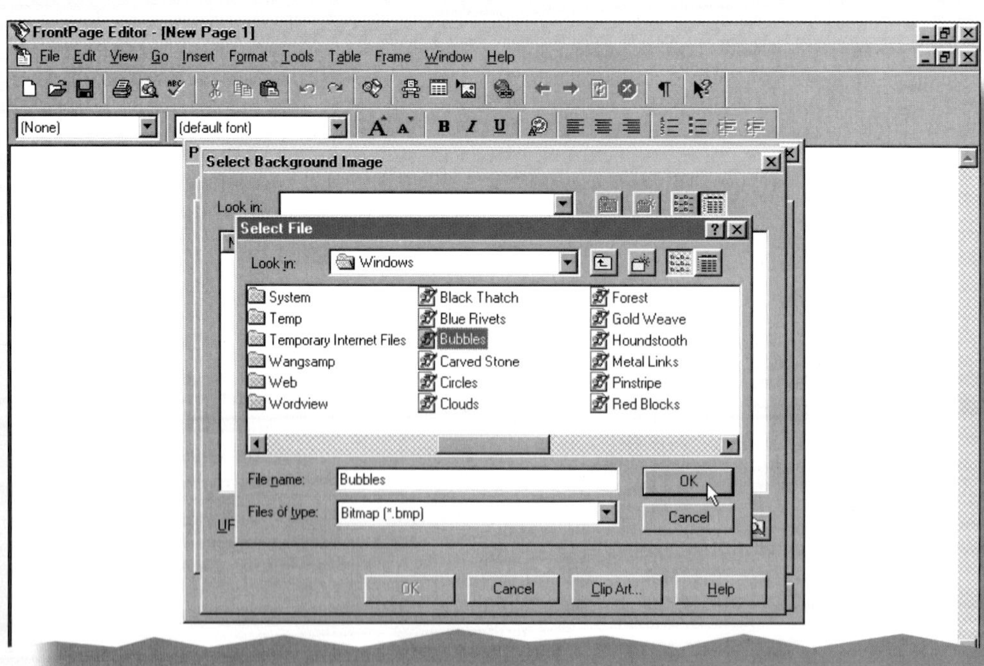

FIGURE 3-85

2 Creating an Image Map

Instructions: Perform the following steps with a computer.

1. Start FrontPage 98.
2. When the Getting Started dialog box displays, click the Cancel button.
3. Click Tools on the menu bar and then click Show FrontPage Editor.
4. Click the Insert Image button on the Standard toolbar. When the Insert Image dialog box displays, click the Clip Art button.
5. When the Microsoft Clip Gallery dialog box displays, scroll down the categories list box and then click Maps.
6. Double-click the black map of the world. Resize the map to make it larger (Figure 3-86).
7. Create hotspots on the major continents (North America, South America, Africa, Europe, Asia, Australia). Assign a file name for the URL that represents the continent name and has a file extension of htm. For example, the URL for the Africa hotspot would be africa.htm.
8. Click the HTML tab at the bottom of the window to display the HTML tags for the image map. Print the HTML, write your name on the printout, and hand it in to your instructor.

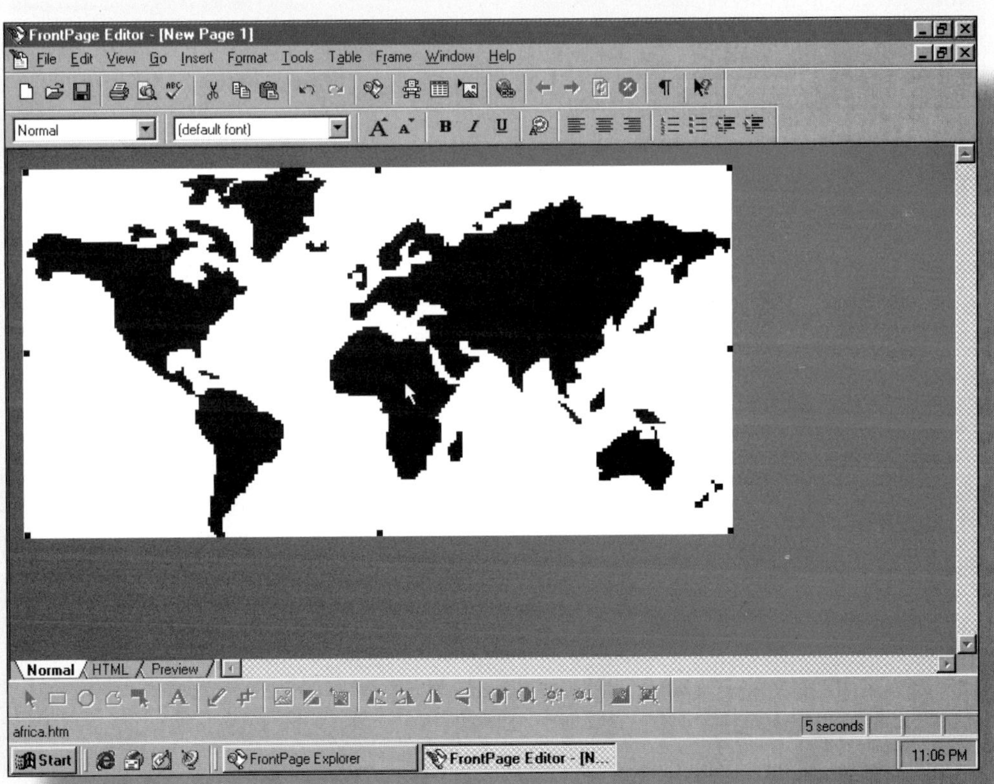

FIGURE 3-86

3 Creating a Thumbnail Image

Instructions: Perform the following steps with a computer.

1. Start FrontPage 98.
2. When the Getting Started dialog box displays, click the Cancel button.
3. Click Tools on the menu bar and then click Show FrontPage Editor.
4. Click the Insert Image button on the Standard toolbar. When the Insert Image dialog box displays, click the Clip Art button.
5. Click the Pictures tab in the Microsoft Clip Gallery dialog box. Click All Categories in the categories list box.
6. Scroll through the list of available pictures. When you find one you like, insert it in the Web page by double-clicking the picture.
7. Make the picture a thumbnail image using the AutoThumbnail command (Figure 3-87).
8. Click the HTML tags to display the HTML for the thumbnail image.
9. Print the HTML, write your name on the printout, and hand it in to your instructor.

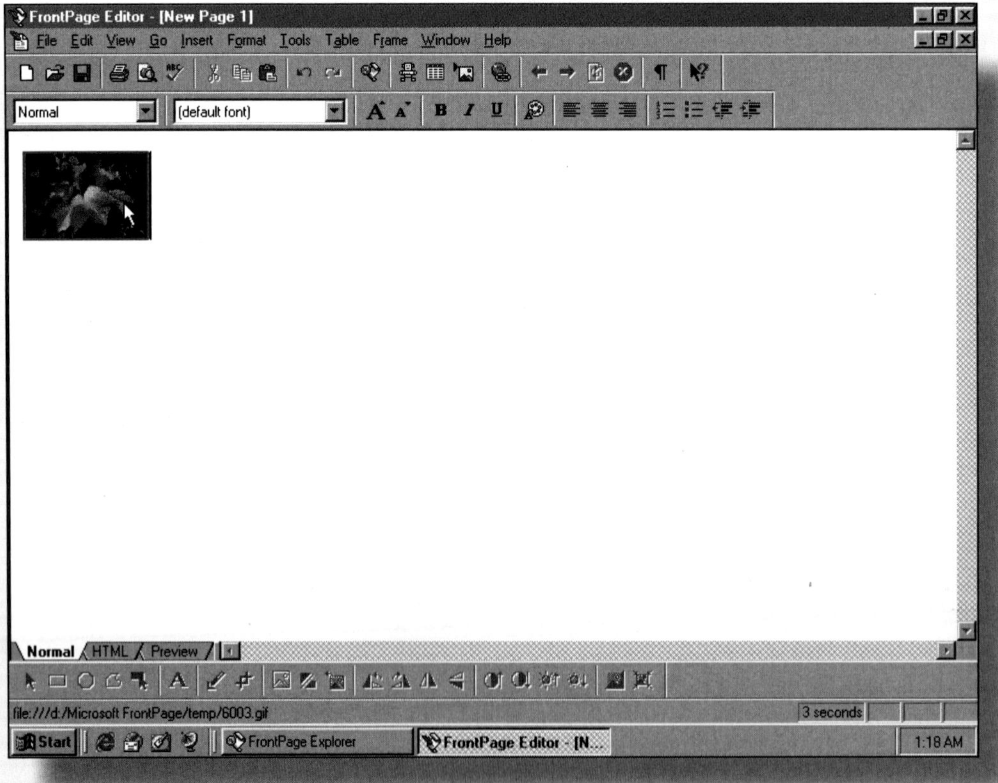

FIGURE 3-87

Cases and Places

The difficulty of these case studies varies:
◗ are the least difficult; ◗◗ are more difficult; and ◗◗◗ are the most difficult.

1 ◗ You can learn about the use of image maps by studying how other Web developers use them. Find and print three Web pages, each containing an image map. Write a report that details the advantages and disadvantages of each image map. Include in the report a diagram for each image map that describes the hotspots and their targets.

2 ◗ Not all the clip art, buttons, dividers, and other images you find on the Web are free. Some of it is copyrighted. Research the legal issues surrounding the use of materials found on the Web and write a report detailing your findings.

3 ◗◗ In addition to images, you also can include sound and movies on your Web pages. Search the Web for libraries of sounds and movies. Create a Web page containing links to some of these resources.

4 ◗◗ Graphics editors, such as Windows Paint, allow you to create and edit images. Many editors are available for download on the Internet. Find out about four different graphics editors and report on their features and limitations. Include information such as the types of supported image file formats and special effects.

5 ◗◗◗ The GIF89a format supports special images called animated GIFs. These animated images support limited movement. Find out how to create an animated GIF. What types of animated GIF editors are available? What are some of the objects and other information you would need to create an animated GIF?

6 ◗◗◗ The current formal specification for HTML is HTML 4.0. Find out if formal specifications exist for the JPEG and GIF file formats. Write a report that briefly describes the contents of GIF and JPEG files. Are any new techniques or features being considered for inclusion in the next set of specifications?

7 ◗◗◗ Image maps can be created using one of several different styles. These styles include client-side, server-side, NCSA, CERN, and Netscape. Research the different image map styles and write a report describing each format and when you might use each one.